Constitutionalism, Identity, Difference, and Legitimacy

Constitutionalism, Identity, Difference, and Legitimacy

Theoretical Perspectives

Edited by Michel Rosenfeld

Duke University Press *Durham and London 1994*

Originally published as a special issue of the *Cardozo Law
Review*, "Comparative Constitutionalism: Theoretical
Perspectives on the Role of Constitutions in the Interplay
Between Identity and Diversity," vol. 14, nos. 3–4 (Janu-
ary 1993).

For Susan

CONTENTS

ACKNOWLEDGMENTS

The essays gathered in this volume were first presented at a conference entitled "Comparative Constitutionalism: Theoretical Perspectives on the Role of Constitutions in the Interplay Between Identity and Difference," which took place on October 13-14, 1991, at the Benjamin N. Cardozo School of Law in New York City under the auspices of the Jacob Burns Institute for Advanced Legal Studies and the Cardozo–New School Project on Constitutionalism. Among the many persons who were instrumental in conceiving and organizing this conference, I wish to single out for special thanks Professor András Sajó and Jean McMahon, the 1991-92 Administrative Editor of the *Cardozo Law Review*. In addition, I wish to thank my research assistant Magda Jimenez for her very able assistance in the preparation of this volume.

I

Introduction

MODERN CONSTITUTIONALISM AS INTERPLAY BETWEEN IDENTITY AND DIVERSITY

Michel Rosenfeld

The spirit of constitutionalism has so dramatically soared of late that it seems poised to achieve a worldwide sweep. Moreover, two recent sets of events have invigorated constitutionalism and propelled it to the forefront. First, the bicentennial celebrations of the American Constitution and the French Declaration of the Rights of Man have underscored the importance and durability of modern constitutionalism. Second, sweeping changes towards constitutionalism have taken place since 1989 in Eastern and Central Europe as well as in what used to be the Soviet Union.[1] Furthermore, the collapse of authoritarian socialist regimes has paved the way for the completion of the worldwide thrust towards constitutionalism that began shortly after the end of World War II. Starting with the adoption of the Japanese Constitution and the West German Basic Law, this trend continued with the embrace of constitutionalism in Western European countries such as Greece, Portugal, and Spain, which later spread to such Latin American countries as Argentina and Brazil.

There appears to be no accepted definition of constitutionalism[2] but, in the broadest terms, modern constitutionalism requires imposing limits on the powers of government, adherence to the rule of law, and the protection of fundamental rights. Moreover, although not all constitutions conform to the demands of constitutionalism, and although constitutionalism is not dependent on the existence of a written constitution,[3] the realization of the spirit of constitutionalism generally goes hand in hand with the implementation of a written constitution. As the number of diverse constitutions purporting to adhere to the fundamental tenets of constitutionalism proliferates, however, the relationship between constitution and constitutionalism and the very boundaries of the concept of constitutionalism tend to become increasingly blurred. This, in turn, calls for the providing of new perspectives on modern constitutionalism and its relation to

---

[1] *See, e.g.*, Jon Elster, *Constitutionalism in Eastern Europe: An Introduction*, 58 U. CHI. L. REV. 447 (1991).

[2] *See* Louis Henkin, *A New Birth of Constitutionalism: Genetic Influences and Genetic Defects*, *infra* p. 39, 40.

[3] The United Kingdom provides a notorious example of adherence to the fundamental tenets of constitutionalism without the existence of a written constitution.

modern constitutions from the standpoint of theoretical perspectives that are both anchored in particular national and cultural settings and open to broader comparative concerns.

The essays published in this book all make significant contributions to the task of bringing to bear fruitful theoretical perspectives on several of the most thorny problems raised by the relationship between constitutions and constitutionalism. Moreover, given the vast array of issues that fall within the scope of the relationship between constitutions and constitutionalism, the following essays focus on a central concern raised by various attempts to implant constitutionalism through the deployment of a constitutional order. This central concern is that of the proper role of constitutions and constitutionalism in forging a fruitful interplay between the reinforcement of identity and the preservation of diversity.

The roles that may be assumed by constitutionalism and constitutions in relation to the interplay between identity and diversity are complex and multifaceted. Furthermore, the relevant nexuses between identity and diversity are themselves numerous as well as fairly intricate. Strictly speaking, it is not a matter of any single identity emerging against a backdrop of multiple differences. Rather, issues concerning constitutionalism and constitutions arise in sociopolitical settings demarcated by clashes between competing identities. Among other identities, there are likely to be national, regional, linguistic, religious, ethnic, political, generational, class, and ideological identities. Moreover, it is far from obvious how these competing identities ought to be combined or divided to frame the kind of interplay between identity and diversity that is likely to conform with the fundamental tenets of constitutionalism.

The pursuit of the central values embodied in constitutionalism only makes sense in relation to sociopolitical settings that can be construed as revolving around the two opposite poles of identity, and diversity or difference. Indeed, without some predominant identity, such as that of the sovereign nation or of the constitutional self, it is difficult to imagine how one could justify the imposition of a constitutional order. In contrast, if a sociopolitical setting were so homogeneous as to lack differences susceptible to becoming implicated in political conflicts, there would appear to be no need for imposing the kind of constraints usually associated with constitutionalism. More specifically, each of the three general features of constitutionalism identified above—namely, limited government, adherence to the rule of law, and protection of fundamental rights—acquires its legitimacy in relation to a sociopolitical reality oriented towards conflicting poles of identity and difference. Limited government is thus justified as a means to acknowledge, and profitably to make use of, the conflict produced by the confrontation between the partial identity and the partial schism that characterizes the relationship between the governors and the governed. Without partial identity—as in the case of foreign occupation—the government would lack constitutional legitimacy altogether; without significant difference, however, there would be no point in limiting government, as the governors would be indistinguishable from the governed.

Adherence to the rule of law also acquires particularly significant normative force in the context of a setting marked by the deployment of intricate links between partial identity and partial differentiation. Commitment to the rule of law evinces a determination to mark a firm demarcation between the generation of rules of conduct designed to regulate the governed, and the application of such rules to particular cases. This is usually accomplished through separation of the function of legislation, which is firmly and directly anchored in the realm of the political, from the function of adjudication, which is supposed to remain as removed as possible from the political arena. Application of a law to a particular case would lack legitimacy unless there were a partial identity between the persons involved in the particular case and the persons who achieve political expression through the legislative process (or at least through the legislative process as constrained by adherence to relevant constitutional norms). Alternatively, unless there were at least some partial differences between those who achieve political expression through legislation and those who are subject to such legislation, there would be no need for submission to the rule of law, as the will of the collectivity acting as one could achieve full realization through the political process.[4]

Protection of fundamental rights, the third general feature of modern constitutionalism, also implies the existence of an ongoing tension between identity and difference. The difference involved is that between the individual citizen and the collectivity or ruling majority. Without that difference the individual would not really require protection against government intrusions into her zone of fundamental interests. Commitment to the protection of fundamental rights, however, generally implies at least two different though usually re-

---

[4] *Cf.* Michel Rosenfeld, *Deconstruction and Legal Interpretation: Conflict, Indeterminacy and the Temptations of New Legal Formalism*, 11 CARDOZO L. REV. 1211, 1229 (1990) ("General rules of law universally applicable to all actors regardless of their group affiliations . . . can be viewed as evincing attempts at reconciliation of self and other within an order of duties and entitlements that transcends the divisions arising from the clash of divergent group interests.").

lated kinds of identity. First, consensus concerning *which* rights ought to be deemed fundamental and hence granted constitutional protection bespeaks some measure of identity between the framers of a constitution and those subjected to the corresponding constitutional order. Second, beyond the latter identity (and even conceivably if the latter identity is lacking), there is another kind of identity that links together each member of society as a bearer of the same constitutional rights. For example, if a constitution postulates that all persons are entitled to equal respect and dignity, it generates a basis of identity among persons who may in several other respects conceive of themselves as being more different than alike.[5]

As already mentioned, a working constitutional order must revolve around a predominant identity. For example, in the United States that identity, at least at the most abstract level, is that of "We, the People." Moreover, the predominant identity in question depends for its creation and maintenance on the operation of a process that simultaneously stresses certain identities and minimizes certain differences. Thus, for instance, in a society marked by the existence of ethnic homogeneity and religious diversity, the development of a viable constitutional identity might well depend on emphasizing ethnic pride, while at the same time downplaying religious differences.[6] Furthermore, that part of the process under consideration which consists of valorizing certain identities may be driven either by an essentially inclusionary or a fundamentally exclusionary approach. An inclusionary approach searches for similarities that can serve to bind a group of people together. An exclusionary approach, in contrast, seeks to isolate and exploit certain differences in order to produce a negative association among all those who can draw a common identity because they are different from others who are marked by the differences involved.[7] In short, a predominant constitutional identity may rely pri-

---

[5] For an example of a constitution that postulates human dignity as fundamental, see GRUNDGESETZ [GG] (federal constitution) art. I (F.R.G.).

[6] While the downplaying of religious differences might be essential to the preservation of the predominant identity on which the relevant constitutional order depends for its survival, religious differences need not be altogether ignored by the constitution. Quite to the contrary, the downplaying of religious differences in relation to the framing of the predominant identity would seem in all likelihood to necessitate the adoption of constitutional provisions guaranteeing respect for religious diversity. Hence, whereas religious differences would not figure in the definition of the predominant constitutional identity, they would be properly accounted for in the overall interplay between constitutionally relevant identity and diversity.

[7] In a large number of cases, whether the approach taken to establish an identity is inclusionary or exclusionary depends ultimately on the circumstances surrounding its adoption. Take, for example, the case of forging an identity on the basis of race. It would appear that if all whites identify as belonging to the same group because of the similarity of their skin color, they are making use of an inclusionary approach, whereas if they define themselves as a group

marily on stressing certain identities or on emphasizing certain differences.

Not only are there different ways of putting together a predominant constitutional identity, but such identity is unlikely to be constructed at once or to remain unchanged over a substantial period of time. To illustrate this, let us return to "We, the People." First, it is not altogether clear who are the "We" or who are the "People." Second, it is not obvious what keeps this "We, the People" together. Moreover, that latter inquiry has both a spatial and a temporal dimension: it is not evident what keeps together the multiple and diverse population now located on American soil, and it is not readily apparent what preserves the fundamental identity of that population over the course of several generations.

Even if it were clear to whom "We, the People" refers, the nature of the predominant identity animating the United States Constitution could not be sufficiently delineated without a grasp of the relevant ways in which those who make up "We, the People" are bound to one another in order to form a unitary constitutional self. Curiously, the key source of the nature of the predominant American constitutional identity—namely, the proposition that "all men are created equal"— is not found in the Constitution but in the Declaration of Independence. In any event, by linking "We, the People" with "all men are created equal"—a proposition that is counterfactual to the extent that it postulates a moral equality among persons rather than refers to any particular factual equality[8]—one can derive as the predominant constitutional identity that of a group of individuals who ought to relate to one another as moral equals.

Viewing "all men are created equal" in a historical perspective reveals an important dichotomy between the predominant constitutional identity promoted by American constitutionalism and that implied by the United States Constitution prior to the adoption of the Civil War amendments. Indeed, as David Richards indicates in his contribution, the authors of the Declaration of Independence intended "*all* men" to refer to blacks as well as to whites.[9] Yet the United States Constitution of 1787, with its implicit recognition of

---

on the basis of not being brown or black, they seem to be engaging in a negative approach. In fact, both approaches may be equally negative to the extent that their bases for identity are no more than skin deep. Alternatively, if American blacks forge a racial identity based on their shared history of slavery and oppression, then their approach could be genuinely categorized as inclusionary.

8 *See* MICHEL ROSENFELD, AFFIRMATIVE ACTION AND JUSTICE: A PHILOSOPHICAL AND CONSTITUTIONAL INQUIRY 21 (1991).

9 David A.J. Richards, *Revolution and Constitutionalism in America*, *infra* p. 85, 135-36.

slavery,[10] can only be reconciled with the proposition that "all men are created equal" if the latter is understood as referring to whites but not to blacks. Accordingly, the predominant identity underlying American constitutionalism was at best only partially given expression by the 1787 Constitution. It would take over three quarters of a century and a bloody civil war before the constitution could be fully reconciled with the predominant identity which was supposed to shape the constitutional self of the American people.

Another important issue affecting the interplay between identity and diversity is raised by the dichotomy between "all men are created equal" taken in its broadest sense—as encompassing not only *all* men but also women—and taken in the restrictive sense susceptible of reconciliation with the 1787 Constitution. That issue concerns the role of equality in the context of modern constitutionalism.

The idea of equality is inextricably linked to modern constitutionalism, which emerged against the backdrop of absolutism and authoritarianism. Indeed, modern constitutionalism took root in opposition to the privileges of status and birth characteristic of the feudal order. Accordingly, modern constitutionalism requires a levelling of status-based hierarchies in favor of an order grounded on the premise that all human beings are equal, with an inherent capacity for moral choice, self-respect, and dignity.[11] The equality inherent in modern constitutionalism, however, imposes constraints only at the highest levels of abstraction, and is thus consistent with a wide range of more concrete conceptions of equality, ranging from the libertarian paradigm to the most egalitarian paradigms.[12] But even though it remains very abstract, the equality implicit in modern constitutionalism plays a major role in shaping the basic structure of a constitutional order that conforms to the dictates of constitutionalism. Indeed, while insufficient to determine the nature of the specific fundamental rights that ought to be constitutionalized, the abstract equality inher-

---

[10] U.S. CONST. art. I, §§ 2, 9.

[11] The equality implicit in modern constitutionalism is meant to be prescriptive (or counterfactual) rather than descriptive, and it forms the backbone of liberal political theory. *See* ROSENFELD, *supra* note 8, at 20-21.

[12] The libertarian paradigm, originating in the work of John Locke, postulates that all individuals are equally free; that is, they are equally entitled to pursue their life, liberty and property. *See* JOHN LOCKE, THE SECOND TREATISE OF GOVERNMENT § 6 (J.W. Gough ed., 1966). In other words, the libertarian paradigm prescribes formal equality among individuals and generally proscribes interfering with property rights in the pursuit of welfare objectives. *See* ROBERT NOZICK, ANARCHY, STATE AND UTOPIA 150-51 (1974). Egalitarian paradigms, on the other hand, legitimate redistributing property for purposes of satisfying welfare needs, and generally endorse the prescription "to each according to his or her needs." For a more extended discussion of the egalitarian conception of justice, *see* ROSENFELD, *supra* note 8, at 116-18.

ent in modern constitutionalism imposes the requirement that all individuals be constitutionally guaranteed the *same* fundamental rights. Accordingly, such abstract equality underlies at least one of three major requirements of modern constitutionalism, namely the constitutional protection of fundamental rights.[13]

Equality is itself necessarily linked to the interplay between identity and difference, thus further tightening the complex nexus between that interplay and constitutionalism. There has been a general tendency to associate equality with identity and inequality or inferiority with difference.[14] Thus, racial, gender, and religious differences, for example, have been used to impose badges of inferiority. In addition, at least as against those who are of a different race, gender, or religion, those who belong to the same race, gender, or religion, tend to treat one another as equal. Upon further analysis, it becomes clear that inequality can be perpetrated through promotion of a forced identity as much as it can through the exploitation of differences. For instance, in a bilingual society one may equally deny equal treatment to the members of a linguistic minority by discriminating against them and treating them as inferiors, or by forbidding all discrimination but forcing all citizens, including those who belong to the linguistic minority, to learn and use the dominant language.[15] To comport with the requirements of equality, therefore, one should only make use of uncoerced identities.

Because of the long history of using certain differences as badges of inferiority, equality is often cast in terms of disregarding specific differences.[16] Moreover, in the case of the abstract equality that inheres in modern constitutionalism, it is necessary to ignore all factual differences that distinguish one individual from the next in order to promote the counterfactual identity that goes hand in hand with equal moral worth. However, to the extent that modern constitutionalism requires, or is compatible with, the protection of fundamental equality rights involving conceptions of equality that are more concrete than those implied by abstract equality, merely disregarding certain differences would simply not do. Take, for example, religious differences.

---

[13] The abstract equality inherent in modern constitutionalism may also be said to underly another of the three major requirements imposed by modern constitutionalism, namely adherence to the rule of law. Indeed, this latter requirement implies that laws should be equally applicable to all people; in other words, all persons should be equal *before* and *under* the law, regardless of the content of such law.

[14] *See* ROSENFELD, *supra* note 8, at 223.

[15] *Id.*

[16] *See, e.g.*, Plessy v. Ferguson, 163 U.S. 537, 539 (1896) (Harlan, J., dissenting) (famous dictum that the Constitution is "color blind").

To be sure, these ought to be disregarded for purposes of assuring most basic civil and political rights. Nevertheless, there are certain equalities, such as the equality of each individual to freely exercise his own religion,[17] which often require that religious differences be taken into account. Indeed, a generally applicable law may well have a disparate impact on different religions, inhibiting the practice of certain religions while not interfering with that of others. In that case, religious differences should *ceteris paribus* be taken into account to constrain application of the law in question to permit the adherents of all the religions involved to practice equally freely their chosen religion.[18] Accordingly, considerations concerning equality as related to modern constitutionalism suggest that voluntarily assumed or accepted identities be taken into account, as well as differences, insofar as they are invoked for the purpose of enhancing the protection of fundamental interests. Alternatively, differences ought to be disregarded whenever drawing upon them would likely result in a dilution of constitutionally significant equality concerns.

The foregoing observations reveal that, depending on the circumstances, constitutionally relevant identities can emerge in various ways—sometimes in spite of differences, sometimes by ignoring them, and sometimes by taking them into account and properly valorizing them. Consistent with this, constitutional identity can take many different forms, and evolve over time, because it is often immersed in an ongoing process marked by substantial changes. Constitutional identity can thus be bolstered through the use of gag rules that permit shifting the focus from areas of discord capable of producing unbridgeable divisions to areas of accord susceptible of providing indispensable rallying points for the preservation of a common identity.[19] Furthermore, constitutional identity may even be profitably pursued when certain fundamental differences cannot be neatly suppressed, ignored, accommodated, or incorporated. This could be done through the institution of what Arthur Jacobson has termed a "transitional constitution."[20] According to Jacobson, "a transitional constitution postpones the accommodation of political paradoxes using unstable principles instead for carrying on in the absence of agreement on one

---

[17] In the United States, the free exercise of religion is guaranteed by the First Amendment to the Constitution. U.S. CONST. amend. I.

[18] *See generally* Michael McConnell, *Accommodation of Religion*, 1985 SUP. CT. REV. 1 (1985); Ruti Teitel, *A Critique of Religion as Politics in the Public Sphere*, 78 CORNELL L. REV. 747 (1993).

[19] *See* Stephen Holmes, *Gag Rules or the Politics of Omission, in* CONSTITUTIONALISM AND DEMOCRACY 19-58 (Jon Elster & Rune Slagstad eds., 1988).

[20] *See* Arthur J. Jacobson, *Transitional Constitutions, infra* p. 413, 413.

or more elements of the basic framework."[21] Accordingly, when the drive towards constitutional identity is powerful enough, it can endure for some time, even in the face of clashing differences producing political paradoxes without apparent foreseeable resolution.

There can be several different ways of fulfilling the principal requirements of modern constitutionalism, depending on the character of the predominant constitutional identity and on the relationship between that identity and other relevant constitutional identities. To illustrate this point, one need only briefly compare the different ways in which eighteenth-century American and French constitutionalism, respectively, sought to implant limited government. In the American conception, limited government is best achieved through a division of powers. Such division is set in place both through horizontal and vertical means. The horizontal division, secured through the separation of powers within the federal government, is meant to give roughly equal powers to the legislative, executive, and judicial branches of government.[22] The vertical division is maintained through federalism which apportions powers between the federal government and the respective governments of the various states.[23] Moreover, underlying the American commitment to the division of powers is the belief that, even in a democracy, unchecked political power tends toward abuse,[24] which can be prevented through the implementation of a system of "checks and balances."

The French Constitution of 1793, in contrast, proclaims the supremacy of the national legislative branch,[25] thus enshrining the notion that democratic values are best preserved through undivided state power. This notion, moreover, is derived from the French belief that limited government is best achieved through democratic government based on universal and rational values, guided by Jean-Jacques Rousseau's conception of the general will.[26] Thus, in the French vi-

---

[21] *Id.* at 413-14.

[22] *See* U.S. CONST. arts. I, II, III (enumerating respectively the legislative, executive, and judiciary powers of the United States government).

[23] Federalism thus seeks to promote both the national identity of the United States and the respective identities of the states. Federalism also seeks to mediate between these identities and to allow them to coexist in harmony. The use of federalism in search of harmony between federal and state concerns, however, by no means guarantees a smooth or permanent apportionment of powers. *Compare* National League of Cities v. Usery, 426 U.S. 833 (1976) (federalism prohibits imposing certain federal labor standards on employees of a state) *with* Garcia v. San Antonio Metro. Transit Auth., 469 U.S. 528 (1985) (federalism permits imposing the same labor standards on employees of a state).

[24] *See, e.g.*, THE FEDERALIST No. 57 (James Madison).

[25] *See* FR. CONST. of 1793, art. I.

[26] *See* JEAN-JACQUES ROUSSEAU, THE SOCIAL CONTRACT 15-18 (Washington Square Press 1967) (1762).

sion, rational democratic self-government seeking to give expression to the general will looms as the optimal antidote to the arbitrary rule of absolute monarchy.

Different constitutional identities may well account for the multiplicity of paths capable of satisfying the fundamental requirements of modern constitutionalism. It must be stressed, however, that evolving sociopolitical conditions can significantly constrain the available choices. Furthermore, the pursuit of the fundamental values inherent in modern constitutionalism in the face of these constraints is likely to require a readjustment, if not a reshaping, of certain relevant constitutional identities. For instance, although in the United States the separation of powers and federalism continue to provide the principal structural constraints on unchecked democratic power, they have undergone important changes since their implantation over two hundred years ago. One notable change in the separation of powers area is the relatively dramatic increase in the powers of the President—particularly in foreign affairs—at the expense of those of Congress.[27] In the foreign affairs area, this shift in power is undoubtedly linked to the fact that the complexity and dazzling speed of contemporary international relations have made concentration of foreign affairs power in the hands of the President seem almost indispensable.[28]

In the area of federalism, however, the original balance of power between the federal government and that of the states has been virtually turned on its head. The 1787 Constitution established a federal government of limited enumerated powers[29] in order to leave a large degree of autonomy to the individual states.[30] Today, however, the vast expansion of federal regulation has severely crippled state power in a number of important areas. There are two principal reasons, moreover, for this dramatic reversal in favor of the federal government. First, the nationalization of the American economy, accompanied by an increasingly expansive judicial interpretation of the power of the federal government to regulate commerce among the states, has evolved to the point that no state activity that may have any effect on the national economy is now immune from federal regulation.[31] Second, basic civil and political rights are systematically nationalized

---

[27] Congress, however, has made periodic efforts to recover part of its lost powers. *See, e.g.,* War Powers Resolution, 50 U.S.C. § 1541 (1973).

[28] *See, e.g.,* United States v. Curtis-Wright Export Corp., 299 U.S. 304 (1936).

[29] *See* U.S. CONST. arts. I, II, III (respectively, the enumeration of powers of Congress, the federal executive, and the federal judiciary).

[30] *Id.* at amend. X ("The powers not delegated to the United States by the Constitution nor prohibited by it to the States, are reserved to the States respectively, or to the people.").

[31] *See, e.g.,* Wickard v. Filburn, 317 U.S. 111 (1942).

through incorporation of virtually the entire Federal Bill of Rights by the Fourteenth Amendment.[32]

In France where, unlike in the United States, the spirit of constitutionalism has presided over the enactment of various constitutions, structural changes have been much more dramatic in relation to the 1793 model based on legislative supremacy. Most notably, pursuant to the 1958 Constitution, the French President has acquired vastly increased powers that substantially mitigate those of the national legislature.[33] Furthermore, over the last twenty years, the French Constitutional Council has exercised an increasingly vigorous constitutional control over laws, thus providing France, for the first time, with a full fledged system of judicial review relating to the constitutionality of laws promulgated by the Parliament.[34] Significantly, however, these important constitutional changes have not fundamentally shaken the French belief that the mission of their constitutional democracy is to give expression to the general will. To be sure, the latter can no longer be given sufficient definition by the legislative process standing alone. Instead, as Dominique Rousseau points out in his contribution to this volume, in contemporary France the shaping of the general will depends on the executive and on the Constitutional Council as well as on the legislature.[35]

Consideration of the above-mentioned changes in the respective constitutional landscapes of the United States and France suggests the existence of an intricate process of dialectic interaction between constitutional identities, constitutional structural devices, and various stages of sociopolitical development. Thus, constitutional identities seem bound to contribute to the definition of particular structural devices and to place their imprint on the sociopolitical environment that they confront. Similarly, important changes in the sociopolitical environment may well require the adjustment or replacement of existing constitutional structural devices as well as a corresponding adaptation, transformation, or remolding of relevant constitutional identities.

Constitutionalism engages a complex interplay between identity and diversity at so many different levels that it seems altogether futile to search for any particular identity or difference as being indispensable to a legitimate constitutional scheme. Because of this, and because

---

[32] U.S. CONST. amend. XIV.

[33] FR. CONST. of 1958, tit. II.

[34] See generally DOMINIQUE ROUSSEAU, DROIT DU CONTENTIEUX CONSTITUTIONNEL ch. II (2d ed. 1992).

[35] Dominique Rousseau, The Constitutional Judge: Master or Slave of the Constitution?, infra p. 261, 276-81.

predominant constitutional identities tend to vary significantly from culture to culture, it seems highly unlikely that specific constitutional structures and provisions could successfully survive wholesale transplantation from one country to another. Modern constitutionalism, however, does impose certain definite broad requirements—such as limited government, adherence to the rule of law, protection of fundamental interests, and compliance with the demands of abstract equality—that are bound to circumscribe the number of possible legitimate orderings of relevant identities and differences. Accordingly, if constitutionalism implies certain points of reference with respect to identities and differences, these are most likely to concern the *relational links* between identity and diversity, and between the interplay of these and prevailing or evolving sociopolitical conditions.

The various essays published in this volume center around a cluster of important themes that are particularly apt to reveal the kind of relational links between identity and diversity which might be expected to go hand in hand with the deployment of modern constitutionalism. The important themes in question are: the relation between constitutionalism and constitutions; identity, difference, self, and other in the context of constitution making; the identity of the constitutional subject and its relation to the search for authoritative constitutional meaning; the struggle between identity and difference in the context of the constitutional apportionment of freedom and equality among individuals and groups; and the role of property in delimiting the constitutional boundaries between self and other in the context of the relation between the individual and the state.

The relationship between constitution and constitutionalism is particularly important because constitutions are especially apt vehicles for the institutionalization of the essential requisites of constitutionalism. Louis Henkin's essay focuses on this important relationship and demonstrates how shortcomings—or, in his own words, "genetic defects"—found in actual constitutions inhibit the full realization of constitutionalism. Henkin examines two constitutional settings, namely the eighteenth-century United States Constitution and the mid-twentieth century international human rights covenants, and finds them both wanting. Henkin points to two important genetic defects found in the eighteenth-century American constitutional scheme. First, the separation of powers and federalism provisions are inadequate to promote a sufficiently representative and democratic government. Second, important fundamental rights, like basic equality rights, are left unprotected. Furthermore, noting that the twentieth-century human rights model has brought about a modification of eighteenth-century liberalism through commitment to communitarianism, Henkin criticizes the twentieth-century model for failing to provide a means to prevent abuses of state limitations of fundamental rights in the name of protecting the public interest. Henkin concludes that this latter genetic defect cannot be remedied in the context of an international community still strongly committed to the paramount importance of state sovereignty rights.

From the perspective of the interplay between identity and diversity, two principal points emerge from Henkin's discussion. First, central to constitutionalism is its prescriptive dimension, enabling it to furnish normative criteria for the critical evaluation of existing constitutions. Second, growing in importance are international covenants for the delimitation of contemporary constitutional identities. Indeed, with the growing number and power of supranational political orderings, relevant constitutional identities are not only increasingly likely to be formed at supranational levels, but also to be significantly shaped by clashes between supranational, national, and regional identities.[36]

The essays by Jon Elster, David Richards, Ulrich Preuss, and Andrew Arato confront various aspects of the relationship between identity, difference, self, and other in the context of constitution making. Constitution making raises questions of identity both across the political landscape and across the temporal boundaries marked by intergenerational succession. Specifically, constitution making requires addressing the question of the identities of the relevant political forces and entities in relation to the definition and legitimation of an appropriate constitutional self. Finding such identity, however, appears to be no easy matter in so far as constitution makers often operate in a political environment characterized either by too great a rupture with the preceding order or, on the contrary, by a break insufficient to permit an adequate demarcation of the new order from the old one. In the former case, the magnitude of revolutionary changes may make it difficult to sustain the requisite degree of identity; in the latter case, the lack of significant change may fail to produce the requisite difference to permit the successful grounding of a new constitutional identity.[37]

Constitution making also raises the question of maintaining the

---

36 For an extended discussion of the conflicts that surround efforts to reconcile national and supranational constitutional concerns in the context of the European Community, see LAURENT COHEN-TANUGI, L'EUROPE EN DANGER (1992).

37 *Cf.* Andrew Arato, *Dilemmas Arising from the Power to Create Constitutions in Eastern Europe*, *infra* p. 165, 165-66 (discussing Hannah Arendt and the antinomy between permanent revolution and conservative tradition).

essential identity of the newly created constitutional self over time in order to secure a sufficient link between the generation of constitution makers and numerous succeeding generations. Carving a constitutional identity over time is crucial in relation to the legitimation of imposing the constitutional scheme devised by the constitution makers upon subsequent generations. Indeed, in the absence of a common identity spanning over time, it is difficult to justify why members of subsequent generations should be bound by the constitutional choices of their long dead ancestors.[38]

Both Jon Elster and David Richards analyze constitution making as it arose in the eighteenth century. Elster compares the French and American experiences, whereas Richards concentrates on the American, but both provide important insights applicable to constitution making in general. Elster demonstrates that constitution making necessarily involves a bootstrapping operation, whereby a constituent assembly severs its ties with the authorities that brought it into being.[39] Moreover, Elster explains that, not only must the constituent assembly disengage itself from past generations, but it must also find a way to bind future generations. Thus, the bootstrapping that necessarily accompanies the creation of a new constitutional order requires the constitution makers to simultaneously introduce a measure of differentiation with respect to relevant past identities, and to project towards the future an identity that is likely to be embraced by yet unborn generations. According to Elster, it is impossible to isolate a general set of conditions that would ensure the success of constitutional bootstrapping. Nevertheless, it is instructive to consider that, as Elster points out, in the United States, where constitution making only produced a partial break with the past, the new constitutional order proved a success. In contrast, the Constitutional Assembly in France achieved a clean break with the past, but its work soon began unravelling. Based on this comparison, one might speculate that successful constitutional bootstrapping requires a delicate balancing act whereby, with respect to the past, differences should outweigh without completely dwarfing identities whereas, with respect to the future, identities should predominate over differences without seeking to suppress the latter. Indeed, only if constitutional identity is flexible enough to accommodate the differences inevitably arising over time is

---

[38] The problem of the legitimation of a particular constitutional order over time could be obviated if constitutionalism imposed sufficiently exhaustive criteria for constitutional legitimacy. As the preceding discussion indicates, however, the selection of constitutionally relevant identities and differences is conditioned, at least in part, by historically and culturally contingent factors.

[39] See Jon Elster, Constitutional Bootstrapping in Philadelphia and Paris, infra p. 57.

it likely to hold any appeal for those who are far removed in time from the constitution makers.

Focusing exclusively on the American case, David Richards also explores the relationship between constitution making and revolutionary change. Richards stresses the key role played by "abstractness in the ascription of constitutional meaning" in the preservation of the identity of the constitutional community over time.[40] Such abstractness makes for a broadly defined identity capable of cementing intergenerational differences becoming integrated within the flow of a dynamically conceived constitutional order.

The abstractness of predominant constitutional identity, however, is a double-edged sword. Not only does it facilitate the integration of differences, but also it allows for the subversion of constitutionalism through the introduction of wedges between abstract and concrete levels of identity. Richards illustrates this latter tendency through his discussion of the historical implications of the acceptance and accommodation of slavery within the American constitutional scheme before adoption of the Civil War amendments. As previously mentioned, the predominant American constitutional identity marking a revolutionary change from the British monarchical scheme, is in significant part encapsuled in the proposition that "all men are created equal." But because this general proposition could not be readily reconciled with the existence of slavery, it became necessary, as Richards observes, to manufacture an intrinsically racial national identity. This, in turn, required a systematic ideological dehumanization of the slave race that saw its culmination in the infamous *Dred Scott* decision.[41]

The tension between an abstract constitutional identity based on equality and its concrete counterpart driven by a need to recognize the legitimacy of slavery, as Richards demonstrates, led to an unbearable impasse. Resolution of this impasse and the genuine alignment of abstract and concrete constitutional identity required, according to Richards, no less than a revolution. This revolution—the second American Revolution—was the Civil War which culminated in the adoption of the Thirteenth, Fourteenth and Fifteenth Amendments to the Constitution which made it possible to reconcile abstract and concrete constitutional identity. Thus, for the United States to achieve a working constitutional identity conforming to the vision of its founding fathers, it was necessary to carry out two revolutions. The first of

---

40 Richards, *supra* note 9, at 140.
41 Scott v. Sanford, 60 U.S. 393 (1856).

these was necessary to implant American constitutionalism; the second, to salvage it.

Ulrich Preuss and Andrew Arato explore important theoretical questions regarding constitution making with special focus on recent constitutional developments in Eastern and Central Europe. Preuss claims that constitution making is the secular equivalent of divine creation "*ex nihilo*."[42] Furthermore, he conceives of constitution making as a revolutionary act which both consolidates and puts an end to the revolution that made it possible. Accordingly, constitution making involves both a revolutionary rupture and a domestication of revolutionary forces in order to become channeled into the flow of a newly emerging institutional order. The shape of this new constitutional order depends, as Preuss emphasizes, on the nature of the constitutional subject.

Underlying the identity of the constitutional subject is a conception of the nation. Preuss contrasts two different conceptions of the nation. On one hand is the French political idea of the nation as a rational and deliberative community of citizens bound together by a social contract designed to implement the general will. On the other hand is the German and Eastern European image of the nation as a prepolitical community characterized by ethnic homogeneity. Furthermore, Preuss asserts that the constituent power of a people always encompasses both an ethnicist and a demotic component.

The constitutional subject cannot do away with either ethnicist or demotic influences. Indeed, without the former, such a subject would be reduced to a rootless abstraction devoid of life; without the latter, in contrast, such a subject would be so blindly driven by prepolitical forces that it would be completely incapable of generating any genuine constitutional order. As Preuss sees it, constitutionalism requires imposing restraints on the impulsive drive of ethos through the deployment of institutional devices designed to control the influence of prepolitical forces on the shaping of politics. The constitutional subject must therefore use constitution making as a means of subjugating ethos to demos. In Preuss's words, "it is the very rationale of the constitution to transform the unfathomable power of the ethos into the responsible authority of the demos."

Andrew Arato approaches the relationship between constitution making and forging a constitutional identity from the standpoint of the attempted implantation of constitutionalism in the absence of a genuine revolution. Drawing on the recent transitions to democracy

---

[42] *See* Ulrich K. Preuss, *Constitutional Powermaking for the New Polity: Some Deliberations on the Relations Between Constituent Power and the Constitution*, *infra* p. 143.

in Hungary and Poland—which involved accommodation rather than violent repudiation of the outgoing regimes[43]—Arato critically assesses the possible ways in which a viable constitutional identity might take hold where there has been no clear rupture with the past.

Unlike in the United States, where the popular sovereign assumed the role of the constitutional subject for purposes of constitution making, the constitutional subject in Eastern Europe has been drawn from the plurality of organized collectivities of civil society. Moreover, whereas the popular sovereign emerging triumphant from the revolution lurks as the natural agent for launching democratic constitutionalism, as Arato points out, the murky constitutional subject that has arisen in Eastern Europe may well prove unequal to the task. Indeed, the popular sovereign acting on the heels of revolutionary rupture can tap the extraordinary energy required to engage in what Bruce Ackerman has termed "constitutional politics" as opposed to "normal politics."[44] Without such rupture, however, the identity of the constitutional subject may not be sufficiently distinct to prevent the eruption of normal politics into the very process of constitution making. As Arato observes, in Eastern Europe, where constitutionalism has been launched through constitutional amendments rather than through adoption of new constitutions, and where existing parliaments have assumed the constitution-making role rather than specially convened constituent assemblies, ordinary politics have so thoroughly permeated the constitution-making process as to raise serious doubts concerning the possibility of successfully instituting democratic constitutionalism.

The problems surrounding the implantation of constitutionalism in Eastern Europe should not lead, however, to outright rejection of civil society as a potentially fruitful constitutional subject. Indeed, given the convergence of political forces in contemporary settings, Arato argues that the making of constitutional politics should not be left to the popular sovereign alone. Instead, Arato proposes that the contemporary constitutional subject should combine reference both to the popular sovereign and to the public sphere encompassed by civil society as a way to promote a brand of democratic constitutional poli-

---

[43] *See* Arato, *supra* note 37, at 180-81.

[44] *See* Bruce A. Ackerman, *Neo-Federalism?, in* CONSTITUTIONALISM AND DEMOCRACY, *supra* note 19, at 153, 162-63. "[C]onstitutional politics . . . is characterized by Publian appeals to the common good, ratified by a mobilized mass of American citizens expressing their assent through extraordinary institutional forms . . . . [C]onstitutional politics . . . should be permitted to dominate the nation's life only during rare periods of heightened political consciousness." At other times, we have "normal politics" where "factions try to manipulate the constitutional forms of political life to pursue their own narrow interests." *Id*. at 162-63.

tics which would not ultimately rest exclusively on legislative bodies or on the atomized population.

Constitutionalism has been described as being in essence antidemocratic.[45] To the extent that a tyrannical majority threatens limited government or fundamental rights, moreover, it seems imperative that constitutionalism should be used to curb majority rule. Pursuant to Arato's assessment, however, the pervasive deployment in contemporary settings of statist institutional devices and the entrenchment of liberal constitutionalism threaten to drown the voices of democracy and thus alienate the constitutional subject from the flow of constitutional politics. Under these circumstances, the challenge is to frame a constitutional subject capable of engaging in deliberative and rational democratic constitutional politics. Relying on Arato's insights, one might well opt for a constitutional subject that draws simultaneously from the popular sovereign and from the more mediated collective identities produced by civil society.

The next group of essays address various aspects of the relationship between the identity of the constitutional subject and the establishment of authoritative constitutional meaning. Much of the controversy surrounding this relationship centers on the legitimacy of judicial review. As the maker of the constitution, the constitutional subject must often generate broadly phrased open-ended constitutional provisions[46] that are flexible enough to accommodate intergenerational differences without compromising the overall identity that furnishes the essential link between the constitution makers and their descendants.[47] Moreover, the identity involved need not be frozen in time, but may be conceived as an evolving one that is further molded by each succeeding generation.[48] But the combination of vague and general constitutional provisions with an evolving constitutional identity make for much uncertainty and debate concerning what ought to qualify as authoritative constitutional meaning. To ac-

---

[45] *See, e.g.*, Jon Elster, *Introduction, in* CONSTITUTIONALISM AND DEMOCRACY, *supra* note 19, at 2 ("Constitutionalism refers to limits on majority decisions.").

[46] *See, e.g.*, U.S. CONST. amend. XIV, § 1 (the Due Process and Equal Protection Clauses).

[47] *Cf.* McCulloch v. Maryland, 17 U.S. (4 Wheat.) 316, 415 (1819) ("[Constitutional provisions are] intended to endure for ages to come, and consequently, to be adapted to the various *crises* of human affairs. To have prescribed the means by which government should, in all future time, execute its powers, would have been to change, entirely, the character of the [constitution], and give it the properties of a legal code.").

[48] Many legal scholars in the United States have argued against confining constitutional interpretation to the discovery and implementation of the "original intent" of the constitution makers. *See, e.g.*, Paul Brest, *The Misconceived Quest for the Original Understanding*, 60 B.U. L. REV. 204 (1980); Richard S. Kay, *Adherence to the Original Intentions in Constitutional Adjudication: Three Objections and Responses*, 82 NW. U. L. REV. 226 (1988).

commodate the interplay between a constantly evolving constitutional identity and the steady flow of differences that must be legitimately integrated within the constitutional order, it may well be necessary to repeatedly define the constitutional subject without provoking any fundamental loss in its identity. Whether the constitutional judge is ready for this delicate task, and whether it is possible to devise consistent normative criteria to evaluate the interpretive work of the constitutional judge, are the questions that strike at the heart of this matter.

The essays by Bernhard Schlink, George Fletcher, Ruti Teitel, and Robin West explore, on one hand, the relationship between constitutional culture, national identity and authoritative constitutional meaning. The essays by Aharon Barak, Dominique Rousseau, and Carlos Nino, on the other hand, focus more specifically on the role of the constitutional judge and of judicial review in relation to the establishment of authoritative constitutional meaning.

Bernhard Schlink examines the connection between national identity, constitutional culture and constitution in the context of contemporary Germany. As conceived by Schlink, constitutional culture emerges not only from the constitution but also from the historical and institutional treatment of the constitution in the hands of, among others, judges, legislators, bureaucrats and legal scholars.[49] Schlink focuses particularly on a recent change in the constitutional culture of Germany. This change has two principal components: first, a shift from a conception of fundamental constitutional rights qua rights to a conception of such rights as principles; and second, an evolution in the relationship between constitutional jurisprudence and the constitutional court, resulting in the court acquiring greater power and latitude in setting the boundaries of constitutional rights.

The principal difference between rights qua rights, or subjective rights,[50] and rights as principles, or objective rights,[51] is that subjective rights are essentially deontological in nature whereas objective rights are predominantly teleological.[52] Enforcing fundamental rights as objective rights, moreover, apparently requires a much more active constitutional court. As Schlink points out, to the extent that the constitutional court treats rights as objective principles, it must weigh

---

[49] *See* Bernhard Schlink, *German Constitutional Culture in Transition, infra* p. 197, 197-98.

[50] Schlink defines subjective rights as entitlements of the individual subject. *Id*. at 199.

[51] Schlink defines objective rights as "maxims according to which social relationships, as well as relationships between state and society are ordered." *Id*. at 199.

[52] Schlink does not use this terminology, but he does refer to subjective rights as entitlements. *See id*. at 199. He also refers to objective rights as rules of optimization. *Id*. at 199-201.

utilities and determine social consequences as a precondition to the protection of rights. This requires the constitutional court to decide policy issues, and since questions concerning optimal social relations rarely have univocal determinate answers, it makes for significant uncertainty concerning the proper interpretation of the scope of fundamental rights.

By treating fundamental rights as teleological rather than as deontological, the German constitutional court has, in Schlink's judgement, moved away from the protection of individual freedoms in order to become another forum for the resolution of social and political problems. Thus, as Schlink observes, the losers in the legislative arena get a second chance to have the policies that they promote adopted by turning to the constitutional court. Moreover, according to Schlink, what accounts for the change in constitutional culture leading to an expanded role for the constitutional court is the fact that, after the experiences of the Weimar Republic and of the Third Reich, Germans tend to view politics as "dirty" while regarding law as "clean." Ironically, however, by propelling policy decisions into the domain of law, contemporary German constitutional culture gives rise not to a genuine escape from politics, but rather to an increasingly pervasive politicization of law.

The clash between deontological and teleological conceptions of fundamental constitutional rights certainly looms as highly relevant beyond the confines of contemporary German constitutional culture. Moreover, the tendency towards an increasingly teleological vision of rights does not appear to be solely dependent on the desire to escape from politics to law. Another plausible reason for the shift towards teleological rights is, in general, the changing nature of the modern state and, in particular, the pervasive nature of bureaucratic administration in the welfare state and the blurring of the boundary between the public and private sectors. As long as government remains relatively limited, and the line between public and private remains fairly clearly drawn, rights as entitlements may carve out a sufficient zone of individual freedom *from* governmental intrusion to comply with the essential dictates of constitutionalism.[53] However, if state administration becomes pervasive and the boundary between private and public largely blurred, mere freedom *from* government intrusion may be inadequate to sustain the values inherent in fundamental rights.[54] In

---

[53] This conforms essentially to the Lockean vision of autonomous private individuals free to pursue their individual happiness in the face of limited government. *See generally* LOCKE, *supra* note 12.

[54] For an elaboration of this last point in relation to freedom of expression in the context of

that case, a change of identity in the sociopolitical fabric of the relevant constitutional community would seem responsible for the need to shift from a deontological to a teleological approach to fundamental rights. Hence, contemporary developments may well make the increasing politicization of constitutional law virtually inevitable. For our present purposes, the most important consequence of the politicization of constitutional law is that it apparently renders the relationship between constitutional culture, national identity, and authoritative constitutional meaning much more problematic.

Whereas Schlink concentrates on how national identity contributes to the shaping of constitutional culture and to the overall structuring of the practice of constitutional interpretation, the contributions by George Fletcher, Ruti Teitel, and Robin West focus on the possible uses of identity as an interpretive tool in the search for authoritative constitutional meaning. Thus, Fletcher asserts that, in certain cases, it is legitimate to resolve a dispute in terms of the constitutional decision maker's constitutional identity.[55] For example, in Germany, the constitutional court's abortion decision was shaped by that country's strong commitment to the protection of life bolstered by its desire to distance itself from Hitler's contempt for human life.

Drawing on the American experience, both Teitel and West make clear that reliance on identity as an interpretive tool does not necessarily pave the way to authoritative constitutional meaning. The reason for this is that there is no single national identity shared by everyone which may be drawn upon to give determinate shape to constitutional rights. Instead, there are likely to be competing identities, giving rise to different arrays of constitutional rights. Teitel argues that the Rehnquist Court has fashioned a reactionary constitutional identity designed to stem the flow of political change.[56] Consistent with that reactionary identity, constitutional rights are conceived as finite elements in a zero sum game, where each grant of a right to an individual is taken as having to correspond with compromising an interest of the majority or with endangering an existing tradition.

West, on the other hand, evokes two different constitutional identities, a liberal one and a progressive one, with respect to the constitutional protection of freedom of speech.[57] West demonstrates fur-

---

American broadcasting, see Owen Fiss, *Free Speech and Social Structure*, 71 IOWA L. REV. 1405 (1986).

[55] *See* George P. Fletcher, *Constitutional Identity*, *infra* p. 223.

[56] *See* Ruti G. Teitel, *Reactionary Constitutional Identity*, *infra* p. 223, 233-34.

[57] *See* Robin West, *Toward a First Amendment Jurisprudence of Respect: A Comment on George Fletcher's* Constitutional Identity, *infra* p. 245, 245.

ther that reliance on the liberal paradigm leads to an individualistic conception of free speech rights, whereas adoption of the progressive paradigm results in a communitarian elaboration of the same rights.

Where there is consensus on the relevant element of the national identity, drawing upon that identity is likely to contribute to the determination of authoritative meaning. Where changing and competing identities predominate, however, references to identity are likely to exacerbate disagreements concerning authoritative constitutional meanings. Moreover, treating part of the national identity as if it represented the whole creates the risk of subverting constitutional identity to the mere political identity of a particular faction.

Aharon Barak examines the relationship between judicial interpretation and the establishment of authoritative constitutional meaning; he brings to this task his unique perspective as both a justice on the Supreme Court of Israel and a prominent legal scholar. Departing from the observation that there is no "true" interpretation of the constitutional text, Barak emphasizes that there are usually several "proper" interpretations, thus leaving a legitimate place for the exercise of judicial discretion.[58] Such judicial discretion, however, is not unlimited, as Barak asserts that the constitutional judge's interpretive practice must be "rooted in history and tradition."[59] As envisaged by Barak, the constitutional judge must not be restricted to the perspective of the constitution's framers, and constitutional interpretation should not be limited to a search for original intent or for the subjective purpose of the constitution. Rather, Barak believes that the proper role of the judge is to interpret the constitution in a manner that is consistent with its objective purpose—that is, with the fundamental contemporary values and policies that establish the identity of the community as a continuation of an evolving identity rooted in history and tradition. These constraints preclude a judge from legitimately relying on personal value preferences as a basis for constitutional interpretations. Moreover, by requiring that judges reconcile past and present identities and by directing them to carry out their interpretive tasks in a way that controls majorities and protects individual dignity and liberty, the constraints in question preclude certain paths of constitutional interpretation even if they leave more than one such path open. More specifically, these constraints do not justify a constitutional judge picking and choosing among all existing conflicting identities. Indeed, in this context, a judge's legitimate power to choose seems limited to those existing conflicting identities which can

---

[58] *See* Aharon Barak, *Hermeneutics and Constitutional Interpretation*, *infra* p. 253, 258-60.
[59] *Id*. at 259.

be reconciled with an open path of interpretation. Finally, to the extent that the constitutional judge scrupulously adheres to the requisite constraints, it seems less likely that the identity of the part will be easily passed for that of the whole.

Focusing exclusively on the French experience, Dominique Rousseau elaborates a strong defense of the role of the constitutional judge and of judicial control in the context of the evolving identity of democracy, as shaped by the values underlying contemporary constitutionalism. Like Arato, Rousseau thinks that modern constitutionalism must draw on civil society as well as on political society.[60] In contrast to Arato, however, Rousseau does not believe that constitutionalism requires an expansion of democratic politics. Instead, Rousseau embraces the view that the enhancement of constitutionalism depends on strengthening liberal constitutionalism, which in turn calls for an elevation of the role of the constitutional judge.[61] Ultimately, there may be no significant disagreement between Arato and Rousseau concerning the optimal relationship among the indispensable ingredients of modern constitutionalism. The differences between the two may be a mere reflection of the fact that Arato concentrates on Eastern Europe where there has been a dearth of democratic politics, whereas Rousseau deals with France where majoritarian politics has traditionally reigned virtually unchecked.

Tracking a trend similar to that discussed by Schlink in relation to Germany, Rousseau notes that French political institutions have fallen into disrepute and that French politicians are currently held in low esteem. Unlike in Germany where politics fell into disrepute because of the highly reprehensible policies of the Third Reich, in France the loss of confidence in politics appears to stem from frustrations with shortcomings inherent in the institutional structures of government. Indeed, as Rousseau emphasizes, the alignment of the legislative majority with the government—that is, the prime minister and his cabinet—reduces the general will to the will of the majority.[62]

---

60 Rousseau, *supra* note 35, at 276-81.

61 Rousseau does not use the term "liberal constitutionalism," but asserts that constitutionalism is better served by a greater balance in the relationship between the government, the legislative branch, and the constitutional council. *Id*. at 267-70.

62 *Cf.* Michel Rosenfeld, *Contract and Justice: The Relation Between Classical Contract Law and Social Contract Theory*, 70 IOWA L. REV. 769 (1985).

As used by [Jean-Jacques] Rousseau, the notion of the general will is certainly somewhat mysterious and not altogether consistent. But it is clearly not reducible to an individual's particular will or to the will of the majority (in the sense of a mere aggregate of individual wills). It has been described as "a highly voluntarist formulation of the traditional conception of the common good or the common interest."

Rescuing the general will from inevitable degradation into the will of the majority necessitates, according to Rousseau, a change in the French constitutional order. That change, in turn, requires granting increased powers to the constitutional judge in order to effectuate a shift from democratic politics to constitutional democracy. Rousseau does not believe that the constitutional judge acting alone can guarantee the articulation and implementation of the general will. Rather, Rousseau envisages the general will emerging from the interaction between the constitutional judge, legislators, members of the government, and a number of nongovernmental actors, such as legal scholars, journalists, and trade association representatives. Furthermore, Rousseau does not entrust the responsibility to conform to the general will exclusively to a structural realignment of relevant interactions between political agents and civil society representatives. Also, he urges reliance on the constitutionalization and judicial implementation of the substantive values promoted by the international human rights movement. In short, in Rousseau's conception, judicial review plays an essential role in the establishment of the identity of constitutional democracy, both in terms of ensuring the proper institutional alignment and promoting the requisite normative values best designed to reinvigorate pursuit of the general will.

Carlos Nino tackles the central problems raised by the relationship between judicial review and the establishment of authoritative constitutional meaning from the standpoint of a systematic philosophical approach. Zeroing in on the countermajoritarian difficulty raised by judicial review, Nino searches for a philosophical justification of the practice of leaving it up to a largely unaccountable and often unrepresentative judicial elite to circumscribe the nature and scope of fundamental constitutional rights.[63] Nino concludes that a philosophical justification of the practice of judicial review can be articulated, provided that the practice in question is set within a dialectical structure. In other words, while no single straightforward line of argument leads to a satisfactory justification of judicial review, such a justification can be formulated nonetheless through a careful integration and balancing of arguments, which, taken separately, run in opposite directions.

In the broadest terms, Nino locates the philosophical foundation of judicial review at the heart of the dialectic between constitutionalism and democracy. The relationship between constitutionalism and

---

Id. at 868 (citations omitted).

[63] *See* Carlos Santiago Nino, *A Philosophical Reconstruction of Judicial Review, infra* p. 285.

democracy is problematic if not downright contradictory. Sometimes, constitutionalism and democracy are conceived as being antagonistic,[64] while at other times, as being essentially mutually dependent and mutually reinforcing.[65] To the extent that constitutionalism is conceived as essentially antidemocratic, moreover, judicial review would appear to be easy to justify as a most useful, if not necessary, adjunct to the constitutional curbing of democratic excesses. In contrast, the more constitutionalism and democracy are viewed as being convergent, the more it would seem unjustified to leave the last word in constitutional interpretation to an unelected judicial elite.

Nino's analysis reveals that the relevant correlations between judicial review and the interplay between constitutionalism and democracy are not as straightforward as might at first appear. The case for the proposition that judicial review is justified in light of the constitution's superiority over laws which are the product of democratic politics is made forcefully, Nino points out, by Chief Justice John Marshall in *Marbury v. Madison*.[66] That case, however, is not as airtight as it initially appears because, as Nino observes, many laws that are contrary to the constitution may, for a number of reasons, have to be considered valid. Because of this difficulty, Nino argues that determination of the ultimate implications of the constitution cannot be left to judicial review alone; instead, they must be derived from extralegal norms. The content of these norms, in turn, depends on the results of a process of democratic deliberation. Accordingly, we seem to have come full circle, with the ultimate meaning of the constitution depending somehow on democracy, thus apparently negating the legitimacy of judicial review. Nonetheless, by a further twist of the dialectic, it turns out that deliberative democracy itself depends for its survival on the operation of certain nondemocratic constraints designed to bolster the integrity of the democratic process and individual autonomy. Judicial review happens to be the appropriate vehicle for the implementation of the constraints designed to save democracy from its tendency towards self-destruction.

In sum, consistent with Nino's analysis, constitutionalism legitimates judicial review not as the rule, but as an exception to democratic deliberation. Moreover, under this conception, the justification

---

64 *See* Ackerman, *supra* note 44 and accompanying text.

65 *See, e.g.*, Stephen Holmes, *Precommitment and the Paradox of Democracy, in* CONSTITUTIONALISM AND DEMOCRACY, *supra* note 19, at 195, 197 ("The existence of an irreconcilable "tension" between constitutionalism and democracy is one of the core myths of modern political thought . . . . [C]onstitutionalism and democracy are mutually supportive . . . .").

66 *See* Nino, *supra* note 63, at 287-89 (citing Marbury v. Madison, 5 U.S. (1 Cranch) 137 (1803).

of judicial review is interstitial, as it serves to preserve a dialectical balance between what Nino regards as the three crucial facets of constitutionalism: democratic deliberation, respect for individual rights, and adherence to the rule of law. Thus, while judicial review cannot be identified with any one of the three facets of constitutionalism, it nevertheless plays a pivotal role in framing the identity of constitutionalism as a three-faceted concept.

The next group of essays, by András Sajó, Frederick Schauer, and Marty Slaughter, address issues related to the struggle between identity and difference in the context of the constitutional apportionment of freedom and equality among individuals and groups. Both freedom and equality rights entail taking differences into account. Freedom of expression, for example, depends on the toleration of a wide diversity of views. Similarly, genuine equality—that is, equality that is not predicated on any coerced levelling of differences—requires accommodating differences relied upon to enhance dignity and self-respect. On the other hand, preservation of constitutional order seems bound to require some constraints on the proliferation of differences. Thus, freedom of expression may not best serve the values of constitutionalism through an unlimited protection of the broadest conceivable array of different expressions.[67] In short, in the context of constitutionalism, accommodation of differences must be constrained to the extent necessary to preserve the unity engendered by the predominant constitutional identity. Accordingly, the determination of the legitimate scope of constitutional protection of individual and group differences, like the definition of constitutional identity, involves consideration of the interplay between identity and diversity. It should, therefore, come as no surprise that the present group of essays should broach some of the same themes as the preceding essays. The principal distinction between this group of essays and the previous ones is that whereas the latter approached the interplay between identity and diversity primarily from the perspective of establishing or preserving identity, the essays in this group place a greater emphasis on the protection of differences when dealing with issues relating to the same interplay.

András Sajó's essay affords us yet another opportunity to consider the problem of intergenerational links between the constitution makers and members of subsequent generations, but it deals with this

---

[67] For example, it is not clear that constitutionalism is well served by a wide protection of extremist speech. For a discussion of the vexing issues raised with respect to the constitutional protection of extremist speech, see Michel Rosenfeld, *Extremist Speech and The Paradox of Tolerance*, 100 HARV. L. REV. 1457 (1987) (book review).

problem from the perspective of the subsequent generations' interest in holding on to their differences without having to abandon their adherence to the prevailing constitutional order. According to Sajó, the constitution-making generation is the preferred generation to the extent that it can write its value preferences into the constitution.[68] Moreover, since it is not possible to discover the value preferences of yet unborn generations, even the most concerned constitution makers will be unable to inscribe future value preferences into the constitution that they are drafting. Nevertheless, as Sajó points out, it is possible to reduce the burden on subsequent generations through adoption of generation-neutral structural constraints such as the separation of powers. In any event, the hold of past value preferences should not be so strong as to cripple the capacity for public participation of subsequent generations.

Sufficient consideration for the differences of future generations is particularly difficult to find in the case of counterrevolutionary or restoration constitutions. These constitutions, as Sajó emphasizes, involve a return to the past. Thus, in the recent transition to constitutionalism in Hungary, the generation of the constitution makers experienced a clear conflict in relation to the establishment of property rights. This conflict was between groups representing the interests of a past generation including former owners and groups of younger propertyless persons. As Sajó notes, in Hungary the constitution-making generation is living a conflict between generations.

In the final analysis, too little accommodation of intergenerational differences seems as threatening to constitutionalism as too great an emphasis on such differences. Overemphasis of differences would tend to blur constitutional identity to the point of undermining the requisite continuity between constitutional past and future. Underemphasis of differences, however, threatens to alienate future generations from the prevailing constitutional identity and could well result in driving them away from the established constitutional order.

Frederick Schauer explores the relationship between cultural difference and establishing authoritative constitutional meaning in the context of free speech rights. As Schauer notes, freedom of speech provisions are typically couched in broad language which makes for significant indeterminacy.[69] Similarly phrased free speech provisions may, however, be given different meanings depending on differences

---

[68] *See* András Sajó, *Preferred Generations: A Paradox of Restoration Constitutions, infra* p. 335, 339-40.

[69] *See* Frederick Schauer, *Free Speech and the Cultural Contingency of Constitutional Categories, infra* p. 353, 356.

in the respective cultural settings in which they are embedded. Schauer points out, for example, that the fact that neo-Nazi speech is protected speech in the United States but not in Germany reflects cultural-historical differences between the two countries. Thus, whereas in the United States "slippery slope" arguments regarding neo-Nazi speech have proven successful, in Germany such arguments do not sound convincing.

It obviously follows from Schauer's analysis that constitutional provisions cannot be exported wholesale from one culture to the next, as the nature and scope of the rights protected in the second culture would end up being quite different than their counterparts in the first culture. But it also may be the case that cultural differences may render certain constitutional provisions important in one culture while making similar provisions superfluous in another.[70]

As earlier noted, the equality implied in constitutionalism and constitutional equality sometimes requires ignoring certain differences, while at other times demanding that such differences be acknowledged and taken into account. Insofar as constitutional identity incorporates equality as an important ingredient, such identity, at times and in certain contexts, is constructed in part by ignoring certain differences,[71] whereas at other times and in other contexts it is constructed in part by drawing upon certain differences.[72] A context with respect to which it is appropriate to ignore differences may be referred to as a "sphere of assimilation." A context, in relation to which it is proper to account for differences, is a "sphere of differentiation."[73]

Constitutionalism, by virtue of its commitment to equality and to the interplay between identity and diversity, requires the existence of both spheres of assimilation and of spheres of differentiation.[74] It is not clear, however, what the relative distribution of spheres of differentiation to spheres of assimilation ought to be, or even, in some cases, which spheres should be designated as spheres of assimilation, and which as spheres of differentiation. To a large extent, the answers to these questions depend on how broad one's conception is of the

---

[70] See Agnes Heller, Comment, 14 CARDOZO L. REV. 881, 883 (1993).

[71] For example, insofar as constitutional identity is predicated on the moral equality of all persons, it must ignore certain factually based individual differences, such as intelligence, strength, and education.

[72] See supra pp. 9-10 (discussion of freedom of religion).

[73] See ROSENFELD, supra note 8, at 224.

[74] If differences were never disregarded, it would seem impossible to construct a common identity or a basis for equality. However, if all differences were ignored, there might be an empty identity and perfect equality, but every person would remain completely alienated from the prevailing constitutional order.

proper scope of legitimate differences that ought to be given constitutional protection. Broadly speaking, one can distinguish between two basic kinds of conceptions of the scope of legitimate differences referred to respectively as monoculturalism and multiculturalism. Monoculturalism is associated with the promotion of dominant or hegemonic values and it requires a strong predominance of spheres of assimilation over spheres of differentiation.[75]

Multiculturalism, on the other hand, accords a far more important role to spheres of differentiation and can be divided into two main positions: pluralism, which is essentially individualistic in nature, and separatism, which is predicated on a collectivist vision. Pluralism is contrasted to monoculturalism by its much greater tolerance for difference. Pluralism, moreover, envisages a voluntary and gradual assimilation (of, among other things, education) regarding the public sphere together with encouragement and preservation of diversity within the private sphere.[76] By contrast, separatism posits that relevant differences are those that set apart one group from the next, and in particular those that are constitutive of group identity and those that loom as essential to the survival of the group as culturally and historically distinct. Accordingly, whereas monoculturalism ignores or suppresses differences, pluralism recognizes differences but subordinates them to commonalities, and separatism exalts differences even to the exclusion of commonalities to the extent that these differences are constitutive of group identity and group solidarity.

Marty Slaughter examines the dynamics of the dialectic between identity and difference in relation to the construction of a national constitutional identity from a multiculturalist perspective.[77] As Slaughter demonstrates, the dialectic between identity and difference involves much more than determining when to recognize and when to ignore given differences. Appearances, moreover, may be deceptive. Thus, the pursuit of pluralism, for instance, need not result in the straightforward subordination of difference. Instead, as Slaughter points out, it is possible for the pluralist to contain difference by trivializing and marginalizing it rather than by simply downplaying it.

---

75 Cf. Talal Asad, Ethnography, Literature, and Politics: Some Readings and Uses of Salman Rushdie's The Satanic Verses, 5 CULTURAL ANTHROPOLOGY 239, 260 (1990) (discussing British "core values" as hegemonic interests imposed on immigrant minorities as a condition for acceptance as members in the British political community).

76 There is no consensus on the definition of pluralism. Compare Diane Ravich, Multiculturalism: E Pluribus Plures, in DEBATING P.C.: THE CONTROVERSY OVER POLITICAL CORRECTNESS ON COLLEGE CAMPUSES 271 (Paul Berman ed., 1992) with Barbara Ehrenreich, The Challenge for the Left, in DEBATING P.C., supra at 333.

77 See M.M. Slaughter, The Multicultural Self: Questions of Subjectivity, Questions of Power, infra p. 369, 369.

Consistent with Slaughter's views, the key to achieving a legitimate equilibrium between national identity and cultural differences is to make possible the expression of differences in an environment shorn of dominance and oppression. From this standpoint, pluralism is inadequate to the extent that it relegates the expression of cultural differences to the private sphere. Moreover, the mere fact that a particular difference is asserted voluntarily is no guarantee that it is not the product of oppression or dominance. Indeed, as Slaughter reminds us, discrimination and persecution may prompt its victims to define themselves as an absence, such as when Jews embrace an image that negates the one propagated by anti-Semites.

Based on Slaughter's analysis, the achievement of an optimal balance between identity and difference depends less on the divide between monoculturalism and multiculturalism than on that between the individual and the group as the proper subject of constitutional rights. Drawing upon the American experience with the conflict between individual and collective rights—in the context of the tribal customs of Native Americans and in that of preferential admissions for racial minorities—Slaughter concludes that the individualistic pluralism driven by the Enlightenment value system that permeates the American constitutional order falls far short of providing an adequate shield against oppression and subordination of those who are not integrated into the dominant culture. Accordingly, Slaughter calls for a constitutional order relying on collective rights and on separatist policies.

By advocating a constitutionalism oriented toward multicultural separatism and group rights, Slaughter poses a formidable challenge to prevalent conceptions of constitutionalism. Even if one agrees with Slaughter that constitutionally protected group rights are necessary to achieve a proper balance between identity and difference, separatist policies may well do more to undermine the constitutional state than to rid it of subordination and oppression. Furthermore, whereas contemporary constitutionalism is undoubtedly compatible with the recognition of certain collective rights, it seems highly uncertain that constitutionalism could countenance the systematic subordination of individual rights to group rights demanded by adherence to separatist policies. Be that as it may, however, Slaughter's essay raises the crucial question of how far modern constitutionalism can be stretched beyond its roots in the normative order of the Enlightenment.

The final group of essays, by Cass Sunstein and Arthur Jacobson, reflect on the role of property in delimiting the constitutional boundaries between self and other in the context of the relation between the individual and the state. Moreover, these essays address constitutional issues relating to property rights under the particularly difficult circumstances confronting the formerly socialist societies of Eastern and Central Europe in their transitions to constitutional democracies.

Property occupies a central place among the fundamental interests that should be afforded constitutional protection in order to secure a boundary between the individual and the state, and between the private and the public spheres.[78] Actually, given a broad Lockean conception of property, according to which property encompasses not only possessions but also life and liberty,[79] constitutional protection of the right to private property might well suffice to enable every person to establish and preserve her own identity against that promoted by the collectivity through majority rule. Indeed, by allowing each individual enough private space to develop and flourish, the constitutional right to property appears to promote the formation and expression of those differences that serve to circumscribe a person's own identity.[80] Moreover, the private identities protected by property rights need not be confined to those identities that inhere in the atomistic individual severed from communal links. As a result of the development of the private institutions that make up civil society, collective private identities can emerge which stand in contrast to both their public counterparts and the identities of atomistic individuals.

Changes in the nature of property relations,[81] and the blurring of the public/private distinction,[82] cast significant doubt on the continuing viability of property rights as the primary guarantors of individual identity. This raises the question of whether the demands of constitutionalism require supplementing or replacing property rights by a bundle of other fundamental rights designed to bolster individual identity against the state—such as liberty, equality, privacy, and social welfare rights—or whether the demise of traditional property relationships seriously undermines modern constitutionalism's chances

---

78 *See generally* Jennifer Nedelsky, *American Constitutionalism and the Paradox of Private Property*, in CONSTITUTIONALISM AND DEMOCRACY, *supra* note 21, at 241.

79 *See* LOCKE, *supra* note 12, at 1187 ("Man . . . hath by nature . . . to preserve his property—that is, his life, liberty and estate . . . .").

80 If implementation of private property rights would suffice to allow every person enough space to become self-sufficient and to ward off unwanted intrusions, then such property rights would safeguard the privacy interests that are currently protected by separate privacy rights covering both spacial and decisional privacy.

81 *See* Nedelsky, *supra* note 78; *see also* Charles Reich, *The New Property*, 73 YALE L.J. 733 (1964).

82 *See generally* Symposium, *The Public/Private Distinction*, 130 U. PA. L. REV. 1289-1608 (1982).

of success.[83]

The relationship between private property rights and modern constitutionalism strikes at the heart of the recent transitions to constitutional democracies in Eastern Europe. These transitions provide a particularly fruitful setting for the contrasting views of Sunstein and Jacobson. Stressing the severe deficiencies of socialist societies due to lack of adequate recognition of private property rights, Sunstein argues that it is essential for the emerging democracies of Eastern Europe to afford constitutional protection to private property rights.[84] Moreover, given the history of socialist emphasis on social welfare interests to the detriment of negative liberty and property interests, Sunstein insists that the new democracies of Eastern Europe should refrain from constitutionalizing positive social welfare rights.

Sunstein believes that the constitutionalization of negative private property rights in Eastern Europe is essential, not only to promote economic development, but also to combat an implanted tradition bent on eradicating all boundaries between the individual and the state. More generally, Sunstein maintains that, contrary to common wisdom, constitutions should go against the culture and mores of those whom they regulate to ward off the harms that are likely to be perpetrated through the deployment of ordinary political processes. Consistent with this view, constitutions should not merely reflect existing national identity, but should also channel desirable changes in that identity through the institutionalization of checks designed to neutralize the worst national tendencies.

Sunstein's assessment of the Eastern European constitutional predicament leads to the conclusion that traditional negative private property rights are still a viable constitutional vehicle for establishing a working boundary between individual and state in societies in which such boundaries had been systematically obliterated. The transition from socialism to constitutional democracies sanctioning private property relations, however, is in many key respects very different from the transition from feudalism or absolute monarchy to constitutional democracy. Accordingly, it is not clear that adoption of an eighteenth-century conception of private property rights could culminate in a successful transition in the formerly socialist states.

Jacobson's essay offers a critical assessment of Sunstein's suggestion, and raises significant questions concerning its likelihood of success. Focusing on the unique circumstances in Eastern Europe,

---

[83] This latter possibility and its implications is the subject of Jennifer Nedelsky's analysis. *See* Nedelsky, *supra* note 78.

[84] *See* Cass R. Sunstein, *On Property and Constitutionalism*, *infra* p. 383, 385-93.

Jacobson notes the paradox of having to undermine the institution of property by destroying socialist property in order to institute viable property rights.[85] More generally, given the existing distribution of power over productive property in Eastern European countries, it seems at best uncertain which conception of property and which combination of constitutional and ordinary rights would best secure a successful transition to constitutional democracy in the various countries of Eastern Europe. Thus, even in the context of societies which have clearly suffered from the lack of adequate traditional private property rights, it remains an open question whether such rights can still be relied upon to play a major role in sustaining a workable boundary between the individual and the state.

In conclusion, whereas the essays included in this book focus on diverse aspects of constitutionalism, and whereas they frequently differ on important points, they all converge on the most salient essential aspects of modern constitutionalism. Modern constitutionalism cannot be reduced to any particular form or any specific identity or difference. Accordingly, cross-cultural transplantation of constitutional provisions is always dangerous, as an unreflected generalization from experience in a single culture is always likely to be wrong. Alternatively, certain recurring relational links between identity and diversity appear to play a key role in sustaining the fundamental values inherent in modern constitutionalism, and tend to lend validity to the pursuit of cross-cultural analyses. Finally, evolving sociopolitical conditions pose new challenges requiring reexamination of established constitutional institutions and, on occasion, the formulation of new constitutional structures and rights.

---

85 *See* Jacobson, *supra* note 20, at 413-14.

II

The Rebirth of Constitutionalism

A NEW BIRTH OF CONSTITUTIONALISM: GENETIC INFLUENCES AND GENETIC DEFECTS

Louis Henkin

INTRODUCTION

The title of this Article makes three statements and promises to pursue two themes. It notes the revolutionary developments of recent years which have brought new commitment in various parts of the world to a political ideology of "constitutionalism." It suggests that the spread of constitutionalism owes much to particular sources and models. It implies that the principal sources or models of constitutionalism may have carried with them some inherent deficiencies that may muddy the concept of constitutionalism and may trouble newly developing constitutional systems.

Sources of political ideas and models for institutions or instruments are rarely single or simple, and they are notoriously difficult to identify. The ideas that fed the spread of constitutionalism, and the earlier expressions of constitutionalism that shaped recent constitutions, cannot be determined with confidence. Locke, Montesquieu, Kant, Rousseau, and their successors (Bentham, Mill, the socialists) have fed the stream of relevant ideas, but contemporary framers of constitutions rarely go back to original sources for guidance. There can be little doubt, however, of the immediate influence of two prominent instruments of constitutional character: the United States Constitution and its Bill of Rights, now 200 years old, and the International Bill of Rights—the common designation for the Universal Declaration of Human Rights and the two principal international covenants on human rights[1]—born in our time and still maturing.[2]

Part I of this Article sets forth, in summary form, the principal

---

[1] Universal Declaration of Human Rights, G.A. Res. 217A (III), U.N. Doc. A/810, at 71, (1948); International Covenant on Civil and Political Rights, Dec. 16, 1966, 999 U.N.T.S. 171; International Covenant on Economic, Social and Cultural Rights, Dec. 16, 1966, 993 U.N.T.S. 3.

[2] No doubt other influences should be credited. England contributed to the idea of limited government, beginning with the Magna Carta, and to the idea of parliamentary government, through the Glorious Revolution and the Bill of Rights (1688). The French Declaration of the Rights of Man and of the Citizen helped spread the idea of inherent rights around the world. The French Declaration itself borrowed from American instruments. The Declaration did not survive in France, but was resurrected after the Second World War. *See* Louis Henkin, *Revolutions and Constitutions*, 49 LA. L. REV. 1023, 1027-34 (1989) [hereinafter Henkin,

elements of constitutionalism. Part II summarizes the contributions of United States constitutional jurisprudence and those of the international human rights movement to the principles and content of constitutionalism. Part III indicates that, by today's standards, both those sources suffer significant deficiencies that suggest the need for care in copying or borrowing from them.

The United States Constitution and its Bill of Rights are products of the eighteenth century, reflecting not only the ideas of the time but also the political forces that presided over their birth—contributing to the "genetic defects" in the title of this Article. The political-constitutional history of the United States has developed constitutional ideas and has remedied some of the original deficiencies, but important defects remain. The International Bill of Rights consists of twentieth-century instruments reflecting contemporary ideas. But these instruments also have defects which are largely the result of deep commitments to state "sovereignty," of ideological divisions in the international political system during their development, and of the politics of their adoption.[3] Unlike the United States, the international human rights movement has not had effective institutions and sufficient time to overcome the original defects. Surely, framers of new constitutions who look to these two sources and who would copy their text or imitate their institutions must proceed with care and discrimination and—to pursue the metaphor—might consider genetic constitutional engineering and treatment.

I.   WHAT IS CONSTITUTIONALISM?

Constitutionalism is nowhere defined. We speak of it as if its meaning is self-evident, or that we know it when we see it. Constitutionalism is commonly identified with a written constitution, yet not

---

Revolutions]. France also contributed to parliamentary democracy, and with Germany and the United Kingdom helped develop the welfare state. *Id.* at 1031-34.

In a number of respects, notably the movement to a Constitutional Court (as distinguished from constitutional review by the ordinary national judiciary as in the United States), the Basic Law of the Federal Republic of Germany has served as a model, and various other European constitutions have doubtless been studied by constitution makers in Eastern and Central Europe and elsewhere. Many of those instruments also derived ideas and followed examples from the United States and from the international human rights movement.

[3] *See, e.g.*, Louis Henkin, *Rights: American and Human*, 79 COLUM. L. REV. 405, 408-11 (1979), *reprinted in* LOUIS HENKIN, THE AGE OF RIGHTS 141, 144-45 (1990).

all constitutional texts are committed to the principles and serve the ends of constitutionalism. A constitution generally provides a blueprint for governance and government, but the system that is blueprinted may not satisfy the demands of constitutionalism. Some constitutions merely describe the existing system of government, proclaim societal goals, promise programs and policies, or serve other purposes that may not be intimately related to the concerns of constitutionalism.[4]

The following sets out, in summary form, my understanding of the principal demands of constitutionalism.

1. Contemporary constitutionalism is based on popular sovereignty. "The people" is the locus of "sovereignty"; the will of the people is the source of authority and the basis of legitimate government. The people alone can ordain and establish the constitution and the system of government. The people remain responsible for the system which they establish.

2. A constitutionalistic constitution is prescriptive; it is law; it is supreme law. Government must conform to the constitutional blueprint and to any limitations the constitution imposes. There can be no legitimate government other than as constitutionally ordained.

3. With popular sovereignty have come related ideas, namely, government ruled by law and governed by democratic principles. Constitutionalism therefore requires commitment to political democracy and to representative government. Even in times of national emergency, the people remain sovereign. Constitutionalism excludes government by decree, except as authorized by the constitution and subject to control by democratic political institutions.

4. Out of popular sovereignty and democratic government come dependent commitments to the following: limited government; separation of powers or other checks and balances; civilian control of the military; police governed by law and judicial control; and an independent judiciary.

5. Constitutionalism requires that government respect and ensure individual rights, which generally are those same rights recognized by the Universal Declaration of Human Rights. Rights may be subject to some limitations in the public interest, but such limitations themselves have limits. Some rights may be sus-

---

[4] The constitutions of the former Union of Soviet Socialist Republics and of China may be said to serve purposes not closely related to the concerns of constitutionalism. *See* LOUIS HENKIN, THE RIGHTS OF MAN TODAY 55-73 (1978).

pended in times of national emergency, but the derogation from rights in an emergency must be determined by constitutional bodies and subject to democratic review and scrutiny, must be strictly necessary, and must be temporary.

6. Constitutional governance includes institutions to monitor and assure respect for the constitutional blueprint, for limitations on government, and for individual rights.

7. Today, constitutionalism may also imply respect for "self-determination"—the right of "peoples" to choose, change, or terminate their political affiliation.

II.   Contemporary Influences For Constitutionalism

A.   *The United States*

It is neither chauvinistic nor unduly self-congratulatory to claim for the United States major credit for establishing and spreading the constitutionalist ideology. Our Declaration of Independence includes perhaps the most famous articulation of the principles of popular sovereignty, of limited and accountable government, and of individual rights. The United States Constitution also provided essential precedents. Ours was the first written constitution—a prescriptive constitution that is supreme law, that governs the governors, that cannot be suspended, and that is not subject to derogations even in national emergency.[5] The United States Constitution is difficult to amend.[6] The United States, which sought an alternative to the Westminster parliamentary system, developed the "presidential system" as a model of democratic government.[7] The United States adopted the first national, constitutional, lasting Bill of Rights.[8] The United States established constitutional review by the judiciary.

The United States Constitution has been an inspiration to others. It spread the idea of inherent human rights, and its Bill of Rights served as a source and a model. The United States concepts of consti-

---

[5] Only the privilege of the writ of habeas corpus may be suspended, and only "when in Cases of Rebellion or Invasion the public Safety may require it." U.S. CONST. art. I, § 9, cl. 2. It is established that only Congress can suspend habeas corpus.

[6] *See* U.S. CONST. art. V. The process for amendment was designed to reflect popular sovereignty and principles of constitutional legitimacy as the Framers saw them.

[7] *See* U.S. CONST. art. II. The United States also provided the idea and the example of federalism, currently an object of much attention in Eastern and Central Europe and elsewhere. Constitutionalism does not prescribe decentralization in principle or in any particular form, but centralization may have implications for other values. *See infra* p. 539.

[8] The English Bill of Rights contained a provision against excessive bail and cruel and unusual punishment, but the rest of it was essentially a bill of parliamentary rights not of individual rights. The French Declaration was adopted earlier but drew on American ideas and instruments. *See* Henkin, *Revolutions, supra* note 2, at 1023-36, 1046-47.

tutional monitoring and constitutional review have been widely imitated.[9] Above all, the United States has set an example of a successful "culture" of constitutionalism.

B. *The International Human Rights Movement*

A second major influence for constitutionalism since the Second World War has been the international human rights movement. This movement, the product of various influences (including the constitutional history of the United States), has promoted and inspired universal commitment to the principal ideas associated with constitutionalism. The United Nations Charter achieved universal commitment to the idea of individual human rights.[10] The Universal Declaration of Human Rights has been the vehicle for universalizing that commitment, establishing the source of human rights in a conception of human dignity, and giving content to the idea.[11] The Declaration also established economic-social rights *as rights* on par with civil-political rights.[12] The Declaration gave content and universalized the commitment to democracy, including universal suffrage, representative government, and equal access to public office and participation in government.[13] The International Covenants, the Optional Protocol, and later specialized conventions extended and confirmed these commitments and established also the principle and practice of international monitoring and scrutiny.[14] The European and American conventions expanded international remedies. The African Charter on Human and Peoples' Rights has demonstrated the universality of the human rights idea and provided new emphasis to the concept of "peoples' rights."[15]

---

[9] *See, e.g.*, Louis Favoreu, *Constitutional Review in Europe, in* CONSTITUTIONALISM AND RIGHTS: THE INFLUENCE OF THE UNITED STATES CONSTITUTION ABROAD 38 (Louis Henkin & Albert J. Rosenthal eds., 1990).

[10] *See* U.N. CHARTER pmbl.; *id.* art. 1; *id.* arts. 55-56.

[11] *See* Universal Declaration of Human Rights, *supra* note 1, pmbl.

[12] *Id.* arts. 22-28.

[13] *See, e.g., id.* art. 21; *see also* International Covenant on Civil and Political Rights, *supra* note 1, art. 25.

[14] *See* International Covenant on Civil and Political Rights, *supra* note 1, arts. 41-42; International Covenant on Economic, Social and Cultural Rights, *supra* note 1, arts. 16-22; International Convention on the Elimination of All Forms of Racial Discrimination, Dec. 21, 1965, 660 U.N.T.S. 195; Convention on the Elimination of All Forms of Discrimination against Women, Dec. 18, 1979, 19 I.L.M. 34; Convention on the Prevention and Punishment of the Crime of Genocide, Dec. 9, 1948, 78 U.N.T.S. 277.

[15] *See* Banjul Charter on Human and Peoples' Rights, June 28, 1981, Organization of African Unity [OAU] Doc. CAB/LEG/67/3/Rev. 5.

III.   GENETIC DEFECTS

Both the United States and the international human rights movement are entitled to celebrate their contributions to constitutionalism,
but neither of those "parents" represents a fully-developed constitutionalism.[16] Each has some defects. Each source can be copied or
emulated only with care and discrimination.

A.   *Deficiencies of the United States Model*

In light of contemporary constitutionalism, the system of government established by the United States Constitution was deficient in
key respects. At its inception, the Constitution did not reflect strong
commitment to popular sovereignty, to democracy, or to representative government. "We the People" ordained and established the Constitution, but those who authorized and approved the Constitution
represented a small fraction of the inhabitants of the United States.
The system of government established by the Constitution was not
democratic and not representative. Only one branch of the legislature
was representative and was, therefore, called the House of Representatives. The Senate represented states, not people. The President represented no one. Even the House of Representatives was elected by a
process that would not satisfy the requirements of constitutionalism
today, since only a small proportion of the inhabitants voted for representatives. Women, slaves, most free blacks, and those who did not
meet property qualifications did not vote for their representatives.[17]

Today, the United States system would presumably pass the requirements of constitutionalism. Senators are elected by the citizens
of their states.[18] All citizens vote for the president in fact if not in
theory or in form.[19] As a result of imaginative constitutional construction of the Bill of Rights and of the Equal Protection Clause of
the Fourteenth Amendment, all citizens now have the right to vote

---

[16] Others who have contributed to constitutionalism also continue to suffer defects. English constitutionalism has produced government with insufficient limitations. Parliamentary
supremacy, once the pride of constitutional ideology, is now particularly vulnerable to criticism that it provides no respect for individual rights. *See, e.g.*, Anthony Lester, *Fundamental
Rights in the United Kingdom: The Law and the British Constitution*, 125 U. PA. L. REV. 337
(1976). France is still finding its way between a presidential and a parliamentary system of
government. Also, its system for constitutional review cannot look at laws after they come
into effect, and does not respond to individual complaint. *See* Henkin, *Revolutions, supra* note
3, at 1047.

[17] Some did not even count for the purpose of being represented. Only three-fifths of the
slave population were included in the enumeration. U.S. CONST. art. I, § 2, cl. 3.

[18] *See* U.S. CONST. amend. XVII, § 1.

[19] *See* U.S. CONST. art. II, § 1.

for representatives, for senators, and for the president.[20]

The ideology of constitutionalism is not sufficiently developed or precise to determine whether our presidential system and our kind of bicameral legislature meet the requirements of "will of the people," "democracy," and "representative government." Our jurisprudence has no coherent view of representative government, and the election of senators by states rather than according to population, and the system of electing the president, need justification and rationalization. As conceived, the presidency was perhaps too weak; now it has perhaps grown too strong. Surely, checks and balances are not working as planned. Does our system satisfy the demands of constitutionalism? Surely, constitutional text, and even the jurisprudence that emanates from the opinions of the Supreme Court, do not tell a whole, coherent constitutionalistic story.

1. *Federalism*

Federalism is not an essential element of constitutionalism, but the political variations it affords have been conducive to other values. Federalism may be relevant to popular sovereignty, democracy, self-determination, and protection for individual rights. Recent events have heightened interest in United States federalism, but United States federalism has no theory, and its mosaic of compromises is hardly an ideal model. United States federalism, moreover, is incompletely articulated. The authority of the federal government is not fully expressed in the enumerations of the legislative powers of Congress. The power of Congress to regulate commerce with foreign nations and among the several states has grown far beyond the text and the conception of the Framers. The power to tax and spend for the general welfare has reshaped the federal system. The express grants to the federal government, the express limitations on the states, and the Tenth Amendment hardly define state powers today.[21]

2. *Individual Rights*

Formally, the United States Bill of Rights consists of the first ten amendments to the United States Constitution. But any examination of constitutional rights in the United States must include also the rights provisions in the original Constitution,[22] the later amendments to the Constitution (notably those that constituted the peace treaty of the Civil War), and the interpretations and elaborations of rights by

---

[20] *See* Wesberry v. Sanders, 376 U.S. 1 (1964); Reynolds v. Sims, 377 U.S. 533 (1964).

[21] *See* U.S. CONST. art. I, § 10; *id.* art. IV.

[22] *See* U.S. CONST. art. I, § 9; *id.* art. III, § 2; *id.* art. IV, § 2.

the Supreme Court that began just before the Second World War.[23]

Since the beginning of our nation's existence, the Constitution's protection for rights has suffered serious deficiency.[24] Even after the Bill of Rights was added by constitutional amendment, important rights were not protected. For example, the Bill of Rights did not bar slavery. It did not secure, or even mention, equality. It did not guarantee the right to vote, to hold office, or to participate in government. As written, it did not secure individual autonomy and liberty, but safeguarded only certain enumerated liberties. The First Amendment protected the free exercise of religion and the freedoms of speech, press, and assembly, but not the freedom of association.[25] The Bill of Rights provided for due process of law, but apparently did not protect against torture or inhumane treatment. It did not include many civil and personal rights, or freedoms of choice in personal, social, or economic matters. It did not establish or safeguard rights of citizenship. The Constitution required that government respect rights, but it did not require that government secure these rights against violations by private persons. The Constitution did not provide punishment for those who violate rights or provide compensation for victims of violation. The Framers doubtless were committed to other rights and other freedoms and to stronger protections and remedies, but they were content to leave those rights and freedoms to the law and the political process—to the common law and to state constitutions.

Many of the defects and deficiencies in the Bill of Rights were remedied by later amendments, and many more were remedied by imaginative constitutional interpretation. The Civil War Amendments abolished slavery, established citizenship, and required the states to provide due process and equal protection of the laws. Later amendments provided for direct election of senators and forbade discrimination in voting on grounds of race, gender, property, or age. By imaginative interpretation, the Supreme Court found a right of association and greatly extended the protection for freedom of expression, press, and religion.[26] The Court found that the liberty protected by the Fifth Amendment included essential autonomy,[27] and that "due

---

[23] See LOUIS HENKIN, *Constitutional Rights—Two Hundred Years Later, in* THE AGE OF RIGHTS 109 (1990) [hereinafter HENKIN, *Two Hundred Years Later*].

[24] *Id.* at 114-15; *see also* Louis Henkin, *A Decent Respect to the Opinions of Mankind*, 25 J. MARSHALL L. REV. 215, 216-19 (1992) [hereinafter Henkin, *Opinions of Mankind*].

[25] Later, the right of association was distilled from the rights enumerated in that Amendment. *See, e.g.*, Roberts v. United States Jaycees, 468 U.S. 609 (1984); NAACP v. Alabama, 377 U.S. 288 (1964); NAACP v. Button, 371 U.S. 415 (1963).

[26] *See* HENKIN, *Two Hundred Years Later, supra* note 23, at 118-20.

[27] *See* Allgeyer v. Louisiana, 165 U.S. 578 (1897).

process" included substantive protections for autonomy and freedom against arbitrary laws, with special protection for autonomy in intimate matters.[28] By imaginative interpretations, rights safeguarded against federal violations were held to be protected also against state violations,[29] and rights protected against state violations were secured also against federal violations.[30]

But even as amended, and even as developed by interpretation, the constitutional safeguards for rights still fall short of contemporary requirements of constitutionalism and still do not provide an ideal model. Individual autonomy is left to the uncertainties of "liberty" and "substantive due process." There is no guidance as to preference between competing rights, or as to how rights are to be balanced against public interest. There are few rights regarding immigration into the United States,[31] and the right of an alien resident in the United States not to be expelled without cause is still in jeopardy.[32] It is increasingly uncertain whether nationals of other countries enjoy any rights against the United States if it exercises authority over them abroad.[33] There is no constitutional guidance as to what is a just tax system. The Sixteenth Amendment gave Congress the power to impose a progressive income tax, but Congress is not required to do so and it need not assure a just progression; many taxes in the United States today are regressive, falling equally on the rich and on the poor. Above all, the Constitution does not require the United States Government or the state governments to meet the basic human needs of their inhabitants. The entitlements associated with the welfare state, and the economic, social, and cultural rights recognized by the international instruments, are not constitutional rights in the United States.[34]

Elsewhere I have expanded on the deficiencies of our conceptions of equality.[35] Our notion of equality is equality in rights, equality in the service of liberty, equal rights to pursue happiness, and equal protection of the laws. Our notion of equality does not require government to offset inequalities, to compensate for handicaps, or to enhance

---

28 *See, e.g.*, Roe v. Wade, 410 U.S. 113 (1973).

29 *See* Duncan v. Louisiana, 391 U.S. 145 (1968).

30 *See, e.g.*, Bolling v. Sharpe, 347 U.S. 497 (1954).

31 *See* Shaughnessy v. United States *ex rel.* Mezei, 345 U.S. 206 (1953); Chae Chan Ping v. United States, 130 U.S. 581 (1889) (the Chinese Exclusion Case); Garcia-Mir v. Meese, 788 F.2d 1446 (11th Cir. 1986), *cert. denied*, 479 U.S. 889 (1986).

32 *See* Galvan v. Press, 347 U.S. 522 (1954).

33 *See* United States v. Verdugo-Urquidez, 494 U.S. 259 (1990); *see also* Henkin, *Opinions of Mankind*, *supra* note 24, at 230-32.

34 *See, e.g.*, Dandridge v. Williams, 397 U.S. 471 (1970).

35 *See* Henkin, *Opinions of Mankind*, *supra* note 24, at 223-26.

equal opportunity. Does constitutionalism, which our generation is in the process of establishing and refining, require commitment to a richer conception of equality, and to a stronger commitment to equality in competition with claims to liberty and property? Might constitutionalism require government to eliminate gross economic maldistributions, so as to preclude the growth of a permanent underclass?[36]

The United States constitutional system also remains deficient in the safeguards it provides for the rights it recognizes. It protects rights against state action, but not against private violation.[37] It does not require Congress to adopt measures to assure official compliance, to prevent or punish violations, to remedy violations, or to compensate victims. Congress has done some of that,[38] but much remains to be done.

B. Defects of the International Human Rights Model

The international human rights movement is a product of the second half of this century, and international human rights instruments reflect contemporary ideology and the lessons of earlier inadequacies. International human rights instruments are more explicitly committed to democracy and representative government.[39] They have modified eighteenth century liberalism by commitments to communitarianism. In the international model, the conception of rights includes the commitments of the welfare states to economic and social

---

[36] Promoting authentic equal opportunity and reducing maldistribution would seem to be proper public purposes for which government can tax, spend, and even regulate. And I do not see why it cannot be done by "taking race into account." Is equal treatment more weighty in our conception of constitutionalism—in our constitutional balances—than the promotion of equal opportunity and the reduction of inequalities? See Henkin, Opinions of Mankind, supra note 24, at 225.

[37] See DeShaney v. Winnebago County Social Servs. Dep't, 489 U.S. 189, 258-59 (1989) which states the following:

[N]othing in the language of the Due Process Clause itself requires the State to protect the life, liberty, and property of its citizens against invasion by private actors. The Clause is phrased as a limitation on the State's power to act, not as a guarantee of certain minimal levels of safety and security.... [I]ts language cannot fairly be extended to impose an affirmative obligation on the State to ensure that those interests do not come to harm through other means. Nor does history support such an expansive reading of the constitutional text.... Its purpose was to protect the people from the State, not to ensure that the State protected them from each other. The Framers were content to leave the extent of governmental obligation in the latter area to the democratic political processes.

Id.

[38] See, e.g., 42 U.S.C. §§ 1983, 1985 (1988); 18 U.S.C. §§ 241, 242 (1988).

[39] See Universal Declaration of Human Rights, supra note 1, art. 21; International Covenant on Civil and Political Rights, supra note 1, art. 25.

guarantees.[40]

International instruments, however, reflect the resistances of an international political system committed to state "sovereignty" and related state values. Furthermore, they reflect their political genesis in a divided world during the cold war. Conceived and developed by institutions riven by ideological conflict, and by states grossly uneven in their commitment to constitutional rights, the international instruments reflect ambiguities, compromises, and not always successful attempts to bridge large differences. The international instruments are ambiguous in their commitment to popular sovereignty, democracy, and representative government, pretending to be acceptable to the West, to totalitarian communism, and to the variegated political ideology of Third World societies. And international instruments are silent on the relation of economic systems—of free enterprise, socialism, and the spectrum of mixed systems—to democracy and to individual rights.

By today's conceptions of constitutionalism, the International Bill of Rights lacks a clear commitment to liberty and autonomy. The individual is guaranteed liberties, but not liberty. He (she) is entitled to freedom from arbitrary incarceration, to freedom of religion and expression, and to freedom of choice of place of residence.[41]   But there is no overarching commitment to essential autonomy and no specific commitment to the right to make one's own life-choices in the pursuit of happiness—choices of life-style, intimate relations, occupation, and leisure. The international instruments declare a right to *seek* asylum from persecution, but they provide no right to such asylum.[42] The Convention Relating to the Status of Refugees provides only a right not to be pushed back to the territory of the oppressor ("non-refoulement").[43]

Doubtless from the lack of essential consensus, the international instruments also lack a clear commitment to the right to property. The Universal Declaration made that commitment, recognizing the right of every individual to own property and not to be arbitrarily deprived of it,[44] but the Covenants and later conventions raised doubts by failing to establish that right in legally binding instruments.

---

[40] *See* Universal Declaration of Human Rights, *supra* note 1, arts. 22-25; International Covenant on Economic, Social and Cultural Rights, *supra* note 1, arts. 6-15.

[41] *See* Universal Declaration of Human Rights, *supra* note 1, arts. 13, 18-19; International Covenant on Civil and Political Rights, *supra* note 1, arts. 12, 18-19.

[42] *See* Universal Declaration of Human Rights, *supra* note 1, art. 14.

[43] *See* Convention Relating to the Status of Refugees, July 28, 1951, art. 33, 189 U.N.T.S. 150.

[44] *See* Universal Declaration of Human Rights, *supra* note 1, art. 17.

The international instruments lack a clear commitment to economic liberty. Both the Universal Declaration and the International Covenant on Economic, Social and Cultural Rights enumerate the right to work,[45] but both leave its meaning ambiguous, neither choosing between, nor confirming both, a right to choose one's work and a right to guaranteed employment. There is not ambiguity but silence as to whether a society may be based on socialistic or free market principles, whether the individual has freedom of enterprise to make and sell shoes or to offer his (her) services as a taxi-driver.

The international instruments are committed to the idea of equality, but their vision and conception of equality are not clear. They require equal protection of the laws, but it is not clear whether that permits or perhaps even requires unequal treatment to compensate for inequalities. It is not clear whether beyond equal treatment a state is required (or permitted) to take "affirmative action" to equalize opportunity by "leveling the playing field," to compensate for various forms of handicap—for physical handicaps, handicaps in natural endowment, or for the outrages of fortune. It is not clear whether a state is entitled or permitted to attempt to achieve an equal or less unequal society. The International Bill of Rights neglected the rights of minorities, assuming apparently that, in the age of individual rights, the rights of groups of individuals need no special protection. Events have proved that that assumption may be unwarranted.

The international instruments recognize that rights may conflict, and apparently permit states to choose between conflicting rights, but provide no guidance for, or limitations on, the state's choice.[46] In specific instances, the international instruments prescribe the choice to be made, but they do not justify the principle of choice or the particular choice preferred. For example, the Covenant on Civil and Political Rights requires a state to safeguard an individual's honor and reputation, implying presumably that a state must provide protection against slander or libel, perhaps even by making it a crime.[47] It explicitly requires a state to prohibit propaganda for war, and prohibits advocacy of national, racial, or religious hatred that incites discrimination, hostility, or violence.[48]

The international human rights instruments recognize the authority of the state to limit rights in the public interest, and the

---

[45] See id. art. 23; International Covenant on Economic, Social and Cultural Rights, supra note 1, art. 6.

[46] See Universal Declaration of Human Rights, supra note 1, art. 29, cl. 2.

[47] See International Covenant on Civil and Political Rights, supra note 1, art. 17.

[48] See id. arts. 19-20.

formula defining the permissible limitations may be as good as words can provide, but they do not provide effective security against abuse.[49] The provisions permitting derogation of rights in times of national emergency may also be inescapable and drafted as well as could be, but they have been the bane of constitutionalism around the world.

Notoriously, the international instruments are deficient in the commitment they demand of states to assure respect for rights or to accept external scrutiny.

CONCLUSION

Constitutionalism is burgeoning and spreading to parts of the world where it was previously unimaginable, an exhilarating and exalting phenomenon. This new constitutionalism has derived inspiration from a pool of ideas, and example from existing institutions and arrangements. But no model is perfect and none can be readily translated. Certainly any model needs to be adopted and adapted with care.

The United States Constitution and the International Bill of Rights have been major sources of influence, but neither the United States Constitution nor the International Bill of Rights is a complete, perfect realization of constitutionalism. The eighteenth-century Constitution of the United States, even as amended and as modernized, is not up-to-date with twentieth-century requirements of constitutionalism. The international model, created out of compromise and ambiguity, provides too low a common denominator and too uncertain a trumpet for a world of states no longer subject to ideological conflict and now uniformly committed to constitutionalism. The United States model needs to be updated; the international model needs to be made clearer, firmer, and more forthright.

Surely, the United States can claim large credit for the spread of constitutionalism—for the idea, for the content of rights, for developing essential institutions, and for providing an example of a successful living constitutionalism. But jurisprudentially, culturally, and politically, United States constitutionalism still has defects. Such defects are reflected in our numerous, notorious contemporary problems: wide poverty and the stark failure to satisfy the basic human needs of housing, health, and education; de facto segregation and the prospect of a permanent underclass; an unjust tax system; police abuse; inadequate respect for rights of would-be immigrants; and lack of respect for the rights of others as exemplified by search and seizure and inva-

---

[49] *See, e.g., id.* arts. 12, 19.

sion of privacy in other countries, and in kidnappings for law enforcement.[50]

Some of these problems perhaps are not, and should not be deemed, constitutional. The content and limits of constitutionalism, however, are not firm and fixed. Surely, all the human rights problems in the United States derogate from human dignity, the foundation of constitutionalism. And certainly, safeguards against police abuse or kidnappings abroad, and rights for would-be immigrants, are clearly appropriate for constitutional protection. If not all basic human needs are to be guaranteed by the Constitution, surely ambiguous constitutional values and false ideologies ought not be set up as obstacles to comprehensive civil rights acts and comprehensive welfare programs.

Some of the defects of international human rights instruments cannot readily be cured in a system of states still committed to state "sovereignty"—to state values, to state "privacy," and to territorial impermeability.[51] Ordinarily, the human rights movement can only exert political-moral pressure on states to take domestic measures to improve the condition of their constitutionalism. In the last decade of this century, however, the international human rights movement would do well to reconsider compromises and concessions once deemed necessary. With the demise of communism, it should be possible, by interpretation if not by formal amendment, to move the international instruments closer to the ideals of constitutionalism. In particular, the general commitment to governance by the will of the people and to universal suffrage have to be construed to require parliamentary, multi-party government. Democracy is in the details.

It is also necessary to clarify and refine the relations to human rights of a state's economic system. The international human rights ideology has accepted both free enterprise and socialism so long as they have a human face. The demise of communism has raised doubts about the viability of socialism, but it has not put capitalism and free enterprise beyond criticism. Constitutionalism may require substantial economic liberty, but does it preclude substantial state ownership and management? The demise of communism and the rush to privatization and a market economy may warrant the conclusion that a market economy is more efficient, but is efficiency a moral value, an essential element in constitutionalism? A market economy may create a larger pie, but does constitutionalism, perhaps, require

---

[50] *See* Henkin, *Opinions of Mankind, supra* note 24, at 222-32.

[51] *See* Louis Henkin, *International Law: Politics, Values and Functions: General Course on Public International Law, in* 216 RECUEIL DES COURS 208-69 (1989-IV).

better distribution? Socialism was in large part a response to the evils of unbridled capitalism; the demise of socialism does not eliminate the need to address, prevent, and ameliorate those evils.

The International Human Rights movement has been the motor for the spread of constitutionalism around the world. The weaknesses of constitutionalism in different countries are not due wholly to defects in international human rights. But in the new post-cold war world, there is promise for a new effort to improve the content of international human rights, and to remove obstacles to its promotion and enforcement. A stronger, purer international human rights movement will speed and help make firm the establishment of constitutionalism in the next century.

III

Constitutionalism as Bridge Between Self and Other: The Politics and Legitimation of Constitution Making

CONSTITUTIONAL BOOTSTRAPPING IN PHILADELPHIA AND PARIS

Jon Elster

INTRODUCTION

This Article discusses an aspect of the process of constitution making in two constituent assemblies, the Federal Convention in Philadelphia and the Assemblée Constituante in Paris from 1789 to 1791.[1] The issue, briefly described, is one of "constitutional bootstrapping," the process by which a constituent assembly severs its ties with the authorities that have called it into being and arrogates some or all of their powers to itself.

This problem arises quite generally. Unless the constituent assembly is a mere puppet of its creators, it will seek to escape from their control. A particularly striking example occurred when the three occupying powers put in place the process that led to the writing of the West German constitution of 1948. The occupying powers stipulated that the constitution would be ratified by referendum in two-thirds of the Länder. The prime ministers of the Länder preferred ratification by the Landtage, arguing that it would be inappropriate to seek popular ratification for a constitution imposed from outside the Landtage itself. In the end, the Germans got their way.[2] The occupying powers also demanded a veto over the constitution, to make certain that there would not be a strong central government.[3]

---

[1] References to the American proceedings will generally be from the three-volume RECORDS OF THE FEDERAL CONVENTION OF 1787 (Max Farrand ed., 1966) [hereinafter RECORDS]. References to the French proceedings will be to volumes eight through 31 of the ARCHIVES PARLEMENTAIRES SÉRIE I: 1789-1799 (1875-88) (as translated by the author) [hereinafter ARCHIVES PARLEMENTAIRES]. Other pertinent documents are reproduced in ORATEURS DE LA RÉVOLUTION FRANÇAISE I: LES CONSTITUANTS (François Furet & Ran Halévi eds., 1989) [hereinafter ORATEURS]. The proceedings of the committee debates on the verification of credentials are found in PROCÈS-VERBAL DES CONFÉRENCES SUR LA VÉRIFICATION DES POUVOIRS (1789) [hereinafter PROCÈS-VERBAL DES CONFÉRENCES]. Although the latter volume has not been much utilized in accounts of the Assemblée Constituante, it can, due to its compact form and strong focus on one problem, illuminate important aspects of debating strategies.

[2] PETER MERKL, THE ORIGIN OF THE WEST GERMAN REPUBLIC 53-54, 159 (1963).

[3] [T]he French Foreign Secretary, Robert Schuman, declared in a speech that only a federal system of considerable decentralization of German governmental powers was consistent with peace and acceptable to his government. The third draft of the Basic Law, however, contained elements he considered conducive to a centralistic

The effort was, if anything, counterproductive: "The cause of federalism in Germany had been much stronger before the military governors discredited it with their constitutional engineering."[4]

This paper, however, is limited to the convocation and constitution—the *self-constitution*—of the two eighteenth-century assemblies.[5] In both cases, the assembly broke with the past to redefine the national identity. If the delegates had followed their mandates to the letter, the changes would have been less radical. I am not claiming, of course, that the American changes were as severe as the French ones, only that the two assemblies faced similar dilemmas and resolved them in somewhat similar ways.

I. THE CONSTITUTIONAL ISSUES

Since the topic of this Article is the *process* of constitution making rather than the substantive contents of the emerging documents, I shall not go deeply into issues of constitutional doctrine. Nevertheless, a brief survey of the main questions may be useful to prepare for the more process-oriented analyses that follow.

Generally, a constitution contains three kinds of clauses: (1) those governing the machinery of government; (2) those controlling the assignment of rights; and (3) the procedures for amending the constitution itself. Each of these is discussed in turn.

In both eighteenth-century assemblies, the main debates over the machinery of government concerned the organization of the legislature, and the relation between the legislative and the executive powers.[6] Yet this general similarity obscures the fact that, in each assembly, the most burning debates were over issues that had no

---

trend. This was, perhaps, the first time in the history of modern constitutionalism that a victorious power attempted to secure itself against revenge or aggression by "constitutional engineering." Such a policy presupposes a naive belief in the restraining force of constitutional clauses imposed by a foreign power on a defeated nation.

Id. at 120-21.

[4] *Id*. at 126.

[5] In the footnotes I shall also make occasional references to some of the current constitution-making processes in Eastern Europe. *See* Jon Elster, *Constitutionalism in Eastern Europe: An Introduction*, 58 U. CHI. L. REV. 447, 447-82 (1991).

[6] For information about the French debates and their background, I rely heavily on JEAN EGRET, LA RÉVOLUTION DES NOTABLES (1950) and ROBERT D. HARRIS, NECKER AND THE REVOLUTION OF 1789 (1986). For information about the American debates and their background, I have mainly consulted CALVIN C. JILLSON, CONSTITUTION MAKING: CONFLICT AND CONSENSUS IN THE FEDERAL CONVENTION OF 1787 (1988); CATHY D. MATSON & PETER S. ONUF, A UNION OF INTERESTS: POLITICAL AND ECONOMIC THOUGHT IN REVOLUTIONARY AMERICA (1990); and GORDON S. WOOD, THE CREATION OF THE AMERICAN REPUBLIC 1776-1787 (1969).

analogue in the other. America was a federally organized country; France was not. Hence, the debate in Philadelphia over the representation of the small states in the Senate had no direct analogue in France.[7] In addition, the representation of slaveholding territories, while the object of several discussions in the French Assembly,[8] was much less central than at the Convention. France was a monarchy and was universally expected—at least at the time when the Assembly debated the royal veto—to remain one. America was not a monarchy and, apart from Hamilton's proposal for an elective monarch,[9] no one at the Convention in Philadelphia argued that it should become one. Hence, the French debate over the King's veto, including his veto over the constitution itself, could have no American analogue. Moreover, the idea of an absolute veto for the executive—the object of heated debates in Paris—was summarily dismissed in Philadelphia.[10] Also, there were few objections in Philadelphia to the *principle* of bicameralism,[11] which was hotly debated in Paris and, in the end, rejected.

A three-stage sequence occurred in England in the seventeenth century, and in America and France through the eighteenth century. In the first stage, there was a strong monarchy perceived as arbitrary and tyrannical. This monarchy was replaced in the second stage by a parliamentary regime. In the third stage, when it was discovered that Parliament could be just as tyrannical and arbitrary as the King, some form of checks and balances was introduced. In 1787, the Americans went from the second to the third stage. In 1789, the French went from the first to the second stage. The pathologies of the second stage and the transition to the third stage came later. This provides the main reason for the difference in tenor in the two debates. The Americans were concerned with protecting themselves against the solution which the French were in the process of inventing, or reinventing.[12]

Today, the inclusion of a bill of rights in the constitution is a

---

[7] It is noted later, however, that at an abstract level the French discussion of voting by order or by head can be seen as analogous to this debate.

[8] 8 ARCHIVES PARLEMENTAIRES, *supra* note 1, at 164, 186; 26 *id.* at 636; 27 *id.* at 12.

[9] 1 RECORDS, *supra* note 1, at 288.

[10] 1 *id.* at 200.

[11] *See* 1 *id.* at 336; WOOD, *supra* note 6, at 553-62.

[12] "The use of the power of Parliament by one group of its supporters to threaten other groups had shown to men who had previously seen only the royal power as a danger, that a parliament could be as tyrannical as a king." M.J.C. VILE, CONSTITUTIONALISM AND THE SEPARATION OF POWERS 43 (1967). This statement, although concerning England after 1648, is also valid for the United States after 1776 as well as France after 1791.

matter of course.[13] The American and French framers thought differently. Some of the American delegates thought a bill of rights would be dangerous, as it might suggest that every right not included in the enumeration might be freely violated by the government. Because the Constitution restricted governmental powers by enumerating them, it was felt that enumerating the rights might similarly be viewed as restrictive.[14] Delegates from the Southern states had a different objection. "Such bills generally begin with declaring that all men are by nature born free. Now, we should make that declaration with a very bad grace, when a large part of our property consists in men who are actually born slaves."[15] In the end, the arguments against the bill of rights carried the day. At the Assemblée Constituante, voices were raised against adopting a bill of rights before the constitution was wholly written. However, the Assembly's motive was fear of granting too many rights, rather than granting too few. Two of the most prominent moderates, Count Lally-Tolendal[16] and Pierre-Victor Malouet,[17] argued that a bill of rights might give the people exaggerated, confused, and dangerous ideas about their freedoms and liberties, and argued for a postponement. In the atmosphere that reigned at the time they were sitting ducks for the assertion of the Jacobin Guy-Jean-Baptiste Target that "[t]he truth can never be dangerous."[18]

Over and above the issue of specific rights, two more general questions were important to the eighteenth-century assemblies. One was whether rights attach only to individuals, or whether a collectivity can also be the bearer of rights. In Philadelphia, the strongest opponent of states' rights was James Wilson. "Can we forget for whom we are forming a Government? Is it for *men*, or for the imaginary beings called *States*?"[19] Advocates of individual rights argued that states ought to be represented in the federal Assembly proportionally to their population, whereas those who believed in the rights of states argued for equal representation. In such cases where right stands against right the outcome is usually either breakdown or com-

---

13 All constitutions or drafts of constitutions in post-1989 Eastern Europe, for instance, include a bill of rights.

14 3 RECORDS, *supra* note 1, at 143-44 (James Wilson at the Pennsylvania Convention for ratifying the Consititution); WOOD, *supra* note 6, at 537. The Ninth Amendment reflects this concern.

15 3 RECORDS, *supra* note 1, at 256 (Charles Cotesworth Pinckney in the South Carolina House of Representatives).

16 8 ARCHIVES PARLEMENTAIRES, *supra* note 1, at 222.

17 8 *id.* at 322.

18 8 *id.* at 320.

19 1 RECORDS, *supra* note 1, at 483.

promise. In the United States, for example, the compromise was equal representation in the upper house and proportional in the lower. Proposals were also made at the Federal Convention to strike a compromise within the Senate itself,[20] by which the representation of the smaller states would extend beyond proportionality but fall short of equality.[21]

The other question concerned the conditions for granting political rights, notably those to vote and to be elected. Such rights were perceived as conditional, contingent upon contribution to one's country. The idea was not only "no taxation without representation," but equally "no representation without taxation." Abbé Sieyès, for instance, made an influential distinction between active and passive citizens.[22] Women, children, and others who did not contribute to the maintenance of the public establishment should not have the right to influence its policy. "Although all should be able to enjoy the benefits of living in society, only those who make a contribution to the public establishment form the real shareholders in the great social enterprise."[23] Contribution includes not only paying taxes, but also defending one's country. In Philadelphia, Benjamin Franklin emphatically insisted on the idea that "in time of war a country owed much to the lower class of citizens. Our late war was an instance of what they could suffer and perform. If denied the right of suffrage it would debase their spirit and detatch [sic] them from the interest of the country."[24] In Paris, the Duke of Clermont-Tonnerre, a brilliant member of the moderate faction, made a brief reference to the fact that Jews served in the national militia to refute one of several arguments for denying them citizenship and, a fortiori, the right to vote.[25]

Finally, the constituent assembly must choose a procedure for amending the constitution. The harder it is to change the constitution, the more people tend to view it as a given framework for policy rather than as a tool for policy. Of course, they may also come to see it as an intolerable prison, whence the need for an *optimal* rigidity of the constitution. As Lally-Tolendal said in the Assemblée Constituante, "it must be neither easy nor impossible to change it."[26] On one hand, " '[c]onstitutions are chains with which men bind them-

---

[20] 1 *id.* at 405, 488, 490, 510-11; 2 *id.* at 5.

[21] A system of this kind was adopted in the West German constitution of 1948.

[22] For an account of this distinction and its fate, see JEAN-DENIS BREDIN, SIEYÈS: LA CLÉ DE LA RÉVOLUTION FRANÇAISE 158 (1988).

[23] ORATEURS, *supra* note 1, at 1014 (Jon Elster trans.).

[24] 2 RECORDS, *supra* note 1, at 210.

[25] 10 ARCHIVES PARLEMENTAIRES, *supra* note 1, at 756.

[26] 8 *id.* at 517.

selves in their sane moments that they may not die by a suicidal hand in the day of their frenzy.' "[27] On the other hand, we should keep in mind a dictum of constitutional lawyers, ascribed to Justice Robert Jackson: the constitution is not a suicide pact. It must be possible to unbind oneself in an emergency: society must not be confined too tightly.[28]

To strike the right balance between rigidity and flexibility one may use a number of devices, either singly or in combination. First, one can require qualified majority support for changes in the constitution in order to guard against instability, so that the constitution remains unaffected even when majorities fluctuate between forty-nine and fifty-one percent. Second, one can impose delaying or "cooling" devices, such as requiring changes to be passed or proposed by several successive parliaments. This solution was adopted in the French Constitution of 1791. Delays protect society from itself, forcing passionate majorities, whether simple or qualified, to cool down and reconsider their positions. Third, federally organized countries can require that any changes be passed by all, or a qualified majority, of the republics. This solution was adopted at the Federal Convention to protect the states against encroachment of the federal government. This solution may also serve as a delaying device. Finally, one can write periodical revisions into the consititution itself, in order to protect later generations from the tyranny of their predecessors and provide the necessary time for constitutional arrangements to work themselves out, so that they will not be discarded prematurely. This

---

27 JOHN E. FINN, CONSTITUTIONS IN CRISIS 5 (1991) (John Potter Stockton in debates over the Ku Klux Klan Act of 1871). On the general theme of self-binding, see JON ELSTER, ULYSSES AND THE SIRENS ch. 2 (1984); Stephen Holmes, *Precommitment and the Paradox of Democracy, in* CONSTITUTIONALISM AND DEMOCRACY (Jon Elster & Rune Slagstad eds., 1988). On the theme of constitutional self-binding, see Jon Elster, *Intertemporal Choice and Political Theory, in* CHOICES OVER TIME (George Loewenstein & Jon Elster eds., 1992). For a discussion of the putative paradoxes involved in self-binding, see PETER SUBER, THE PARADOX OF SELF-AMENDMENT: A STUDY OF LOGIC, LAW, OMNIPOTENCE, AND CHANGE (1990).

28 Alexis de Tocqueville warned against the excessively stringent amendment procedures proposed for the Constitution.

> I have long thought that, instead of trying to make our forms of government eternal, we should pay attention to making methodical change an easy matter. All things considered, I find that less dangerous than the opposite alternative. I thought one should treat the French people like those lunatics whom one is careful not to bind lest they become infuriated by the constraint.

ALEXIS DE TOCQUEVILLE, RECOLLECTIONS: THE FRENCH REVOLUTION OF 1848, at 181 (George Lawrence trans., 1990). The implication, whether intended or not, is that by making change easier one reduces the desire for change. Needless to say, there could also be more rational motives for loosening the ties.

solution was discussed at length in the French Assembly.[29] To meet the objection that fixed revisions would create unrest among the citizens,[30] the proposal was floated to introduce a random element—linking constitutional conventions to the death of the monarch.[31]

It was stated earlier that this Article focuses on process rather than substance. That assertion can be made more precise. I am trying to construct a framework for understanding the events that *lead up to* the adoption of a constitution. The further fate of that document falls outside the scope of this Article. I am concerned with the upstream causes of the constitution, not with its downstream consequences. (I am also concerned, however, with *anticipated* downstream effects.) Specifically, I shall not try to explain, except for some conclusive speculative remarks, why the American Constitution succeeded whereas the French did not. It is not clear what success means in this connection. Minimally, success must imply that the constitutions *matters*. There are three conditions for this to be the case. The constitutions must have precise, enforceable behavioral implications. Those implications must in fact be enforced, and the enforcement of these implications must be causally linked to the existence of the constitution. More ambitiously, the constitution must *work*. It must prevent actors or institutions from usurping power and enable the political system to make decisions and stick to them. It must prevent tyranny, as well as deadlock and vacillation. Finally, we may require that successful conditions should *last* for some substantial period of time, in the sense that any constitutional changes are made according to rules laid down in the constitution itself.

It is a logical truth that a constitution which works will also matter, and a plausible causal proposition that it will also endure. However, constitutions can last even if they do not matter (the 1936 constitution of the Soviet Union lasted for forty-five years).[32] They can even last and matter even if they do not work very well (the Third French Republic lasted for sixty-five years). For purposes of positive analysis, the best working definition of success requires that the constitution endures and matters, as the notion of what works is inevitably value-laden. To explain why some constitutions succeed and

---

29 31 ARCHIVES PARLEMENTAIRES, *supra* note 1, at 36, 39, 67.

30 Madison made the same objection to Jefferson's proposal of periodical constitutional conventions in the United States. *See* Holmes, *supra* note 27, at 217-18. That proposal, however, was not considered at the Convention.

31 30 ARCHIVES PARLEMENTAIRES, *supra* note 1, at 97.

32 The 1968 Czechoslovak constitution is paradoxical in this respect. Although it never mattered during the Communist period, its provisions have profoundly shaped the post-Communist constitutional developments.

others do not, one can focus on *ex ante* conditions of adoption,[33] or on *ex post* events such as exogenous political struggles[34] or the presence of exceptional personalities.[35]

A closely related issue to this explanatory question is germane to my argument. I shall assume that constitution-makers *aim* at producing a document that will work, matter and endure. There are, however, two possible exceptions to this assertion. Some framers may not care whether the constitution matters; some may not want it to last. The first exception arises regarding statements of intentions that have mainly symbolic value and no enforceable content.[36] Although advocates of such statements usually argue that these clauses may change the values and priorities of the citizens, such effects are largely a matter of faith.[37] The second exception is more relevant in the present context and arises with regard to "constitution-wreckers," members of the old regime who wanted the constitution to fail so as to create the conditions for a restoration.[38] In the Assemblée Constituante, the moderate faction (the "monarchists") believed that the Nobility and upper Clergy were practicing a policy of crisis maximization. Specifically, the Noble and Clerical vote against an upper chamber in the legislature was grounded in a fear that this institution would stabilize the new regime. An alternative and perhaps more plausible explanation involves envy and jealousy: the Nobility did not want to see a new aristocracy created whose members would not be recruited from

---

33 "[N]ear unanimous [constitutional] conventions are more successful than politically divided ones because those who thoroughly agree are better able to write a coherent document than those who do not." William H. Riker, *The Lessons of 1787*, 55 PUBLIC CHOICE 5, 9 (1987). Cases may be distinguished in which the balance of forces is (1) known and uneven, (2) known and balanced, and (3) unknown, where the first is the least and the third is the most favorable to constitutional stability. ADAM PRZEWORSKI, DEMOCRACY AND THE MARKET: POLITICAL AND ECONOMIC REFORMS IN EASTERN EUROPE AND LATIN AMERICA 81 (1991).

34 Without the split of the Second International, the Weimar constitution might have proved more durable.

35 In the inter-war period, one may cite President Masaryk of Czechoslovakia or President Pilsudski of Poland. Today, Walesa, Zhelev, and Havel may have a similarly stabilizing role (in an optimistic scenario).

36 Statements of positive rights, such as the right to work, illustrate this case. It is somewhat inaccurate to say that those who advocate such rights do not care whether the constitution works. Rather, those people want the constitution to work in other respects, so that their favored clause can benefit from the prestige that efficiency confers on the constitution as a whole. Of course, each additional free-rider clause of this kind may detract from the prestige that one is trying to exploit.

37 *See, e.g.*, Gary B. Melton & Michael J. Saks, *The Law as an Instrument of Socialization and Social Structure, in* THE LAW AS A BEHAVIORAL INSTRUMENT 235 (Gary B. Melton ed., 1986).

38 The role of the former Communists in the constituent assemblies of Eastern Europe might be worth examining in this perspective.

its ranks.[39]

A large majority of framers in each of the two assemblies was preoccupied with the durability and effectiveness of the document they were writing. Although there were voices at the Federal Convention arguing for the adoption of a temporary or incomplete constitution which could be improved later, the two most influential framers firmly rebutted this idea. Madison argued that reforming constitutions in other countries had been difficult, even when the documents were acknowledged to be defective. "[T]he fear of Innovation and the Hue & Cry in favor of the Liberty of the people will prevent the necessary Reforms."[40] Hamilton similarly claimed that the present occasion was a chance not to be missed. "It is a miracle that we were now here exercising our tranquil & free deliberations on the subject. It would be madness to trust to future miracles."[41]

The French framers were no less insistent upon the unique nature of their Assembly. Mounier, for example, argued that the strong unicameral Assembly necessary to create the constitution would be inappropriate for ordinary law making.[42] The Consitituent Assembly, created by the King and creating a legislature subject to the King, could not itself be bound by anyone. Summarizing both points, Clermont-Tonnerre observed that the "three-headed hydra"—King, first chamber and second chamber—that the constitution would create could not itself have created a constitution.[43] For Clermont-Tonnerre, the privileged character of the Constituent Assembly, by virtue of which it could be a law unto itself, derived from the extraordinary circumstances in which it operated. "Anarchy is a frightening but necessary transitional stage; the only moment in which a new order of things can be created. It is not in calm times that one can take uni-

---

[39] EGRET, *supra* note 6, at 152.

[40] 1 RECORDS, *supra* note 1, at 478.

[41] 1 *id.* at 467. An additional argument against a temporary constitution is that, if it fails, one could never be sure whether the failure was due to inherent defects or to the fact that it was known to be temporary. *See* JON ELSTER, SOLOMONIC JUDGEMENTS 192 (1989). Regarding West Germany in 1948, it has been argued that agreement on the constitution was facilitated by its provisional nature, "because vested interest could anticipate an early revision favoring issues which they considered vital." MERKL, *supra* note 2, at 84. In fact, Merkl goes on to claim that the provisional nature of the constitution facilitated not only its adoption but its survival: "[N]othing is as lasting as an improvisation." *Id.* I doubt, however, whether this last generalization would stand up to scrutiny. Alexis de Tocqueville's analysis of the French constitution-making process in 1848 suggests the opposite and more plausible view, which is that makeshift documents tend to contain gaps and inconsistencies that make them unworkable.

[42] 8 ARCHIVES PARLEMENTAIRES, *supra* note 1, at 555.

[43] 8 *id.* at 574.

form measures."[44]   The rest of this Article elaborates this argument.

II.   THE CONSTITUTION OF THE CONSTITUENT ASSEMBLY

A number of decisions have to be made in the convocation and constitution of a constituent assembly. First, the assembly must be convoked. Second, a procedure for selecting or electing delegates must be adopted. Third, the mandate of the assembly and of the delegates must be defined in terms of constraints on what needs to be included, and what cannot be included, in the final document. Fourth, once the delegates meet, their credentials have to be verified so that the assembly can be formally constituted. Fifth, an internal decision-making procedure of the assembly must be specified. Sixth and finally, a mode of ratifying the constitution must be established.

These decisions flow either from an external authority or from the assembly itself. The first two decisions must clearly be taken by outside agents. The decision to convene the assembly must be made by preexisting authorities, which, in our two cases, are the Continental Congress and the King of France.[45] The mechanism by which delegates are elected or selected also must be in existence prior to the Assembly itself. In the cases concerned here, and in most others of interest, these two outside authorities do not coincide.[46] Although Louis XVI decided the convocation of the Estates General, he could not pick the delegates. When he tried to obtain the power to verify their credentials, he was rebuffed. In America, whereas the Continental Congress made the decision to convene the Federal Convention, the state legislatures chose the delegates.[47]

The assembly is obviously incapable of deciding the initial convo-

---

[44] 9 *id*. at 461.

[45] That authority could be the constitution itself, if calling for periodical constitutional conventions, an occupying power, as in Japan or West Germany after World War II, a provisional government, as in France in 1848, or Round Table Talks between the old regime and the opposition, such as in Poland, Hungary, and Bulgaria in 1989-90. Although a self-convening assembly is a logical impossibility, the Frankfurt Parliament of 1848 does, to some extent, fit that description. On March 5, 1848, 51 self-selected leaders of the public met in Heidelberg to discuss Germany's future. They convened a *Vorparlament* that met in Frankfurt on March 31, 1848. That body voted for elections to a constituent assembly and set up a committee to help administer them. The assembly then met on May 18, 1848. J.J. SHEEHAN, GERMAN HISTORY 1770-1866, at 674-83 (1989).

[46] Such coincidence would indicate that we are dealing with a mere puppet assembly, with no will of its own. An example of such an assembly is the body of 66 men convened in China by Yuan Shikai, (who was President of China from 1912 to 1916, and served in 1916 as Emperor) in 1914 to give his rule a semblance of legality through a "constitutional compact."

[47] I am not denying the close ties between the legislatures and Congress. However, the legislatures' acting collectively through Congress to call a convention should not be confused with their individual power to select delegates.

cation and delegation. It can, however, arrogate to itself the power to control all other decisions. To varying degrees this is what happened in the two eighteenth-century assemblies. Those assemblies verified their own credentials, and set many of their own rules, sometimes overruling their instructions, sometimes supplementing them. The tension between the assemblies and their conveners—between the creature and its creator—was at the heart of both processes. The state legislatures in Philadelphia, the source of the authority of the delegates, were perceived by many as a major obstacle to the assemblies' efforts. There was a somewhat similar relationship in Paris between the King and the Assembly. The general form of the paradox is simple. On one hand, it seems to be a general principle that if X brings Y into being, then X has an authority superior to that of Y.[48] On the other hand, if Y is brought into being to regulate, among other things, the activities of X, Y would seem to be superior. The paradox can also be summarized in two opposing slogans: "Let the kingmaker beware of the king" and "Let the king beware of the kingmaker." These relationships exist both between the assembly and its convener, and between the delegates and their constituencies. Collectively, the delegates owe their existence to one institution; individually, to another. These facts are crucial to understanding the debates in both assemblies.

In both cases, the delegates at the Federal Convention succeeded in replacing the state legislatures with special conventions as the ratifying bodies. Also, the delegates implicitly overruled Congress when they demanded ratification by nine of the thirteen states instead of the unanimity that governed changes in the Articles of Confederation. The French delegates changed the King's veto *in* the constitution into a merely suspensive one, and his veto *over* the constitution into a mere formality.[49] The French delegates also ignored the instructions of their constituents on several crucial issues. This outcome is not surprising. Almost by definition, the old regime is part of the problem to be solved by a constituent assembly. If the regime is flawed, however, why should the assembly respect its instructions?

---

[48] This principle, however, gives rise to a paradox if the amending clause of a constitution is used to amend itself. *See* SUBER, *supra* note 27.

[49] This kind of outcome is generally obtained. Whenever the assembly is more than a mere puppet body, the convoking authorities rarely succeed in imposing their will on it. The Japanese constitution of 1946 is the only clear case of this situation that comes to my mind. *See* KYOKO INOUE, MACARTHUR'S JAPANESE CONSTITUTION (1991). The Western occupying powers had some influence on the West German constitution of 1948, but substantially less than they had hoped for. *See* MERKL, *supra* note 2, at 103, 117, 120-21, 123. When the assembly is convened by an internal authority, and not a foreign power, the assembly is even less likely to listen to dictates.

The following is a more systematic analysis of the six steps: convocation, selection of delegates, specifying the mandate, verifying the credentials of the delegates, defining procedural rules, and choosing a mode of ratification.

III.   CONVOCATION

In both countries, the assemblies were convoked during and because of a general crisis in the country. As argued elsewhere,[50] this fact is important not only in understanding the origin of the assemblies, but also in trying to explain the nature of the document they produced. In a crisis, time is at a premium. The urgent need to reach agreement has the effect of equalizing bargaining power. In particular, the success of the small states at the Federal Convention in achieving equal representation in the Senate may be related to the time pressure under which the delegates found themselves.

France was in a crisis in 1789.[51] The finances of the kingdom were in a shambles due to military overcommitments. The last harvest had been disastrous, and the winter cruel. Moreover, these acute pressures emerged upon a background of chronic anomie. The hierarchies were crumbling. All classes harbored intense resentments against each other or against the royal administration. Intellectual criticism was rampant. Although the direct object of calling the Estates General was raising revenue, it was ineluctably transformed into a general attack on privilege.

The assertion of a general crisis in America in 1787 is more controversial.[52] Although the economy was prosperous, there was a widespread belief that the country was badly governed.[53] The state legislatures, by this perception, acted on partisan and myopic motives, and Congress was too weak to restrain or coordinate their behavior. Moreover, many believed that this political misbehavior had dire economic consequences, such as the printing of paper money, the cancellation of debts, and the confiscation of private property. For the purpose of explaining behavior at the Convention, the existence of these beliefs is more important than their accuracy.

From comparing the two countries, we can draw the following

---

[50] Jon Elster, Arguing and Bargaining in Two Constituent Assemblies, The Storrs Lectures, Yale Law School (September 24-26, 1991).

[51] A marvelous introduction to the pre-revolutionary situation can be found in ALEXIS DE TOCQUEVILLE, THE OLD REGIME AND THE REVOLUTION (Doubleday 1955) (1856). The best modern overview is PIERRE GOUBERT & DENIS ROCHE, 1 LES FRANÇAIS ET L'ANCIEN RÉGIME, (LA SOCIÉTÉ ET L'ETAT) (1984).

[52] A recent overview is provided in MATSON & ONUF, supra note 6.

[53] WOOD, supra note 6, at ch. 10; JILLSON, supra note 6, at 23-24.

implication. In France, the stage was set for a revolution against privilege and royal power from below. In America, the Constituent Assembly carried out what amounted to a revolution against unfettered democracy and radical republicanism from above.[54] While their respective opponents came from opposite ends of the political spectrum, the French and the American framers each shared the same ideal— that of a deliberative and representative mode of government. In the American context, the implementation of this ideal was perceived by many as a step backward. In France, it was several steps forward.

IV. SELECTING THE DELEGATES

This section discusses the mode of selecting delegates. In the Assemblée Constituante delegates were selected both from the regions and from the three estates. On three points related to this procedure, Necker, the King's finance minister, played a crucial role in persuading the King to deviate from the stipulations of the Assembly of Notables that had met in November 1788.[55] First, he secured acceptance of the principle that the Third Estate should have twice as many delegates as each of the other orders. Second, he ensured that the number of deputies would be proportional to the population and tax contribution of the electoral districts, whereas the notables wanted equal representation for all districts, although these varied in size from 6,000 to 600,000 people. Third, he made it possible for electoral assemblies of the Third Estate to choose as delegates members of the other two orders. Both Mirabeau and Sieyès owed their presence in the Assembly to this innovation. The Provincial Assembly of the Dauphiné, which spearheaded the transformation of the Estates General into a national Assembly, went even further and adopted a kind of converse of the last principle, so that delegates from each estate were elected by votes from members of all three estates.[56] On a national scale, however, little is known about the elections of the 1200 delegates to the French Assembly.[57] Although case studies of the elections in the Dauphiné,[58] Brittany,[59] and Burgundy[60] demonstrate considerable strategic manipulation, no synoptic view is available.

---

[54] *See supra* note 18 and accompanying text.

[55] The following draws on HARRIS, *supra* note 6, at ch.9.

[56] JEAN EGRET, LES DERNIERS ÉTATS DE DAUPHINÉ 153 (1942).

[57] FRANÇOIS FURET, LA RÉVOLUTION 75 (1988).

[58] EGRET, *supra* note 56.

[59] Augustin Cochin, *Comment Furent Élus les Députés aux Etats Généraux*, in LES SOCIÉTÉS DE PENSÉE ET LA DÉMOCRATIE MODERNE 211-31 (1978).

[60] Augustin Cochin, *La Campagne Électorale de 1789 en Bourgogne*, in LES SOCIÉTÉS DE PENSÉE ET LA DÉMOCRATIE MODERNE, *supra* note 59.

The delegates to the Federal Convention were elected indirectly by the state legislatures rather than by the voters. Although there were voices calling for the delegates to be appointed by conventions organized expressly for that purpose,[61] the idea did make its way. As a consequence, the debates at the Convention remained, to some extent, under the shadow of the state legislatures. A further consequence of this mode of election was that the delegates were certain to be part of the power establishment, or deeply familiar with politics at the state and confederate levels. Whether the outcome would have been similar had they been chosen at specially called conventions is, of course, hard to tell.

A constituent assembly is made up of individuals. In some assemblies, this logical truth also reflects a political reality. In the Assemblée Constituante, the majority of the delegates actually voted as individuals because they did not want to be captured by any of the organized groups in the Assembly.[62] This fact explains the fluid, volatile and unpredictable character of the proceedings. For instance, Emmanuel Mounier, the leader of the moderates, refused to strike a deal with the patriots over the issues of bicameralism, the right to veto, and the right to dissolve parliament.[63] One of several possible explanations is that he did not trust the ability of his opponents. The delegates were at nobody's beck and call. I am not implying that they were sturdy individualists who preferred to make their own decisions. They were volatile individually as well as collectively—highly susceptible to the eloquence of a Mirabeau or a Robespierre—subject to moods and fashions, rumors and apprehensions. However, they could not be gathered and delivered as a bloc of votes.[64]

At the Federal Convention, the delegates represented their respective states and voted as a single bloc. However, the delegates from a given state were not always of a single mind. It has been calculated that between them, the states that sent delegates to the Convention contained roughly three dozen well-defined political factions, all but a few of which were represented.[65] Although only three percent of the roughly 5,000 votes cast at the Convention were recorded

---

[61] 1 THE FOUNDERS' CONSTITUTION 188 (Philip B. Kurland & Ralph Lerner eds., 1987) (John Jay to George Washington, January 7, 1787).

[62] Albert Mathiez, *Etude Critique sur les Journées des 5 & 6 Octobre 1789*, 67 REVUE HISTORIQUE 241, 269 (1898).

[63] ORATEURS, *supra* note 1, at 933.

[64] Anyone who has ever tried to gather the mercury from a shattered thermometer will know what I mean.

[65] *See* JILLSON, *supra* note 6, at 4.

as "divided,"[66] many more must have fallen short of unanimity. To be sure, the terms "fluid" and "volatile" apply here as well, but for another reason. What occurred in Philadelphia was the coming together and breaking up of coalitions—five altogether, according to Calvin Jillson[67]—rather than the operation of crowd psychology. Coalitions can shift even if individual preferences remain the same.

V. INDIVIDUAL AND COLLECTIVE MANDATES

Consider next the mandate of the assemblies and of the delegates. It was noted earlier that there are two sources of outside authority— one responsible for the convocation of the assembly, and the other for the election of delegates. Each of these creators will predictably try to constrain their creatures, to ensure that certain questions are not raised or that certain solutions are chosen. The convener will try to limit the collective mandate of the assembly, and the electors will try to limit the individual mandates of the delegates. Equally predictably, the creature will rebel against the creators. As previously suggested, the rebel typically will succeed.

Based upon a distinction made by Talleyrand in the Assemblée Constituante,[68] we may distinguish between three kinds of bound mandates: (1) instructions about how to vote on specific issues; (2) instructions to refuse to debate specific issues; and (3) instructions to withdraw from the assembly if certain decisions are made. These are all attempts to bind individual delegates. In addition, it was argued, both in Paris and Philadelphia, that the assembly itself had a limited mandate in that certain institutions or issues were inappropriate for discussion.

In the French Assembly, individual mandates were involved mainly with respect to three issues: instructions to vote by order or by head, to refuse consent to a loan before the constitution had been adopted, and to support the royal veto. Most delegates eventually decided to ignore their instructions on all three counts. The main question concerning the collective mandate of the Assembly arose, as indicated earlier, in the debate over the royal veto in, and over, the constitution. For many, it was self-evidently true that the Assembly had no mandate to destroy or limit its creator. For others, it was equally evident that the Assembly could do anything it wanted, being the embodiment of the will of the nation.

The delegation from Delaware came to the Federal Convention

---

[66] *Id.* at 208. The delegation split its vote evenly.

[67] *Id.* at 200.

[68] 8 ARCHIVES PARLEMENTAIRES, *supra* note 1, at 201.

with instructions to not accept anything short of equality of votes for all states in the new union. Although the instructions themselves did not amount to more than bound mandates of the first kind,[69] the threat to withdraw was nevertheless made at the outset of the Convention.[70] Delegates from the slaveholding states also threatened to withdraw unless their preferences regarding the slave trade were implemented,[71] but they never referred to any mandate of the first or third kinds.[72] The relevance of this distinction is that threats are more credible if supported by instructions from a superior body.

The Delaware instructions were the only case of individual mandates at the Federal Convention. Far more important, however, was the question of whether the Convention itself had a mandate to propose sweeping changes in the Constitution. Some delegates to the Federal Convention claimed that their instructions did not extend to the kind of wide-ranging reform that was emerging.[73] The advocates for a radical change had two replies. James Wilson weakly said that "he conceived himself authorized to *conclude nothing*, but to be at liberty to *propose any thing*."[74] George Mason argued more robustly that "[i]n certain seasons of public danger it is commendable to exceed power."[75] Randolph, similarly, "was not scrupulous on the point of power."[76] Bootstrap-pulling can be justified by external circumstances. This kind of statement was also frequently made in the French Assembly. The exceptional conditions that create the call for a constituent assembly also justify arrogations of power that would appear illegal under normal circumstances. In the constitution-making process the kingmaker should beware of the king.

VI.   VERIFYING THE CREDENTIALS

Once the delegates have met, their credentials must be verified so that the assembly can start working. In Philadelphia, this potentially tricky step caused no problems. The delegates met, read their credentials, and proceeded with their business. In Paris, the verification debates proved to be a crucial stage in the self-transformation of the

---

[69] 3 RECORDS, *supra* note 1, at 18, 173, 574.

[70] 1 *id.* at 37.

[71] 2 *id.* at 364.

[72] Two delegates from New York State, John Lansing and Robert Yates, actually did withdraw from the Convention. This, however, did not amount to withdrawal of the New York delegation.

[73] *See, e.g.*, 1 RECORDS, *supra* note 1, at 34, 249-250. These delegates, however, did not threaten to withdraw on this account.

[74] 1 *id.* at 253.

[75] 1 *id.* at 346.

[76] 1 *id.* at 255.

Estates General into the National Assembly.[77] Two issues were at stake. First, the Nobility wanted each order to verify the powers of its own delegates, whereas the Third Estate wanted the verification to take place in a joint session of all three orders.[78] The Clergy said from the beginning that it would go along with any agreement reached by the other two orders. Second, when the Nobility saw that its ideas were not succeeding, they accepted a proposal that the King be made the arbiter of contested cases. This, too, was unacceptable to the Third Estate.

The first issue was, to a large extent, a red herring. Much more important was the question of whether the Assembly should vote by order or by head. The Nobility thought that a joint verification procedure would create a prejudice in favor of the vote by head.[79] Although the Third Estate strenuously denied this implication,[80] and even claimed (not implausibly) that voting by order would make common verification even more necessary,[81] there is little doubt that they used this issue to drive in a wedge for the more crucial demand for voting by head. In fact, the ultimate resolution of the crisis came when the Third Estate unilaterally transformed itself into the National Assembly, and invited delegates from the other orders to join them.

Before that happened, however, the committee had examined the compromise proposal to refer contested cases to the King. The King's commissaries argued that having called the Assembly into being, the King also had the right to verify the credentials of the delegates in cases of disagreement between the orders.[82] (The commissaries actually presented this as a concession; in the last Estates General in 1614 the King had the right to decide in cases of disagreement within each order.) The spokesmen for the Third Estate clearly recognized the nature of the dilemma.[83] On one hand, it was unacceptable that the credentials of the Assembly should be judged by an external power, since such a practice might, at the limit, amount to

---

[77] After initial plenary sessions, these debates took place in a small committee with delegates from the three orders. The transcripts from the debates are relatively full, but do not permit us to identify speakers except by their membership in one of the orders. *See* PROCÈS-VERBAL DES CONFÉRENCES, *supra* note 1.

[78] In this joint session each delegate would have one vote. A compromise suggested by the Clergy, which involved having the credentials of a delegate from the Third Estate, was not seriously discussed. *Id*. at 39.

[79] *Id*. at 8.

[80] *Id*. at 9, 95.

[81] *Id*. at 117.

[82] *Id*. at 160.

[83] *Id*. at 75, 86-87.

74   Jon Elster

the King selecting the delegates. On the other hand, self-verification created a vicious circle: How could the Assembly verify the credentials without being constituted, and how could it be constituted without a prior verification of the credentials? The answer of the spokesmen to the dilemma was purely pragmatic: "[I]t is impossible to believe that the majority of those who present themselves as delegates should not have valid credentials."[84] In the end, as noted, the Third Estate broke the Gordian chain by simply declaring itself constituted.

VII.   INTERNAL PROCEDURES

Another aspect of the constitution of the constituent assembly concerns its internal procedural rules. Several issues may arise. The assembly may set a time limit for its proceedings. If also serving as a legislative assembly, the consitituent assembly must allocate its time between law making and constitution making. It may decide to create one or several subcommittees to prepare a draft of the constitution or to discuss special issues. The assembly must decide whether to proceed in closed sessions or open the debates to the public. If the sessions are closed, it must decide whether to inform the public about the proceedings or keep them secret. It must decide on the quorum, on the method of voting, and on the procedure for transforming votes into decisions.

The effect of such procedural rules can be profound for three reasons. First, as we know from social choice theory, the process of aggregating given preferences into a final decision is deeply affected by procedural rules. Second, the preferences that the delegates choose to express may be affected by the rules of the assembly, depending on the incentives they create for tactical voting. Third, the setting of the debates may affect those preferences themselves, depending on the scope that is allowed for argument and persuasion as distinct from mere voting and bargaining. In sum, procedure affects the transformation, expression, and aggregation of preferences in ways that can be crucial to the final outcome.

Consider first the issue of preference aggregation. In both countries, the assembly had to come to grips with the fact of a preexisting partition of the nation into groups of unequal size. In both cases, the

---

[84] *Id*. at 86-87. Even admitting this premise, the dilemma still persists. Assume that the assembly has one hundred delegates, that three of the credentials are contested, and that the uncontested delegates are divided 49 to 48 over the validity of the contested credentials. If, in the vote over one contested case, the other contested cases vote with the minority, the contested credentials will be approved.

question arose as to whether the assembly should proceed on the principle "one man, one vote" or "one group, one vote." This question was resolved differently in the two countries. Another difference is that the groups were defined by geographical criteria in one country, and mainly by social criteria in the other.

In the French Assembly, Necker failed in his attempt to impose the principle that the traditional method of deliberation and voting by order could not be changed except by the agreement of each of the three orders and the approval of the King. Instead, the Third Estate unilaterally imposed common deliberation and voting by head. This outcome, to be sure, was clearly what Necker intended to bring about. The doubling of the votes of the Third Estate would make little difference if voting were to be by order. He had hoped, however, that it would be reached by compromise and negotiation. To that end, he fought, albeit unsuccessfully, against electoral assemblies that instructed their delegates to vote for or against voting by head.

The Convention in Philadelphia implemented a system controlled by majority vote, each state having one vote. Although the Pennsylvanians wanted to refuse the smaller states an equal vote, their proposal was never formally considered.[85] When a committee was formed to forge a compromise on the upper house, James Wilson "objected to the committee because it would decide according to that very rule of voting which was opposed on one side,"[86] but to no avail. Yet equality of votes at the Convention could not in itself ensure that the outcome would be equal representation in the Senate, as decisions were controlled by majority vote among the states, and the small states constituted a minority. The large states failed, but not because the rules of voting in the Convention made equal representation a foregone conclusion.

The American case, upon closer inspection, involved three stages. In the first stage, Congress convoked the assembly. In the second stage, a voting procedure to be used at the Convention was adopted. In the third stage, a voting procedure was adopted for the future Senate. *In all three stages, the principle "one state, one vote" was followed.* It is tempting to read a causal connection into this fact. The Convention adopted the principle for its own proceedings because it was used by the institution that had called the Convention into being. In addition, the principle was proposed for the future because the smaller states at the Convention benefitted from the disproportionate strength which they derived from the principle's use at that

---

[85] 1 RECORDS, *supra* note 1, at 10 n.4, 11.

[86] 1 *id.* at 515.

stage. As already stated, the principle cannot itself explain the final decision of having equal representation in the Senate, but it may have been a contributing, perhaps even pivotal, factor.

There are two mechanisms that could be at work here. On one hand, there is the sheer force of precedence. As Samuel Patterson asked at the Convention, "[i]f a proportional representation be right, why do we not vote so here?"[87] On the other hand, the equality of votes at the Convention increased the voting power of the small states: Since the small states were a minority, this voting procedure could not alone ensure their victory. However, the voting procedure at the Convention increased their bargaining power for logrolling purposes. Whatever the mechanism, a deep continuity is present in the American proceedings. The Articles of Confederation shaped the Convention. Through the Convention, they also shaped the Constitution that was finally adopted. The French Assembly, in contrast, made a much cleaner break with the past. Once the Third Estate had obtained the vote by head, there was nothing to stop them.

The French case has some additional complications. Unlike the Federal Convention, the Assemblée Constituante also functioned as an ordinary legislature. That arrangement, however, may be undesirable, since one main task of a constitutional assembly is to strike the proper balance of power between the legislative and the executive branches of government.[88] Although Malouet's argument that "all assemblies have a natural tendency to extend their authority"[89] was made *in* the Constituent Assembly *about* the Legislative Assembly, it also applies to the Constituent Assembly itself. A constitution written by a legislative assembly might give excessive powers to the legislature. In the abstract, this problem could be solved by means similar to those used in legislative bodies, such as checks and balances. A royal veto over the constitution might, for instance, keep the legislative tendency to self-aggrandizement in check. The Assemblée Constituante adopted another solution—by voting its members ineligible to the first ordinary legislature. It was Robespierre who, in his first great speech, won the Assembly for this "self-denying ordinance."[90]

Although viewed by posterity as a disastrous piece of populist

---

[87] 1 *id.* at 250.

[88] The effects of this dual function can be clearly observed in the recently adopted Bulgarian and Romanian constitutions, which give an almost unprecedented power to parliament and provide virtually no system of checks and balances.

[89] 8 ARCHIVES PARLEMENTAIRES, *supra* note 1, at 590.

[90] 1 J. M. THOMPSON, ROBESPIERRE 134-35 (1988); 26 ARCHIVES PARLEMENTAIRES, *supra* note 1, at 124.

overkill,[91] Robespierre's solution did correspond to a genuine problem. If framers have both the motive and the opportunity to write a special place for themselves into the constitution, they will do so.[92] At the Federal Convention, the motive may have been lacking. Although the framers were guided by the Humean idea that future voters and politicians had to be assumed to be knaves, they viewed themselves as moved by loftier motives.[93] More importantly, however, the opportunity was lacking. It was an understood fact, and outside the control of the delegates, that the Convention would be dissolved forever once the Constitution had been written. In the Assemblée Constituante, by contrast, the founders had to take active steps to remove the opportunity to give themselves a privileged place in the constitution.

Procedure may also have an impact on the transformation and expression of preferences. The key variables here are those of publicity and secrecy. Constitutional proceedings may be closed or open to the public. If they are closed, the deliberations may be kept secret until the constitution is finally adopted. They may also, however, become known to the public before the final adoption of the document. The Federal Convention and the Assemblée Constituante are two polar cases regarding this issue. In the former, the sessions were closed and the deliberations subject to a rule of secrecy respected by all. In the latter, the debates were not only open to the public, but constantly interrupted by the public. As we shall see, publicity can have both undesirable and desirable affects on the quality of debates and of decision making.

One effect of publicity is that when speakers commit themselves to a position in public it becomes more difficult to change that position later. The speaker's prestige, and hence his efficacy in shaping events, is more severely affected when he backs down publicly than when he does so in private. Also, overt commitments may create expectations in the public which cannot be frustrated without incurring serious political costs.[94] This was a major reason why the delegates to

---

[91] FURET, *supra* note 57, at 104.

[92] An analogous problem arose in recent debates over the role of the Senate in the Polish constitution. That body, which was created as part of the Round Table Talks compromise, had little justification after the fall of Communism. However, as the Senate will have a vote on the new constitution, it cannot be expected to abolish itself. Andrezej Rapaczynski, *Constitutional Politics in Poland: A Report on the Constititutional Committee of the Polish Parliament*, 58 U. CHI. L. REV. 595, 615 (1991).

[93] ARTHUR O. LOVEJOY, REFLECTIONS ON HUMAN NATURE 52 (1961); MORTON WHITE, PHILOSOPHY, THE FEDERALIST, AND THE CONSTITUTION 114, 249 (1987).

[94] In France, this idea is captured in a wonderful contemporary comment on the abolition of feudal privileges on the night of August 4, 1789: "The people are penetrated by the benefits

the Federal Convention swore to secrecy. As Madison later said,

> had the members committed themselves publicly at first, they
> would have afterwards supposed consistency required them to
> maintain their ground, whereas by secret discussion no man felt
> himself obliged to retain his opinions any longer than he was satis-
> fied of their propriety and truth, and was open to the force of
> argument.[95]

In the Assemblée Constituante, it was initially envisaged that the
Assembly would meet two days each week, and work in subcommittees on the other days.[96] However, the moderates and the patriots
had very different opinions on these two modes of proceeding. For
Mounier, the committees favored "cool reason and experience, by de-
taching the members from everything that could stimulate their vanity and fear of disapproval."[97] For the patriot Charles-Francois
Bouche, committees tended to weaken the revolutionary fervor.[98] He
preferred the large assemblies, where "souls become stronger and
electrified, and where names, ranks and distinctions count for nothing."[99] Based upon Bouche's proposal, it was decided that the Assembly would sit in plenum each morning and meet in committee in
the afternoon. Soon there were only plenary sessions. The importance of this move, which constituted the beginning of the end for the
moderates, was understood perfectly at the time.[100] It was reinforced
by the move to voting by roll call, a procedure that enabled members
or spectators to identify those who opposed radical measures, and to
circulate lists with their names in Paris.

Finally, consider open versus secret balloting in the constituent
assembly. To my knowledge, no constituent assembly has proceeded
by secret ballot, although some ordinary legislatures do. We may
speculate, nevertheless, about the effect of such practices. The advan-
tages of the secret ballot protect the participants from bribes, threats,
and other forms of overt and covert pressure. People are less likely to

---

they have promised; they will not let themselves be de-penetrated." Mathiez, *supra* note 62, at
265 n.4.

[95] 3 RECORDS, *supra* note 1, at 479. For a fuller discussion of the effects of publicity, see
Jon Elster, *Strategic Uses of Argument, in* BARRIERS TO CONFLICT RESOLUTION (Kenneth
Arrow et al. eds., forthcoming 1993).

[96] Great care was taken to form the subcommittees so as to prevent the emergence of
factions. The subcommittees were essentially formed randomly (using an alphabetical order)
and renewed each month so that the same deputies would never remain together.

[97] ORATEURS, *supra* note 1, at 926 (Jon Elster trans.).

[98] 8 ARCHIVES PARLEMENTAIRES, *supra* note 1, at 307.

[99] 8 *id.*

[100] EGRET, *supra* note 6, at 120. Later, Mounier strongly reproached himself his inactivity
on this occasion. ORATEURS, *supra* note 1, at 927.

conform to others when they can express their beliefs unobserved by other voters. The advantage of the open ballot is that it encourages voter accountability. If people argue in impartial terms for a position that does not correspond fully to their self-interest, the open ballot moves them to vote for the same position.

The following are sketches of two scenarios about the impact of public debate and secret voting on the quality of debates. One would appeal to cognitive-dissonance theory, claiming that people who argue in public-regarding terms are likely to think in those terms as well. There is then no need for an open ballot to make them adhere to their stated views. On the contrary, the secret ballot might be useful in shielding them from pressure. The other scenario is based on the premise that one can, at most, induce people to talk *as if* they believe in impartiality. An open ballot may then be needed to induce them to vote in accordance with their public-regarding statements, if there is a gap between their publicly stated position and their privately held views. The open ballot may then serve as an institutional device to create a similar gap between their vote and their interests. In previous work I have committed myself to something like the first scenario.[101] I now believe that the first step in that scenario is too fragile to justify the second step, and that the second scenario is more robust. No amount of institutional design can produce a *reliable* tendency for speakers to become genuinely motivated by the common good. One can, however, make it in their interests to argue for their positions in public-regarding terms and to express their views in their votes.[102]

One might ask whether this is a desirable way to organize political decision making, given the negative effects of publicity mentioned earlier. However, it may be possible to some extent to have the good effects of publicity without the bad ones. More recent constituent assemblies have usually rested on a combination of secrecy and publicity. First, constitutional drafts are composed in closed committee meetings. Next, the drafts are debated publicly in the constituent assembly or in ratifying assemblies. Finally, the vote takes place in public. In this three-stage procedure, framers at the first stage know that they cannot make deals that cannot be justified in public-regarding terms at the second stage. At the same time, framers are not subject to the negative effects of publicity. They can change their minds or their vote without losing prestige or frustrating the public. Although

---

[101] JON ELSTER, SOUR GRAPES ch. I.5 (1983).

[102] For further discussion of why self-interested framers might find it in their interest to adopt impartial arguments, see Elster, *supra* note 95.

the real decision will often be made at the first stage, they will be constrained by the necessity of surviving public scrutiny.

VIII.   RATIFICATION

The final decision concerns the mode of ratification of the constitution. This act is intended to confer downstream legitimacy on the constitution, to be distinguished from the upstream legitimacy derived from the authorities that call the assembly into being. Whereas ordinary laws need no legitimacy beyond that of having been adopted by a lawfully elected assembly, the constitution may seem to require a second scrutiny. The constitution regulates the most basic aspects of political life. In addition, it is deliberately constructed so as to be difficult to change. For both of these reasons, one might want to have an opportunity to overrule the decision of the constituent assembly itself. Moreover, the knowledge of that possibility will keep the framers within designated limits. Not wanting to be overruled, they will anticipate and feel constrained by the possible censure.

It seems axiomatic that the authorities which call the constituent assembly into being also want the right to veto the final document. However, the framers themselves might not accept the authority of their creator, especially if they have already gone beyond what the mandate permits. Instead, the framers might define themselves as the final and sovereign authority, rejecting any need for ratification. Alternatively, they might appeal directly to the people or to special conventions. These are the respective outcomes that were observed in the French and the American cases.

The right of the King to veto the constitution was a thorny issue in France, especially in the wake of the decree of August 4, 1789 which abolished all feudal dues. As the King hesitated to give his sanction to the decree, the question arose whether his assent was needed at all. Both the King and the Assembly tended to see the other as its creature, invested with powers only through the actions of the creator. Mounier argued that since the King had created the Assembly, he also must have the right to veto its decision.[103] In reply, Target argued that a royal veto over the constitution would be absurd, as if "the constituent power had to ask the permission of the constituted power."[104] When the issue arose again in the last days of the Assembly, the King was formally left free to refuse the constitution.[105] Although some of the King's advisers urged him to strike a

---

[103] 8 ARCHIVES PARLEMENTAIRES, *supra* note 1, at 587.
[104] 8 *id.* at 603.
[105] 30 *id.* at 127.

bargain, he opted for unconditional acceptance.[106] It is fair to say that by that time—after the King's flight to Varennes that undermined his authority—he had no other choice. In reading the debates, it is clear that they did not take place under the shadow of future ratification.

By contrast, that shadow was very much present at the Federal Convention. Although no ratification procedure was laid down in the Convention's convocation, many assumed that the Constitution would eventually have to be ratified by the state legislatures. Reasoning from that premise, they argued that the Constitution ought to be tailored so as to be acceptable to those bodies. Charles Pinckney asserted, for instance, that "the Legislatures would be less likely to promote the adoption of the new Government, if they were to be excluded from all share in it."[107] Ellsworth argued in similar terms that "[i]f we are jealous of the State [governments], they will be so of us."[108] The Constitution would not receive their approval "[i]f on going home I tell them we gave the [General Government] such powers because we could not trust you."[109] Others turned the argument on its head: If the state legislatures had an institutional interest in the outcome, they ought not to be judges in their own cause. Rufus King, for instance, argued for ratification by special conventions on the grounds that "[t]he Legislatures also being to lose power, will be most likely to raise objections."[110] In the end, the latter view was adopted. The Convention decided that the Constitution had to be approved by conventions in nine of the thirteen states. This procedure involved a double break with the Articles of Confederation, which demanded unanimous ratification by the state legislatures for all alterations.

It should be emphasized that the institutional interests of the legislatures were not the only, nor even the main, concern of the delegates in Philadelphia. Much more important was the need to accommodate the material interests of the states, an issue that would have arisen regardless of the mode of state ratification. This downstream concern is closely linked to upstream obligation of the delegates to represent the interests of their constituencies. There is, however, a difference. Whereas delegates from all states are concerned about the ratification by any given state, only the delegates

---

106 NORMAN HAMPSON, PRELUDE TO TERROR: THE CONSTITUENT ASSEMBLY AND THE FAILURE OF CONSENSUS, 1789-1791, at 182 (1988). Actually, a bargain had been struck earlier.
107 1 RECORDS, *supra* note 1, at 132.
108 1 *id*. at 374.
109 1 *id*. at 374.
110 1 *id*. at 123.

from that state have an obligation to represent its interests. The shared concern provides grounds for rational argument. The partisan interest, by contrast, yields only raw material for strategic bargaining. Another difference between upstream delegation and downstream constraints is that the latter define the interests of a constituency as a constraint rather than as an end to be promoted. Even the most impartially minded framer may recognize that, unless those interests are minimally satisfied, the constitution will not be ratified.[111] As Charles Cotesworth Pinckney said at the Federal Convention, even "if himself and all his colleagues were to sign the Constitution and use their personal influence, it would be of no avail towards obtaining the assent of their Constituents" to the prohibition of the slave trade.[112]

CONCLUSION

This Article attempted to state the basic issues of constitution making and describe the situation in which constitution makers make their decisions. Its main intention has been to underline the unique character of the constituent assembly, suspended between the past and future, unbound by earlier generations, yet binding the later ones. This creates a paradox. To be sure, each generation wants to be free to bind its successors, while not being bound by its predecessors.[113] It is logically impossible, however, for all generations to occupy this position. Nevertheless, it may be better for all generations if one of them successfully claims that position than if the basic organization of political life is constantly up for grabs. There is no general set of conditions that ensures success in the bootstrap-pulling enterprise of organizing political life. Moreover, success in the constitution-making stage may lead to failure in the next stage of implementing the constitution. The American framers succeeded only incompletely in liberating themselves from the Articles of Confederation, and perhaps this is why the constitution they wrote proved so durable. The French Assembly, after some false starts, made a clean break with the past, only to see its work unravel. I believe that deliberate attempts by representatives of the old regime to impose restrictions on the founders of the new regime tend to be counterproductive for the reasons mentioned above. However, the past can also shape the present and the future in a more indirect way by offering ready-made proce-

---

111 Robert A. McGuire, *Constitution Making: A Rational Choice Model of the Federal Convention of 1787*, 32 AM. J. POL. SCI. 483, 504 (1988). McGuire does not, however, make the distinction, which I believe to be vital, between interests as maxim and interests as constraint.

112 2 RECORDS, *supra* note 1, at 371.

113 *See supra* note 27.

dures for decision making that provide a natural focal point, *faute de mieux*. When that happens, the outcome may also, perhaps unintentionally, satisfy some of the substantive interests of the old regime and thus avoid the polarization and conflicts that might otherwise destroy the new regime.

REVOLUTION AND CONSTITUTIONALISM
IN AMERICA

David A.J. Richards

The American Civil War is now conventionally termed by American historians as the second American Revolution.[1] The implicit idea of a relationship between the two events is not merely one of temporal succession in the same general territory; the second American Revolution was understood by both the Union and the Confederacy as a controversy over the political theory of the first Revolution and the constitutional terms under which it justified its claims. The Reconstruction Amendments are the culminating constitutionalism of this controversy, and should be understood within the framework of the genre of what Americans understood as their revolutionary constitutionalism. We need initially to examine the tradition of revolution and constitutionalism of 1776-1787,[2] and then turn to the elaboration of that tradition in the revolution and constitutionalism of 1861-1870.

I. AMERICAN REVOLUTIONARY AND CONSTITUTIONAL THOUGHT 1776-1787

It is fundamental to the American legal and political experience that its revolutionary and constitutional projects were conceived as a common enterprise.[3] Two leading advocates of the American Revolution, Thomas Jefferson and John Adams, clearly saw constitutionalism at both the state and national levels as the test of the very legitimacy of the Revolution. Accordingly, Jefferson wrote no less than three constitutions for Virginia, and Adams was the main author of the Massachusetts Constitution of 1780 that was centrally used by the Founders in 1787.[4] The success of American constitutionalism was, for Adams and Jefferson, literally the test of the legitimacy of the

---

[1] See, e.g., JAMES M. MCPHERSON, ABRAHAM LINCOLN AND THE SECOND AMERICAN REVOLUTION (1990).

[2] I develop this account at greater length in DAVID A.J. RICHARDS, FOUNDATIONS OF AMERICAN CONSTITUTIONALISM (1989) [hereinafter FOUNDATIONS].

[3] The following discussion of American revolutionary and constitutional thought is a summary of the much more lengthy and leisurely treatment in FOUNDATIONS, *supra* note 2.

[4] See id. at 19-20, 95, 106, 123-24, 141.

Revolution. In order to understand this attitude, we must examine what I shall hereinafter call the six ingredients of American revolutionary constitutionalism: (a) the political principles of the Revolution, (b) the relationship of those principles to what the Americans regarded as the pathological misinterpretation of the British Constitution by the British Parliament, (c) the analysis of that pathology in light of the history of British constitutionalism and the larger practice of republican and federal experiments over time, (d) the use of such comparative political science in the construction of new structures of government free of the mistakes both of the British Constitution and republican and federal experiments in the past, (e) the weight placed on the experiments in the American states and in the nation between 1776 and 1787 in thinking about institutional alternatives, and (f) the historically unique opportunity self-consciously recognized and seized by Americans in 1787 to develop a new republican experiment that established a new kind of argument more politically legitimate than the arguments of ordinary politics.

A.   *Revolutionary Principles*

Americans, following John Locke, accepted the truth that persons have inalienable human rights, tested the legitimacy of political power against respect for such rights, and justified revolution against Great Britain because of its failure to respect such rights.[5] Both Locke's argument for human rights and its associated limits on political power must be understood within the framework of his central defense of an inalienable right to conscience.[6] That defense—the argument for religious toleration—took objection as a matter of principle to the political imposition of sectarian religious views as the measure of all reasonable religious and moral views. Such imposition illegitimately used political power to entrench systems of religious and political hierarchy that deprived people at large of their reasonable moral freedom as democratic equals. Locke's political theory generalized this insight into a theory of political legitimacy, which constrained political power to respect, not trammel, the equal rights of free people.[7] American religion gave strong support to these political convictions; its Protestant emphasis on the right to conscience naturally took objection to uses of political power inconsistent with re-

---

[5] *See* FOUNDATIONS, *supra* note 2, at ch. 2.

[6] *See id.* at 26-32.

[7] *See id.* at 32, 51-52, 82-83, 88, 146, 148.

spect for equal rights like that to conscience.[8]

B. *Constitutional Principles of the British Constitution*

Americans importantly believed that their revolutionary principles were also fundamental not only to the legitimacy but also to the proper interpretation of the British Constitution.[9] Americans took pride in being participants in the British common-law tradition of dissent that had fired the English Civil War and triumphed in the Glorious Revolution of 1688. When the British Parliament sought to tax them, the Americans rejected this not only on independent grounds of rights, but also as violative of the common-law principles they took to be fundamental to both the legitimacy and proper interpretation of the British Constitution. Americans anachronistically appealed to Lord Coke's conception of British constitutionalism that he had urged against the tyranny of James I, and appealed to common-law principles (no taxation without representation) that apply not only against the monarchy (the gravamen of Coke's argument) but against Parliament. For Americans like Adams, Jefferson, Wilson, Hamilton, and Dickinson,[10] the parliamentary supremacy of the British Constitution had betrayed its own basic principles of legitimacy, and they needed an alternative form of government that could use the bitter lessons of British constitutional corruption to establish a government more faithful to the true principles of the British Constitution. In that sense, American revolutionary thought was based as much on a view of the true nature of British-style constitutionalism as it was on the inalienable rights of persons. The natural test of the legitimacy of the American Revolution, thus understood, would be to produce a more adequate conception of constitutionalism than the British understanding of these matters in 1776.

C. *Analysis of Political Pathologies*

For Americans, the betrayal by the British of their own constitution required an analysis of political power and its corruptibilities, and they bring to bear on this question complex historical reflections. These reflections include not only their own oppression by the British, but a larger inquiry into the pathologies of political power under other forms of government, including classical republicanism (ancient Athens, Sparta, Rome,the Florentine and Venetian republics, and so

---

[8] For a useful general study, see ALAN HEIMERT, RELIGION AND THE AMERICAN MIND: FROM THE GREAT AWAKENING TO THE REVOLUTION (1966).

[9] For a fuller discussion, *see* FOUNDATIONS, *supra* note 2, at 65-77.

[10] *See id.* at 65.

forth).[11] These investigations led to the pivotal role in American constitutional thought of James Madison's theory of faction,[12] and John Adams's theory of fame.[13] The theory of faction identifies as a permanent fact of group political psychology that the group will tend to ignore or denigrate both the rights and interests of those external to the group; the theory of fame analyzes the psychology of leadership as often motivated by drives of comparative emulation, not by more ultimate aims of justice and the public good. Neither Madison nor Adams was a moral skeptic, and neither doubted what each of them had demonstrated to an astonishing degree in their own lives, namely, people's capacity for a sense of justice and the public good. Their objective as constitutional architects was not ultimate moral skepticism, but the permanent tendencies of political power over time that it was reasonable to assume an acceptable form of constitutionalism must take seriously as among the facts of man's political nature. The evolving political thought of James Madison—in a memorandum prepared for his use at the Constitutional Convention, speeches at the Convention, correspondence with Jefferson after the Convention, and finally the now classical argument of *The Federalist* No. 10—exemplifies how this perspective framed the American project of drafting, debating, criticizing, and ratifying the Constitution.

In his important memorandum, "Vices of the Political System of the United States,"[14] Madison analyzed defects not only in the Articles of Confederation but in the state constitutions. In particular, Madison took alarm not only at the bad policies pursued by state laws, but at their unjust failure to respect rights. Such laws brought "into question the fundamental principle of republican Government, that the majority who rule in such Governments, are the safest Guardians both of public Good and of private rights."[15] The difficulty was not only in the representative bodies, but more fundamentally in the political psychology of the people themselves. The mistake of American republicanism up to this point was that it had, consistent with much Whig opposition thought, focused on the political corruptibility of government officials, not on the corruptibility of the people themselves. But Madison had come to see that the facts of political psychology applied to all political actors; republican government was distinguished by the power it gave the people to be political actors, but it could claim no legitimate exemption from the laws of

---

[11] For a fuller discussion, see FOUNDATIONS, *supra* note 2, at ch. 2.

[12] *See id.* at 32-39.

[13] *See id.* at 49-55.

[14] 9 THE PAPERS OF JAMES MADISON 345-58 (Robert A. Rutland et al. eds., 1975).

[15] *Id.* at 354.

political psychology. The political power of the people was as subject to these laws as the power of a hereditary monarch or aristocracy. American constitutionalism had to, consistent with its commitment to the uses of emancipated religious and political intelligence in service of the rights of human nature, take account of these facts and frame its task accordingly.

Madison characterized the facts of political psychology pertinent to the American situation in Humean terms:[16]

"All civilized societies are divided into different interests and factions, as they happen to be creditors or debtors—Rich or poor—husbandmen, merchants or manufacturers—members of different religious sects—followers of different political leaders—inhabitants of different districts—owners of different kinds of property &c &c."[17]

Such factions, by definition, pursue their own private interests at the expense of any fair weight to the interests and rights of others, and the commitment of republican government to majority rule would allow majority factions untrammelled power to achieve their ends at the expense of the public interest and the rights of minorities.

Madison considered three motives as possible limits on the oppressive power of such majority factions: interest, character, and religion. The political psychology of faction was such, however, especially under the circumstances of republican government, that none of them were constitutionally adequate. The ugly truth about faction was that a person's critically independent judgment, as a person of conscience, about his or her long-term interests and common interests and about justice to others would be distorted and even subverted by their group identifications: "However strong this motive [respect for character] may be in individuals, it is considered as very insufficient to restrain them from injustice. In a multitude its efficacy is diminished in proportion to the number which is to share the praise or the blame."[18]

Indeed, Madison underscored the special ferocity of this type of factionalized injustice under the republican system. The sense of justice in a republican community reflects public opinion, but public opinion "is the opinion of the majority" so that "the standard [of critical public opinion] is fixed by those whose conduct is to be measured by it."[19] And religion—so far from being a constraint on majority

---

[16] For a discussion of the Humean influence on Madison's thought, see FOUNDATIONS, *supra* note 2, at 34-37.

[17] 9 THE PAPERS OF JAMES MADISON, *supra* note 14, at 355.

[18] *Id.*

[19] *Id.*

factions—was often its worst expression: "The conduct of every popular assembly acting on oath, the strongest of religious Ties, proves that individuals join without remorse in acts, against which their consciences would revolt if proposed to them under the like sanction, separately in their closets."[20]

Madison reproduced and elaborated this argument in his addresses to the Constitutional Convention on June 6[21] and June 26, 1787[22] and in his letter of October 24, 1787 to Jefferson that both explained and criticized the work of the Convention.[23] At the Convention, Madison argued that it was not enough that new powers be given to the federal government, it must provide "more effectually for the security of private rights, and the steady dispensation of Justice. Interferences with these were evils which had more perhaps than any thing else, produced this convention."[24] The oppressive force of faction was well supported by history and by contemporary examples in America, one example of which Madison acidly brought to stage center: "We have seen the mere distinction of colour made in the most enlightened period of time, a ground of the most oppressive dominion ever exercised by man over man."[25]

A central task of the Constitution was to take seriously the corruptive force of many such factions and "to protect [the people] agst. the transient impressions into which they themselves might be led."[26] Madison later wrote to Jefferson in no uncertain terms about the felt need to address the problem of the oppressions of majority factions of minority rights at the state level:

> The injustice of them has been so frequent and so flagrant as to alarm the most stedfast [sic] friends of Republicanism. I am persuaded I do not err in saying that the evils issuing from these sources contributed more to that uneasiness which produced the Convention, and prepared the public mind for a general reform, than those which accrued to our national character and interest from the inadequacy of the Confederation to its immediate objects.[27]

Indeed, Madison's main criticism of the Constitution was conceptual-

---

[20] 9 THE PAPERS OF JAMES MADISON, *supra* note 14, at 356.

[21] 1 THE RECORDS OF THE FEDERAL CONVENTION OF 1787, at 134-36, 138-39 (Max Farrand ed., 1966).

[22] *Id.* at 421-23.

[23] *See* 10 THE PAPERS OF JAMES MADISON 206-19 (Robert A. Rutland et al. eds., 1977).

[24] 1 THE RECORDS OF THE FEDERAL CONVENTION OF 1787, *supra* note 21, at 134 (Madison's speech of June 6, 1787).

[25] *Id.* at 135.

[26] *Id.* at 421 (Madison's speech of June 26, 1787).

[27] 10 THE PAPERS OF JAMES MADISON, *supra* note 23, at 212.

ized in such terms: it had not gone far enough in affording strong institutional constraints on such majority factions (for example, a Congressional veto on state laws).[28]

In *The Federalist* No. 10, Madison defended the Constitution to the nation at large on the basis of the constraints it imposed on "the violence of faction."[29] Madison defined a faction as follows:

> By a faction I understand a number of citizens, whether amounting to a majority or minority of the whole, who are united and actuated by some common impulse of passion, or of interest, adverse to the rights of other citizens, or to the permanent and aggregate interests of the community.[30]

In his memorandum prepared for the Convention, Madison had earlier pointed to the especially malign force of faction under republican government, namely, its erosion of citizens' capacity for critical moral independence by a public opinion that often is the self-serving opinion of majority factions. The argument of No. 10 generalized this theme.

Republicans valued liberty above all. We know that liberty for Madison[31] crucially included the inalienable right to conscience that made possible religious and political emancipation, including the exercise of public judgment in drafting and ratifying a constitution. But such liberty "is to faction, what air is to fire, an aliment without which it instantly expires."[32] The argument of No. 10 has often been interpreted in light of the special emphasis it gives "the most common and durable source of factions . . . the various and unequal distribution of property."[33] Another important strand of Madison's argument, however, turns on why the uncompromisable republican value placed on liberty of judgment is inconsistent with the kind of uniformity of judgment and action that would preclude faction:

> As long as the reason of man continues fallible, and he is at liberty to exercise it, different opinions will be formed. As long as the connection subsists between his reason and his self-love, his opin-

---

[28] Madison had unsuccessfully defended at the Convention and defended to Jefferson the need for a Congressional veto on the laws of the states. *See id.* at 209-14.

[29] THE FEDERALIST No. 10, at 56 (James Madison) (Jacob E. Cooke ed., 1961).

[30] *Id.* at 57.

[31] For the primacy of the right of conscience in Madison's thought about rights, see his *Memorial and Remonstrance against Religious Assessments, reprinted in* 8 THE PAPERS OF JAMES MADISON 295-306 (Robert A. Rutland ed., 1973), and his essay, *Property, reprinted in* 14 THE PAPERS OF JAMES MADISON 266-68 (Robert A. Rutland et al. eds., 1983).

[32] THE FEDERALIST No. 10, *supra* note 29, at 58.

[33] *Id.* at 59. *See, e.g.,* CHARLES A. BEARD, AN ECONOMIC INTERPRETATION OF THE CONSTITUTION OF THE UNITED STATES 14-15, 153-54 (1941). For cogent criticism of Beard's interpretation, see MORTON WHITE, PHILOSOPHY, THE FEDERALIST, AND THE CONSTITUTION 74-81 (1987). *But see* JENNIFER NEDELSKY, PRIVATE PROPERTY AND THE LIMITS OF AMERICAN CONSTITUTIONALISM (1990).

ions and his passions will have a reciprocal influence on each other; and the former will be objects to which the latter will attach themselves.[34]

In effect, sectarian disagreements, whether religious, economic, or political, will be unleashed by the republican commitment to protection of the liberty of judgment in exercising our faculties—"the first object of government".[35] The disagreements thus unleashed will, under majority rule, lead to sectarian oppression. The argument amplified Madison's earlier theme about the self-subverting character of the untrammelled majoritarianism Americans had associated with republican rule; the subversion of the moral independence of free people by a factionalized public opinion was generalized to the subversion of republican liberties by the factions that those liberties necessarily unleashed. Some constructive alternatives had to be defined that might transcend the horns of this republican dilemma.

D.   *Use of Comparative Political Science*

American reflection on the pathologies of political power exemplifies a larger feature of the American constitutional mind, to wit, its absorption in the best available comparative political science (Machiavelli of the *Discourses*, Harrington, Montesquieu, Hume, and the Scottish social and economist theorists—Smith, Ferguson, and Millar).[36] The Americans of 1787 identified themselves—in the sense made familiar by Machiavelli and Harrington[37]—as founders, concerned to use the best political science available to learn from the history of past institutional mistakes in order to construct a better order. Perhaps more than any other people before or since, they took seriously Harrington's project of designing a written constitution that, in light of such political science, could be an immortal commonwealth for posterity. But, unlike Machiavelli and Harrington, Americans had—in light of the later development of political science in Montesquieu, Hume, and the Scottish theorists—become conspicuously skeptical about the continuing utility of the classical republican models (in particular, Rome and Sparta) that Machiavelli and Harrington so admired.

The American skepticism about the classical republics rested in

---

[34] THE FEDERALIST No. 10, *supra* note 29, at 58.

[35] *Id.*

[36] On Machiavelli's influence on American thought, see FOUNDATIONS, *supra* note 2, at 147, 287, 289, 295; on Harrington, see *id.* at 100-102, 115, 124, 132, 147, 287, 289, 295; on Montesquieu, see *id.* at 101-02, 111, 120-22, 125, 127, 128-29, 130, 147, 287, 289, 295; on Hume, see *id.* at 129, 130, 147, 287, 289, 295; on the Scottish social theorists, see *id.* at 56-59.

[37] *See id.* at 97-101.

part on their basis in militaristic and imperialistic aims no longer suited to the commercial stage of civilization in which commerce could supply a basis for peaceful and mutually advantageous relations among diverse peoples. The normative heart of the American objection was that the classical republics had blatantly violated the fundamental conditions of legitimate government as such, namely, respect for inalienable human rights. Madison in particular expressed this skepticism in terms of distrust of mass political bodies like the Athenian assembly. Such assemblies, lacking any appropriate constraints on political power, give maximum expression to the ferocities of faction, subverting—through the unrestrained political force of group psychology—the moral independence that was, for Madison, fundamental to respect for human rights. Madison puts the point starkly, "[H]ad every Athenian citizen been a Socrates; every Athenian assembly would still have been a mob."[38]

Whereas Montesquieu and Hume used such examples to defend the British Constitution as a preferable form of constitutional government for a large commercial nation in modern circumstances, the American revolutionary and constitutional project was precisely to show that a more legitimate form of constitutionalism than the British was practicable. Accordingly, they defined their task as constructing a new kind of republican government that could learn from the excesses of the classical republics without accepting the anti-republican premises of the British Constitution with its hereditary classes (the monarchy and House of Lords). The use of comparative political science was fundamental to the American enterprise because it enabled them to take up a remarkably intellectually independent stance on the issue before them. It enabled them, for example, to take up the thread lost when the English Civil War was aborted by the Stuart restoration, recapturing the Harringtonian dream of an immortal republican commonwealth that Britain had forgotten. On the other hand, the Americans gave a quite independent interpretation to how that project should—in light of Montesquieu and Hume—be understood in contemporary circumstances, but one not hostage to Montesquieu's and Hume's own preferences for the British Constitution.[39]

---

[38] THE FEDERALIST No. 55, *supra* note 29, at 374 (James Madison). The Athenians appear to have been at least to some extent concerned about this issue; thus, the Athenian constitution included various devices that were meant to throttle the assembly's excesses, including a "writ of unconstitutionality." *See* CHESTER G. STARR, THE BIRTH OF ATHENIAN DEMOCRACY: THE ASSEMBLY IN THE FIFTH CENTURY B.C. 26 (1990).

[39] Hume's utopian republican essay, "Idea of a Perfect Commonwealth" did, however, play an important role in shaping Madison's thought. *See* DAVID HUME, ESSAYS MORAL,

E. *American Political Experience*

Americans tested their constitutional minds not only against past political history, but against their own democratic political experience both before and after the American Revolution. Americans were governed as working democracies when colonies, and, after the revolution, engaged in a wide range of constitutional experiments at the state level and the Articles of Confederation at the national level. The drive to the 1787 Constitution was the conviction that these experiments, both state and national, had not respected the principles of political legitimacy they had invoked against the British Constitution.[40] Jefferson objected, for example, to the Virginia Constitution in that it rested on a legislative despotism as bad as that of parliamentary supremacy,[41] and the Articles of Confederation were discredited by their failures both to limit state power oppressive of human rights and to develop a coherent and effective conception of the national interest.[42] The 1787 Convention critically invoked the lessons of the now discredited state and federal constitutions, and looked hopefully to those state constitutions (notably, John Adams's constitutional structures for Massachusetts as well as those of New York and Maryland) that appeared, by comparison, to afford effective constitutional constraints.[43]

F. *American Constitutionalism as Self-conscious Work of Political Reason*

Americans thought of their constitutional responsibility in terms of using their remarkable political opportunity in 1787 to bring to bear the lessons of political experience on the self-conscious design of a new experiment in republicanism: an enduring commercial republic in a large territory that would respect human rights. Both James Wilson and Alexander Hamilton celebrated America as enjoying a unique historical opportunity,[44] and offered their arguments to one of the most free and democratic processes of constitutional reflection that the world had yet seen. Importantly, Americans resisted the Machiavellian picture of politically ruthless founders, favoring instead a process of deliberative reflection about constitutional construction whose

---

POLITICAL, AND LITERARY 514-29 (Eugene F. Miller ed., Liberty Classics 1985) (1777). For a fuller discussion, see FOUNDATIONS, *supra* note 2, at 111-14.

[40] *See* FOUNDATIONS, *supra* note 2, at 19-20.

[41] *See* THOMAS JEFFERSON, NOTES ON THE STATE OF VIRGINIA 120 (William Peden ed., Univ. of North Carolina Press 1954) (1787).

[42] *See generally* JACK N. RAKOVE, THE BEGINNINGS OF NATIONAL POLITICS (1979).

[43] *See* FOUNDATIONS, *supra* note 2, at 106.

[44] *See id.* at 23.

legitimacy ultimately depended on deliberative ratification.[45] Americans innovated a new kind of political structure, namely, conventions exclusively called for the purpose of constitutional construction and special procedures of democratic ratification of the work of those conventions.[46] This structure was sharply distinguished from ordinary politics by the nature and subject of its reflections, in particular, by the kind of deliberative ratification to which it was subjected. These special procedures crucially marked for Americans the special status of constitutional argument that distinguished it from arguments of ordinary politics. In effect, the ratification procedures appropriate to constitutional argument gave institutional expression to the Lockean political legitimacy of the constitution itself. Because the Constitution had been subjected to such deliberative ratification, it could be reasonably regarded as having satisfied the ultimate test for the legitimacy of political power, namely, that political power could be reasonably justified to all subject to that power as consistent with respect for their human rights and the use of such power to pursue the common interests of all alike.[47] Constitutional argument was for Americans supreme over ordinary political argument because it was reasonably regarded as expressive of this kind of authoritative collective democratic deliberation on permanent issues of the legitimate use of political power.

From this abstract deliberative perspective, Americans accepted the justifiability of the three great structural innovations of American constitutionalism (federalism, the separation of powers, and judicial review)[48] on the ground that they reasonably responded to the republican dilemma. They divided and limited corruptible political power (including the exercise of majority rule) in service of uses of political power more likely overall to respect human rights and serve the public good. Understandably, Americans also required that interpretation of issues of constitutional design must call for a kind of deliberation that is institutionally distinguished from ordinary politics.[49] Americans gravitated to judicial review as an institution more likely to secure such deliberation,[50] and to a demanding amendment procedure more likely to secure such reflection over time.

---

45 *See* FOUNDATIONS, *supra* note 2, at 97-105.
46 *See id.* at 92-97.
47 *See id.* at 131-57.
48 *See id.* at 105-30.
49 *See id.* ch. 4.
50 *See id.* at 126-30.

II.   The Second American Revolution and the
Reconstruction Amendments

The Reconstruction Amendments were the culminating expression of critical reflection on the moral, political, and constitutional crisis of the antebellum period.[51] That long national controversy may have been a necessary condition of the Reconstruction Amendments, but was not sufficient. The moral and political world of 1864-70 that gave rise to these amendments was not the nation of 1860-61. Two related facts in each period mark the difference between them.

First, on March 2, 1861, the Congress of the United States, having given the required two-thirds approval in each house, transmitted to the states its proposed Thirteenth Amendment to the Constitution, which would have constitutionally guaranteed slavery against federal interference in the states.[52] Lincoln, in his first inaugural address, supporting the amendment, observed: "[H]olding such a provision to now be implied constitutional law, I have no objection to its being made express, and irrevocable.[53] On June 15, 1865, the Congress, having approved it by the required two-thirds, sent the later ratified Thirteenth Amendment to the states; the amendment abolished slavery and involuntary servitude in the United States.[54] In his December 6, 1864 annual message to Congress, Lincoln had urged Congress to pass the then pending amendment:

> I venture to recommend the reconsideration and passage of the measure at the present session . . . . It [the recent reelection of Lincoln as president] is the voice of the people now, for the first time, heard upon the question. In a great national crisis, like ours, unanimity of action among those seeking a common is very desirable—almost indispensable. And yet no approach to such unanimity is attainable, unless some deference shall be paid to the will of the majority, simply because it is the will of the majority. In this case the common end is the maintenance of the Union; and, among the means to secure that end, such will, through the election, is most clearly declared in favor of such constitutional amendment . . . Judging by the recent canvass and its result, the purpose of the people, within the loyal States, to maintain the integrity of the

---

[51] I discuss these debates at greater length in David A.J. Richards, Conscience and the Constitution: History, Theory, and Law of the Reconstruction Amendments (forthcoming 1993). The argument here developed is taken from that work.

[52] See David M. Potter, Lincoln and His Party in the Secession Crisis 301 (1942).

[53] Abraham Lincoln, First Inaugural Address (Mar. 4, 1861), in 2 Abraham Lincoln 222 (Don E. Fehrenbacher ed., 1989) [hereinafter 1 Lincoln or 2 Lincoln].

[54] See George H. Hoemann, What God Hath Wrought: The Embodiment of Freedom in the Thirteenth Amendment 130 (1987).

Union, was never more firm, nor more nearly unanimous, than now.[55]

Second, in 1860 the leaders of the radical disunionist wing of the abolitionist movement (in particular, William Lloyd Garrison and Wendell Phillips)[56] were a rather discredited and even despised minority within a minority. Phillips had even welcomed secession[57] in light of the triumph of political abolitionism through constitutional processes.[58] But by 1864 they had become major leaders and shapers of a Northern public opinion increasingly favorable to abolition by constitutional amendment; indeed, Phillips was an influential public advocate of related constitutional amendments guaranteeing equal rights, including voting rights.[59] Lincoln, as president, met with Garrison[60] and Frederick Douglass[61] and profited from their (though not Phillips's)[62] public political support in the election of 1864.

The gap between these two periods was filled not only by public deliberative constitutional debate as the background of the Reconstruction Amendments,[63] but by the greatest and most tragic failure of constitutionalism in American history: the Civil War.[64] To study the Reconstruction Amendments as if they were to be understood as simply continuous with the dominant constitutionalism and politics of the antebellum period is to study the Soviet state without reference to the Russian Revolution or the French republics without the French Revolution or, for that matter, the United States Constitution without the American Revolution. The Reconstruction Amendments were not only made possible by the sectional conflict of arms between the North and South; they were also the expression of essential public

---

[55] Abraham Lincoln, Annual Message to Congress (Dec. 6, 1864), *in* 2 LINCOLN, *supra* note 53, at 658.

[56] These thinkers advocated the separation of the non-slaveholding states from the constitutional union with slaveholding states, a kind of mirror image of the Southern secessionist argument. For a good general study of the internal divisions in the abolitionist movement, see generally LOUIS FILLER, THE CRUSADE AGAINST SLAVERY 1830-1860 (1960).

[57] *See* JAMES M. MCPHERSON, THE STRUGGLE FOR EQUALITY: ABOLITIONISTS AND THE NEGRO IN THE CIVIL WAR AND RECONSTRUCTION 34-36 (1964).

[58] For a good general study, see generally RICHARD H. SEWELL, BALLOTS FOR FREEDOM: ANTISLAVERY POLITICS IN THE UNITED STATES 1837-1860 (1976).

[59] *See generally* MCPHERSON, *supra* note 57.

[60] *See id.* at 271-77.

[61] *See id.* at 213.

[62] *See id.* at 260-66, 268-70, 285.

[63] For a good collection of ongoing constitutional debates during the Civil War, including over the war itself, see UNION PAMPHLETS OF THE CIVIL WAR 1861-1865 (Frank Freidel ed., 1967).

[64] *See generally* JAMES M. MCPHERSON, BATTLE CRY OF FREEDOM: THE CIVIL WAR ERA (1988); PHILLIP SHAW PALUDAN, "A PEOPLE'S CONTEST": THE UNION AND CIVIL WAR 1861-1865 (1988).

reflections on the moral and constitutional meaning of the Civil War in light of a constitutionalism that had tragically failed to bring public reason to bear on the underlying controversy. The most compelling interpretation of those events was that they fulfilled the abolitionist prophecy of "the time for a *second revolution*,"[65] the appeal to the right of revolution against the decadent constitutionalism that had protected and expanded slavery and led to its entrenchment under the Confederacy. That interpretation required not only abolition of slavery but a rethinking of our constitutionalism.

Originally, the Civil War was fought by the North to defend the Union against the moral and constitutional illegitimacy of Southern secession[66] and not to secure the abolition of slavery, a point on which Lincoln insisted in his 1862 letter to Greeley.[67] But as the Civil War wore on, the kinds of terrible human losses that the conflict required called for a moral justification more able and worthy to sustain the will and morale of the North.[68] Lincoln himself, after various attempts to secure some form of voluntary compensated abolition with colonization of freedmen abroad, came to regard immediate uncompensated emancipation as necessary to win the war; he even defended the Emancipation Proclamation in such terms, noting, in particular, the crucial importance of the Proclamation's role in stimulating the presence of blacks (both free and slave) in the Union armies and the importance of that presence to the increasingly successful war effort.[69] By the end of the war, most slaves had been effectively emancipated, and Lincoln recognized that only the constitutional abolition of slavery would and did give the war an enduring moral and constitutional meaning.[70] The Civil War was to be regarded as a revolutionary battle for human rights, and the constitutional abolition of slavery was the symbol of that moral achievement.

The Civil War, the "Second American Revolution," was, like the

---

[65] JOEL TIFFANY, A TREATISE ON THE UNCONSTITUTIONALITY OF AMERICAN SLAVERY 75 (Mnemosyne Publishing Co. 1969) (1849).

[66] *See* 2 LINCOLN, *supra* note 53, at 215-24.

[67] *See id.* at 357-58; for example, "I would save the Union. I would save it the shortest way under the Constitution. . . . If I could save the Union without freeing *any* slave I would do it, and if I could save it by freeing *all* the slaves I would do it; and if I could save it by freeing some and leaving others alone I would also do that." *Id.* at 358.

[68] *See, e.g.*, LEWIS TAPPAN, THE WAR, ITS CAUSE AND REMEDY: IMMEDIATE EMANCIPATION: THE ONLY WISE AND SAFE MODE 102-17 (1861); UNION PAMPHLETS OF THE CIVIL WAR 1861-1865 (Frank Freidel ed., 1967); ORESTES AUGUSTUS BROWNSON, *Brownson on the Rebellion* (1861), *reprinted in id.* at 128.

[69] *See* Abraham Lincoln, Letter to James C. Conkling (Aug. 26, 1863), *reprinted in* 2 LINCOLN, *supra* note 53, at 495-99.

[70] *See* Abraham Lincoln, Annual Message to Congress (Dec. 6, 1864), *id.* at 657-58; Abraham Lincoln, Second Inaugural Address (May 4, 1865), *id.* at 686-87.

First American Revolution, a revolution over constitutional and moral ideals. Like its predecessor, it required a constitutional order that would conserve its astonishing accomplishments in a legacy of principle for posterity. Prior to the Civil War, there had been what many regarded as a sharp distinction between the question of the abstract requirements of justice—namely, that slavery was morally wrong, and should not exist—and the question of the morally tolerable and reasonable burdens that could be placed on the South in accomplishing the abolition of slavery. According to this view, slavery as an institution had been foisted on the South by history; it had not been adopted by the present generation, many of whom would not have adopted it if adoption had been an open question, a point on which Lincoln had insisted in 1854:

> When southern people tell us they are no more responsible for the origin of slavery, than we; I acknowledge the fact. When it is said that the institution exists; and that it is very difficult to get rid of it, in any satisfactory way, I can understand and appreciate the saying. I surely will not blame them for not doing what I should not know how to do myself. If all earthly power were given me, I should not know what to do, as to the existing institution.[71]

Lincoln's initial suggestion was colonization:

> My first impulse would be to free all the slaves, and send them to Liberia,—to their own native land. But a moment's reflection would convince me, that whatever of high hope, (as I think there is) there may be in this, in the long run, its sudden execution is impossible. If they were all landed there in a day, they would all perish in the next ten days; and there are not surplus shipping and surplus money anough in the world to carry them there in many times ten days.[72]

The other possibility, the immediate abolition of slavery, would impose severe economic and personal costs on slaveowners, on society at large, and arguably even on the freedmen; Lincoln had problems with all the options:

> What then? Free them all, and keep them among us as underlings? Is it quite certain that this betters their condition? I think I would not hold one in slavery, at any rate; yet the point is not clear enough for me to denounce people upon. What next? Free them, and make them political and socially, our equals? My own feelings will not admit of this; and if mine would, we well know that those of the great mass of white people will not. Whether this feeling

---

71 Abraham Lincoln, Speech on Kansas-Nebraska Act (Oct. 16, 1854), *in* 1 LINCOLN, *supra* note 53, at 316.

72 *Id.*

accords with justice and sound judgment, is not the sole question, if indeed, it is any part of it. A universal feeling, whether well or ill-founded, can not be safely disregarded. We can not, then, make them equals.[73]

Lincoln concluded, "[I]t does seem to me that systems of gradual emancipation might be adopted; but for their tardiness in this, I will not undertake to judge our brethren of the south."[74] In effect, such Southern "brethren" might not unreasonably (or, for Lincoln, not blamably) conclude, as Thomas Dew had in 1832,[75] that, since all such schemes of abolition and colonization were unworkably unrealistic, then the balance of reasons favored continuing slavery, subject to amelioration of its rigors. In the antebellum period, the judgment of the abstract injustice of slavery was thus consistent with a range of views about whether, when, or how slavery could or should be abolished in light of the balance of considerations of justice overall.

After the Civil War, the distinction between these questions had been subverted by the new moral reality to which the conflict had given rise. Most slaves had not only been emancipated, but, more importantly from the vantage of the emerging conception of Union moral identity, many of them had fought well and nobly in a civil war to save the Union. In response to objections to his emancipation policy, Lincoln made quite clear the new moral status black and white Americans now deserved in light of the great moral testing that was this civil war over national identity:

The war has certainly progressed as favorably for us, since the issue of the proclamation as before. I know as fully as one can know the opinions of others, that some of the commanders of our armies in the field who have given us our most important successes, believe the emancipation policy, and the use of colored troops, constitute the heaviest blow yet dealt to the rebellion . . . You say you will not fight to free negroes. Some of them seem willing to fight for you . . . If they stake their lives for us, they must be prompted by the strongest motive—even the promise of freedom. And the promise being made, must be kept . . . Peace does not appear so distant as it did. I hope it will come soon, and come to stay . . . then, there be some black men who can remember that, with silent tongue, and clenched teeth, and steady eye, and well-poised bayonet, they have helped mankind on to this great consummation; while, I fear, there will be some white ones, unable to forget that,

[73] 1 LINCOLN, *supra* note 53 at 316.

[74] *Id.*

[75] *See* Thomas Roderick Dew, *Abolition of Negro Slavery, reprinted in* THE IDEOLOGY OF SLAVERY: PROSLAVERY THOUGHT IN THE ANTEBELLUM SOUTH, 1830-1860, at 21-77 (Drew Gilpin Faust ed., 1981).

with malignant heart, and deceitful speech, they have strove to hinder it.[76]

If black Americans were now taken with a new moral seriousness by Lincoln and the public he led, the claims of Southern defenders of slavery had, in contrast, negligible moral, political, and constitutional weight; indeed, if anything, as the debates over the Fourteenth Amendment make clear, much could now be said, and was said, in favor of the constitutional disempowerment of the Southern leadership that had precipitated and persevered in the conflict until its bitter end.[77] Their obduracy had led them unjustly and illegitimately to defend slavery as an institution by fighting a war essentially for its protection and expansion, a war whose successful prosecution had required the abolition of slavery. From the perspective of the now triumphant constitutional theory of Union (which deemed secession unconstitutional)[78] Southern leaders had forfeited the protections they had long enjoyed under the Constitution of 1787 precisely because they had abandoned the processes of constitutional deliberation and decision (namely, the constitutionally legitimate result of the presidential election of 1860) in favor of a factionalized and insular pursuit of short-term sectional advantage and pride. In the antebellum period, the claim that the Southern slave states were not republican in the way required by the Guarantee Clause was the view only of radical antislavery constitutional theorists or of increasingly radical political abolitionists like Parker.[79] Secession and civil war—the Southern revolt against constitutional law and process—rendered this theory the dominant understanding of Congressional power over reconstruction.[80] The very facts of secession and civil war were proof of the non-republican character of Southern governments, and slavery (the institution which, in the terms of Lincoln's second inaugural, "[a]ll

---

[76] Abraham Lincoln, Letter to James C. Conkling (Aug. 26, 1863), *reprinted in* 2 LINCOLN, *supra* note 53, at 497-99.

[77] Much of the Congressional debate over the Fourteenth Amendment was not about the substantive terms of section 1, but the terms of political disempowerment of section 2. *See generally* HORACE EDGAR FLACK, THE ADOPTION OF THE FOURTEENTH AMENDMENT (1908); JOSEPH B. JAMES, THE FRAMING OF THE FOURTEENTH AMENDMENT (1956).

[78] For Lincoln's invocation of the theory against secession, see Abraham Lincoln, First Inaugural Address (Mar. 4, 1861), *in* 2 LINCOLN, *supra* note 53, at 217-20.

[79] For a good general discussion, see WILLIAM M. WIECEK, THE GUARANTEE CLAUSE OF THE U.S. CONSTITUTION (1972).

[80] *See generally* MICHAEL LES BENEDICT, A COMPROMISE OF PRINCIPLE: CONGRESSIONAL REPUBLICANS AND RECONSTRUCTION 1863-1869, at 152, 169-70, 215 (1974); ERIC FONER, RECONSTRUCTION: AMERICA'S UNFINISHED REVOLUTION 1863-1877, at 232-33 (1988); ERIC L. MCKITRICK, ANDREW JOHNSON AND RECONSTRUCTION 93-119 (1960); PHILLIP SHAW PALUDAN, "A PEOPLE'S CONTEST": THE UNION AND CIVIL WAR 1861-1865, at 224-25, 252-53 (1988); J.G. RANDALL, CONSTITUTIONAL PROBLEMS UNDER LINCOLN 234-38 (rev. ed. 1963).

knew . . . was, somehow, the cause of the war"[81]) was seen increasingly to be pivotal to the moral and constitutional understanding of their non-republican character. The injustice of slavery was no longer an abstract question. Public reason—for the first time in our constitutional history alive to the claims of black Americans and no longer reasonably bound to the demands of the South—was now, in light of the de facto wreckage of American slavery, required to act on the long delayed demands of justice.

In 1865 America faced the question of how political community and national unity and identity were to be understood in the light of the antebellum debates, the Civil War, and the emancipation of the millions of blacks who had been held in slavery in the South.

The antebellum mainstream understanding was reasonably clear, and clearly racist. Chief Justice Roger Taney gave an authoritative interpretation of American national identity in *Dred Scott v. Sanford*;[82] blacks were "beings of an inferior order, and altogether unfit to associate with the white race, either in social or political relations; and so far inferior, that they had no rights which the white man was bound to respect . . . ."[83] Accordingly, speaking of whether blacks could be members of the political community:

> We think they are not, and that they are not included, and were not intended to be included, under the word "citizens" in the Constitution, and can therefore claim none of the rights and privileges which that instrument provides for and secures to citizens of the United States. On the contrary, they were at that time considered as a subordinate and inferior class of beings, who had been subjugated by the dominant race, and, whether emancipated or not, yet remained subject to their authority, and had no rights or privileges but such as those who held the power and the Government might choose to grant them.[84]

Correspondingly, Taney argued that the words of the Declaration of Independence ("all men are created equal . . . [and] endowed . . . with certain unalienable rights"[85]):

> would seem to embrace the whole human family . . . . But it is too clear for dispute, that the enslaved African race were not intended to be included . . . ; for if the language, as understood in that day, would embrace them, the conduct of the distinguished men who

---

[81] Abraham Lincoln, Second Inaugural Address (Mar. 4, 1865), *in* 2 LINCOLN, *supra* note 53, at 686.

[82] 60 U.S. (19 How.) 393 (1856).

[83] *Id*. at 407.

[84] *Id*. at 404-05.

[85] *Id*. at 410.

framed the Declaration of Independence would have been utterly and flagrantly inconsistent with the principles they asserted; and instead of the sympathy of mankind, to which they so confidently appealed, they would have deserved and received universal rebuke and reprobation.[86]

Both of Taney's originalist claims were historically false: blacks voted in some states at the time of the 1787 Convention,[87] and the Declaration of Independence, understood as a statement of long-term ambition and aspiration, may reasonably be interpreted to mean what it said.[88] However, in his 1858 debates with Douglas, Lincoln thought it important to refute Taney's historical claims about the Declaration,[89] but stated Taney's views of black citizenship "without making any complaint of it at all."[90] Lincoln knew that Taney's history on this point was wrong as well, but made little of it because he agreed in substance with it; though states had constitutional power to make blacks citizens of the state and of the nation, "I should be opposed to the exercise of it."[91] In effect, Taney offered a racial conception of American national identity as constitutionally compelled, while Lincoln believed it was merely permitted and desirable.

This antebellum world of racist complacency was shattered by the Civil War, which made necessary the reexamination of the terms of national unity. Americans were compelled to rethink both their revolutionary constitutionalism and the form it took in the Constitution of 1787. Drawing upon the antebellum moral, political, and constitutional controversies, Americans asked the kinds of fundamental questions about constitutionalism that they had not discussed since 1787; the Reconstruction Amendments were the outcome of these deliberations.

Several important constitutional historians have persuasively argued that the Reconstruction Amendments are best understood both historically and constitutionally as a set of ramifying principles interpretive of the central judgment of political morality at the heart of the abolitionist movement: namely, the fundamental moral wrongness of slavery on grounds of its abridgment of fundamental human rights.[92]

---

[86] *Dred Scott,* 60 U.S. (19 How.) at 410.

[87] *Id.* at 572-74, 576 (Curtis, J., dissenting).

[88] *Id.* at 574-75 (Curtis, J., dissenting).

[89] Abraham Lincoln, Fifth Joint Debate, Galesburg (Oct. 7, 1858), *in* THE LINCOLN-DOUGLAS DEBATES OF 1858, at 219-20 (Robert W. Johannsen ed., 1965); Abraham Lincoln, Seventh Joint Debate, Alton (Oct. 15, 1858), *in id.* at 304.

[90] Abraham Lincoln, Seventh Joint Debate, Alton (Oct. 15, 1858), *in id.* at 302.

[91] Abraham Lincoln, Fourth Joint Debate, Charleston (Sept. 18, 1858), *in id.* at 198.

[92] *See* HAROLD M. HYMAN, A MORE PERFECT UNION: THE IMPACT OF THE CIVIL WAR AND RECONSTRUCTION ON THE CONSTITUTION (1973); HAROLD M. HYMAN & WILLIAM M.

On this view, the Thirteenth Amendment's abolition of slavery and involuntary servitude were not merely prohibitions on certain institutions and practices, but the affirmation of the constitutionally enforceable judgment of political morality that made sense of these prohibitions, namely, a judgment about the substance, nature, and weight of the inalienable human rights of all persons subject to political power in the United States.[93] Both the Fourteenth and Fifteenth Amendments are to be understood as deliberative interpretations of this judgment of political morality along its various normative dimensions. These include the guarantee of inalienable rights and liberties, the requirement that legitimate political power be justifiable to all persons as equals, the fair distribution of political power, and observance of the fair procedures of deliberative due process. The leaders of the Reconstruction Congress, much under the influence of abolitionist political and constitutional morality, agreed about the desirability of constitutional protection for all these principles, disagreeing only on whether separate amendments (the Fourteenth and Fifteenth Amendments, for example) were needed to secure them and on points of strategy about how reasonably to secure ratification of amendments guaranteeing such principles.[94] We need, then, to study the methodologies of analysis and justification used in the deliberations over these amendments as a unity, thus capturing the normative coherence that the amendments have and were understood to have.

Consistent with the historical understanding of the normative integrity of the Reconstruction Amendments, we need to understand their unity in light of the six ingredients of American revolutionary constitutionalism that, suitably interpreted in terms of the context of 1865, were crucially brought to bear on deliberations about the amendments. To a remarkable extent, the Reconstruction Amendments were as much the result of internal reflections on the revolutionary constitutionalism of 1787-88 as they were external criticisms of that constitutionalism in light of the bitter experience of its antebellum decadence.

A.   Revolutionary Principles

Lincoln's famous 1864 letter on the wrongness of slavery memorialized for the nation moral views central to the public mind deliber-

---

WIECEK, EQUAL JUSTICE UNDER LAW: CONSTITUTIONAL DEVELOPMENT 1835-1975 (1982); JACOBUS TENBROEK, EQUAL UNDER LAW (1965).

[93] *See generally* HOEMANN, *supra* note 54.

[94] *See generally* BENEDICT, *supra* note 80. For a useful anthology of relevant readings, see THE RADICAL REPUBLICANS AND RECONSTRUCTION 1861-1870 (Harold M. Hyman ed., 1967).

ating on the constitutional abolition of slavery. One sentence in that letter, echoing a similar passage in Channing's great essay,[95] was conspicuously cited by proponents of the Thirteenth Amendment in the Congressional debates: "If slavery is not wrong, nothing is wrong."[96] Lincoln referred to the antislavery views thus expressed as "my primary abstract judgment on the moral question of slavery,"[97] and members of Congress thought of it similarly as expressing a "philosophical truth."[98] That truth was a natural moral judgment about the origination of natural rights in moral personality which no positive law of vested property rights could legitimately abridge:

> What vested rights are so high or so sacred as a man's right to himself, to his wife and children, to his liberty, and to the fruits of his own industry? Did not our fathers declare that those rights were inalienable? And if a man cannot himself alienate those rights, how can another man alienate them without being himself a robber of the vested rights of his brother-man?[99]

Democratically legitimate power cannot accept the claims of popular sovereignty of:

> [the] right of one people to enslave another people to whom nature has given equal rights of freedom. Sir, civil liberty, in my judgment, has no such interpretation, no such meaning; and no man who regards himself as made in the image of his Maker, solely responsible to his Maker for his thoughts and actions, can recognize a sentiment which lowers him in his own estimation, in the estimation of Heaven, and before the face of the whole world.[100]

Such distortions of legitimate democracy were "conceived more than thirty years ago, and John C. Calhoun was present at its conception."[101] Its basis was "tyrannic and despotic power" of the sort "exercised abroad for the purpose of restricting liberty of opinion . . .

---

[95] "Is there any moral truth more deeply rooted in us, than that such a degradation [slavery] would be an infinite wrong? And, if this impression be a delusion, on what single moral conviction can we rely?" William Ellery Channing, *Slavery, in* THE WORKS OF WILLIAM E. CHANNING 692-93 (Burt Franklin, 1970).

[96] Abraham Lincoln, Letter to Albert G. Hodges (Apr. 4, 1864), *in* 2 LINCOLN, *supra* note 53, at 585. For citations to this statement by Lincoln, see CONG. GLOBE, 38th Cong., 2d Sess. 138 (1865) (Rep. Ashley): "My Speaker, *If slavery is not wrong, nothing is wrong.* Thus simply and truthfully has spoken our worthy Chief Magistrate." *See also id.* at 237 (Rep. Smith): "Mr. Speaker, in my judgment there never was a sounder or a more philosophical truth communicated by any man than that of the President of the United States, when he wrote to Colonel Hodges, of Frankfort, Kentucky, that 'if slavery is not wrong, nothing is wrong.' "

[97] Abraham Lincoln, Letter to Albert G. Hodges (Apr. 4, 1864), *reprinted in* 2 LINCOLN, *supra* note 53, at 585.

[98] CONG. GLOBE, *supra* note 96, at 237 (Rep. Smith).

[99] *Id.* at 200 (Rep. Farnsworth).

[100] *Id.* at 154 (Rep. Davis).

[101] *Id.*

where . . . the despotism of Church and State attempted to control the minds of men."[102]

The abstract moral judgment underlying the Thirteenth Amendment expresses the truth, following Locke, that persons have inalienable human rights, that the legitimacy of political power must be tested against respect for such rights, and that revolution is justified against forms of political power that fail to respect such rights. As stated earlier, Locke's argument for human rights and associated limits on political power must be construed within the structure of his seminal defense of an inalienable right to conscience, the argument for toleration, and a resulting skepticism about the uses of political power to self-entrench hierarchies of "natural" privilege that deprive persons of their reasonable moral freedom as democratic equals. All these elements of Lockean skepticism were a crucial part of the most philosophically elaborate defense of the Thirteenth Amendment, which was made by Representative James Wilson when he introduced the amendment on the floor of the House of Representatives on March 19, 1864.[103]

Wilson began and ended his address by appealing to the great change in American public opinion stimulated by the Civil War: "[a] public opinion now existing in this country in opposition to this power [that] is the result of slavery overleaping itself, rather than of the determination of freemen to form it."[104] The Civil War "awakened to its true and real life the moral sense of the nation,"[105] a sense that had lain dormant for "half a century . . . when slavery controlled the national mind."[106] In contrast to the Founders, what we have learned both from the antebellum controversies and from the Civil War is the imperative moral need for revolutionary political action against slavery:

> Mr. Chairman, the position which this nation maintains to-day in relation to the true character of slavery is more perfect than that which the founders of the Government occupied. They believed that slavery was so directly opposed to justice, so distinctly arrayed against divine law, so utterly depraved and desperately wicked, that its own aggregation of enormities would speedily accomplish its dissolution. We recognize their faith as most correct, except in its conclusion. We see that the death can only be accomplished by an executioner. Slavery will not kill itself.[107]

---

102 CONG. GLOBE, *supra* note 96, at 155 (citing examples of Holland, Spain, and Britain).
103 CONG. GLOBE, 38th Cong., 1st Sess. 1199-1206 (1864) (Rep. Wilson).
104 *Id.* at 1199.
105 *Id.* at 1200.
106 *Id.* at 1201.
107 CONG. GLOBE, *supra* note 103, at 1202.

The nation, in fighting a just civil war now seen to be essentially against slavery, recovered the revolutionary political morality of the American Revolution that justified war on grounds of defending human rights:

> The spirit of patriotism has returned to us clothed with a resurrectional brightness like unto that which shall light the heirs of glory to the abode of the eternal Father. Manhood, as it stood proudly erect in the grand, colossal, symmetrical proportions known to the early days of the Republic, again gives sublimity to American character . . . . An awakened, invigorated concentrated national conscience revivifies our observance of justice . . . . Our Red Sea passage promises to be as propitious as was that of God's chosen people when the waters parted and presented the sea-bed for their escape from the hosts upon whom these waters closed and effected the burial appointed by Him who had declared, "Let my people go."[108]

The task now was to forge a constitutionalism that would memorialize and give adequate institutional expression to "the grand volcanic action that is upheaving the great moral ideas which underlie the Republic."[109]

Wilson's emphasis on a judgment of moral right forged by morally good action reflects the abolitionist distrust for the familiar proslavery uses of the intellect to distort or suppress the requirements of ethical impartiality: "We have tried to reason it [the wrongness of slavery] away, to practice arts which should carry us around it, or over it, or under it."[110] But he also offers an argument for why this judgment of political morality is sound, which is based on toleration, clearly derived from the same argument made by the abolitionists.[111]

The right to revolution was, in Lockean political theory, centrally linked to the right to conscience because only the required guarantees for the moral independence of critical conscience would enable it to make the kinds of judgments on the basis of which the right to revolution might legitimately be asserted. As Locke explained, "I myself can only be Judge in my own Conscience . . . ."[112] The abridgment by the state of the rights to conscience and free speech would

---

[108] *Id.*

[109] *Id.*

[110] *Id.* at 1200.

[111] For a fuller elaboration of this point, see RICHARDS, *supra* note 51, at ch.3.

[112] JOHN LOCKE, TWO TREATISES OF GOVERNMENT § 21, at 300 (Peter Laslett ed., 2nd ed. 1970) (1690); *see also id.* § 168, at 398, § 209, at 422-23, § 242, at 445. For commentary, see FOUNDATIONS, *supra* note 2, at 78-97.

illegitimately allow it to determine what was considered valid or proper criticism of the state or, even worse, to set the critical intellectual and ethical standards of public reason. In effect, dominant political powers would self-entrench an epistemology that would immunize its powers from the kind of independent critical assessment central to the tests under which the legitimacy of any political power should be assessed, namely, respect for rights and pursuit of the public interest. For this reason, abridgment of the right to conscience was one of the central grounds on which the right to revolution might be claimed.

Thus the normative heart of Wilson's argument of revolutionary justification for the Civil War was put in terms of the illegitimate abridgment of the inalienable rights of conscience, free speech, and assembly. For example, with respect to freedom of conscience:

> The bitter, cruel, relentless persecutions of the Methodists in the South, almost as void of pity as those which were visited upon the Huguenots in France, tell how utterly slavery disregards the right to a free exercise of religion. No religion which recognizes God's eternal attribute of justice and breathes that spirit of love which applies to all men the sublime commandment, "Whatsoever ye would that men should do unto you, do ye even so to them," can ever be allowed free exercise where slavery curses men and defies God. No religious denomination can flourish or even be tolerated where slavery rules without surrendering the choicest jewels of its faith into keeping of that infidel power which withholds the Bible from the poor. Religion, "consisting in the performance of all known duties to God and our fellow-men," never has been and never will be allowed free exercise in any community where slavery dwarfs the consciences of men.[113]

And with respect to free speech:

> How much better has free discussion fared at the hands of the black censor who guards the interests of slavery against the expression of the thoughts of freemen? On what rood of this Republic cursed by slavery have men been free to declare their approval of the divine doctrines of the Declaration of Independence? Where, except in the free States of this Union, have the nation's toiling millions been permitted to assert their great protective doctrine, "The laborer is worthy of his hire?" What member of our great free labor force, North or South, could stand up in the presence of the despotism which owns men and combat the atrocious assertion that "Slavery is the natural and normal condition of the laboring man, whether white or black," with the noble declaration that "La-

---

[113] CONG. GLOBE, *supra* note 103, at 1202.

bor being the sure foundation of the nation's prosperity should be performed by free men, for they alone have an interest in the preservation of free government," with any assurance that his life would not be exacted at the price of his temerity? In all this broad land not one could be found. The press has been padlocked, and men's lips have been sealed. Constitutional defense of free discussion by speech or press has been a rope of sand south of the line which marked the limit of dignified free labor in this country. South of that line an organized element of death was surely sapping the foundations of our free institutions, reversing the theory of our Government, dwarfing our civilization, contracting the national conscience, compassing the destruction of everything calculated to preserve the republican character of our Constitution; and no man in the immediate presence of this rapidly accumulating ruin dared to raise a voice of warning. Submission and silence were inexorably exacted. Such, sir, is the free discussion which slavery tolerates.[114]

And the right of free assembly to protest grievances

has been as completely disregarded as the other rights I have mentioned by the terrorism which guards the citadel of slavery. If slavery persecuted religionists, denied the privilege of free discussion, prevented free elections, trampled upon all of the constitutional guarantees belonging to the citizen, peaceable assemblages of the people to consider these grievances with a view to petition the Government for redress could not be held. If non-slaveholding whites became alarmed at the bold announcement that "slavery is the natural and normal condition of the laboring man, whether white or black," seeing therein the commencement of an effort intended to result in the enslavement of labor instead of the mere enslavement of the African race, they were not privileged to peaceably assemble and petition the Government in regard thereto, or to discuss the barbarism and to arouse the people in opposition to it. Slavery held political and social power sufficient to crush all such attempts on the part of the injured people. Slavery could hold its assemblages, discuss, resolve, petition, threaten, disregard its constitutional obligations, trample upon the right of labor, do anything its despotic disposition might direct; but freedom and freemen must be deaf, dumb, and blind. Throughout all the dominions of slavery republican government, constitutional liberty, the blessing of our free institutions were mere fables.[115]

From the contractualist perspective of Lockean political theory that Wilson assumes, the abridgment of such rights—at the very core

---

[114] CONG. GLOBE, *supra* note 103, at 1202.
[115] *Id.*

of the inalienable human rights that government is instituted to secure—deprives political power of legitimacy, and justifies the right to
revolution in order to secure those rights in a form of constitutionalism that will, at a minimum, better protect them. Americans in 1864-
65 were thus, on grounds of abstract natural right, at least as well
justified as the American revolutionaries of 1776 in rejecting the illegitimate political claims made on behalf of the Southern slave power,
revolting against such power, and forging new constitutional forms
adequate to their just grievances.

B.   *Constitutional Principles of the American Constitution*

American constitutional revolutionaries like Wilson in 1864 importantly believed that their revolutionary principles were fundamental not only to the legitimacy, but also to the proper interpretation of
the United States Constitution. In the same way that the revolutionaries of 1776 justified themselves not only on the basis of natural
rights but on the basis of a better interpretation of the principles of the
constitution against which they were revolting, the revolutionaries of
1864-65 appealed interpretively to the American constitutionalism
they still revered.

Their continuing reverence for the Constitution of 1787 appears
in their failure to take seriously the more radical constitutional alternative of reconsidering the Founders' rejection of the model of British
parliamentary supremacy, a proposal urged upon them by Sidney
George Fisher in 1862.[116] Fisher's proposal was not frivolous. The
British Constitution, rejected by Americans in 1776 on revolutionary
grounds of violating natural rights, had successfully and democratically abolished slavery in the West Indies in 1833-38 largely because
the institution of parliamentary supremacy, in which West Indian
planters were not well represented, had sufficient power and incentive
to act on humane moral principles in response to a well-organized and
politically astute British abolitionist movement (a movement intimately connected to the American abolitionists).[117] In morally ironic
contrast, the United States Constitution, proposed and defended as a
better constitutional process to protect inalienable human rights, had
so entrenched Southern slaveholding power constitutionally (through
the 3/5 Clause)[118] that America was to abolish slavery comparatively

---

[116] *See* SIDNEY G. FISHER, THE TRIAL OF THE CONSTITUTION (1862). For commentary
on Fisher in general, see PHILLIP S. PALUDAN, A COVENANT WITH DEATH: THE CONSTITU-
TION, LAW, AND EQUALITY IN THE CIVIL WAR ERA 170-218 (1975).

[117] *See generally* DAVID B. DAVIS, THE PROBLEM OF SLAVERY IN THE AGE OF REVOLU-
TION 1770-1823 (1975); DAVID B. DAVIS, SLAVERY AND HUMAN PROGRESS (1984).

[118] On the political importance of the constitutionally enhanced representation of the South

late, after even Imperial Russia[119] (Brazil[120] and Cuba[121] did so even later). The argument might reasonably be made that, in light of the comparative experience of Britain and the United States on the greatest issue of human rights in the nineteenth century, British parliamentary democracy was, on grounds of Lockean political theory, the preferable constitutionalism. America, in this view, had taken a wrong turn in 1776 and 1787, and should now return to the parent constitutionalism it had unwisely rejected.[122]

American revolutionary constitutionalists like Wilson in 1864 knew that radical changes in American constitutionalism were needed, but they framed their task in light of the various antebellum constitutional theories that, as previously seen, criticized as interpretively mistaken the direction in which American constitutionalism had been taken by the politics of Douglas and by the judiciary of Taney. To differing degrees and extents, the constitutional theories of union, radical disunion, and moderate and radical antislavery[123] criticized American constitutionalism both internally and externally. Internal criticism supplied a theory of interpretive mistake in light of which various influential and even authoritative interpretations of the Constitution could be reasonably regarded as wrong and mistaken (Calhoun's theory of nullification and secession, Douglas's popular sovereignty, and Taney's views in *Dred Scott* of both citizenship and the national powers of Congress in the territories).[124] Both radical disunionism and antislavery profoundly questioned the Constitution of 1787 itself: disunionism by attacking it directly as pro-slavery and thus worthy of revolution, radical antislavery more circuitously by draining the pro-slavery clauses of the Constitution of their evident historical meaning because, otherwise, revolutionary Americans of 1776 and 1787 "would sooner have had it [the Constitution] burned

---

on crucial sectional issues, see DWIGHT L. DUMOND, ANTISLAVERY: THE CRUSADE FOR FREEDOM IN AMERICA 63-75, 106-07 (1966).

[119] Serfdom was abolished in Russia in 1861. *See generally* PETER KOLCHIN, UNFREE LABOR: AMERICAN SLAVERY AND RUSSIAN SERFDOM (1987).

[120] Slaves in Brazil were emancipated in 1888. *See* DAVIS, SLAVERY AND HUMAN PROGRESS, *supra* note 117, at 291-98.

[121] Slavery was abolished in Cuba in 1886. *See id.* at 285-91.

[122] For a related form of argument that American constitutionalism should profitably be interpreted on the model of British parliamentary government, see WOODROW WILSON, CONGRESSIONAL GOVERNMENT: A STUDY IN AMERICAN POLITICS (The Johns Hopkins University Press, 1981) (1881). For useful commentary, see NIELS A. THORSEN, THE POLITICAL THOUGHT OF WOODROW WILSON 1875-1910 (1988).

[123] I explore these theories at greater length in RICHARDS, *supra* note 51, at chs. 2-3. For a good study of the distinctions among these views, see WILLIAM M. WIECEK, THE SOURCES OF ANTISLAVERY CONSTITUTIONALISM IN AMERICA, 1760-1848 (1977).

[124] For fuller development of these criticisms, see RICHARDS, *supra* note 51, at chs. 2-3.

by the hands of the common hangman"[125] and we, when awake to our revolutionary rights of conscience, would demand, in Tiffany's words, *"change* or *revolution."*[126]

In 1864, Wilson, speaking to a nation now alive to its revolutionary rights and responsibilities, made his case for the Thirteenth Amendment not only on the abstract ground of natural rights but on the interpretive ground, supported by radical antislavery, that the Constitution, properly interpreted, had protected the inalienable rights of conscience, free speech, and assembly against the states. Borrowing an argument made by Goodell[127] and clearly stated by Tiffany,[128] Wilson suggested that the Supremacy Clause[129] and the Privileges and Immunities Clause[130] extended the protections of the First Amendment against the states, protections which the Southern states—controlled by the slave power—had egregiously abridged. Wilson might have made the argument at this point not as an interpretive one but as a claim of political theory. Even if the Constitution did not extend the Bill of Rights to the states, the failure of the states to respect such rights deprived them of political legitimacy and, from the revolutionary perspective of the nation in 1864, slavery should be abolished to remove the main temptation to such political illegitimacy. But Wilson's interpretive stance on the meaning of the Constitution was motivated by exactly what motivated radical antislavery: an interpretation of the Constitution so that it would conform with Lockean political theory. Unlike them, he had behind him "the grand volcanic action"[131] of national revolutionary moral public opinion wrought by the Civil War. From the perspective of such revolutionary constitutionalism, the Constitution, to be worthy of allegiance, must be interpreted in this way, and slavery was to be abolished in order that such interpretive mistake might not recur.

---

[125] LYSANDER SPOONER, THE UNCONSTITUTIONALITY OF SLAVERY 119 (1860).

[126] TIFFANY, *supra* note 65, at 99.

[127] *See* WILLIAM GOODELL, VIEWS OF AMERICAN CONSTITUTIONAL LAW IN ITS BEARING UPON AMERICAN SLAVERY 75-77 (1844).

[128] *See* TIFFANY, *supra* note 65, at 84-97.

[129] CONG. GLOBE, *supra* note 103, at 1202.

This Constitution, and the laws of the United States which shall be made in pursuance thereof; and all treaties made, or which shall be made, under the authority of the United States, shall be the supreme law of the land; and the Judges in every State shall be bound thereby, anything in the Constitution or laws of any State to the contrary notwithstanding.

U.S. CONST. art. VI, cl. 2.

[130] "The citizens of each State shall be entitled to all privileges and immunities of citizens in the several States." U.S. CONST. art. IV, § 2, cl. 1, *cited in* CONG. GLOBE, *supra* note 103, at 1202.

[131] *Id.* at 1203.

Representative John A. Bingham, the architect of Section 1 of the Fourteenth Amendment, had been a close friend of Joshua Giddings,[132] an important advocate of moderate not radical antislavery;[133] and he correspondingly took the road not taken by Wilson, acknowledging more of a gap between political theory and the proper interpretation of the Constitution of 1787 than Wilson conceded. Bingham certainly believed and argued that, as a matter of political theory, no state had the authority to violate inalienable human rights like those guaranteed by the First Amendment. In contrast to Wilson, he thought the Constitution, properly interpreted, had applied the standard to the states as a standard that, at best, they were to enforce, and had not applied the principle against the states by adequate federally enforceable guarantees. In the debate over the first version of Section 1 introduced in the House of Representatives,[134] Bingham, like Wilson, pointed to the Supremacy Clause and Privileges and Immunities Clause (also the Due Process Clause) as imposing obligations on the states to respect human rights, but, properly interpreted, "these great provisions of the Constitution, this immortal bill of rights embodied in the Constitution, rested for its execution and enforcement hitherto upon the fidelity of the States."[135] The point of Section 1 was, Bingham argued, "to arm the Congress of the United States, by the consent of the people of the United States, with the power to enforce the bill of rights as it stands in the Constitution today,"[136] that is, to give the federal government adequate power to guarantee respect for human rights by the states. Bingham recognized as clearly as Wilson the revolutionary character of the constitutional moment; in response to the suggestion that Congress could not constitutionally approve any amendment in the absence of the Southern states from Congress, he noted an analogous argument had been made against the ratification of the Constitution of 1787 on terms forbidden by the Articles of Confederation, and argued the same response applied here as there, namely:

---

[132] See GEORGE W. JULIAN, THE LIFE OF JOSHUA R. GIDDINGS 398-99 (1892).

[133] Moderate antislavery accepted that the Constitution did not prohibit slavery in the states that had it; radical antislavery argued that the Constitution, properly understood, forbade slavery even in the states. See generally WIECEK, supra note 123.

[134] The version read:

> The Congress shall have power to make all laws which shall be necessary and proper to secure to the citizens of each State all privileges and immunities of citizens in the several States, and to all persons in the several States equal protection in the rights of life, liberty, and property.

CONG. GLOBE, 39th Cong., 1st Sess. 1034 (1866) (Statement of Rep. Bingham).

[135] Id.

[136] Id. at 1088.

that the right of the people to self-preservation justifies it; it rests upon the transcendent right of nature, and nature's God. That right is still in the people and has justified their action through all this trial. It is the inherent right of the people. It cannot be taken from them. It has survived the storms and tempests of this great conflict of arms.[137]

But the very legitimacy of the revolutionary moment required, for Bingham, clarity that Section 1 of the Fourteenth Amendment worked revolutionary change, not merely a correction of interpretive mistake. In the debate over the second version of Section 1 introduced in the House,[138] he made clear the gap between political legitimacy and constitutional guarantees that Section 1 filled. With respect to political legitimacy:

No State ever had the right, under the forms or law or otherwise, to deny to any freeman the equal protection of the laws or to abridge the privileges or immunities of any citizen of the Republic, although many of them have assumed and exercised the power, and that without remedy.[139]

Section 1 would fill this gap by enabling:

the people . . . by express authority of the Constitution to do that by congressional enactment which hitherto they have not had the power to do; that is, to protect by national law the privileges and immunities of all the citizens of the Republic and the inborn rights of every person within its jurisdiction whenever the same shall be abridged or denied by the unconstitutional acts of any State.[140]

Bingham, like Wilson, nonetheless fit his conception of the need for the Reconstruction Amendments very much within the framework of the principles of American constitutionalism (which Section 1 extends in certain required ways). While they disagreed on points of internal criticism that largely reflect interpretive divergences in antebellum abolitionist constitutional theories, they agreed both on the ultimate revolutionary foundations of the amendments and the need—in light of the revolutionary moment—to see the amendments as being as much interpretive as critical of the Constitution of 1787.

---

[137] CONG. GLOBE, *supra* note 134, at 1089.

[138] The second version read:

No state shall make or enforce any law which shall abridge the privileges or immunities of citizens of the United States; nor shall any State deprive any person of life, liberty, or property without due process of law, nor deny to any person within its jurisdiction the equal protection of the laws.

CONG. GLOBE, *supra* note 134, at 2461.

[139] *Id.* at 2542.

[140] *Id.*

C. *Analysis of Political Pathology*

For the revolutionary Americans of 1776, the betrayal by the British of their own constitutionalism required an analysis of political power and its corruptibilities, and they brought to bear on this question complex historical reflections. Investigations of this sort led to the pivotal role in American constitutional thought, as seen earlier, of the theories of faction and of fame. Neither theory rested on ultimate moral skepticism, but rather took seriously facts gathered from the study of comparative political science about political psychology, *i.e.*, man's nature in the group psychology characteristic of political life. The great architects of American constitutionalism, James Madison and John Adams, did not believe, in contrast to Rousseau,[141] that man's political nature would be ethically transformed by the responsibilities of politics under a republican form of government; the political corruptibilities of group psychology in politics would persist, albeit in varying ways and with different emphases, under any form of politics, including republican politics. The task of an enlightened constitutionalism was to use these facts of political psychology in the design of constitutional institutions that, consistent with democratic rights of voting and participation, would channel and structure republican political power in ways more likely to secure respect for inalienable human rights and the use of political power for the public good.

Madison, in particular, had anatomized the political psychology of faction acutely as a form of group identification and insularity that could corrupt conscience itself, respect for which was the foundation of inalienable human rights. Moreover, he had suggested two elaborations of the theory of faction that would be central to the thinking of the revolutionary constitutionalists of 1865. First, Madison worried in his despairing October 24, 1787 letter to Jefferson that the Constitution of 1787 had not taken sufficient account of the need for national constitutional structures (like a Congressional veto over state laws) that might address what had proven under the Articles of Confederation to be the worst form of political pathology, namely, state factions. Second, Madison identified group political psychology based on race as one of the worst forms of faction—"the most oppressive dominion ever exercised by man over man."[142] To a remarkable degree, the thoughts on political psychology of the proponents of the

---

[141] For an extended exploration of this comparison, see David A. J. Richards, *Revolution and Constitutionalism in America and France*, 60 MISS. L.J. 311 (1990).

[142] Speech by James Madison (June 6, 1787), *in* 1 THE RECORDS OF THE FEDERAL CONVENTION OF 1787, *supra* note 21, at 134.

Reconstruction Amendments worked within and analytically elaborated the framework of Madison's thoughts about these factions.

Proponents of the Reconstruction Amendments took different views of where the Constitution had gone wrong: some, like Wilson, emphasizing interpretive mistakes, others, like Bingham, focussing on foundational mistakes in institutional design. But they all shared the common interest central to American revolutionary constitutionalism of both understanding the nature of the political psychology that had led to the American revolutionary crisis of constitutional legitimacy and the framing of a constitutionalism adequate to this analysis.

Such an analysis had two components, one normative, the other empirical. The normative component rested on the central principles of political legitimacy, in particular, respect for inalienable human rights. The empirical component examined the main types of political threats to which various rights tended to be subject. In Lockean constitutional thought, religious persecution was a paradigm example of such a faction, and the argument for toleration correspondingly had both a normative and an empirical component to explain its nature and appropriate constitutional remedy. The normative component was the inalienable right to conscience and the kind of justification for public power that it required; the empirical component was the political enforcement at large of sectarian views that both corrupted reasonable standards of critical inquiry and deprived persons of their moral powers to make such inquiries. Both components were crucial to the analysis of each faction central to the design of the Reconstruction Amendments, namely, the slave power and irrational race prejudice (or racism).

The idea of a slave power was a central contribution of political abolitionism to antebellum moral and constitutional debate.[143] Its normative component was defined by the unjustifiable abridgements of inalienable human rights central to the maintenance and expansion of the political power of the defenders of slavery; its empirical component was the political enforcement on society at large of sectarian moral and constitutional views that crippled reasonable standards of debate and deprived persons of their rights to personal and moral self-government. As previously cited, the most brilliant expression of this analysis in the Congressional debates on the Reconstruction Amendments was James Wilson's speech proposing a Thirteenth Amendment to the House of Representatives. Wilson's discussion of the unjustified abridgement by Southern states of the inalienable rights of

---

[143] *See generally* DAVID B. DAVIS, THE SLAVE POWER CONSPIRACY AND THE PARANOID STYLE (1969).

conscience, free speech, and assembly was offered by him as part of his larger analysis of the political faction that had grown up around the defense and expansion of slavery as an institution. The faction was identified by its normative abridgement of the rights of all persons (slave and free) to conscience, free speech, and assembly and empirically by its increasingly parochial and insular modes of essentially sectarian argument in terms of which such abridgments were thought to be justified. The distorted uses to which the Constitution of 1787 had been put in the antebellum period were then explained in terms of the political power that this faction had achieved under the Constitution (for example, in *Dred Scott*). Wilson argued that the Founders had also recognized the evil of slavery, but they mistakenly thought an institution "so directly opposed to justice, so distinctly arrayed against divine law, so utterly depraved and desperately wicked, . . . would speedily accomplish its dissolution."[144] Experience had proven them tragically wrong: An institution like slavery, itself based on the abridgement of human rights, had given rise to a political faction, precisely within the terms of Madison's theory, "a number of citizens . . . , who are united and actuated by some common impulse of passion, or of interest, adverse to the rights of others citizens, or to the permanent and aggregate interests of the community."[145] This political faction, united by its economic interests in slavery as an institution, had abused the constitutional protections accorded slavery not to end it but to entrench and extend it on terms that required further violations of inalienable human rights of conscience, free speech, and assembly.

The Constitution of 1787, designed to channel both faction and fame in service of a republican political theory of respecting rights and pursuit of the public good, was responsible for the growth and effective political power of a pathological faction that had undermined its political legitimacy. The political science of the Founders, so wisely skeptical about the corruptibilities of political power, had recognized its corruption even of conscience itself, and thus the principle of toleration of the First Amendment had removed from national power altogether the force of sectarian factions that threatened the very foundations of political legitimacy. But they had failed to act on the insight, so worrying to Madison, that the same argument applied at the state level and that state-supported slavery, like religious persecution, was in its nature corruptive even of conscience itself and thus could not be regarded as a normal form of political faction whose

---

144 CONG. GLOBE, *supra* note 103, at 1203.
145 *See* THE FEDERALIST, *supra* note 29, at 57.

temptations to radical evil could be ameliorated and compromised by democratic politics. The theory of the slave power thus rested on the abolitionist argument about the radical and incommensurable republican evil of slavery, drawing from that normative argument an explanation of the political and constitutional decadence that Lincoln had so brilliantly articulated for the American public in the Lincoln-Douglas debates.[146] A constitution, structuring political power to respect rights and the public good, could not, as Wilson argued in light of American experience, accord political power to the radical republican evil of slavery without undermining its own legitimacy. Indeed, as history had shown, the radical political evil of the institution, once accorded any constitutional protection at all, had gradually subverted constitutionalism itself. A legitimate constitutionalism and slavery could not co-exist.

The abolition of slavery gave rise to a related elaboration of the theory of faction, namely, concern for the faction of irrational race prejudice. The Confederacy had been justified by its vice-president, Alexander Stephens, in terms of the racial truth underlying Southern slavery:

> Our new government is founded upon exactly the opposite idea [to Jefferson's ideal of equal human rights]; its foundations are laid, its corner-stone rests upon the great truth, that the negro is not equal to the white man; that slavery—subordination to the superior race—is his natural and normal condition. [Applause] This, our new government, is the first, in the history of the world, based on this great physical, philosophical, and moral truth.[147]

The force of this theory was so strong in the Confederacy that, in its dying days when leaders like Jefferson Davis and General Lee urged the use of blacks in Southern armies, its Congress refused; as Davis explained, "[i]f the Confederacy falls, there should be written on its tombstone, 'Died of a theory.' "[148] The abolition of slavery did not, of its own force, morally transform the public force in the South of the views defended by Stephens in 1861, but gave new opportunities for their political perpetuation in the form of the Southern Black Codes designed, on racial grounds, to deprive the freedmen of rights. In proposing national legislation (eventually to be the Civil Rights Act of 1866) to strike down these laws, Senator Trumbull described them:

> The laws in the slaveholding States have made a distinction against

---

[146] See THE LINCOLN-DOUGLAS DEBATES (Robert W. Johannsen ed., 1965).

[147] Alexander Stephens, *Sketch of the Corner-Stone Speech, in* HENRY CLEVELAND, ALEXANDER H. STEPHENS IN PUBLIC AND PRIVATE 721 (1866).

[148] 1 JEFFERSON DAVIS, THE RISE AND FALL OF THE CONFEDERATE GOVERNMENT 443 (D. Appleton and Co., 1938) (1881).

persons of African descent on account of their color, whether free
or slave. I have before me the statutes of Mississippi. They provide that if any colored person, any free negro or mulatto, shall
come into that State for the purpose of residing there, he shall be
sold into slavery for life. If any person of African descent residing
in the State travels from one county to another without having a
pass or a certificate of his freedom, he is liable to be committed to
jail and to be dealt with as a person who is in the State without
authority. Other provisions of the statute prohibit any negro or
mulatto from having fire-arms, and one provision of the statute
declares that for "exercising the functions of a minister of the Gospel free negroes and mulattoes, on conviction, may be punished by
any number of lashes not exceeding thirty-nine on the bare back,
and shall pay the costs." Other provisions of the statutes of Mississippi subject him to trial before two justices of the peace and five
slaveholders for violating the provisions of this law. The statutes
of South Carolina make it a highly penal offense for any person,
white or colored, to teach slaves; and similar provisions are to be
found running through all the statutes of the late slaveholding
States.[149]

Trumbull argued that the Enforcement Clause of the Thirteenth
Amendment conferred power on Congress to pass this legislation, but
some Republicans, notably John A. Bingham[150] (opposed, strikingly,
by James Wilson[151]), argued that the application of such legislation
nation-wide required a constitutional amendment. The Fourteenth
Amendment was proposed and approved in part to quiet any constitutional doubts about national power to enforce such legislation.[152]

Section 1 of the Fourteenth Amendment reads:

All persons born or naturalized in the United States and subject to
the jurisdiction thereof, are citizens of the United States and of the
State wherein they reside. No State shall make or enforce any law
which shall abridge the privileges or immunities of citizens of the
United States; nor shall any State deprive any person of life, liberty, or property, without due process of law; nor deny to any person within its jurisdiction the equal protection of the laws.[153]

Its Citizenship Clause, of course, constitutionalized the once radical
abolitionist argument that persons subject to political power should be
citizens. The remaining clauses of the Fourteenth Amendment con-

---

[149] CONG. GLOBE, supra note 134, at 474 (Statement of Sen. Trumbull).

[150] See id. at 1291-92 (Statement of Rep. Bingham).

[151] See CONG. GLOBE, supra note 103, at 1294-95.

[152] See generally HORACE EDGAR FLACK, THE ADOPTION OF THE FOURTEENTH AMEND-
MENT (1908); JOSEPH B. JAMES, THE FRAMING OF THE FOURTEENTH AMENDMENT (1956).

[153] U.S. CONST. amend. XIV, § 1.

stitutionalized the related argument of Lockean political theory that all such persons should be guaranteed equal protection of their basic rights as the reasonable reciprocal condition of the duties of allegiance. Its clear constitutional legitimation of the Civil Rights Act of 1866 was pointed to by Senator Howard, introducing the amendment in the Senate, in terms that reveal concern for the faction of race prejudice:

> The last two clauses of the first section of the amendment disable a State from depriving not merely a citizen of the United States, but any person, whoever he may be, of life, liberty, or property without due process of law, or from denying to him the equal protection of the laws of the State. This abolishes all class legislation in the States and does away with the injustice of subjecting one caste of persons to a code not applicable to another. It prohibits the hanging of a black man for a crime for which the white man is not to be hanged. It protects the black man in his fundamental rights as a citizen with the same shield which it throws over the white man. Is it not time, Mr. President, that we extend to the black man, I had almost call it the poor privilege of the equal protection of the law? Ought not the time to be now passed when one measure of justice is to be meted out to a member of one caste while another and a different measure is meted out to the member of another caste, both castes being alike citizens of the United States, both bound to obey the same laws, to sustain the burdens of the same Government, and both equally responsible to justice and to God for the deeds done in the body?[154]

In light of the experience of the Civil War, Republicans had come to regard "prejudice against race," of the sort clearly reflected in Stephens's defense, as irrational and unjust.[155] Furthermore, they perceived the expression of such prejudice through laws, like the Southern Black Codes, as unconstitutional under Section 1 of the Fourteenth Amendment and thus within the power of Congress to strike down under Section 5, the enforcement clause of the amendment.

Of course, the Republicans, who agreed that racial prejudice was irrational, had a range of varying views about what counted as unreasonable race prejudice and, thus, how the concept should be interpreted and applied.[156] But in light of antebellum mainstream views

---

[154] CONG. GLOBE, *supra* note 134, at 2766 (statement of Sen. Howard).

[155] *See id.* at 2034 (citing and discussing Stephens). *See generally* WILLIAM E. NELSON, THE FOURTEENTH AMENDMENT: FROM POLITICAL PRINCIPLE TO JUDICIAL DOCTRINE 124-25 (1988).

[156] *See, e.g.*, NELSON, *supra* note 155, at 133 (anti-miscegenation laws), 133-36 (state-sponsored racial segregation).

on racial questions both in the North and the South, the identification of racial prejudice (or racism) as a faction at all confirms the remarkable impact on public constitutional thought of the Civil War; prior to the war, only the abolitionists had generated any views critical of American racism as such.[157] The same constitutional analysis of the antebellum period that had led to the theory of the slave power evolved, under the impact of abolition and the Southern reaction, into the theory of racism as a political faction. This analysis, of course, has direct antebellum antecedents in abolitionist moral and political thought. The underlying analysis tracked rather exactly the comparable analysis of the slave power, from which it derived. The normative component of the analysis was the abridgment of rights on sectarian grounds themselves hostage to the support of practices like slavery and racial discrimination. Such practices were thus not only immunized from impartial criticism and assessment, but unjustly fostered the kinds of cultural differences (now interpreted as natural) on the basis of which subjugation and discrimination were ostensibly justified. The empirical component was the paradox of intolerance so clearly displayed in American antebellum politics:[158] an intolerant exclusion of a racial minority from the political community immunized itself from reasonable criticism by manufacturing a conception of national identity, as intrinsically racial, based on irrationalist distortion of fact and history (see *Dred Scott*). Racist degradation could, no more than slavery or religious intolerance, be permitted political expression if American revolutionary constitutionalism was, in light of experience, to forge a constitutionalism that was politically legitimate.

All these themes were brilliantly analyzed in Senator Charles Sumner's long speech in the Senate of February 6-7, 1866 later published as *The Equal Rights of All*.[159] Sumner's aim was, even without

---

[157] For a notable example of this abolitionist genre, see L. MARIA CHILD, AN APPEAL IN FAVOR OF AMERICANS CALLED AFRICANS (Arno Press, 1968) (1836).

[158] By the paradox of intolerance, I mean to identify the tendency of sectarian intolerance to entrench its claims by censorship precisely when those claims most require reasonable discussion and debate in society at large. For further discussion and elaboration, see RICHARDS, *supra* note 51, at ch. 3.

[159] CHARLES SUMNER, THE EQUAL RIGHTS OF ALL: THE GREAT GUARANTEE AND PRESENT NECESSITY FOR THE SAKE OF SECURITY AND TO MAINTAIN A REPUBLICAN GOVERNMENT, *reprinted in* 8 CHARLES SUMNER: HIS COMPLETE WORKS, 115-269 (1969) [hereinafter EQUAL RIGHTS OF ALL]. Sumner's speech was actually offered in opposition to what he took to be the inadequacies of the Fourteenth Amendment (in particular, its failure to extend the franchise to the freedmen), and was bitterly resented by other Republicans for failure to support the great practical advance in securing the freedmen's rights that the Fourteenth Amendment represented. The speech's general analysis of issues of principle was, nonetheless, admired even by those Republicans, like Representative Dawes, who condemned

constitutional amendments like the Fourteenth and Fifteenth, constitutionally to defend the extension of the franchise to black Americans by national law on the ground of the Guaranty Clause (appealing to the interpretive approach of radical antislavery constitutional theory) and the Enforcement Clause of the Thirteenth Amendment.[160] He put his argument in terms of an American revolutionary constitutionalism, derived from Locke, that quite self-consciously united the revolutionaries of 1776 and 1866.[161] American revolutionaries like Otis[162] and constitutionalists like Madison (citing Madison on racism as the worst faction)[163] had recognized the claims of blacks to equal inalienable rights. The recent abolition of slavery had, however, unleashed on the freedmen the hatred of an embittered South,[164] and it was now incumbent on American revolutionary constitutionalists to accord them adequate protections against this vicious form of faction. Sumner directly analogized race hatred to a kind of religious persecution:

> It is nothing less than a caste, which is irreligious as well as unrepublican. A caste exists only in defiance of the first principles of Christianity and the first principles of a republic. It is heathenism in religion and tyranny in government. The Brahmins and the Sudras in India, from generation to generation, have been separated, as the two races are still separated in these States. If a Sudra presumed to sit on a Brahmin's carpet, he was punished with banishment. But our recent Rebels undertake to play the part of Brahmins, and exclude citizens, with better title than themselves, from essential rights, simply on the ground of caste, which, according to its Portuguese origin (*casta*), is only another term for race.[165]

The constitutional task before us, Sumner concluded, was to insure that the Constitution would never again be distorted by "[t]he Gospel according to Calhoun," namely, "that this august Republic, founded to sustain the rights of Human Nature, is nothing but 'a white man's government.' "[166] Constitutional interpretation must recover its roots in ethical impartiality: "The promises of the Fathers must be sacredly fulfilled. This is the commanding rule, superseding all other rules. This is a great victory of the war,—perhaps the greatest. It is nothing

---

Sumner's failure to apply the principles properly to the current situation. *See* DAVID DONALD, CHARLES SUMNER AND THE RIGHTS OF MAN 246 (1970).

[160] *See* EQUAL RIGHTS OF ALL, *supra* note 159, at 215-19.

[161] *See id.* at 155-56, 158-59.

[162] *See id.* at 164.

[163] *See id.* at 180.

[164] *See id.* at 131-32, 222-23.

[165] *Id.* at 210-11.

[166] *Id.* at 234-35.

less than the emancipation of the Constitution itself."[167]

D.   *Comparative Political Science*

American revolutionary constitutionalism in 1787 was acutely self-conscious of its repudiation of the utility of classical republican models for the task of designing an enduring constitution for a commercial republic in a large territory committed to respect for human rights. No American constitutionalist was a more profound student of the differences between ancient and modern republics or used it to more brilliant effect than James Madison in No. 10 of *The Federalist.* Madison did not draw explicit attention, however, to an implicit aspect of the contrast, namely, the central role of slavery in the ancient republics and its disfavored and hopefully declining status in a commercial republic committed to human rights.

The contrast, however, became absolutely central to the antebellum constitutional theories—in particular, those of Union and of moderate and radical antislavery—whose thought culminated in the Reconstruction Amendments. Southern pro-slavery constitutional theory had, since Calhoun, embraced the ancient slave republics of Greece and Rome as models for its own conception of national identity, emphasizing heroism and imperialistic expansion led by a class accorded by slavery the time and incentive to pursue public excellence and glory.[168] Antislavery constitutional theory properly saw such Southern theory as deeply anachronistic and fundamentally hostile, as it was, to both the political science and political and economic philosophy of Madisonian constitutionalism. Lincoln's clear articulation of discordant principles that doom the house divided made this point eloquently.[169] This thesis was also propounded by both Karl Marx[170] and John Stuart Mill,[171] who later argued that the defeat of the South was necessary in the worldwide struggle for the advance of progressive values of modernity against a reactionary historicism. All the major proponents of radical antislavery—Goodell,[172] Spooner,[173] and

---

[167] EQUAL RIGHTS OF ALL, *supra* note 159, at 219.

[168] For a probing discussion of Southern pro-slavery views, see KENNETH S. GREENBERG, MASTERS AND STATESMEN: THE POLITICAL CULTURE OF AMERICAN SLAVERY (1985).

[169] *See* Abraham Lincoln, "House Divided" Speech at Springfield, Illinois (June 16, 1858), *in* 2 LINCOLN, *supra* note 53, at 434.

[170] *See generally* KARL MARX, ON AMERICA AND THE CIVIL WAR (Saul K. Padover ed., 1972).

[171] *See generally* JOHN STUART MILL, THE CONTEST IN AMERICA, *reprinted in* UNION PAMPHLETS OF THE CIVIL WAR, *supra* note 63, at 326-44.

[172] *See* GOODELL, *supra* note 127, at 44-47.

[173] *See* SPOONER, *supra* note 125, at 105-14.

Tiffany[174]—made the same point in the form of arguments based on the Guarantee Clause that slavery was anti-republican. Theodore Parker published a particularly well-argued form of the theory in 1858[175] that much influenced Senator Charles Sumner and others.[176]

Consistent with his views of Bible interpretation in light of values of ethical impartiality, Parker argued that the constitutional conception of American democracy—"government over all, by all, and for the sake of all"[177]—must be best interpreted in terms of its background theory of the protection of inalienable human rights. Such rights were "founded not on Facts of Observation in Human History, but on Facts of Consciousness in human Nature itself."[178] The constitutional conception of a republic in the Guarantee Clause must be interpreted, in the same way the British common law was construed "in the Somerset case"[179] to invalidate slavery, in light of the best interpretation of such rights available to us as interpreters now:

> [T]here must be a Progressive Interpretation of many institutions and statutes. Thus the Common Law of England did not change, but ship-money became illegal; and slavery perished by interpretation. No number of decisions by learned Judges, no royal usage, no popular acquiescence for centuries, could withstand the demand for natural Justice made by the increased knowledge, virtue and humanity of the progressive People.[180]

The interpretation of a written constitution like the United States Constitution must be understood in light of the best interpretation to be accorded its text in light of such values, ascribing to it a possibly abstract concept not properly reduced to how its Founders may have understood its concrete meaning in their situation.[181] The classical republics were a radically inapposite precedent for the interpretation of the American republic because the American Constitution was, in contrast to them, clearly based on the protection of inalienable human rights:

> A constitutional representative Democracy did not exist in the old times . . . . I know there are men in Virginia and South Carolina, who quote Aristotle and Cicero in favor of American slavery; they

---

174 See TIFFANY, supra note 65, at 107-14.

175 THEODORE PARKER, THE RELATION OF SLAVERY TO A REPUBLICAN FORM OF GOVERNMENT (Boston, William L. Kent & Co. 1858).

176 HANS L. TREFOUSSE, THE RADICAL REPUBLICANS: LINCOLN'S VANGUARD FOR RACIAL JUSTICE 267 (1969).

177 PARKER, supra note 175, at 5.

178 Id. at 9.

179 Id. at 11.

180 Id. at 14.

181 Id. at 10-11.

seem to have read the translations of these authors only to get arguments against the Natural Rights of Mankind. Similar men have studied the Old Testament but to find out that Abraham was a slaveholder, that Moses authorized bondage; they have read the New only to find divine inspiration in the words of Paul, which they wrest into this: "Slaves, obey your masters!".[182]

The best interpretation of the Guaranty Clause, understood to be founded on the protection of basic human rights, now conferred power on Congress to abolish slavery in the states.

In the antebellum period, the conflicting constitutional interpretations of American republican government of a Calhoun and a Parker sketched out, to borrow Anne Norton's phrase, alternative Americas[183]—one nostalgic for the glories of the ancient world, the other committed to a self-consciously progressive conception of human rights. After the Civil War, Americans had to make the best sense they could of earlier events in light of the revolutionary constitutionalism to which the war had given rise. That perspective explains why the Reconstruction Congress chose Parker's alternative reading of America not only by adopting, as we have seen, the Guaranty Clause as the theory of reconstruction, but by taking the kind of interpretive and critical stance on American constitutionalism in general that his approach called for.

Parker wrote of "a progressive demoralization of the Constitution,"[184] pointing, as Lincoln also did in his debates with Douglas, to both the politics of Douglas and the jurisprudence of Taney. Such interpretive distortion was a central concern of the revolutionary constitutionalists of 1865. Not all of them agreed with Charles Sumner's earlier discussed expansive reading of the Guaranty Clause (making unnecessary the Fourteenth and Fifteenth Amendments), but Sumner provided a plausible metainterpretive analysis of how the demoralization of constitutional interpretation had taken place. The problem in both Bible and constitutional interpretation, Sumner argued, was that the sectarian conviction of the moral validity of slavery determined interpretation: textual authority for slavery and discrimination were only found "because they have first secured a license in his own soul."[185] Nothing in the text of the Constitution compelled Calhoun

---

182 PARKER, *supra* note 175, at 14.

183 *See generally* ANNE NORTON, ALTERNATIVE AMERICAS: A READING OF ANTEBELLUM POLITICAL CULTURE (1986).

184 PARKER, *supra* note 175, at 15.

185 Charles Sumner, *The Antislavery Enterprise, reprinted in* 8 CHARLES SUMNER: HIS COMPLETE WORKS, *supra* note 159, at 20. *See also* Charles Sumner, *The Barbarism of Slavery, reprinted in id.* at 223-27.

or Taney to read the Constitution in the positivistic way they did (Calhoun in terms of state sovereignty, Taney in terms of historical positivism); rather, each brought to the Constitution a rights-skepticism that distorted interpretation to protect fixed positions devoted to sectional interests. The only prophylaxis against the recurrence of such interpretive distortion was, Sumner argued, to demand that "[f]rom this time forward it [the Constitution] must be interpreted in harmony with the Declaration of Independence, so that Human Rights shall always prevail."[186]

E.   American Political Experience

Americans had tested their constitutional minds in 1787 not only against comparative political science, but against their own democratic experience both before the revolution as colonies and after the revolution in a wide range of constitutional experiments at the state level and the Articles of Confederation at the national level. The 1787 Convention was motivated by the conviction that these experiments, state and federal, had not respected the principles of legitimacy they had invoked as revolutionaries against the British Constitution. The Constitution of 1787 accordingly transferred much political power from the states to the national government in order to render its exercise more legitimate.

Reference has already been made to Madison's concerns that, consistent with the theory of faction, sufficient constitutional power had not been accorded the national government to moderate the malign insularity and parochialism of state factions. American political experience during the antebellum period confirmed the wisdom of Madison's fears, and that experience played a central role in the deliberations on the Reconstruction Amendments. Such state factions had not only, as we have seen, distorted the interpretation of the Constitution itself, but had flagrantly violated without remedy their constitutional obligations both under the federal and their own state constitutions. The indictment of the slave power made both points. The slave power, operating in the states without federally enforceable constraint, had abridged basic inalienable human rights like those to conscience, speech, and assembly, rights ostensibly guaranteed by the state constitutions. It had also abridged rights guaranteed at the federal level, for example, not enforcing the rights of blacks and whites under the Privileges and Immunities Clause,[187] and securing the

---

[186] EQUAL RIGHTS OF ALL, *supra* note 159, at 219.

[187] On South Carolina's exclusion of black sailors, see WILLIAM W. FREEHLING, PRELUDE TO CIVIL WAR: THE NULLIFICATION CONTROVERSY IN SOUTH CAROLINA, 1816-1836, at

abridgment of rights of abolitionists to use the federal mails under the First Amendment.[188] From the perspective of Lockean political theory, both forms of political power—federal and state—must respect rights and pursue the public good, and the Constitution was justified in 1787 in such terms. Political experience had decisively shown that the Constitution had not only over time failed to meet these tests; its constitutional protection of slavery had led to the Constitution itself becoming an interpretive sword and shield for the aggressive violation of inalienable human rights. The last chapter in this declension of the Constitution from its background republican morality was its invocation by the South as a justification for secession and civil war. The Constitution, thus interpreted by the South, had become a just object of the right to revolution on behalf of the Union. The task in the wake of the success of the second revolution was to preserve America's newly recovered revolutionary constitutionalism in a constitutionalism that would profit from America's bitter antebellum political experience of the devastating and malign consequences of a defective constitutionalism.

F. *Constitutional Justification and Community*

The deliberative procedures of both ratification and amendment of the United States Constitution marked its distinctive status as authoritative supreme law over all other law that was the product of ordinary politics. These procedures were an original contribution of the American Founders to constitutional thought and practice, innovating a distinctive institutional procedure meant more closely to approximate what Locke regarded as necessary to the legitimacy of any government, namely, that the government must be reasonably acceptable to all as protecting their inalienable human rights.[189] Locke himself supposed that government could only feasibly be formed by the political decision procedure of majority rule.[190] But the American Founders—well familiar with the oppressions of majority rule in ordinary politics—innovated special procedures of constitutional ratification and amendment that would, as political decision procedures,

---

111-16, 206-07 (1966); on the case of Prudence Crandall, who had been forbidden by Connecticut state law from teaching free blacks, see HYMAN & WIECEK, *supra* note 92, at 94-95; for Chief Justice Taney on the issue of blacks having no status to claim protection under the Privileges and Immunities Clause, see Dred Scott v. Sanford, 60 U.S. (19 How.) at 404-05, 414-17, 422-23 (1857).

[188] *See generally* RUSSELL B. NYE, FETTERED FREEDOM: CIVIL LIBERTIES AND THE SLAVERY CONTROVERSY 1830-1860 (1963).

[189] *See* FOUNDATIONS, *supra* note 2, at 140-42.

[190] *Id.* at 87-88.

more plausibly bear the interpretation of being reasonably acceptable to all in the required way.   Constitutional law would be authoritatively supreme over all other law because it had been and would continue to be (if properly interpreted) subjected to more demanding and stringent tests of ultimate political legitimacy than other laws, namely, that it was reasonably justifiable to all as protecting rights and advancing the public interests of all alike.

The nature of constitutional ratification and interpretation was one of the central items of interpretive controversy in the antebellum period between Southern pro-slavery theories and the constitutional theory of Union. Southern advocates of the compact theory, as early as St. George Tucker in 1803[191] and as late as Alexander Stephens in 1868,[192] had given ratification a positivistic interpretation putting decisive weight on ratification by separate states, not by vote of the people as a whole, as evidence of the ultimacy of state sovereignty with the interpretive consequences Southern theorists variously drew from that fact, namely, the narrow construction of national powers in favor of the broad reserved powers of the states. Proponents of the theory of Union, notably Justice Story,[193] emphasized in contrast the crucial significance of ratification by separately elected constitutional conventions wholly independent of the standing state governments. They argued that such a historically unique procedure must be interpreted—consistent with the most natural reading of the words of the Preamble ("We, the People")—as resting the authority of the Constitution directly on the rights of the people that the Constitution preserved, protected, and defended against all governments—state and federal. Accordingly, the Constitution was to be interpreted to affirm a broad national power to protect such rights of the person. The disagreement was not over facts, but an interpretive one that appealed, at bottom, to different understandings of how the Constitution should be interpreted in light of political theory, Lockean or otherwise. Calhoun's rights-skepticism directly shaped his way of reading the relevant materials;[194] other Southern theorists, who accepted rights-based

---

191 *See* St. George Tucker, *View of the Constitution of the United States, reprinted in* 1 BLACKSTONE'S COMMENTARIES *140-41 (1803).

192 *See generally* ALEXANDER STEPHENS, A CONSTITUTIONAL VIEW OF THE LATE WAR BETWEEN THE STATES (Chicago, Ill., Zeigler, McCurdy & Co., vol. I, 1868, vol. II, 1870).

193 *See* JOSEPH STORY, COMMENTARIES ON THE CONSTITUTION OF THE UNITED STATES (Da Capo Press 1970) (1833); *see also, e.g.,* I STEPHENS, *supra* note 192, at 245, 313-17, 321-26.

194 *See* JOHN C. CALHOUN, A DISQUISITION ON GOVERNMENT (Richard K. Cralle ed., Peter Smith 1943) (1853). For useful commentary, see AUGUST O. SPAIN, THE POLITICAL THEORY OF JOHN C. CALHOUN (1951).

political theories (Tucker,[195] John Taylor of Caroline,[196] Stephens[197]), thought of such rights as best ultimately defended by state institutions and construed ratification and constitutional interpretation accordingly. Proponents of the theory of Union, like Story, identified the nation as the best ultimate vehicle of the articulation and enforcement of human rights, and thus thought of ratification and constitutional interpretation in the way they did.

From the perspective of the constitutional revolutionaries of 1865, the constitutional procedures of ratification and amendment were properly interpreted in terms of the theory of Union, and that carried with it a comparable view of constitutional interpretation. At the beginning of the Civil War, Lincoln,[198] Francis Lieber,[199] Edward Everett,[200] and Joel Parker[201] had all justified resistance to secession on grounds of the constitutional theory of Union. By the end of the war, the self-conscious constitutional revolutionaries of 1865 had to interpret both the antebellum period and the Civil War itself in light both of the theory of Union and the moderate and radical antislavery views to which they increasingly turned to make sense of their responsibilities of constitutional reconstruction. In terms of these views, secession and civil war by the Southern states confirmed their antirepublican character, their obdurate refusal not only to respect the inalienable right to freedom of their slaves and the rights of freedmen to basic rights like conscience, but to make war on the national institutions whose ultimate moral and constitutional responsibility was to secure the equal rights of all. In such circumstances, procedures of constitutional amendment, rooted in Lockean political theory, must be interpreted in light of both the Guaranty Clause and the background Lockean political theory of the Constitution. On the former ground, Congress, reasonably regarding its task under the Guaranty

---

195 On the strict construction of the Constitution as a treaty among states, see Tucker, *supra* note 191, at 143.

196 *See generally* JOHN TAYLOR, CONSTRUCTION CONSTRUED AND CONSTITUTIONS VINDICATED (Da Capo Press 1970) (1820); JOHN TAYLOR, NEW VIEWS OF THE CONSTITUTION OF THE UNITED STATES (Da Capo Press 1971) (1823).

197 *See generally* STEPHENS, *supra* note 192.

198 *See* Abraham Lincoln, First Inaugural Address (Mar. 4, 1861), *in* 2 LINCOLN, *supra* note 53, at 217-18.

199 *See* Francis Lieber, WHAT IS OUR CONSTITUTION—LEAGUE, PACT, OR GOVERNMENT? (1861), *reprinted in* FRANCIS LIEBER, 2 CONTRIBUTIONS TO POLITICAL SCIENCE 87-136 (London, J.B. Lippincott & Co. 1881).

200 *See* Edward Everett, The Causes and Conduct of the Civil War, (originally delivered Oct. 16, 1861), *in* EDWARD EVERETT, 4 ORATIONS AND SPEECHES ON VARIOUS OCCASIONS 464-90 (Boston, Little, Brown and Co. 1868).

201 *See* JOEL PARKER, THE RIGHT OF SECESSION (1861), *reprinted in* UNION PAMPHLETS OF THE CIVIL WAR 1861-1865, *supra* note 63, at 55-85.

Clause to propose constitutional amendments that would insure republican governments in the South, may reasonably exclude non-republican Southern states from their constitutional position in the Union until they agree to and conform with the amendments. And on the ground of political theory, the Civil War was ultimately politically justified on the ground of the revolutionary right of a people to recover its inalienable rights—both those of blacks and whites—from their political oppressors who had dominated Southern politics; the constitutionalism that gave ultimate vindication to that revolutionary right could not justifiably allow the oppressors to determine its terms. In light of the events of the Civil War, it would not be reasonable to interpret the procedure of constitutional amendment, clearly meant to express the requirements of Lockean political legitimacy, to frustrate amendments that, for the first time in American history, permitted the Constitution reasonably to be justified to all as politically legitimate.

The Reconstruction Amendments were in fact the product of the most profound deliberation on American constitutionalism from the perspective of its background political theory since the Constitutional Convention of 1787, and reflect, in much more direct textual fashion than the Constitution of 1787, the impact of that political theory. Its impact is evident both in the substantive terms of the amendments (in particular, those of the Fourteenth) and in the national institutions accorded the central role in the interpretation and enforcement of those terms.

Both the Citizenship Clause[202] and the Privileges and Immunities Clause[203] of the Fourteenth Amendment were derived from the requirements of Lockean political theory that all persons in a political community sharing its benefits and burdens have a right to be treated as citizens and as equals with respect for their inalienable human rights. Weld, of course, stated the argument as the basis for his criticism of American slavery,[204] and Tiffany put it in the form of a radical antislavery interpretation of the Constitution of 1787.[205] The Fourteenth Amendment unambiguously constitutionalized these arguments on the Lockean terms of the respect for rights required, as

---

[202] "All persons born or naturalized in the United States, and subject to the jurisdiction thereof, are citizens of the United States and of the State wherein they reside." U.S. CONST. amend. XIV, § 1.

[203] "No State shall make or enforce any law which shall abridge the privileges or immunities of citizens of the United States." U.S. CONST. amend. XIV, § 1.

[204] See THEODORE DWIGHT WELD, AMERICAN SLAVERY AS IT IS 150 (Arno Press 1968) (1839).

[205] See TIFFANY, supra note 65.

Bingham put it, "to bear true allegiance to the Constitution and laws of the United States."[206] The textual adoption of the birthright theory of American citizenship must be understood against the background of the clear moral right of black Americans to be treated as citizens under a Lockean theory of justice[207] and the authoritative interpretation of the Constitution of 1787 to the contrary in *Dred Scott*. And the Privileges and Immunities Clause extended to all citizens the protection of their basic human rights that is the very test, on Lockean grounds, of the legitimacy of any political power at all.

The revolutionary constitutionalists of 1865 were quite clear that the terms of an amendment like the Fourteenth resulted from an assessment of the 1787 Constitution in light of such political theory. It is the theory Bingham assumed when he insisted that the Fourteenth Amendment

> takes from no State any right that ever pertained to it. No State ever had the right, under the forms of law or otherwise to deny to any freeman the equal protection of the laws or to abridge the privileges or immunities of any citizen of the Republic, although many of them have assumed and exercised that power, and that without remedy.[208]

The working assumption of the Constitution of 1787, that states could largely be depended on not to violate inalienable human rights, had, as Madison anticipated, proved false; amendments were needed to insure that this lacuna of political legitimacy was filled.

The Privileges and Immunities Clause extended to all American citizens protection of their inalienable human rights from the states, the main source of the abuse of human rights in the antebellum period. The language of the clause, adapted from that of the Privileges and Immunities Clause of Article IV,[209] reflected the interpretation of the latter as protecting what Bingham called "the inborn rights of every person."[210] The clause of Article IV, sometimes called the Comity Clause, required each state to guarantee citizens of other states "all privileges and immunities of citizens in the several states," an ambiguous phrase that could extend only to such rights as a state

---

206 CONG. GLOBE, *supra* note 134, at 2542.

207 For an excellent study of various theories of American citizenship, see JAMES H. KETTNER, THE DEVELOPMENT OF AMERICAN CITIZENSHIP 1608-1870 (1978). For a Lockean interpretation of the Citizenship Clause that controversially excludes illegal aliens, see PETER H. SCHUCK & ROGERS M. SMITH, CITIZENSHIP WITHOUT CONSENT: ILLEGAL ALIENS IN THE AMERICAN POLITY (1985).

208 CONG. GLOBE, *supra* note 150, at 2542 (Rep. Bingham).

209 "The Citizens of each State shall be entitled to all Privileges and Immunities of Citizens in the several States." U.S. CONST. art. IV, § 2, cl. 1.

210 CONG. GLOBE, *supra* note 134, at 2542.

in fact extended to its own citizens or to a substantive standard of basic human rights owed to all citizens as such. Bingham clearly interpreted the phrase in the latter way,[211] and thus construed the clause in the Fourteenth Amendment as protecting against the states all such rights of citizens of the United States. Bingham's interpretation of Article IV reflected the construction of the clause given by Judge Bushrod Washington in *Corfield v. Coryell*,[212] relevant sections of which were, in fact, cited to this effect by Senator Trumbull in the debates over the Civil Rights Act of 1866[213] and Senator Howard upon introducing the Fourteenth Amendment in the Senate.[214] Judge Washington had interpreted the clause in terms of the rights of American citizens as such: "[W]e feel no hesitation in confining these expressions to those privileges and immunities which are, in their nature, fundamental; which belong, of right, to the citizens of all free governments . . . ."[215]

As we have seen, Bingham referred to these as "the inborn rights of every person" and cited the prohibition on cruel and unusual punishments in the Eighth Amendment as an example;[216] Senator Howard in the Senate, after quoting *Corfield* on the nature of these rights, went on:

> To these privileges and immunities, whatever they may be—for they are and cannot be fully defined in their entire extent and precise nature—to these should be added the personal rights guaranteed and secured by the first eight amendments of the Constitution; such as the freedom of speech and of the press; the right of the people peaceably to assemble and petition the Government for a redress of grievances, a right appertaining to each and all the people; the right to keep and to bear arms; the right to be exempted from the quartering of soldiers in a house without the consent of the owner; the right to be exempt from unreasonable searches and seizures, and from any search or seizure except by virtue of a warrant issued upon a formal oath or affidavit; the right of an accused

---

211 For Bingham's earlier expressed views to the same effect, see John A. Bingham, The Constitution of the United States and the Proslavery Provisions of the 1857 Oregon Constitution (delivered in the House of Representatives in 1859), *in* TENBROEK, *supra* note 92, at 321-41. Bingham said of the Comity Clause: "There is an ellipsis in the language employed in the Constitution, but its meaning is self-evident that it is 'the privileges and immunities of citizens of the United States in the several States' that it guaranties." *Id.* at 333. He later specified these rights as "[t]he equality of all to the right to live; to the right to know; to argue and to utter, according to conscience; to work and enjoy the project of their toil." *Id.* at 339-40.

212 Corfield v. Coryell, 6 F. Cas. 546 (C.C.E.D.Pa. 1823) (No. 3,230).

213 *See* CONG. GLOBE, *supra* note 134, at 474.

214 *See id.* at 2765.

215 *Corfield*, 6 F. Cas. at 551.

216 *See* CONG. GLOBE, *supra* note 134, at 2542.

person to be informed of the nature of the accusation against him, and his right to be tried by an impartial jury of the vicinage; and also the right to be secure against excessive bail and against cruel and unusual punishments.

Now, sir, here is a mass of privileges, immunities, and rights, some of them secured by the second section of the fourth article of the Constitution, which I have recited, some by the first eight amendments of the Constitution; and it is a fact well worthy of attention that the course of decision of our courts and the present settled doctrine is, that all these immunities, privileges, rights, thus guaranteed by the Constitution or recognized by it, are secured to the citizen solely as a citizen of the United States and as a party in their courts.[217]

It is rather trivializing of the political theory that motivated the Privileges and Immunities Clause to reduce it to the terms of the incorporation debate between Justice Black[218] and Charles Fairman.[219] Fairman's cavalier attribution of confusion to Bingham reflects less on Bingham than on Fairman's inability to take seriously the political theory Bingham propounded as requiring a guarantee of basic rights against the states. Moreover, Justice Black's use of Senator Howard's illustration does not give weight to what is essentially an interpretive judgment of the basic rights that must be secured to all as a condition of the legitimacy of political power. The Privileges and Immunities Clause, so clearly based on political theory, must be interpreted in light of such theory, and neither Fairman nor Black did justice to this demand.[220]

The Constitution of 1787 left interpretively open its relationship to the political theory stated in the Declaration of Independence, and that gap was aggressively filled by forms of pro-slavery constitutional theory that denied the central role in constitutional interpretation of the political theory of human rights. If both the Citizenship Clause and the Privileges and Immunities Clause were grounded in such political theory, the Equal Protection Clause was a direct and clear statement of it, bringing the implicit theory of the 1787 Constitution to center stage as the explicit governing theory of the Constitution. If the Constitution of 1787 was ultimately justified as a set of institutions that would tend overall to protect the equal rights of all, the Four-

---

217 CONG. GLOBE, *supra* note 134, at 2765.

218 *See, e.g.,* Duncan v. Louisiana, 391 U.S. 145, 162 (1968) (Black, J., concurring); Adamson v. California, 332 U.S. 46, 68 (1947) (Black, J., dissenting).

219 *See, e.g.,* Charles Fairman, *Does the Fourteenth Amendment Incorporate the Bill of Rights?: The Original Understanding*, 2 STAN. L. REV. 5 (1949).

220 For further development of this theme, see RICHARDS, *supra* note 51, at ch. 6.

teenth Amendment imposed that justificatory requirement directly on the states, whose abuses of human rights had been the scandal and shame of the antebellum period; because the Fourteenth Amendment in this way clarifies the general theory of the Constitution, the requirement of equal protection has been correctly construed to be applicable as well to the national government.[221] We have already seen that one deprivation of such equal rights, that grounded in racism, was a paradigm interpretive case for a violation of equal protection in 1866, and the jurisprudence of equal protection understandably starts from that interpretive paradigm.[222]

If the Fourteenth Amendment stated the affirmative principles of justice that undergirded the prohibition of the radical evil of slavery by the Thirteenth Amendment, the Fifteenth Amendment (forbidding abridgment of the right to vote "on account of race, color, or previous condition of servitude")[223] expressed a companion judgment of the fair distribution of political power required to support and sustain both the prohibitions of the Thirteenth Amendment and the affirmations of justice of the Fourteenth Amendment. By far the most historically controversial of the Reconstruction Amendments, its requirement of black suffrage had been repeatedly rejected in Northern state votes during much of the relevant period,[224] and only the more indirect procedures of constitutional amendment secured its ratification.[225]

All the substantive provisions of the Reconstruction Amendments were subject to authoritative interpretation and enforcement by national institutions. It was Francis Lieber who, during the antebellum period, had most deeply explored the connection between universal human rights and national identity; and his own influential proposals for constitutional amendments at the end of the Civil War centered on concepts of federally enforceable guarantees of national citizenship and national rights as terms of allegiance;[226] many Repub-

---

[221] See, e.g., Bolling v. Sharpe, 347 U.S. 497 (1954) (unconstitutionality of state-sponsored racial segregation applied to federal government). *Bolling* grounded its doctrine on the Due Process Clause of the Fifth Amendment. Because of my own skepticism about the use of due process to protect substantive rights, RICHARDS, *supra* note 51, at ch. 6, I would argue that the result in this case would be better grounded on the implicit theory of justification of the 1787 Constitution, the nature and weight of which was clarified by the Equal Protection Clause of the Fourteenth Amendment.

[222] See RICHARDS, *supra* note 51, at ch. 5.

[223] U.S. CONST. amend. XV, § 1.

[224] See WILLIAM GILLETTE, THE RIGHT TO VOTE: POLITICS AND THE PASSAGE OF THE FIFTEENTH AMENDMENT 25-27, 167-68 (1969).

[225] See generally id.

[226] See FRANCIS LIEBER, AMENDMENTS OF THE CONSTITUTION (1865), *reprinted in* LIEBER, *supra* note 199, at 137-79.

licans, as diverse as Bingham[227] and Sumner,[228] defended constitutional reconstruction in such terms. The Civil War, Lieber argued, enabled Americans as a people to critically assess the flaws in their constitutionalism, "to see rugged ground or deep abysses where from a distant view nothing but level plains had appeared."[229] The main flaw was slavery and the associated doctrine of state's rights with their attack on American nationality.[230] Slavery therefore must be abolished,[231] and national guarantees of equal rights must be imposed, to protect Black Americans from a prejudice that Lieber, the German expatriate, analogized to the European treatment of Jews.[232]

Almost all antebellum constitutional theorists (except notably Calhoun) paid at least lip service to political theories of human rights, but Lieber had not only seen the validity of Madison's 1787 worries about the Constitution, he had put the point on a more profound basis. According to Lieber, the only legitimate basis for national political identity was the protection of the universal human rights of all persons subject to the political power of the relevant community. But universal human rights, by virtue of their abstract character and their demands on ethical impartiality, must be articulated, interpreted, and enforced as standards by the national institutions most capable of bringing to the task the kind of abstract and impartial justice that was required. The Southern doctrines of nullification, secession, and state's rights were a transparent mockery of these demands, a fact shown by the utility of such doctrines in shielding from scrutiny the radical evil of American slavery. Calhoun justified his constitutionalism as a protection of minorities, but in fact his view gave regional majorities complete sovereignty over minorities, including, in South Carolina, the abridgment of the inalienable rights of the black slaves who were, numerically, a majority. Such intellectual obfuscation, ideological distortion of the language and thought of constitutionalism, and self-serving amoralism were made possible by the authority the Constitution had accorded the states over issues of human rights. The

---

227 Mr. Speaker, it appears to me that this very provision of the bill of rights brought in question this day, upon this trial before the House, more than any other provision of the Constitution, makes that unity of government which constitutes us one people, by which and through which American nationality came to be, and only by the enforcement of which can American nationality continue to be.
CONG. GLOBE, *supra* note 134, at 1090.

228 *See* Charles Sumner, *Are We a Nation?* (1867), *reprinted in* 8 CHARLES SUMNER: HIS COMPLETE WORKS, *supra* note 159, at 7-65.

229 Lieber, *supra* note 199, at 147-48.

230 *Id*. at 150.

231 *Id*. at 169-72.

232 *Id*. at 173-74.

moral and constitutional meaning of the Civil War, for the generation which had fought it ultimately to defend the integrity of American revolutionary constitutionalism, must be that the protection of human rights be placed authoritatively in the hands of the nation.

Lieber's analysis fit securely in the framework of the great structures of American constitutionalism, which it left undisturbed. The task was not to change the federal system into a parliamentary democracy, but to make better use of the existing structures so that they might achieve their ends, yielding more impartial judgments on how to secure political power that respected rights and pursued the public interest. Congress had a general enforcement power under each of the three Reconstruction Amendments that, consistent with the constitutional theory of Union, was to be at least as broadly interpreted to advance human rights as the Fugitive Slave Clause in *Prigg* had been interpreted by Justice Story (in the name of the theory of Union)[233] to advance slavery.[234] Importantly, the original draft of Section 1 of the Fourteenth Amendment, that had focused on giving Congress power, had been changed to directly prohibit state power probably in response to a criticism of Representative Hotchkiss:

> It should be a constitutional right that cannot be wrested from any class of citizens, or from the citizens of any State by mere legislation. But this amendment proposes to leave it to the caprice of Congress; and your legislation upon the subject would depend upon the political majority of Congress, and not upon two thirds of Congress and three fourths of the States. Now, I desire that the very privileges for which the gentleman is contending shall be secured to the citizens; but I want them secured by a constitutional amendment that legislation cannot override.[235]

The judiciary was the federal institution (much admired by Lieber) that, consistent with the theory of the 1787 Constitution, would afford an authoritative public forum for deliberative debate, articulation, and enforcement of these principles in the face of a nascent Congress. Of course, the judiciary, like any other branch of government, may make interpretive mistakes, and must be subject to constant critical scrutiny and public debate to maintain its ultimate accountability to the public community of reason, the ethical end of constitutional government. It remains to be explored how, in light of

---

233 *See* Prigg v. Pennsylvania, 41 U.S. (16 Pet.) 539 (1842). For commentary on *Prigg*, see ROBERT M. COVER, JUSTICE ACCUSED: ANTISLAVERY AND THE JUDICIAL PROCESS 166-68 (1975).

234 *See* CONG. GLOBE, *supra* note 103, at 1294.

235 CONG. GLOBE, *supra* note 134, at 1095 (statement of Rep. Hotchkiss).

the argument here developed, interpretation of the Reconstruction Amendments should be understood.

Of course, it does not follow from the fact that the founders of a constitution or some amendment thereof took a certain view of how it should be interpreted in the circumstances of the founding or even a view of how it should later be interpreted, that those views are authoritative on how constitutional interpretation should be understood by a later generation. It is, of course, of interest that the Founders of the 1787 Constitution did not take the view of constitutional interpretation sometimes called originalist;[236] but a Lockean constitution, like that of the United States, rests on the reasonable consent of the present generation, not on the authority of a previous generation who are, from the perspective of Lockean political theory, no more authoritative than Filmer's fictive patriarchs.[237] But Americans, in light of the arguments in No. 49 of *The Federalist*, have found reflection on the arguments of the Founders—made in a period of rather remarkable impartiality and public intelligence focused on the permanent problems of constitutional government—useful in understanding how the task of constitutional interpretation might best be understood by a contemporary generation. If we find this to be true of the Founders of 1787 (with the admitted tragic flaws in their work), it must be true, a fortiori, of the work of the founders of the Reconstruction Amendments, the most fundamental deliberation since 1787 on the flaws of American constitutionalism in the spirit of the founding and a self-conscious enterprise to bring that spirit to bear on the self-correcting reconstruction of the Constitution.

From this perspective, we make the best interpretive sense of the text and background history of the Reconstruction Amendments, including their place in the overall tradition of American constitutionalism, if we construe them to demand that the kind of political power in question be justifiable to all (respecting rights and pursuing the public interest) in light of the most exacting standards of ethical impartiality and public reason in our circumstances. Each provision of the Reconstruction Amendments has behind it, as we have seen, a historically based concern about some threat to political legitimacy posed by the interpretation or misinterpretation of the Constitution of 1787, and the text and history call for a national deliberative process appealing to the political theory of human rights to make sense of what these

---

236 The now classic contemporary study is H. JEFFERSON POWELL, THE ORIGINAL UNDERSTANDING OF ORIGINAL INTENT (1985), *reprinted in* JACK N. RAKOVE, INTERPRETING THE CONSTITUTION: THE DEBATE OVER ORIGINAL INTENT 53-115 (1990).

237 *See* FOUNDATIONS, *supra* note 2, at 131-57.

threats are and how they should be remedied. A text and history, so conscious of past interpretive mistakes, must reasonably be interpreted to take instruction from those mistakes and not repeat them yet again in the interpretation of amendments centrally concerned to remedy them. The most central mistake was the failure to bring to bear on constitutional interpretation the right kind of impartial reflection on and enforcement of basic human rights; the political theory of human rights must accordingly play a central role in the interpretation of the Reconstruction Amendments.

Many ancillary manifestations of this central interpretive mistake are illustrated in the study of antebellum constitutional theories:[238] Calhoun's rights-skeptical utilitarianism in political theory and his positivism in law, Douglas's popular sovereignty, Taney's originalism, and the like. Such study should also usefully inform us about recurrent temptations to interpretive mistake, ways in which antebellum constitutionalism manifested its central interpretive failure to take rights seriously in understanding the ambitions and terms of the Constitution.

The arguments of the deepest antebellum moral and political critics of these failures (Theodore Parker, Francis Lieber, and Charles Sumner) urge a different interpretive attitude altogether, one based on interpreting constitutional traditions of respect for human rights in terms of what they took to be the best available contemporary theory of human rights, an anti-utilitarian neo-Kantian transcendentalism rooted in equal respect for basic moral powers. Our interpretive responsibilities must be understood in a similar way, making the best sense of what the Reconstruction Amendments clearly require (protection of human rights against certain political threats) in light of the best contemporary understanding of rights-based political legitimacy. The Reconstruction Amendments, in the spirit of No. 49 of *The Federalist*, should remind us of the gravest moment of interpretive constitutional decadence in our history and consequently the need to bring to bear on constitutional interpretation the best arguments available to us about the nature, weight, and scope of human rights, including whatever advances in political theory today (over that of 1866) better clarify the structure of such arguments. The call for ethical impartiality, at the heart of the political theory of the Reconstruction Amendments, must be at the heart of their interpretation; such impartiality must in its nature be open to all the resources of public reason, including advances in social and political theory that render those demands more perspicuous. If, for example, the kind of neo-Kantian rights-

---

238 For such a study, see RICHARDS, *supra* note 51.

based argument emphasized by Lieber and Parker is today best articulated by a form of contemporary contractualism, as I believe, such argument should take its proper place in the interpretation of the enduring meaning of constitutional guarantees of basic human rights.

The enduring moral and constitutional meaning of the Reconstruction Amendments was their decisive rejection of the racial conception of the American political community clearly defended by Taney and not clearly rejected in the antebellum period, even by Lincoln. The Civil War compelled Americans to articulate a higher level of ethical community than anything in the antebellum period would have suggested to be possible or probable. Americans did so through the rediscovery and reinterpretation of their revolutionary constitutionalism and its internal ethical demands for a politics of public reason; those demands repudiated, on grounds of principle, the radical evil that their flawed constitutionalism had spawned, an evil that, like a monstrous child grown to overpowering maturity, had almost devoured them. The Reconstruction Amendments, a self-conscious expression of American revolutionary constitutionalism, interpreted American constitutionalism as a moral community of universal human rights open and accessible to all on terms of its only legitimate demands, public reason—what I have elsewhere called a historically continuous community of principle.[239]

The proper explication of the idea of the continuing legitimacy of a written constitution over time, with the claims for legitimacy made by American constitutionalism, rests on this idea of a community of principle, a commitment to institutions premised on enduring values like respect for human rights that each generation of citizens must understand as constitutive of their constitutional identity as a people. The Reconstruction Amendments speak, on the basis of the gravest failure of constitutionalism in our history, about the normative demands of this idea that must be understood and elaborated consistent with its background political theory. If the point of the idea was, as Madison argued in No. 49 of *The Federalist*, to memorialize these requirements as demands in terms of which each generation of Americans must aspire to define its identity as a people, constitutional interpretation, consistent with this project, must ascribe to constitutional guarantees in general, and the Reconstruction Amendments in particular, that level of abstract moral understanding that allows such guarantees to be interpreted in this way, as a historically continuous strand of principles to which each generation must bring its best understanding of how such guarantees are most reasonably applied.

---

[239] *See* FOUNDATIONS, *supra* note 2, at 145-57.

This tendency to abstractness in the ascription of constitutional meaning both preserves the continuity of the community over time (as normative demands that can be seen to be strands of principle at the core of our moral struggles and ethical growth as a people) and yet enables each generation to understand its own interpretive responsibilities in terms of bringing its own internal powers of public reason most fully to bear on the progressive meaning of human rights in its own contextual circumstances.[240]   American constitutionalism, one of the greatest political legacies historically bequeathed to any people, is thus an interpretive challenge to each generation's powers of universal moral reason.

This tendency to abstractness in constitutional interpretation derives from its basic normative aspirations to justify political power to all persons in light of public reasons that they could accept as reasonable protections of basic rights and the public interest. Such justification must, by its nature, seek the more general features of moral personality and human circumstances in terms of which such an aspiration to universal justification can be sensibly articulated. Such an aspiration does not dilute normative ideas but enriches them, revealing larger patterns of justification that are reasonably required and thus leads the political community to revise its understanding of what human rights are and require. The interpretation of equal protection in this way reveals, for example, a larger abstract structure of threats to basic human rights and the need for the same analysis, as a matter of principle, in contexts that might otherwise seem unrelated (for example, anti-Semitism, racism, sexism, and homophobia).[241] The nature and weight of basic human rights must, as a matter of principle, be analyzed in the same way; in this way, an abstract human right like that to intimate personal life can reasonably be understood to raise issues of constitutional privacy in issues that might otherwise seem as disparate as contraception, abortion, and homosexual relations.[242] Constitutional interpretation of this sort enriches the moral vocabulary and sensitivity of us all, enabling us to interpret our constitutional history more truly and richly as resting on profound moral insights into basic ethical principles of legitimate government from which all persons, as a matter of principle, can and should profit. Indeed, such interpretation *requires* precisely the contextual sensitivity to those relevant matters of fact and value that change over

---

[240] On this tendency to abstractness, see FOUNDATIONS, *supra* note 2, at 167-68, 170, 241, 271.

[241] For further elaboration of this view, see RICHARDS, *supra* note 51, at chs. 3, 5.

[242] *See* DAVID A.J. RICHARDS, TOLERATION AND THE CONSTITUTION 231-281 (1986).

time and that, as a matter of public reason, must change our understanding of how basic principles should be understood. If the progressive moral vision of political community of the Reconstruction Amendments means anything, it means that the claims of political community—both its scope and its demands—must now be subjected to impartial reasonable justification in terms of abstract moral principles, conceptions, and ideals. Constitutional interpretation, consistent with this project, must invite and use the full resources of public reason.

The failure of constitutional interpretation to meet this demand is illustrated not only in the antebellum interpretive mistakes I have already noted, but in later interpretive mistakes that fail in comparable ways to make good sense of the Reconstruction Amendments themselves. The positivism and rights-skeptical utilitarianism of Calhoun are echoed by those of Learned Hand;[243] the popular sovereignty of Stephen Douglas by the majoritarianism of Ely;[244] the originalism of Taney by that of Bork.[245] An understanding of such recurrent temptations to interpretive mistake must explore both their failure to interpret our history properly and their related failure to take seriously the rights-based political theory of American constitutionalism. Judicial interpretive mistakes regarding the meaning of the Reconstruction Amendments rest on both failures. The critical examination of such mistakes often best clarifies the constitutional demands of public reason on historical and moral intelligence by revealing the nature of the failure to meet such demands—the ignorance and misuse of history, the polemical abuse of science, the failure responsibly to bring public reason to bear on the basic interpretive issues of ascribing to constitutional principles the level and kind of moral abstraction that allows them to be regarded as justifiable in contemporary circumstances in the right way.[246] Accordingly, a good substantive theory of constitutional interpretation must also incorporate a complementary theory of interpretive mistake; these tasks are mutually illuminating.

To interpret the Reconstruction Amendments in the right way is to require that political power be justified on the terms of the guarantees of universal human rights appealed to by the American revolu-

---

243 *See* LEARNED HAND, THE BILL OF RIGHTS (1968).

244 *See* JOHN HART ELY, DEMOCRACY AND DISTRUST: A THEORY OF JUDICIAL REVIEW (1980).

245 *See* ROBERT BORK, THE TEMPTING OF AMERICA: THE POLITICAL SEDUCTION OF THE LAW (1990).

246 *See, e.g.*, RICHARDS, *supra* note 51, at chs. 5-7.

tionaries of 1776 to whom Lincoln paid homage in the speech of his political youth:

> Let every American, every lover of liberty, every well wisher to his posterity, swear by the blood of the Revolution, never to violate in the least particular, the laws of the country; and never to tolerate their violation by others. As the patriots of seventy-six did to the support of the Declaration of Independence, so to the suppose of the Constitution and Laws, let every American pledge his life, his property and his sacred honor; . . . in short, let it become the *political religion* of the nation; and let the old and the young, the rich and the poor, the grave and the gay, of all sexes and tongues, and colors and conditions, sacrifice unceasingly upon its altars.[247]

Our interpretive responsibility today is to render the Constitution worthy of such allegiance and homage, grounded in the always refreshed and reinvigorated memory of the demands of our revolutionary constitutionalism.

---

[247] Abraham Lincoln, Address to Young Men's Lyceum (Jan. 27, 1838), *reprinted in* 1 LINCOLN, *supra* note 53, at 32-33.

CONSTITUTIONAL POWERMAKING FOR THE NEW POLITY: SOME DELIBERATIONS ON THE RELATIONS BETWEEN CONSTITUENT POWER AND THE CONSTITUTION

Ulrich K. Preuss

I. THE AMBIVALENT RELATIONS BETWEEN REVOLUTION AND CONSTITUTION

The power to make a constitution is the power to create a political order *ex nihilo*. Of course, in reality there is no such thing as a *nihil*, therefore new constitutions are empirically instituted on the ruins of an order which has collapsed after a revolution, a lost war, or a similar catastrophic event. In modern terms, constitution means the active making of a new order, as opposed to its gradual emergence in the course of a continual historical development. Constitution making involves the idea of an authority and an author whose willpower is the ultimate cause of the polity. This is an idea that could only spring from the natural law assumption that "all men are by nature equally free," since only the voluntary act of free men could justify their duty to comply to any kind of human rule. Hence, only the collective acts of free men could be accepted as the legitimate source of political rule. While this concept became particularly powerful during the French Revolution, it was Edmund Burke, the most prominent and influential antirevolutionary theorist of that time, who made a strong case for a quite different understanding of constitutions. According to Burke, constitutions are "made by the peculiar circumstances, occasions, tempers, dispositions, and moral, civil, and social habitudes of the people, which disclose themselves only in a long space of time."[1]

However, in the constitutional tradition of the European continent, the grounding of the constitution in men's will prevailed and

---

[1] Edmund Burke, Speech in the House of Commons against Pitt's proposal for a committee to consider parliamentary reform (May 7, 1782), *in* ENGLISH HISTORICAL DOCUMENTS 1714-1783, at 226 (D.B. Horn & Mary Ransome eds., 1957).

entailed significant consequences for the meaning of constitution making. For instance, the author of the constitution cannot become subject to it; he is the extra-constitutional origin of the constitution. Another consequence is that "making one's will dependent on previous wills' decisions is tantamount to mortgaging our freedom, to transforming ourselves from autonomous into heteronomous beings."[2] This would be incompatible with the theoretical foundations of modernity which presume that the structures and values of the political order are neither innate nor revealed by God, but rationally fabricated by men. The concept of a constituent power invented by a theologian, is a famous example of what has been called political theology: The constituent power is the secularized version of the divine power to create the world *ex nihilo*, to create an order without being subject to it.[3] The will of the constituent power aims at transforming itself into an objective and enduring incarnation, a constitution, but it cannot simultaneously submit itself to its own creation without losing its character as the supreme secular power.

Not surprisingly, the relationship between revolution and constitution is extremely ambivalent. On the one hand, the experience of the last two hundred years has proved that the leading forces of the revolution endeavor to congeal the achievements of the revolution, particularly the new distribution of political power, in a constitution—a legal document which bears the unequivocal authority of a written text superior to all other laws of the land. However important the character of the constitution as a written text may be—here again, it can be compared with the theological significance of the Holy Scriptures—its lasting authority depends on the persistence of its author's authority. Feher, in his subtle analysis, observed that "a constitution based on will can only endure as long as those persons whose wills backed the document."[4] That is why in modern history there are many revolutionaries who prefer a permanent revolution to the creation of a constitution. The very meaning of "constituent power" is the transmutation of the creative, unorganized, and untamed power of the revolution into the constituted powers of a particular political regime. This definition implies that after the constituent power has created the constitution, every power which claims political legitimacy

---

2 Ferenc Feher, *Voice and Text in Constitutionalism*, 14 CARDOZO L. REV., 705, 706 (1993).

3 CARL SCHMITT, POLITICAL THEOLOGY: FOUR CHAPTERS ON THE CONCEPT OF SOVEREIGNTY (George Schwab trans., 1985); *see also* ERNST-WOLFGANG BÖCKENFÖRDE, STAAT, VERFASSUNG, DEMOKRATIE: STUDIEN ZUR VERFASSUNGSTHEORIE UND ZUM VERFASSUNGSRECHT 90-112 (1991).

4 Feher, *supra* note 2, at 706.

has become subject to it. There is no place for any kind of extra-constitutional power.

By making a constitution, the revolutionary forces are digging their own graves; the constitution is the final act of the revolution. At least, this is the idea of transforming the singular and unitary constituent power into the plurality of constituted powers. This assumption shall be discussed further below.[5] According to this idea, the ensuing political process is not controlled by the revolutionaries, but by the constitution. More precisely, it is controlled by social forces that are the beneficiaries of the revolution without having necessarily participated in initiating and waging it.

The constitution liberates social forces which had been suppressed by the old regime. However, frequently it also creates the political and institutional preconditions for the emergence of totally new social and political actors. The present situation in some Eastern and Central European countries supports this implication of constitutionalism; creating new political actors and exposing them, as well as the revolutionaries themselves, to the uncertainties of the political process organized by the constitution.[6]

Put in a pointed manner, constitution making is an act of self-liquidation of the revolution. A typical feature of all modern revolutions is the split of the revolutionary forces into those who shun their own political decapitation, proclaiming the permanent revolution or at least an institutional device which guarantees the permanent rule of the revolutionary elites, and those who want to use their constituent power for the foundation of a new polity. In the latter case, two alternative interpretations and self-interpretations, respectively called "radical-democratic" and "institutionalist," may be distinguished.

According to the radical-democratic model, constitutions sanctify democratic revolutions by solemnly confirming that through revolutionary actions, the people have recaptured their constituent power which is regarded as being unrestricted by any rules, institutions, or superior orders, and is directed only by its unrestrained willpower. Constitutions are the authentic embodiment and expression of this will. Under this interpretation, the constitution aims at perpetuating the major achievements of the revolution and tends to incorporate many of the revolution's social promises. Since not all political issues

---

5 *See infra* part II.A.

6 *See* Adam Przeworski, *Democracy as a Contingent Outcome of Conflicts, in* CONSTITU-TIONALISM AND DEMOCRACY 59-80 (Jon Elster & Rune Slagstad eds., 1986); *see also* Adam Przeworski, *Some Problems in the Study of the Transition to Democracy, in* TRANSITION FROM AUTHORITARIAN RULE: COMPARATIVE PERSPECTIVES 47-63 (G. O'Donell et al. eds., 1986).

can be included in the constitution, the framers are anxious to devise an institutional order that makes the will of the people the ultimate arbiter in all relevant political conflicts that will necessarily emerge in the future. The people are supposed to become the reliable guard of their revolutionary achievements and future preservation.

This is easily understandable if it is recognized that revolutions that generate this kind of constitution involve at least some elements of a social revolution, associating the term "people" more or less consciously with the lower classes, the poor and miserable.[7] Hence, constitutions of this radical-democratic type usually not only promise relief of the people's misery, but also establish the institutional superiority of the elected representation of the people over the other branches of government. The assumption is that the popularly elected body *is* the people, and in order to achieve the greatest possible congruity of the actual popular will and that of its representative body, additional safeguards are provided. Plebiscites and proportional representation, a type of imperative mandate to the elected deputies, are the most familiar characteristics.

Whenever major social and political conflicts arise, the power to find a solution must be delegated to the people, since in a *genuine* democracy there is no superior wisdom than that of the people. Consequently, supporters of radical-democratic constitutions aspire to preserve the revolutionary high-spiritedness of the people and rely more or less explicitly on the same civic virtues that have initially engendered the revolution. Ideally, they are committed to maintaining a permanent revolution and leveling the difference between revolutionary and normal politics. Not surprisingly, constitutions which focus on the people's will by making it the ultimate source of social and political order are vulnerable to the volatile and disorderly passions of politics. As the French case displays, this form of constitution has proven rather unstable.

In contrast, institutionalist settlements of revolutions use the revolutionary civic spirit to create institutions which allow the people to return to their normal lives and to normal politics after the goals of the revolution have been achieved. They rely on the wisdom of institutions and on the proper operation of social mechanisms rather than on the immediate willpower of the people (and the continuance of their civic virtues characteristic of the revolutionary period).

Institutionalist framers are reluctant to include substantive policies in the constitution because this may complicate and hinder the

---

[7] HANNAH ARENDT, ON REVOLUTION 69 (Greenwood Press 1982) (1963).

adjustment of such policies to new circumstances, and thus weaken the creative capacity of political institutions. In an institutionalist framework, constitutions are not the solution to problems, but rather institutional instruments of problem-solving; they are possibility-engendering, rather than devices used to consolidate a particular policy willed by the people, in a particular situation, under particular conditions. The people submit themselves to rules (the separation of powers or the independence of the judiciary) that, though not determining political outcomes, guarantee that the actual political outcomes are consistent with what the people would have willed in the revolution if they had anticipated the new circumstances. Institutionalist constitutions "congeal" neither the actual empirical nor the future hypothetical will of the revolutionary generation. Rather, they institutionalize the capacity of the people to form and to enforce their will in post-revolutionary times of *normal politics* without being forced to permanently revitalize the spirit of the revolution, and to adjust it to ever changing social and political circumstances. In other words, institutionalist constitutions, largely skeptical and even suspicious of the very revolution from which they originate, determine the close and definite termination of the revolution, setting a clear-cut hiatus between revolutionary and normal politics.

Institutionalist constitutions even tend to become hostile toward any attempt to reinvigorate the revolutionary spirit, since they provide regular social mechanisms which guarantee political outcomes that should have the same or even better effect than revolutionary politics, without being as costly.

II. Constituent Power of the People, the Concept of Nation and the Constitution

There is no question that the Eastern and Central European revolutions of 1989 reflect the institutional alternative. Although this alternative was thought to operate as a problem-solving institutional device, there are indications that it has also generated unanticipated problems. In almost all of the affected countries—Bulgaria, Czechoslovakia, Hungary, Poland, not to speak of Yugoslavia—we are confronted with the problem that the constituent power has not been sedimented and domesticated in a constitution which provides the institutional tools for the creative and peaceful solution to the respective country's problems. The foundation of a new polity requires more than just the superiority of the society over the bureaucratic sphere of the state. To gain (or to regain) an active role in the organization of individual's lives and their social relations with each other, the society, which is not a homogeneous entity, has to develop its capacity to act as a collectivity. The idea of a constituent power presupposes this capacity. However, the question is whether the constituent power, which is supposed to constitute a polity, must have a preexisting collective identity to be able to act as a secularized God and serve as the ultimate source of political legitimacy for a constitution. It has been said that "[a] constitution not only constitutes a structure of power and authority, it constitutes a people in a certain way."[8] But the interrelations between the people and the constitution may well have the reverse character: Do we have to assume that the people must have a prior collective identity in order to possess the capacity to exercise a constituent power?

"We the people of the United States . . . do ordain and establish this Constitution . . . ."[9] Does this mean that the collectivity of the people exists prior to the constitution or is it the very act of constitution making which creates the collectivity and, consequently, its constituent power? Initially, this is an entirely academic problem. However, in view of the constitution-giving processes in Eastern and Central Europe, the question has vital significance. Obviously, it refers to the self-interpretation of those societies in terms of their national identity.

Is the constitution the manifestation of the national identity of a particular people, or is it an act of political self-organization of a civil society? Is the constituent power of the people essentially the power of an ethnically homogeneous nation, or is it the capacity of a pluralist and diverse society to govern itself? Evidently, the relationship between collective identity and constitution making must be considered. What do we mean if we speak of "constituent power"; more precisely, who is its subject? Does the constitution really absorb the constituent power? Does it only exist in the rare historical moments in which new constitutions are generated? Or does the constituent power survive as a constitutional element in that the constitution embodies the tension of a dual power structure, namely the rivalry between the manifestly established constituted powers and the constituent power's claim to embody the "true" spirit and collective identity of the polity?

A. *Who Constitutes the Nation—the* Demos *or the* Ethnos?

When Abbé Sieyès, in his famous pamphlet *What is the Third*

---

[8] SHELDON S. WOLIN, THE PRESENCE OF THE PAST: ESSAYS ON THE STATE AND THE CONSTITUTION 9 (1989).

[9] U.S. CONST. pmbl.

Estate?,[10] justified the claim of the third estate not just to represent, but to be the whole nation,[11] he had to find arguments to prove that the nation was independent of any superior power that could legitimately determine its will. His major theoretical invention was the distinction between constituent and constituted power.[12]

Its lasting relevance can be found in two elements. First, the constitution is not based and dependent upon tradition, historical legacy, or religious revelation, but originates in a secular willpower. Second, the concept of the constituent power of the nation implies that the empirical subject of this power is the people, not the monarch or an aristocratic elite. Equal liberty for every human being as it had been solemnly proclaimed in the Declaration of the Rights of Man and the Citizen, the supreme power of the nation, could only harmonize with the inherently democratic premise of the nation's sovereignty—the latter was the collective expression of the former.

> The nation is prior to everything. It is the source of everything. Its will is always legal; indeed it is the law itself.
>
> . . . .
>
> Not only is the nation not subject to a constitution, but it *cannot* be and *must* not be . . . .
>
> . . . .
>
> . . . That would put it in danger of losing its liberty for ever, for tyranny, under the pretext of giving the People a constitution, would only need a momentary success to bind it so closely by procedural rules that it would lose the ability to express its own will . . . . The manner in which a nation exercises its will does not matter[,] . . . any procedure is adequate, and its will is always the supreme law.[13]

The nation's will is the preconstitutional source of the constitution, and the constitution is the institutionalization of the nation's will. The existence and the continual operation of the constitution are inspired and fed by this preconstitutional power. But what is the nation? Sieyès had an unequivocal answer to this question. A nation is "[a] body of associates living under *common* laws and *represented* by the same *legislative assembly*."[14] The nation is constituted by the entirety of the denizens of a particular territory who, by the very act of forming a political entity and being subject to common laws, acquire

---

10 EMMANUEL JOSEPH SIEYÈS, WHAT IS THE THIRD ESTATE? (S.E. Finer ed. & M. Blondel trans., 1963) (1789).

11 *Id.* at 58.

12 *Id.* at 122-23.

13 *Id.* at 124, 126-28.

14 *Id.* at 58.

the status of citizenship. The nation consists of the totality of its citizenry.[15]

This understanding of what constitutes a nation diverges significantly from a concept that has been prevailing in Germany and in Eastern Europe. According to this understanding, the nation is a prepolitical community which is constituted by the commonness of such properties as origin, race, language, religion, culture, history, and the like. In this sense, a nation must be distinguished from a nation-state, which is a political organization that incorporates a nation. But with this understanding a nation can exist independently of a state.

According to the terminology established by the German historian Friedrich Meinecke at the beginning of this century,[16] the French concept of nation, based on the idea of citizenship, is an example of a *state* nation.[17] In contrast, the German perception includes the idea of a *culture* nation. Whereas in the French concept the nation is the entirety of the *demos*, in the German and East European concept the nation is a group defined in terms of ethnicity—the nation is the *ethnos*.[18] The nation based on common citizenship is necessarily a *state* nation, whereas the *culture* nation can be entirely stateless, such as the Polish nation between 1795 and 1918.

On the other hand, a nation can be politically organized in a plurality of states—like Germany before the foundation of the Bismarck Reich in 1871, and between 1949 and 1990. Very rarely is one homogeneous *ethnos* politically organized in one nation; normally the *ethnos* and the *demos* of a state are incongruous. This fundamental conceptual difference in the understanding of what constitutes a nation entails important variations in the concept and the perception of fundamental political ideas. For example, Francis pointed out that national freedom and self-determination assume different meanings:

> In Western Europe it meant that the demotic nation took over the government of an existing sovereign state, thereby safeguarding its self-determination. In the freedom movement that spread from Germany east and south, however, the term "self-determination" meant the liberation of a preestablished ethnic society from alien influence and foreign domination.[19]

---

[15] *See also* ERIC J. HOBSBAWM, NATIONS AND NATIONALISM SINCE 1780: PROGRAMME, MYTH, REALITY 14-45 (1990).

[16] FRIEDRICH MEINECKE, COSMOPOLITANISM AND THE NATIONAL STATE (Robert B. Kimber trans., Princeton University Press 1970) (1963).

[17] *Id.* at 7-8.

[18] *See* E.K. FRANCIS, INTERETHNIC RELATIONS: AN ESSAY IN SOCIOLOGICAL THEORY 43-115 (1976).

[19] *Id.* at 78.

B.   *The French Concept: Equal Citizenship as the Ground of the Nation*

No less important are the consequences for the idea of the constituent power of the nation. Evidently, the French political idea of the nation—the nation-state formed by the totality of its citizens—has its theoretical roots in the social contract constructions of the natural law theorists of the seventeenth and eighteenth centuries, Rousseau in particular. The constituent willpower of the nation is the general will of Rousseau's social contract. This power is formed not by the expression of a transpersonal entity, but rather by the entirety of the participating individuals; that is why the constituent power of the nation is inseparably connected with the principle of democratic sovereignty.[20] The constituent power is not simply the power to make a constitution.

Conceptually, it cannot be attributed to any single person, even a monarch, although this attempt was undertaken by some constitutional theorists in the nineteenth century—not surprisingly, it failed. Essentially, the constituent power is the power of a collective body, which by the very act of constitution-giving, exercises its right to self-rule. The constituent power of the nation presupposes the idea of a demotic entirety of individuals—the citizenry—an entirety which originates from this very act of creating common laws and a common representative body.

In fact, the political foundation of the nation is what was really formed in France at the end of the 18th century. It is true that the French monarchy had already claimed to embody the French nation. But evidently, this claim did not refer to the entirety of the people living within the boundaries of the kingdom. Nor did it refer to a prepolitical entity such as the lingual community of all Frenchmen. Rather, this was the absolutist monarchy's affirmation of superiority over the particularism of the intermediary powers of feudalism. In a political sense, there was no French nation before the revolution, or before its establishment through the exercise of its constituent power by the third estate.

Contrary to the German case, before the revolution there was not even a common French language which could have served as the con-

---

[20] *See* KARL LOEWENSTEIN, VOLK UND PARLAMENT: NACH DER STAATSTHEORIE DER FRANZÖSISCHEN NATIONALVERSAMMLUNG VON 1789, at 278-82 (1922); EGON ZWEIG, DIE LEHRE VOM POUVOIR CONSTITUANT: EIN BEITRAG ZUM STAATSRECHT DER FRANZÖSISCHEN REVOLUTION 2 (1909).

stitutive element of the nation. As a survey carried out in 1794 reports, "in only fifteen departments was the French language in exclusive use. In all probability, the majority of French citizens was either unable to speak French at all or spoke it with great difficulty."[21] Hence, the diffusion of the French language became a major administrative task of the nation-state. The idea of common citizenship presupposed a common sphere of public debate and reasoning. Moreover, the citizens had to be able to understand and to read the laws which were supposed to express the common will of the nation. Therefore, it was not the commonness of the language that constituted the nation, but, conversely, it was the nation that required and created the commonness of the language.

C.   The Predominantly Ethnicist Notion of the People in Eastern Europe

I have dealt with the question of what constitutes the nation at some length because it is still of great importance in the ongoing processes of constitution making in Central and Eastern Europe. Also, I want to mention in passing that the unification and significant emergence of xenophobia in Germany can be interpreted in this conceptual framework, considering the collective identity of different countries. As the Yugoslavian case manifestly displays, in Central, Eastern, and Southeastern Europe the concept of the nation-state is primarily defined in terms of ethnic homogeneity. The meaning of nation-state is that a nation, in the ethnic sense of this term (defined in terms of the commonness of language and/or religion, culture, origin, etc.), acquires its political existence in its own state. The nation is a prestatist, prepolitical, existential and almost eternal entity, whereas the state is a quasi-accidental and ephemeral phenomenon, which supports the survival of the nation in history, but is not really the embodiment of the essence of the nation. However, the political self-determination of the nation requires statehood; but it is a statehood based on ethnic homogeneity. It is the self-determination of the *ethnos*, directed against alien influence, rather than the political self-rule and freedom of the *demos*, which is directed against political oppression and social inequality.

Ironically, this ethnicist notion of the nation-state was definitively encouraged by an American, namely President Wilson, who after World War I declared the universal right to national self-determination. This right was polemically directed against the three

---

[21] FRANCIS, *supra* note 18, at 73-74.

major multinational European empires of that time—Austria, Russia and the Osmanian Empire. As we experience national self-determination in our days, the purported solution of the problems of those since-vanished empires has possibly created more new problems than it has solved.

Wilson was the representative of a nation which encompassed a multinational society and was constituted by the commonness of citizenship and the common belief in the constitution.[22] Hence, he probably had an understanding of the implications of his proclamation quite different from that of his European addressees. Be that as it may, what is most relevant in the debate about the relation between constitutions and the constituent power is the conclusion that in the framework of an ethnic conception of the nation the constituent power of the nation does not necessarily coincide with the principle of democratic sovereignty (just as national self-determination is not the same as democratic freedom).

D. *Carl Schmitt's Ethnicist Concept of Democracy*

In order to clarify the theoretical implications and consequences of this fundamental conceptual divergence, I want to refer briefly to a constitutional theorist who represents the Central and Eastern European approach to the understanding of nationhood in a most illuminating and provocative manner. I mean the German jurist and political theorist Carl Schmitt, who may be regarded as the most influential theoretical antipode to the French and American concept of the relations between the constituent power of the nation and democracy. His approach is particularly pertinent for discussion because his reasoning refers to the Weimar constitution; a constitution which had been devised by its authors as the constitution embodying the liberal and democratic traditions of the American and the French revolutions, that Schmitt undertook to reinterpret in an ethnicist manner.[23] We cannot exclude the possibility that the constitutions being devised in Central and Eastern Europe, which are generally worded like traditional Western constitutions, will fall prey to a similar reinterpretation.

What is essential in this reinterpretation is the introduction of an ethnicist understanding of democracy, the substitution of the *ethnos* for the *demos*.[24] For Schmitt, the political character of a democratic

---

[22] For the problematic implications of this concept, see WOLIN, *supra* note 8.

[23] CARL SCHMITT, VERFASSUNGSLEHRE (1928).

[24] *Id.* at 234.

order was not characterized by good rules but by good rulers,[25] whereby "good" represents the prenormative existential quality of the people. In a purely empirical sense, the people is only a multitude of individuals within a distinct territory; but in a political sense, the people exist in the ethnic and cultural oneness of this multitude, which entails its capacity to realize its otherness in relation both to other peoples and the liberal-universalist category of mankind.[26] For him, the essence of the political in a democratic order is the will of the people to preserve their distinctive property and oneness, and to impose this will on the economic, social, cultural, and political cleavages of the modern society.[27]

In the first instance, this means the exclusion of all inhomogeneous members of society from their affiliation to the people, and as a consequence, from the enjoyment of equal political right—like the right to vote, to free speech, and to free assembly.[28] Moreover, from this it follows that the people, in this existential and quasi-naturalistic sense of a preconstitutional homogeneous entity, become the antipode of the people in the sense of citizenry. The people, although the holders of sovereignty, cannot exercise their sovereign power other than according to the standards of the constitution; therefore, their political will is channeled and mediated in manifold ways.

It comes as no surprise that Schmitt regarded the constitutionally unalienated people, in their ethnic and national sameness, as the "true" foundation of democracy.[29] Democracy is the rule of the people's will, whose essence is collective authenticity; this quality cannot be achieved by mere aggregation of private individual wills, the attribute of elections in liberal democracies. Referring to Rousseau, at the same time misunderstanding him, Schmitt contends that the best precondition for the inherent authenticity and existential oneness of the people's will is the unqualified immediacy of its expression.[30]

The ideal model is the assembly of a small community, which is not available in the extended territory of the modern nation-state; but his concept of genuine democracy is derived from this ideal hypothesis. Only an actually assembled people is a people and only an actually assembled people can do what distinctively belongs to the actions of this people: it can acclaim, that is, express its consent or its rejec-

[25] *Id.* at 252.
[26] *Id.* at 227.
[27] *Id.* at 237.
[28] *Id.* at 228, 234; *see also* CARL SCHMITT, THE CRISIS OF PARLIAMENTARY DEMOCRACY 9 (Ellen Kennedy trans., MIT Press 1985) (1923).
[29] SCHMITT, *supra* note 23, at 235.
[30] *Id.* at 229.

tion through simple shouts, yells, cheers, or boos; hallow a leader or a proposal; venerate the king or anybody else; or reject acclamation through silence or grumbling.[31]

Within the institutional framework of mass democracy, the utmost attainable degree of authenticity and congruity of the people's will, with its very essence, is to be achieved through representation.[32] By representation, Schmitt does not mean the complex process of constitutional aggregation of the many divergent and antagonistic interests and opinions, channelled and processed through rights, procedures, institutions, associations, et cetera characteristic of constitutional democracy.[33] Rather, he suggests a kind of symbolic reappearance of the essential qualities of the people and their incarnation in a person who has the capacity to express the "true" self of the people.[34]

This concept of democratic representation clearly reveals the close connection between democracy and authoritarian rule—an affinity which led Schmitt to the (at a first glance paradoxical) contention that a true dictatorship can only be founded on a democratic basis.[35] According to this view, democracy and dictatorship are not essentially antagonistic; rather, dictatorship is a kind of democracy if the dictator successfully claims to incarnate the identity of the people.

III. THE FOUNDATION OF THE POLITY: COLLECTIVE IDENTITY OR THE CONSTITUTION?

Given the fact that the concepts of nation and people are amenable to divergent interpretations and that the principle of national sovereignty can entail democratic and ethnocratic consequences as well, it is open to question if the polity and its power rests on national identity or on its constitution. Obviously, the character of the constituent power determines the character of the constitution; although, it is not quite clear in what manner.

A. The Relation Between the Constituent Power and the Constituted Powers

Can we, depending on the basic structure of the constituent power, conceive of different concepts of individual rights, of the idea of separation of powers, of the elements of democratic rule, or of the

---

31 *Id*. at 243-44.
32 *Id*. at 239.
33 *Id*. at 242.
34 *Id*. at 242.
35 *Id.* at 237; *see also* CARL SCHMITT, DIE DIKTATUR XII (1921).

machinery of government? Before turning to this question, I want to make a few remarks about the question of whether the constituent power dissolves itself in the process of constitution making. Is the constituent power consumed by the very act of creating a constitution, or does it survive as a permanent element of the constitution? As stated above, the concept of constituent power is an important part of the doctrine of popular sovereignty.[36] The meaning of constituent power is self-determination, as opposed to the imposition or the revelation of an order. This is why modern constitutions can only be understood as institutional devices which embody the self-binding capacity of a group.[37] Self-determination and self-binding are by no means incompatible. However, it is far from clear whether self-determination involves the right to unbind oneself—to repeal the commitments which have been stipulated in the constitution. Does the constitution absorb the constituent power, a "power from which forms originate but which itself cannot be formed"?[38] Or is the constituent power a latent element of the constitution that is determined to reemerge manifestly, to act as the guardian of the revolution and to preserve the original and undomesticated spirit of the act of foundation against those who, while obeying the letter of the constitution, delude its very spirit? In other words, is the constituent power predisposed to act as a permanent threat to the legality of the constitution?

The significant political implications of these questions can hardly be overlooked. The latter alternative implies that the constitution is exposed to the permanent threat of its own annihilation; whereas the former implies that the constituent power is mediated forever, and that the foundation of the polity will remain a historical event for the overwhelming majority of its members to which they have no personal connection whatsoever.

I should mention that in contemporary Germany this question has become an issue of practical constitutional law, not just of constitutional and political theory. The Basic Law, amended in the process of the unification of the Federal Republic with the German Democratic Republic, contains a final article (Article 146) which, to my knowledge, is truly unique among all of the provisions in the present constitutions of the world.[39] In its original version, which was valid until 1990, this article stipulated that the Basic Law would cease to be

---

36 *See supra* text accompanying notes 23-35.

37 Stephen Holmes, *Precommitment and the Paradox of Democracy, in* CONSTITUTIONALISM AND DEMOCRACY 195-240 (Jon Elster & Rune Slagstad eds., 1988).

38 PETER SCHNEIDER, AUSNAHMEZUSTAND UND NORM: EINE STUDIE ZUR RECHTSLEHRE VON CARL SCHMITT 100 (1957).

39 GRUNDGESETZ [Constitution] [GG] art. 146 (F.R.G.), *reprinted in* 6 CONSTITUTIONS

in force on the day on which a constitution adopted by a free decision of the German people came into force.[40] The underlying idea is evident: Given the expectation of the framers in 1949 that a united German nation-state would soon be reestablished, the Basic Law was to be replaced by a full-fledged constitution sanctioned by the whole German people.

It should be emphasized that Article 146 is not an "amendment rule"—a rule stipulating how to change the Basic Law. Constitutions can be revised fundamentally, but the revisions are subject to the rules of the constitution itself. In contrast, no constitution can contain rules which allow its abolishment altogether; this would permit revolution, whereas it is the very meaning of constitutions to avoid revolutions and to make them dispensable. Political revolutions change political institutions in ways that those institutions prohibit; whereas constitutional amendments change political institutions in ways which the constitution authorizes.

Article 146 is a paradoxical combination of these two sentences. It allows the people to annihilate the Basic Law and replace it with a completely new constitution, without binding the democratic sovereign to any procedural or substantive rules beforehand—the people can abolish the constituted powers and claim their unrestrained constituent power without running the risks of a revolution. This amounts to the constitutional permission to make a revolution, which again is a paradox, because the authority of the constituted powers cannot imply the liberty of self-annihilation. The authorities of the constituted powers act only as trustees of the constituent power, the will of the constituent power being superior to theirs. In the words of Sieyès, "[N]o type of delegated power can in any way alter the conditions of its delegation."[41]

Article 146 of the Basic Law is a unique constitutional response to a unique political predicament. But this does not mean that in all normal cases the constituent power is totally consumed in the act of constitution making. For Sieyès there was no question that the constituent power of the sovereign nation could not be restricted, much less abolished by the constitution:

> [A] nation can neither alienate nor waive its right to will; and whatever its decisions, it cannot lose the right to alter them as soon as its interest requires. Secondly, with whom would this nation

---

OF THE COUNTRIES OF THE WORLD 79, 161 (Albert P. Blaustein & Gisbert H. Flanz eds., 1992).

40 *Id.*

41 SIEYÈS, *supra* note 10, at 124-25.

have entered into such a contract? I see how it can *bind* its members, its mandataries, and all those who belong to it; but can it in any sense impose on itself duties towards itself? What is a contract with oneself? Since both parties are the same will, they are obviously always able to free themselves from the purported engagement.[42]

However, the implementation of Sieyès's doctrine during the deliberations of the National Assembly required concessions to the necessities of practical life. Since the nation in an extended territory cannot act and express its will immediately, it is necessary to establish some rules and procedures which enable the sovereign to act according to its supreme position in the polity. In the French case, this meant the unequivocal distinction between the ordinary legislative body—the Parliament—which was a constituted power in the framework of the separation of powers and whose powers were restricted to the legislative functions, and the Convention or National Assembly (called the Revision Assembly) which, though a representative body as well, was the representative of the entire nation with the unrestricted authority of the constituent power.[43] Apparently the American constitution, which in Article V provides for the convocation of a convention for proposing amendments, served as the model for the distinct and separate institutionalization of the normal legislative power and the extraordinary constituent power. However, it is not fully clear if the amendment process stipulated in Article V refers to the constituent power, or to the constituted powers. The term "Convention"[44]—which evidently alluded to the Convention of Philadelphia, whose constituent power was accepted and confirmed by the majority—and its distinct mode of origination are arguments in favor of construing the character of the Convention as a constituent power. The Convention is something other than a normal legislative body. In justifying the constituent power of the Philadelphia Convention, Madison explicitly referred to the right of the people to "abolish or alter their governments as to them shall seem most likely to effect their safety and happiness."[45] This is a straightforward hint to their right to revolution. In his explication of the amendment procedures and the amending power of Article V he used almost the same words, speaking of the competence of a society to "alter or abolish its estab-

---

[42] *Id.* at 127.

[43] LOEWENSTEIN, *supra* note 20, at 287.

[44] Article V of the United States Constitution provides in relevant part: "The Congress, whenever two thirds of both Houses shall deem it necessary . . . shall call a Convention for proposing Amendments . . . ." U.S. CONST. art V.

[45] THE FEDERALIST No. 40, at 253 (James Madison) (Clinton Rossiter ed., 1961).

lished government."[46]

Given that the Convention carries the entirety of the power of the polity, not just its legislative power, it is very close to the constituent power. On the other hand, it cannot be overlooked that not only the power of the legislative bodies but also the authority of the Convention is restricted by the Constitution—an instance which gives reason to assume that the Convention is not a constituent, but a constituted power.

I do not want to give conclusive answers to this question, rather the reference to the Convention of the American Constitution and to the French Revision Assembly are meant to show that the constituent power does not fully vanish through the very act of constitution making. Nonetheless it is domesticated; it loses its unfathomable and formless character and acquires a quasi-constituted status. This ambivalent status is clearly expressed in the French Constitution of 1791:

> The National Constituent Assembly declares that the nation has the inalienable right to amend its Constitution, and considering that the national interest is better served by making use of the means provided for in the Constitution itself, of the right to reform such articles which experience shall show the expediency of, decrees the formation of an Assembly of Revision, in the following manner . . . .[47]

Although the constituent power is tamed insofar as it becomes subject to the rationalizing force of a procedural rule, it remains a potential power which may check the misuse of authority by the constituted powers. This is so because there is one element which establishes its superiority over all constituted powers and which was expressly verbalized in the French Constitution of 1793, namely, that it "unites in itself the highest power."[48] This consolidated power can only be assigned to a nonconstituted power, because a constituted power which unites all power is self-contradictory. The meaning of constitution is the guarantee of rights and the separation of powers,[49] and this is why only the nonconstituted power, namely the people, can own the con-

---

46 THE FEDERALIST No. 39, at 246 (James Madison) (Clinton Rossiter ed., 1961).

47 LA CONSTITUTION [CONST.] of 1791, tit. VII, art. 1 (Fr.), *reprinted in* HENRY C. LOCK-WOOD, CONSTITUTIONAL HISTORY OF FRANCE 273, 301 (New York, Rand McNally 1890).

48 LA CONSTITUTION [CONST.] of 1793, art. 116 (Fr.), *reprinted in* LOCKWOOD, *supra* note 47, at 305, 312.

49 DECLARATION OF THE RIGHTS OF MAN AND THE CITIZEN art. 16 (FR. 1789), *reprinted in* FIVE CONSTITUTIONS 267, 269 (S.E. Finer ed., 1979). Article 16 provides: "A society in which rights are not secured nor the separation of powers established is a society without a constitution." *Id.*

stituent power.[50]

But the reverse is also true. Whenever the constitution empowers the people to act beyond the exercise of the citizens' right to vote and to express their collective will, there is always a touch of constituent power and of out-rivaling the legitimacy of the constituted powers—be it the superior legitimacy of a law enacted in a plebiscitarian procedure over the authority of a parliamentarian law, or the superiority of the authority and the power of a president elected directly by the people over the power and authority of the government which is elected by the parliament. The dualism of the presidential powers, the powers of the parliament, and the government in the Weimar constitution is a telling example for the latent presence of the constituent power in the operation of the constitution. This may be considered as a negative example for the persistence of the constituent power in the constitution.

On the other hand, there are also negative examples for the malfunctioning of the political process if the direct participation of the people in the political process is almost totally excluded. This is the case in contemporary Germany whose constitutional pattern has been termed a "representative absolutism." This may be exaggerated, however, and in this paper I am not going to analyze the constitutional properties of Germany. What is important for the consideration of the relation between constitution and constituent power is the observation that a total and permanent exclusion of the unorganized constituent power of the people from the realm of politics tends to produce a formalism and rigidity of the constituted powers. This threatens to devalue constitutional democracy altogether.

B. *The Basis of Society: Blood or Contract?*

There is still another kind of argument which pertains to the question, of whether, and to what degree, the constituent power persists and determines the character of the constitution. Hypothetically, the character of the constituent power is likely to determine the structure of the constitution it generates. Hence, whenever a constitution is created, the question arises: What is the substance of the constituent power? Is it a prepolitical commonness of a group of people who form a polity in order to transform their quasi-natural community into a political entity? Is the substance of the constituent power the irrationality of the blood; or is it the freedom and independence that nature has assigned to every individual and that, as we know,

---

[50] CARL J. FRIEDRICH, CONSTITUTIONAL GOVERNMENT AND DEMOCRACY: THEORY AND PRACTICE IN EUROPE AND AMERICA 21 (1941).

became the basic condition for entering into a social compact? The alternative is precisely identified by Rousseau in *The Social Contract*.

> The oldest of all societies, and the only natural one, is that of the family; yet children remain tied to their father by nature only so long as they need him for their preservation. As soon as this need ends, the natural bond is dissolved. Once the children are freed from the obedience they owe their father, and the father is freed from his responsibilities towards them, both parties equally regain their independence. *If they continue to remain united, it is no longer nature, but their own choice, which unites them*; and the family as such is kept in being only by agreement.
>
> This *common liberty* is a consequence of man's nature.[51]

To be sure, Rousseau speaks of the foundation of civil society, not of the process of constitution making. We must distinguish both steps, although empirically they will normally coincide. It is hardly conceivable that in real life the formation of a group out of a multitude of individuals, and the determination of the structure according to which the group is enabled to act as an entity, can be separated from each other. However, the distinction is analytically important because the generation of a constitution for a group presupposes the very existence of the group. Hence, before the group gives itself a constitution (e.g., by establishing a kingdom), it must clarify who is subject to this constitutional determination, and who is entitled to participate in this decision. In other words, who is a member of the group.

Quoting Grotius, who had contended that a people may give itself to a king, Rousseau argues:

> Therefore, according to Grotius a people is *a people* even before the gift to the king is made. The gift itself is a civil act; it presupposes public deliberation. Hence, before considering the act by which a people submits to a king, we ought to scrutinize the act by which people become *a* people, for that act, being necessarily antecedent to the other, is the real foundation of society.[52]

Given Rousseau's natural law approach, according to which the state of nature is characterized by the isolated dispersion of human animals, not by the existence of natural communities, the foundation of society rests on a contract:

> Indeed, if there were no earlier agreement, then how, unless the election were unanimous, could there be any obligation on the minority to accept the decision of the majority? What right have the

---

51 JEAN-JACQUES ROUSSEAU, THE SOCIAL CONTRACT 50 (Maurice Cranston trans., Penguin Books 1968) (1762) (emphasis added).

52 *Id.* at 59 (emphasis added).

hundred who want to have a master to vote on behalf of the ten who do not? The law of majority-voting itself rests on a covenant, and implies that there has been on at least one occasion unanimity.[53]

A similar argument exists in Locke's social contract theory, though it is diluted by his famous theory of tacit consent. But this does not concern us here.

What is important is that both Rousseau and Locke assume that the formation and the coherence of a social group rests on the individual's decision to participate in the group. Although their visions of a civil society are extremely antithetical, the methodological approach of their reasoning is the same; both Rousseau and Locke start with an individualistic construction of society. Obviously, this determines the character of the constituent power of this society. A society which has been formed because this was the appropriate response to the needs and interests of free and equal individuals can exercise its constituent power only for the common good of its individual members.

This is why Locke does not regard the constituent power as omnipotent, but as limited by the goal of society and of a government—namely, the aim to protect the individual's life, liberty, and property. Rousseau presupposes the omnipotence of the constituent power (i.e., the sovereignty of the entirety of all members of civil society), but this too is a consequence of his individualistic approach. The sovereign, and the omnipotence of its constituent power, follow from an act of delegation by each and every individual that participates in the social contract; in Rousseau's words, "[E]ach one of us puts into the community his person and all his powers under the supreme direction of the general will; and as a body, we incorporate every member as an indivisible part of the whole."[54]

The contract includes a promise of everybody, to everybody, to put his or her person and goods totally into the community. It is this absolutism of the individual's self-commitment which leads Rousseau to the conclusion that the sovereign who originates from this act cannot violate anybody's rights: "[A]s every individual gives himself absolutely, the conditions are the same for all, and precisely because they are the same for all, it is in no one's interest to make the conditions onerous for others."[55]

Rousseau contends that it is the very character of the social contract that generates the kind of social solidarity necessary for the in-

---

[53] *Id.*
[54] *Id.* at 61.
[55] *Id.* at 60.

herent justice and orientation towards the common good of society. The omnipotence of the constituent power is not only no threat to the individual's rights, but at the same time is the safeguard for the realization of the common good. The conditions of the formation of the general will guarantee that the constituent power will necessarily create a constitution which satisfies the needs of all members of the society.

I am highlighting this implication because there is an argument which contends the opposite, and even Rousseau himself seems to adhere to its reasoning.[56] The assertion is that the coherence of a polity cannot entirely be created and sustained by the contract of free and equal individuals. According to this contention, some minimum conditions of prepolitical unity are required; the most important conditions being ethnic homogeneity (commonness of origin, language, religion, customs, and the like). Rousseau asks the question: Which people are fit to receive the kind of constitution which he has in mind? He answers the question, postulating that the type of people for such a constitution would be "a people which, finding itself already bound together by some original association, interest or agreement[,] . . . combines the cohesion of an ancient people with the malleability of a new one."[57] His assumption of a preconstitutional union and coherence of the people would limit the validity of his contention that his construction of the social contract generates the solidarity which binds a multitude of individuals to a social group. More important for our contemporary problems is the question of whether the constitutional state presupposes some minimum degree of prepolitical sameness and homogeneity of the constituent power.

This is of course the contention of all nationalist theorists. But there are also liberals who argue the same way. For instance, John Stuart Mill maintained that the governed should decide over their government, but that the governors and the governed should belong to the same nation (defined by Mill as a union constituted by common sympathies, mostly generated by the commonness of language, religion, origin, etc.).[58]

> Free institutions are next to impossible in a country made up of different nationalities. Among a people without fellow-feeling, especially if they read and speak different languages, the united public opinion, necessary to the working of representative government,

---

[56] See id.

[57] Id. at 95.

[58] JOHN STUART MILL, CONSIDERATIONS ON REPRESENTATIVE GOVERNMENT 308-10 (London, Longman, Green, Longman, Roberts & Green, 3d ed. 1865).

cannot exist. . . . The same books, newspapers, pamphlets, speeches, do not reach [the different sections of the country]. . . . The same incidents, the same acts, the same system of government, affect them in different ways . . . .[59]

If Mill is right, multinational states like Switzerland or the United States could not exist. On the other hand, the dissolution of the Soviet Union and of Yugoslavia, or the ethnic tensions in Bulgaria, Czechoslovakia, or Romania carry sufficient evidence that a constitution whose creator cannot refer to a prepolitical collective identity—the most important being nationhood—might not be able to generate the coherence which the constitutional state needs for its functioning. It is open to question if this observation applies to all constitutional states. But wherever it holds true, it would strongly indicate that the domestication of the irrational forces of politics has not yet been fully successful.

CONCLUSION

I do not mean to discredit the feelings of national identity which we find in almost every country of the world. But the idea of modern constitutionalism is the separation of fellow-feelings of a nation from the structure of government and the rights of individuals given from the constitution.

The constituent power of the people will always encompass the ethnic and the demotic elements of the people. But it is the very rationale of the constitution to transform the unfathomable power of the *ethnos* into responsible authority of the *demos*. Therefore, the constitution, although created by the constituent power, must always fight against the tendency of its own creator to infuse prepolitical elements into the structures of politics. The constituent power is simultaneously the creator of the constitution and a permanent threat to it. Yet, both functions are necessary for the vitality of the constitution.

---

[59] *Id.* at 310.

DILEMMAS ARISING FROM THE POWER
TO CREATE CONSTITUTIONS IN
EASTERN EUROPE

Andrew Arato

INTRODUCTION

Three years have passed since the dramatic events of 1989, and it is time to recall the outcome of Hannah Arendt's analysis of revolutions.[1] According to Arendt, the history of modern revolution has been dominated by the antinomic paradigms of a permanent revolution that fails to make a new beginning on freedom, and a conservative revolution that forgets its origins, or converts them into mere tradition. This diagnosis certainly retains its power. While it is too early to speak of outcomes in Eastern Europe, the interpretations of the actors themselves, whether or not they use the term revolution, have already begun to reproduce the very antinomy Arendt analyzed. This time, paradoxically, it is elements of a new nationalist right that clamor for a total break with the past and the indefinite continuation of radical revolution, while the liberals and remnants of the democratic left, who have done far more to change the earlier regime, now affirm continuity and the rule of law. Once again a third alternative has been ignored. While the revolutionaries' slogan is "restoration," and the liberals call for "imitation," very few people recognize the necessity, or even the possibility, of innovation, of new historical creation.

Hannah Arendt, of course, insisted on the establishment of a *novus ordo saeclorum* as the most important task of modern revolutions. We should recall that she believed that constitution making alone could create the new order, and that a republican constitution could provide a way of transcending the antinomy of permanent revolution and revolutionary amnesia. In order to realize this goal, it was necessary to resolve the fundamental problem of preserving public freedom beyond its revolutionary beginnings.

Arendt's original solution to the problem of institutionalizing public freedom—a Jeffersonian argument for workers' (citizens')

---

[1] HANNAH ARENDT, ON REVOLUTION (1965).

councils—is now obsolete. In fact, she tacitly admitted defeat by placing the emergence of such politics at historical ruptures when "the dialectic stood still,"[2] in effect removing the explosions of democracy from historical time. How could she do otherwise, standing at the crossroads of the revolutionary tradition of a failed revolution and the non-revolutionary tradition of a successful one? But are we in a better position to search for the excluded third alternative following the unexpected reemergence of "revolution" in Eastern Europe in 1989? Answering affirmatively, have we been perhaps misled by a year when once again the dialectic stood still?

At this moment there are two theoretical options available that look beyond the antinomies of permanent and conservative, social and political revolutions. One option retraces the road of Arendt's one successful revolution—the American—and argues, in opposition to her verdict, that the eighteenth-century experience of public freedom *was* successfully institutionalized in a dualism of constitutional and normal politics.[3] In this conception, constitutional politics refers to movements of citizens, participating publicly through extraordinary but legal political forms, oriented primarily to making or revising constitutions. The second conception argues that a new program of self-limitation, capable of combining radical social change with the making of free constitutions, has emerged in East Central Europe.[4] While the two conceptions are linked together by the idea of self-limitation, there are crucial differences between them. The philosophical core of Bruce Ackerman's argument is based on the eighteenth-century American theory of popular sovereignty, according to which valid constitutions and constitutional revisions are acts of the sovereign people outside of all duly-constituted legislatures.[5] In contrast,

---

[2] The expression comes from Walter Benjamin in CHARLES BAUDELAIRE: A LYRIC POET IN THE ERA OF HIGH CAPITALISM 171 (1973), and was fully developed in the essay *Theses on the Philosophy of History*, the original of which was given to Hannah Arendt. *See* WALTER BENJAMIN, *Theses on the Philosophy of History, in* ILLUMINATIONS 253 (Hannah Arendt ed., 1969).

[3] Bruce A. Ackerman, *Neo-federalism?* [hereinafter Ackerman], *in* CONSTITUTIONALISM AND DEMOCRACY 153 (Jon Elster & Rune Slagstad eds., 1988). Unfortunately, I was unable to take Ackerman's WE THE PEOPLE (1991) into account, as it appeared after the completion of this Article.

[4] ULRICH PREUSS, REVOLUTION, FORTSCHRITT UND VERFASSUNG (1990); Ulrich Preuss, The Influence of Carl Schmitt on the Legal Discourse of the Federal Republic of Germany (unpublished paper delivered at the conference "Carl Schmitt and the Challenge to Democratic Theory," New School for Social Research, February 17, 1990, on file with author) [hereinafter Preuss, Influence of Carl Schmitt]; Ulrich Preuss, The (Central) Round Table in the Former German Democratic Republic (1991) (unpublished manuscript, on file with author) [hereinafter Preuss, Round Table].

[5] *See generally* GORDON S. WOOD, THE CREATION OF THE AMERICAN REPUBLIC 1776-1787 (1972).

Ulrich Preuss disputes the European theory of a unified constituent power capable of exercising all dimensions of sovereignty, and applauds the absence in East Central Europe of a reference to the sovereign people as the subject of constitution making. Preuss stresses the replacement of the sovereign people with a pluralistic emphasis on the organized collectivities of civil society.[6] While Ackerman seeks to defend a genuine form of revolutionary legitimacy, Preuss seems to prefer constitutional continuity, propagated by the new constitution makers not only as the shield of stability and legality, but also of constitutional innovation.

I believe that these two perspectives, born of different constitutional traditions, may be more complementary than it would first appear. The democratic consistency of the American idea of constitution-making power, which, unlike the European theory of the *pouvoir constituant* rightly excludes legislative and executive powers from the constitutional convention, does not benefit from its claim of privileged access to that mythical entity, the sovereign people. But the idea of a genuine new beginning in constitutionality need not be entirely sacrificed to a justifiable fear of revolutionary semantics based on the relation of friend and enemy outside of all normative limitations.[7] Taken together the two conceptions give us democratic constitutional politics whose referent is civil society and its public sphere rather than established legislative bodies or the atomized population, a politics with an elective affinity for the dimension of fundamental lawmaking. This politics, worthy of institutionalization in settled constitutions, represents, in my view, the center piece of a theory of democratic constitutionalism.

I will not attempt to synthesize the most promising American and European approaches to democratic constitutionalism in this Article. Instead, I will first explore some of the theoretical bases for insisting on this somewhat unusual notion; then I will examine the political conditions which make possible such an innovative version of constitutionalism, focusing on the dilemmas raised by constitution making in Eastern Europe.

I. Democratic Constitutionalism

We define constitutionalism as a political form in which a body of fundamental laws establishes the powers of government and institu-

---

[6] *See* Preuss, Influence of Carl Schmitt, *supra* note 4.

[7] Presumably, Preuss would support incorporating the democratic spirit of the transitions in settled constitutionalism. This can best be achieved by linking constituent and constituted power.

tionalizes important limits for its operation.[8] Ordinarily these limits are understood in the liberal sense, as disabilities of the legislature, and by implication, the executive. They are meant to affirm the existence of, or carve out and stabilize, a realm differentiated from the state, that is, civil society understood in the rather defensive liberal sense. Fundamental rights, civil rights, and political rights understood on the model of civil rights, such as freedoms and liberties, represent the major building blocks of liberal constitutionalism.

Constitutionalism in the liberal sense, along with the judicial review which enforces it, is often understood to be in conflict with democracy. This common understanding is largely mistaken, and not only because limitation and self-limitation in politics can often be forms of empowerment. While conflicts between liberalism and democracy or between rights and political participation are possible, they are not automatically involved when the rights of minorities or individuals are defended against the strictures of legislation or executive order. Most supposed instances of conflict between liberal constitutionalism and democracy are such only from a narrow legal point of view that identifies modern political systems as democratic, as defined in general civics textbooks that provide only the *official* narratives concerning the workings of government. From a sociological point of view, many of the same conflicts turn out to be between liberal rights and oligarchic-statist claims of governments having various degrees of democratic legitimacy.[9]

If, however, we understand constitutionalism first and foremost as a limitation on the modern state, and not on democratic forms of power, and, moreover, if we entertain the possibility of a three-sided conflict between liberal, democratic, and statist principles, a second dimension of constitutionalism comes to the fore. This involves a defense of democratic participation in the face of the state, whose logic involves not only the drive for efficiency,[10] but also the perpetuation of existing power and prerogatives of officials. Next to (and in addi-

---

[8] Stephen Holmes rightly distinguishes between enabling and disabling limits, but tends to argue that both represent an increase in democratic power to do things in the present. Stephen Holmes, *Precommitment and the Paradox of Democracy, in* CONSTITUTIONALISM AND DEMOCRACY, *supra* note 3, at 195. I accept the distinction, but not the automatic reference to democratic power. Moreover some limits, such as constitutional rights, involve an increase in power for an entity (the political system or the state) only in the broad sociological sense, and not in any specifically legal-political sense. *See* NIKLAS LUHMANN, GRUNDRECHTE ALS INSTITUTION (1965).

[9] See LUHMANN, *supra* note 8, on the "function" of fundamental rights; see also NIKLAS LUHMANN, LEGITIMATION DURCH VERFAHREN (1975), on the two narratives types—official and informal—which we use to describe democratic politics.

[10] Jon Elster, *Introduction, in* CONSTITUTIONALISM AND DEMOCRACY, *supra* note 3, at 1.

tion to) liberal constitutionalism, there is a need to assert the imperatives of democratic constitutionalism.[11]

In recent literature on American constitutionalism and judicial review, two important, and in my view complementary, attempts have been made to establish the idea of democratic constitutionalism. In J.H. Ely's *Democracy and Distrust*,[12] judicial review by appointed-for-life officials without democratic accountability is justified by the need to keep democratic procedures open—a task which generally cannot be left to elected officials who may have a personal interest in keeping the process closed. As important as this emphasis may be, Ely's argument may be faulted both for leaving the internal mechanism of the "democratic" process untouched—on the input side, protecting the citizen solely in his capacity as a voter (who is to have equal access) while on the output side, protecting the citizen solely in his capacity as a beneficiary (who is to receive equal treatment). It is in this context that we should locate Ackerman's argument.[13] Ackerman attempts to go beyond Ely (whom he treats somewhat unfairly) by discovering in *The Federalist Papers* a program for a dualistic politics in which constitutional politics represents a more democratic, if extraordinary, option next to normal interest-group pluralistic politics. While Ackerman may rightly be criticized for conceding too much of normal politics to a version of pluralism without democratic principle,[14] it is his insistence on a radical democratic constitutional politics that acquires special relevance today. Indeed, while Ely's understanding of the democratic correction of normal politics may still be contained under an expanded notion of liberal constitutionalism, because it is still focused on the defense of rights, even if on democratic political rights, Ackerman's reassertion of a form of power which is, within its sphere, more democratic than normal electoral and parliamentary politics, establishes the equal status of democratic constitutionalism.

At least it does so in principle. The operation of the framework of American constitutionalism does not leave much room for an element of radical democracy. In particular, it seems difficult to identify judicial review as intrinsically involved in provoking a radical demo-

---

[11] Despite the potential for conflict between individuals' rights and the opinions and wills of majorities, I am convinced that liberal and democratic constitutionalism are mutually reinforcing.

[12] JOHN HART ELY, DEMOCRACY AND DISTRUST: A THEORY OF JUDICIAL REVIEW (1980).

[13] Ackerman, *supra* note 3.

[14] Cass R. Sunstein, *Constitutions and Democracies: An Epilogue, in* CONSTITUTIONALISM AND DEMOCRACY, *supra* note 3, at 327.

cratic response.[15] In fact, the ambiguity between principle and prag-
matism is already included Ackerman's major source. The principle
of the superior, constituent power of the people is present in *The Federalist Papers*.[16] Ackerman accurately describes it as the culmination
of a generation of revolutionary experience.[17] The incorporation of
this principle in the constitution is, however, balanced by the desire to
build in the foundations of a traditional legitimacy.[18] Thus it could be
said that the early defenders of the United States Constitution used
the principle of the democratic superiority of the constituent power
over the legislature to bring the whole period of constitutional politics
to an end, and to establish the legislatures all the more firmly.[19] In
any case, if the making of the United States Constitution was legitimated by a new American revolutionary-democratic principle, this
principle was built into the settled constitution at best in a contradictory manner. This is shown by the uneasy status of constitutional
conventions in Article V of the United States Constitution, which re-
stores the role of ordinary legislatures in constitutional politics.[20]
And while in great, quasi-revolutionary moments of United States history, the amendment process, especially in the case of the post-Civil

---

[15] Ackerman, *supra* note 3, at 172. A defense of rights by the court cannot ordinarily be
identified with a challenge by the court to the population to abolish that right through constitutional amendment. Such a view tends to sacrifice liberal constitutionalism to the democratic
one!

[16] *See* THE FEDERALIST Nos. 40, 53 (James Madison), No. 78 (Alexander Hamilton).

[17] As does Gordon Wood. Ackerman, *supra* note 3, at 157; WOOD, *supra* note 5, at 306-
43, 519-64. In light of Wood's evidence, and a dispassionate reading of *The Federalist Papers*,
it is certainly wrong to dismiss Ackerman's reading of this text as "imaginative," but not
supported by his source (Holmes, *supra* note 8, at 218 n.79) even if the relevant citations
(which are not the only ones possible) are assembled somewhat carelessly. What Holmes's
discussion amply proves, however, is the presence of a very different, and in my view neo-
traditional, interpretation of constitutions in *The Federalist Papers*. Recall, if you will, the
Platonism of THE FEDERALIST No. 49 (James Madison), which states that one would not have
to stimulate the future unreflective veneration of the constitution in a nation of philosophers,
which, however, is obviously impossible. Similarly, Sunstein's critique only establishes the
presence of a strong republican strain in Madison's view of normal politics, not the absence of
a pluralist strain. In effect, then, the conceptions of both normal and constitutional politics are
internally ambiguous in the document, a fact which can lead to four distinct interpretations.
They are 1) democratic-pluralist, 2) democratic-republican, 3) neo-traditional-pluralist, and
4) neo-traditional-republican. A more complex interpretation would then insist on the importance of dualistic politics, precisely because it reinforces republican elements with respect to
pluralistic normal politics. This interpretation might accommodate the tension between democratic and neo-traditional constitutional politics by differentiating, which Holmes does not,
between the democratic character of constitutional revision and its level of difficulty, and by
considering the possibility of identity formation and reference to tradition without quasi-reli-
gious veneration.

[18] *See* THE FEDERALIST No. 49 (James Madison).

[19] This seems to be Wood's final verdict. WOOD, *supra* note 5, at 593-618.

[20] The point is fudged by Hamilton. *See* THE FEDERALIST No. 85 (Alexander Hamilton).

War amendments—though without the provocation of judicial review—could play a radical democratic role, the traditional element in
constitutional legitimacy which was stressed by Arendt has certainly
come to the fore. Dualistic democratic politics today seems more to
be the basis of an immanent criticism than a description of the actual
framework of our constitutional reality. The critics of Ackerman are
right to point this out, even if they cannot thereby vitiate the normative interest of the dualistic program.[21]

Is the program viable on the level of normative-theoretical considerations? Let us concede to the critics of all radical democracy
that any attempt to establish large-scale popular participation on the
level of normal politics is doomed to fail in modern societies; it is
scarcely thinkable that a democratic constituency in a large-scale,
complex society with radical time constraints would not delegate day-
to-day control over legislation, execution, and adjudication to specialized political bodies, such as organs of the state.[22] Assuming though
not here demonstrating, a discourse theoretical conception of the plurality of democracies,[23] the dualistic fall-back position provided by
Ackerman becomes all the more attractive. There are, in fact, important reasons why constitutional politics can, and therefore should, involve a wider and more democratic form of participation than normal
politics. In what follows, I will enumerate and briefly discuss some of
these reasons.

A.   *Plurality of Democracy*

On the most abstract and entirely normative level, I would stress
the need to combine different forms and types of democracy. Assum-

---

[21] Several perspectives on the dualistic politics in American society are possible: One can
take a normatively positive attitude that is empirically skeptical, such as Arendt does; a normatively positive and empirically optimistic view, such as Ackerman's; an empirically skeptical and normatively negative view, such as that held by Holmes; and, finally, a viewpoint
which is optimistic about a possible republican correction of normal politics, but on a purely
republican, rather than dualistic, basis, which has been espoused by Sunstein. The most serious objection to the argument as presented here would come from Holmes, who would insist
on vastly limiting the channel of constitutional politics, for the sake of democracy as well as
political efficiency. These two objectives do not amount to the same thing, though Holmes
seems to think they do. In my view, great limits on the utilization of the power to revise
constitutions empower the state rather than any democratic constituency. At best, effectiveness is purchased at the cost of democratic legitimacy. But in conflict or crisis situations, the
relative low level of democratic legitimacy would diminish the ability of the state to act, hence
to be effective.

[22] This does not mean that "normal politics" cannot be democratically corrected at the
procedural level, nor even that extra-ordinary political mobilization as well as long term trends
in the political culture cannot introduce greater democratic responsiveness and accountability.

[23] JEAN L. COHEN & ANDREW ARATO, *Discourse Ethics and Civil Society, in* CIVIL SOCI-
ETY AND POLITICAL THEORY 345-420 (1992).

ing a discursive theory of democratic legitimacy, I wish at the same time to maintain that it is impossible to fully and definitively embody the normative-rational presuppositions of discourse in empirical institutions of public life. For reasons that are in part contingent (the stress on private happiness in modern cultures), and in part theoretical (time constraints), all types of democratic institutions in public life have built-in forms of exclusion, constraints of discussion, and probable asymmetries among participants. However, the forms that non-democracy takes within various types of democracy are significantly different. Thus in principle, other things being equal, it is highly desirable to combine different types of democratic institutions and processes (direct and representative, centralistic and federal, civil and political) in a given constitutional framework.

B. *Separation of Normal and Constitutional Channels*

The idea of the plurality of democracy has special relevance to the problem of democratic constitutionalism, because it is highly desirable that constitution making and revision operate on a different democratic "channel" than normal legislative politics. In this context, the argument of *The Federalist Papers*, systematizing the already prevalent American rejection of parliamentary constitution making and revision, remains the best starting point. It is still lamentably true that this idea is poorly understood by many Europeans. According to Madison, whenever legislatures retain the power of constitutional revision, they are in position to establish themselves as oligarchical replacements of the power they claim only to represent.[24] Evidently, when questions of changing the operations or institutional relationships of the legislature are the themes of constitutional revision, the legislature should not be the body with power to judge the issue on its own behalf. Even more importantly, if constitutionalism is to be a limit on the operation of the legislative branch of government, it is unwise to allow the same legislature the power to alter the relevant limits according to its own design.[25] Whether a constitutional convention doubles as a legislative and policy-making body, or working legislatures retain constitution-making powers, the divisions in interests of ordinary politics permeate a process in which principles should have the dominant role. In times of rapid change and dislocation, either variant, for example, the second French constitutional as-

---

[24] See THE FEDERALIST No. 53 (James Madison) and the more grudging acceptance of this point by Hamilton in THE FEDERALIST No. 85 (Alexander Hamilton).

[25] This is true even if the limits do empower. Disabling (as against enabling) limits do not empower in the specific aspect under discussion.

sembly or *Convention Nationale*, which drafted an unenacted constitution, and the Long Parliament, which operated during the English civil war, can lead to dictatorship. In this context, neither restrictions on the legislature, nor the need to produce qualified majorities change anything in principle—they only link the avoidance of ill effects to contingent electoral outcomes. Putting constituent powers in the hands of legislatures can either lead to a frivolous use of constitutional revision, which produces patchwork constitutions without legitimacy, or to increased constitutional inflexibility of even supposedly flexible constitutions in order to counteract potential constitutional chaos. Misplaced constituent powers can even lead to bizarre combinations of these two options: total inflexibility in some areas and frivolous use of amendments in others.

C. *The Democratic Surplus of Constitutional Politics*

The democratic legitimacy of normal state operations would be weakened if the state and its agencies could maintain the same type of control over the making of rules as they possess under these rules over ordinary legislation. On the other hand, democratic legitimacy would be clearly strengthened if the extraordinary processes of constitutional rule-making could involve a widening of democratic participation. However, neither populist arguments, such as those of James Madison and the Abbé Sieyès,[26] nor existential-political arguments, such as Schmitt's, are acceptable today for the normative superiority of constituent politics. Constitutional politics has no privileged access, either to "the people" or to the deepest layers of our political identity. Nor is it a good idea to elevate constitutional politics by linking normal politics under liberal democracies exclusively to liberal, as opposed to democratic, standards.[27] What is true is that constitutional politics, due to its extraordinary nature, has the potential to promote the public participation of individuals otherwise dedicated

---

[26] Schmitt and Arendt each discuss Sieyès. *See* CARL SCHMITT, VERFASSUNSGLEHRE 77-80 (1928); ARENDT, *supra* note 1, at 154, 160-63.

[27] *See* Ackerman, *supra* note 3, at 153-54. While I think Ackerman's phrase "democratically inferior," *id.* at 163-64, is well chosen, I do not see the reason for his total denial of democratic justification for electoral-representative party politics whether or not we introduce the idea of its republican correction. *See* Sunstein, *supra* note 14. While normal politics in the American sense is important from the point of view of the search for private happiness, it also provides a form of political participation for those who do not choose a public, political life. Nor do I believe that Ackerman's one passage critical of the element of populist justification for constitutional politics, Ackerman, *supra* note 3, at 186 n.60, provides an adequate replacement for it. The interesting idea of vastly enriching the vocabulary of Americans through the availability of higher law-making politics does not prove the democratic superiority of this political channel.

to private happiness, and whose political involvement is inevitably a shifting one. While organizing that occurs outside the legislature may create nothing more than another assembly, constitutional politics limited to relatively few broad issues of principle could be, and often is, organized to give the direct democratic element a greater, though fortunately, rarely an exclusive, role. Yet the democratic surplus of constitutional politics lies on an even more fundamental level. Assuming that democracy is fundamentally deliberation and dialogue, much depends on the structure of the public sphere in which discussion is institutionalized. Here Habermas's ground-breaking work on the public[28] can easily mislead those who follow him: The structure of parliamentary publicity never was and never could be based on the unconstrained communication possible in a cultural or literary public sphere located in civil society rather than the state. In parliaments the complexity of issues and the constraints of decision-making lead to formal and substantive limitations on the time available for debate.[29] Given the relative specificity and lesser complexity of the parameters involved in constitutional revision, and even in constitution making, as well as the lesser demand for quick decision-making than is found in policy questions, constitutional politics may take place in the far less constrained public spheres of civil society. Even special legislatures and expert commissions involved in constitution making need not isolate themselves from ongoing public discussion in which those most concerned can participate in an organized fashion. The legitimacy of a constitution, as the American experience from 1776 right up to the final ratification of the Bill of Rights indicates, has much to gain from a long and open period of public discussion of the basic principles.[30]

---

[28] JÜRGEN HABERMAS, THE STRUCTURAL TRANSFORMATION OF THE PUBLIC SPHERE: AN INQUIRY INTO A CATEGORY OF BOURGEOIS SOCIETY (Thomas Burger & Frederick Lawrence trans., 1989).

[29] On the latter of these, see Stephen Holmes, *Gag Rules or the Politics of Omission, in* CONSTITUTIONALISM AND DEMOCRACY, *supra* note 3, at 19.

[30] In my view it is the stress on open, extended and multi-levelled public discussion that shifts the final principle of constitution making from the abstract concept of "the people" to civil society, rather than the representations of the institutions of civil society in a constitution-making body. *Cf.* Preuss, Round Table, *supra* note 4. The people as a whole can participate in the framing of a constitution only by electing delegates, voting in ratification or by more immediate forms of identification, *e.g.*, acclamation, demonstration etc. The principle of extended public discussion, though not dispensing with election and voting, puts the stress on deliberation by individuals organized in "publics" and associations. While not excluding the participation of the unorganized, this approach multiplies the influence of organized and associated individuals.

D. *Constitution as Institutionalization of Revolutionary Change*

Even if opposed to the idea of the veneration of constitutions, we should not give up the desideratum of constitutional stability, which is important both for limiting and identity-forming functions of constitutions. Starting with Madison's reply to Jefferson in *The Federalist* No. 49, the democratic claims of constitutional politics have been typically rejected on behalf of stability. Indeed, the discussion today remains under the shadow of the long Jefferson-Madison debate.[31] Three issues, however, are conflated in the reference to Jefferson, who came to believe not only in democratic, but also frequent and potentially total, hence revolutionary, revisions of existing constitutions. The level of difficulty does not directly vary with the democratic character of the process of constitutional revision. Indeed, a purely parliamentary procedure, in my view quite undemocratic, is certainly the easiest and quickest way to change a constitution. Moreover, only Jefferson's own preferred road—frequent constitutional conventions—potentially implies repetition of the Convention of 1787, which changed a commission to amend the constitution into the power to make a completely new constitution. It is possible to eliminate this option, or better still to make any recourse to it procedurally far more difficult than other procedures of amendment.[32] Thus, it is possible to keep the process of even frequent revision entirely *within* the constitution, a point disregarded by Madison in *The Federalist* No. 49, but insisted on by Hamilton (in a different context) in *The Federalist* No. 85.[33]

For now these arguments will suffice to make the idea of dualistic politics worth discussing. I would like to repeat that I am skeptical of the claim that present-day United States politics actually takes this form. To be sure, American constitutional revisions (those which are not linked to judicial review), and judicial review (linked to changes

---

[31] *See especially* Holmes, *supra* note 8.

[32] I would not argue that the never-tried road of a new constitutional convention provided for in Article V is more difficult procedurally per se. It is avoided, perhaps, because it is relatively easy. More likely, of course, as it has often been said, it is the danger of wholesale revision which prohibits the use of this potentially revolutionary option.

[33] It is logically possible, but politically unlikely that one could change the essence of a constitution through a single amendment. *See, e.g.*, CARL SCHMITT, *supra* note 26, at 102-06. Schmitt sought to portray such a change as invalid and even impossible, but it is not entirely clear in what sense. One of his examples, the "impossibility" to simply amend the power to amend itself, is an interesting example for his thesis. *Id.* at 103. Nevertheless, even changing the power to amend might make a democratic constitution more, rather than less, consistent internally—in Schmitt's own terms, more consistent with its own spirit—especially if the original draft incorporated fundamental inconsistencies. Technically, of course, one can change the power to amend without a revolution.

in the political culture, and even movements, but not to constitutional revision), have provided links between extraordinary levels of public involvement and commitment and constitutional politics, in a broader sense than simply revising the written constitution would have done. Moreover, since the Constitution itself has not successfully institutionalized both the normal and radical democratic tracks in our political life, extraordinary politics has repeatedly established links to normal political processes as well.

Does this speak for a continuum between extraordinary and ordinary, between constitutional and normal politics? Perhaps. But this may be because our channels for extraordinary politics are not only relatively closed on the constitutional level, but also because even in the United States this level is insufficiently distinguished from the politics of established legislatures. There is, nevertheless, a strong case to be made for the assumption that constitutional politics and, in the fullest sense, public politics, have great potential affinity. The trouble is that where the link is not now well-established, it is difficult to foresee the use of existing procedures of constitutional revision to produce a fundamental shift toward the institutionalization of dualistic politics. Legislatures are generally reluctant to give up even minor powers, and the power to amend constitutions is clearly a major power. Except in revolutions, the amendment process itself may be the most difficult to amend.[34]

II. Constitution Making in Eastern Europe

Here lies the link between the theory presented so far and the "revolutions" in East Central Europe: Not only does 1989 represent a year of extraordinary democratic, and in some sense revolutionary, politics, but it is also a year that begins a new epoch of constitution making. The need to make new constitutions should once again raise the question of how the new or renewed meaning of public life could be incorporated in fundamental law.

It certainly lies within the power of the new constitution-makers to institutionalize a future dualistic politics in which constitutional politics would carry a democratic surplus. Much depends in this context not only on the nature of the proposed drafts, but also on the self-understanding of current constitution-makers. Both are burdened by ambiguities. The leading ideas of the day—"restoration" and "imitation"—certainly do not point to innovative forms of democratic constitutionalism. At the same time, however, all current constitution-

---

[34] Again, for political reasons, and not for legal ones, as Schmitt seems to imply!

makers face a special need: to increase the reserves of democratic legitimacy. Mere imitation of institutional frameworks elsewhere is hard to raise to the level of a norm, especially when these have already shown their negative sides, as well as their inflexibility in the face of novel historical challenges. The imitation of liberal institutions seems especially difficult in strongly democratizing contexts, where the idea of democratic revolution has become fully conscious for the first time, and where citizens are ill-prepared to forget their needs and interests. At the same time, restoration is an inherently divisive and unstable goal in complex societies which have, to put it mildly, complex histories. In fact, only in some uniquely fortunate modern historical constellations could a deficit of democratic legitimacy be compensated for by a species of traditional legitimation, based on both the traditionalization of the present and a relatively unproblematic relationship with the past. Therefore, I maintain that democratic constitutionalism, as I have presented it here, represents one way to redress the emergent legitimation problems of the new democracies.[35] Its key assumption is that the state's power will be limited through the distinction of *constituant* and *constitué*, institutionalized in the constitution itself as a democratic power to revise and amend.

Even if we disregard competing ideologies and visions of constitutionalism, there are formidable difficulties intrinsic to the project that are exacerbated in the peculiar Eastern European "revolutions," that are, among other things, "revolutions against the Revolution." I see four great problem areas: the relationship between the power to make new constitutions and the old constitutions themselves; the identity of the constitution-making body; the presence of elements of the future normal politics in current constitutional politics; and finally, the difficulty of establishing the spirit and logic of present constitutional politics as embodied in the new constitution, in the future *pouvoir constitué*.

---

[35] I am not proposing that imitation and tradition be abandoned. There is much that is worth imitating in the West, and specific national histories can be critically affirmed. I stay within the Weberian theory to the extent that I believe that an empirical framework of legitimation will inevitably be a composite. *See, e.g.*, 1 MAX WEBER, ECONOMY AND SOCIETY (Guenther Roth & Claus Wittich trans., 1978). But I do believe that a legitimation complex needs to have a core of principles, which, given the Eastern European struggle for the liberation and democratization of civil society (as well as independent normative considerations) point to a combination of liberal and democratic constitutionalism. This Article focuses only on the democratic dimension of this project.

A.   *The Old* Constitué *in the* Constituant

Constitution-makers in Europe have good reason to fear the revival of the old idea of *le pouvoir constituant*. In Carl Schmitt's version for example, this idea involves democracy by way of affective identification with leaders or elites, as well as a dark and potentially violent reservation in the face of all duly-constituted authority.[36] Even Hannah Arendt's transmutation of the principle into that of public freedom did not dispose of all doubt, since it depended on a historically unique example of the inherited constituted bodies of American political society that anticipated the new principle and could therefore be integrated easily into the new constitutional order.[37] To be sure, confronting old regimes far less attractive than the one faced by Sieyès, the Eastern European constitution-makers, conscious of history, had all the more reason to fear the temptation to adopt his notion that the constituent power is in the state of nature. As Arendt showed, this idea was logically connected to a claim of plenitude of powers by subsequent constituent assemblies and the logic of permanent revolution. The Eastern Europeans of 1989, however, faced a new situation. At a time when the military forces in the hands of the old regime were intact, the slogan of Sieyès, with its concommitant implication that all power must belong to a new constituent assembly, would have been a call for civil war. The "gentle" and "legal" revolutionaries had equally good normative as well as strategic reasons to avoid this road, since they explicitly rejected the Jacobin-Bolshevik tradition of the revolution to which it always led.

It was, however, difficult to reject revolutionary legitimacy while accomplishing a revolution. As Preuss has shown in several works, the circle was squared by tentatively postulating the legitimacy of the old constitution, and by using its method of amendment to produce a new one.[38] Thus the Eastern European participants in the various Round Tables sought to avoid even a temporarily lawless state, by postulating constitutional continuity with the old regimes, and leaving legislative and executive power, whatever their actual value, in old hands throughout the transition.[39] Thus, in Poland, Hungary, Bulgaria, and the German Democratic Republic, the democratic opposi-

---

[36] *See* SCHMITT, *supra* note 26.

[37] *See* ARENDT, *supra* note 1.

[38] *See* sources cited *supra* note 4.

[39] Even the legislatures in Poland and Hungary, and the constitutional assemblies in Bulgaria and Romania, which were subsequently freely elected, maintained a procedural continuity with the old order, symbolized especially by the procedure of amendment. In the Czech and Slovak Republic, a difficult case due to the problem of federalism, the utilization of the old procedure, and the old constitution led to constitutional impasse.

tions sought to carry out "legal" and "constitutional" revolutions.[40]

But utilization of the old constitutions was based on a *double fiction*. The old written constitutions were mere fictions in Soviet-type societies. They were forms of window-dressing on an unwritten constitution in which the Communist party was the only sovereign, and its various organs the actual possessors of power. At the first real use of the old, formal constitutions, a break occurred in the actual structure of constitutionality. In some countries, though not in all of them, the moment of the break can actually be dated. In the German Democratic Republic, the government formed under the "old" constitution was effectively a provisional government. In Hungary and Poland, on the other hand, the old regimes began to take reluctant measures toward constitutionalism before any negotiations. That is, they began to turn their paper constitutions into real ones (in some respects, therefore, actually attempting to make them less liberal!). So the actual moment of the break is difficult to establish.

It is useful to keep Carl Schmitt's key thesis in mind: Whatever the formal limits of the amendment process, its procedures cannot be used, either for logical or fundamental political reasons, to amend a constitution out of existence, or to create a new one.[41] If this proves possible, it will only be because the old constitution is already *politically* dead. Following the amendment procedure so extensively in this case seems itself to be fictional, in other words so much play-acting, which may have a social-psychological motivation, but certainly has no legal justification.[42] In this context, the first use of the amendment procedure to introduce or eliminate any key provision in fundamental

---

[40] The idea of legal and constitutional revolution is, of course, far more paradoxical than those of "gentle" and even "negotiated" as the Czech and Slovak example, a far more classical revolution than the others, shows. Gentle, that is, non-violent, can mean simply that the other side, in this case suddenly minus Soviet military support, was suddenly unable to fight a rapid change of power. Negotiated in this case meant not that immense and one-sided pressure was not used, but only that two unequal sides used negotiation to disengage without violence which they rejected for very different reasons. Neither term represents a break with the revolutionary idea of rupture, even if in the Czechoslovak case the empty forms of legality were adhered to. Parliamentary deliberations operated under tremendous outside pressure and, unlike the German Democratic Republic, actual extra-constitutional interference (packing of the parliament). Legal or constitutional revolution meant, above all in Poland and Hungary, that the old legal forms and procedures were to an extent allowed to operate under their own logic, producing some consequences unintended by the main parties in the negotiations. To be sure the terms "negotiated and non-violent" are generally implied by the terms "legal and constitutional." The opposite is not true.

[41] SCHMITT, *supra* note 26, at 102.

[42] In a note that reveals a contemptuous attitude for the actual (rather than ideal) German people, "whose desire for legal appearances is stronger than its political sense," Schmitt asserts that this people might more readily accept the restoration of the hereditary monarchy of the Hohenzollerns, and the implied abrogation of the Weimar Constitution, if this was done by a

contradiction with the spirit of Communist "constitutionalism" would signify a constitutional break merely disguised by procedural continuity.

Fictions may have important consequences, however, which can be both positive and negative. In the Polish and Hungarian examples, the semblance of constitutional continuity provided for a transition within unchallenged rules that allowed both sides to agree upon the terms that would vastly diminish (in Poland), or largely eliminate (in Hungary), the powers of one of them. In each case, the transitions were possible only if the losing side did not have to fear revolutionary justice and revolutionary populism. The constitutional transition provided a genuinely legal model of justice and a semantics of self-limitation which worked for both sides. Not only the losers gained in this process; as they knew from the history of revolutions, the winners too, indeed the whole society, had good reason to fear the triumph of a revolutionary logic.

To some extent, the determined use of constitutional fictions turned precepts into legal realities.[43] In order to accomplish their goals, the Round Tables had to presume and work under the double constitutional reality of Soviet-type societies, and so could not entrust the fate of the agreements to the good will of fundamentally Communist parliaments. (It was assumed from the outset that the Communist Party would obtain a two-thirds majority of parliamentary votes more or less in the old way.) At least in Hungary, the insistence on a constitutional fiction made the outcomes far less predictable than they would have been under the old "dual" system, and less predictible than the majority of the Round Table participants would have liked. In this way, the utilization of the old procedures became less fictional: The formal political game was suddenly played for real. Thus the

---

constitutional amendment pursuant to Article 76 of the Weimar Constitution. SCHMITT, *supra* note 26, at 104. He turned out to be more or less right, unfortunately.

[43] The highly important Zétényi-Takács law, decided by the Constitutional Court of the Hungarian Republic on March 3, 1992, Alkotmánybíróság (manuscript version, on file with author), which declared the unconstitutionality of an act of parliament seeking to bypass an already expired statute of limitations and to pursue retroactive justice, is the best example of the legal fiction of continuity turning into legal reality. The court defined the very meaning and normative force of the Hungarian change of systems from the legal point of view by the state of affairs that "the Constitution and the organic laws that introduced revolutionary changes from the political point of view were established through adhering to the rules of the earlier legal order with regard to law making, in a formally unimpeachable manner." Manuscript at 6. This argument is deeply connected to the Eastern European idea of a self-limiting revolution. The justification for turning fictions into realities lies in the single sentence: "[O]ne cannot establish a state resting on the rule of law in spite of the rule of law." Manuscript at 7. Thus if we seek to establish the rule of law we must act *as if* we were already operating under it.

Hungarian opposition-within-the-opposition was able to use a recently-enacted law on referenda, which had been passed by the last Kadarist parliament in February, 1989, to amend the constitution beyond the scope of the Round Table agreements,[44] while this old parliament used its prerogatives to alter some of the same agreements as well.[45]

Finally, and most significantly in the present context, the fiction of continuity came to imply that nowhere, not even in Hungary, were all important features of the inherited constitutions actually changed. All the constitutions that were presidential remained so. In Hungary, the existing parliamentary system proved stronger than attempts to introduce a presidential system. Only in Poland, where the presidency was strengthened and a new chamber of parliament was introduced as a trade-off, was there an exception to the trend. Equally important, and in my view, unfortunate, the old status of parliaments (if merely formal) as quasi-constitutive assemblies, was maintained in most of these countries by preserving the old method of constitutional amendment.[46] This fact seems to confirm Schmitt's claim that it would be highly implausible to use the method of amendment to essentially alter the amendment procedure itself.[47] If using the existing procedure to replace the constitution only disguises a very real break, the survival of the procedure points to the incompleteness of this break in a fundamental area, which helps produce a form of parliamentary sovereignty rather than democratic constitutionalism.

---

[44] Referenda, mentioned in the 1972 Constitution, and legally regulated by Act XI of 1987, art. 3.E ("a referendum shall be regulated by an Act of Parliament"), became a method of constitutional amendment, probably through oversight.

[45] The conversion of fictions into operative law could have legally absurd consequences where the legal provisions were haphazardly put together. The most obvious instance was the fate of a directly elected presidency. This *constitutional* provision (in my view potentially authoritarian) was agreed to by the National Round Table; passed by two-thirds of the old parliament; narrowly defeated in the Referendum of the Four Yeses of November 1989; and passed by the old parliament once again, a decision whose validity was upheld by the constitutional court. After free elections the law was given up in an agreement between the two largest, now opposing, parties, and replaced by parliament by two-thirds vote by the parliamentary election of the president. Finally, an attempt to restore direct presidential elections (in spite of the majority of votes) failed in a referendum because voting fell far below the required 50 percent.

[46] The Czech and Slovak Republic is only an apparent exception to this rule because of its move to a more genuine federalism. Even there the procedure of constitution making seems to involve a surviving, strongly federalist amendment rule from the Constitution of 1968, which was never before used. It turned out to be unusable, with very negative consequences. The actual exception is Poland, whose Round Table established a bicameral parliament for the first time.

[47] SCHMITT, *supra* note 26, at 103.

B.   *The Identity of the* Constituent

In Ulrich Preuss's presentation,[48] the use of the old constitutional rules to frame the transition blocked the emergence of the classical *pouvoir constituant* of European revolutions, along with its political embodiment, the sovereign constituent assembly. According to Preuss, the *pouvoir constituant* was replaced by civil society as the key system of reference of the constitution-making process. Here was a second answer of the Eastern Europeans to Sieyès: Constitution making need not remain in "the state of nature" during the transition, not only because it assumes the constitutional rules of the previous system, but also because it refers for validation to the organized groups, bodies, and institutions of civil society, and not to the unified, unstructured people as a whole. In this depiction, civil society somehow becomes the stand-in for the *pouvoir constituant*, and the alternative framework to a unitary sovereignty.

There are two ways to interpret Preuss's claim, as it pertains to the Eastern European experience. On the one side, a stronger version of the argument refers to the Round Tables that refused the status of a constituent assembly, and where a plurality of participants acted not according to the logic of power, but as befits the undistorted discursive processes possible in civil society. Preuss's own experience with the Central Round Table of the former German Democratic Republic[49] represents the empirical background for this version.

In a more plausible, weaker version, civil society would not be seen as a substitute for both the *pouvoir constituant* and the constituent assembly. Rather, concern for civil society, which may exist only in a rather undeveloped form, leads only to the renunciation of the model of a unified, unlimited, sovereign constitution-making power. In theory this merely negative determination would also leave the door open for participation by groups within a civil society in a major constitution-making forum, such as occurred in the former German Democratic Republic. However, it may also lead, and in Hungary did lead, to a pluralization (fragmentation?) of the constituent process, with each group acting within the limits of existing law. This meant that a bewildering array of groups and ideologies could and did play a role in the constituent process: the National Round Table; the old parliament; the Referendum of the Four Yeses of November 1989 (which determined the manner of electing the president, and required the Communist party to disband the militia, account for its property,

---

[48] Ulrich K. Preuss, *Constitutional Powermaking for the New Polity: Some Deliberations on the Relations Between Constituent Power and the Constitution*, *supra* p. 143.

[49] Preuss, Round Table, *supra* note 4.

and leave the workplace); the negotiators of the two leading parties following the free election (the Hungrian Democratic Forum and the Alliance of Free Democrats); the new parliament; and last, but certainly not least, the Constitutional Court.

Both options had their drawbacks. The presence in the German Democratic Republic of many equal partners probably reduced the political weight of the few organizations with popular and growing followings. In the end no one was in a position to fight for the acceptance of the constitution thus formulated.[50] The constitution-makers, in their refusal to act strategically, were defenseless against those groups that were willing to do so. Breaking their self-limitation and accepting governmental responsibility further weakened the groups of civil society which were represented at the Round Table.

In Hungary, the renunciation of a classical constituent power and constituent assembly[51] empowered an incipient pluralistic, but political rather than civil, society. Two opposition political organizations were dominant from the beginning of the National Round Table, and there was little problem with enacting most of what they agreed upon, especially given the simple parliamentary process of amendment carried over from the Communist constitution. On the other hand, the two most important stages of constitution making, embodied in the agreements of the National Round Table in September 1989, and the Hungarian Democratic Forum-Alliance of Free Democrats pact in April 1990, smacked of exclusionary elite compromise. This was corrected in the first case by the Referendum of November 1989, which became, under the provisions of existing law, another constitution-making, rather than-ratifying, instance. The plurality of constitution-making bodies, as well as of the political forces that played the most important role may have represented some, but only some, of the plurality of a slowly institutionalized civil society. From a legal point of view, however, this type of process led at the same time to important inconsistencies of formulation, weakening the coherence and identity-forming power of the constitution. This had the unfortunate consequence of putting the appropriately

---

[50] It is another matter that by the time the constitution was formulated, the issue of unification vastly overshadowed that of constitution making. As Preuss argues, even in the context of the drive for unity there were good reasons to formulate a constitution for the former German Democratic Republic. Those interested, the makers of the revolution, did not have the power to push through such a constitution, and the procedures of the Round Table, which were otherwise attractive, were partially responsible. Of course, the March 1990 election decided the issue. Its outcome also shows, however, that the dissidents went too far in an antipolitical direction, and not far enough in involving a nascent political society in the process of fighting for and making a constitution.

[51] The latter was actually considered and discussed in late 1988 and early 1989.

strong Constitutional Court and later processes of judicial review in difficult positions. Given the context of a patchwork constitutional document that nevertheless does amount to a minimum basis of a liberal constitutionalism, the court inevitably becomes overactive, and, in the view of a number of people, perhaps overly creative and political.[52] No matter how it is justified, a high level of court activism on behalf of rights becomes precarious when the constitution has insufficient democratic legitimacy. Today, after a feverish period of constitution making, the demand for a new constitution is once again heard in Hungary.

In summary, although the break with a unified constituent power, establishment of the role of constitution-making groups other than sitting parliaments, and involvement in the process of unconstrained, extended public discussion are all important, the establishment of a public body relying on open, discursive processes of interaction, which has no strategic capabilities as the central constitution-making forum, and a process which altogether bypasses a central body, both represent difficult, and perhaps, counter-productive, institutionalizations of these desiderata.[53]

To be sure, in most countries there has been a return to parliamentary constitution making. While there are structural differences (division of labor, house-rules, length of tenure) between the constituent assemblies and regularly elected parliaments, they are alike in one respect: They combine constitutional and policy interests, constituent and legislative powers. As these parliaments are deeply involved in the processes and conflicts of ordinary politics, and are in the position to tailor constitutional requirements to party political needs which emerge after the first election, it is indeed an open question whether such bodies can generate democratic legitimacy for the constitutions

---

[52] I do not include myself in that group. For an examination of this viewpoint, see the debate between B.T. [Tamàs Bauer], *A bölcsek tanácsa*, BESZÉLŐ, May 4, 1991, at 11, Gábor Halmai, *Parlamentarizmus kontra alkotmányosság*, BESZÉLŐ, May 11, 1991, at 36, András Arató, *A bölcsek tancsa védelmében*, BESZÉLŐ, May 18, 1991, at 40, Gáspár Miklós Tamás, *Birói jogalkotás és parlamenti mindenhatóság*, BESZÉLŐ, May 25, 1991, at 37 and András Sajó, *Alkotmánybiróság a fürdökádban*, BESZÉLŐ, May 25, 1991, at 38.

[53] Nevertheless I do not share the view of those in Hungary who today maintain that the cleanest solution would have been the establishment of a constituent assembly in 1989, instead of the Round Table negotiations. At that time, this would have implied both a revolutionary posing of the question of power that the Hungarian population clearly did not want as well as the possible concentration of all power in the hands of the constituent. Even if less likely, the calling of a constituent council today, while procedurally legitimate executive and legislative powers continue to operate, would be a far better solution. To be sure, new decision rules would be needed regarding the ratification of the constitution. These might involve the new council and the parliament as well as forms of popular participation.

they produce.[54] What is wrong with all of them is that they incorporate too many of the interests of an already-constituted future politics in the politics of constitution making.

C. *The New* Constitué *in the* Constituant

While participants in the Hungarian and German Democratic Republic Round Tables were obsessed by their lack of legitimacy,[55] the Polish participants were unconcerned with this problem.[56] Unlike the small groups in Hungary and the German Democratic Republic, Solidarity had a charismatic central figure and nationally known leaders, was the largest popular movement in Polish society, and was able to draw on vast reserves of more or less active social support as a result of its ten-year struggle. The problem, however, was that the negotiating partner possessed sovereign power, but no legitimacy. As all dualistic proposals—from Michnik's *New Evolutionism*[57] to Kis's *Social Contract*[58]—assumed a historic compromise with Communist power had to be legitimated in part by a merely negative legitimacy: This is the best we can do, given the geo-political setting.

As a result of the dramatically changed circumstances just one year later, this negative legitimacy disappeared, opening up a serious legitimation deficit for the previous agreement. In the end, the circumstances of a bargain between old and new elites (in which, as it turned out, mostly useless things were conceded to the Communists),

---

[54] A case in point is the Bulgarian Constitution passed in July, 1991, a document which seems acceptable in terms of its content to many members of the opposition who reject it because of its origins. James Madison's advice, offered in THE FEDERALIST No. 40, which was to overlook the origins and focus on the constitution itself, is apparently not easy to follow. Granted, the argument used by the opposition is that there was still a Communist majority in the parliament. Since this was the result of a free election, the argument is not a particularly convincing one. It seems that everyone notices the danger of parliamentary majoritarianism when someone else is in the majority. The trick would be to take the next logical step.

[55] András Bozóky, Hungary's Road to Systemic Change: The Opposition Roundtable (June 1991) (unpublished manuscript, on file with author); Preuss, Round Table, *supra* note 4.

[56] It was striking that as late as June 1990, unlike their Hungarian colleagues, the Polish participants in an American Council of Learned Societies conference on Comparative Constitutionalism in Pécs, Hungary still laughed at the suggestion that their round table had any legitimation problem whatsoever. By this time however, the new group around Walesa had already made the charge of a red-pink bargain. This opened up a legitimation problem for the Mazoviecki government more clearly than the loss of support for economic reasons. The point however is not that Solidarity lacked legitimacy at the time of the agreements. At that time, as the elections showed, Solidarity still maintained overwhelming support as the representative of society, based not on votes but on the history of the 1980s.

[57] ADAM MICHNIK, *New Evolutionism*, *in* LETTERS FROM PRISON AND OTHER ESSAYS 135 (1980).

[58] János Kis et al., *Társadalmi Szerződés*, BESZÉLÖ, June 1987 (Special Issue).

clearly helped to erode the very real social support of the first post-Communist government in Poland.

The lack of legitimacy on all sides, of government and opposition, of Round Table and Parliament, was clearly debated at the Hungarian Round Table. But the first response—that no legitimacy was needed—only sufficed so long as the Round Table and the parliamentary acts based upon it could be restricted to a democratic minimum needed for regulating the transition. When even this minimum came to imply the full-scale rewriting of the constitution, this position collapsed. What other legitimating options were available?

1.   *Revolutionary Legitimacy*

All the Round Tables, even the one-sided Czechoslovakian affair, renounced revolutionary legitimacy, which would have involved a claim of complete identity with the people in whose name and *future* interest a total rupture with the *past* would have been announced. This option, equivalent to a claim of fully sovereign constituent power was unacceptable in "revolutions against the Revolution."

2.   *Electoral Legitimacy*

The Hungarian Round Table claimed a potential retroactive democratic legitimacy. If, as the argument went, the population voted under the new electoral rules within the new procedural framework, this would legitimate the agreements after the fact. Such a tacit form of democratic legitimation (and one on which all democratic normal politics relies), is very doubtful in the case of constitution making. With the partial and indirect exception of the important Referendum of 1989, the electorate was not asked to vote on the new constitution, but to vote under it or to stay politically passive. Under such conditions, the low level of participation in the first year of free elections in Hungary had to have negative consequences for the legitimacy of the system.

3.   *Discursive Legitimacy*

The Round Table of the former German Democratic Republic, like its Hungarian forerunner, claimed neither revolutionary nor any other form of strictly political legitimacy; it passed no decrees nor otherwise formally exercised political power. The new elites relied instead on their power of persuasion in the reconstructed public sphere, a "power" rooted in the superiority of a powerless morality over an immoral power.[59] Unlike its Hungarian counterpart, the former German Democratic Republic Round Table sought to produce a new constitution from the outset, by a method that would partially break with the Communist as well as West German models of constitution making, by requiring not only a two-thirds majority of the *Volkskammer*, but a popular-plebiscitary ratification of the document as well.[60] Thus the actors sought to derive the legitimacy of the constitution from a combination of two democratic methods: a process of communication free of domination among elites; and plebiscitary, direct democratic ratification involving the rest of the population. Only the first of these could be tried, of course, and it produced mixed results. The Habermasian discourse model may have, for a while, generated legitimacy for the deliberations, but apparently did not provide a feasible alternative to a process of constitution making in which strategic considerations could play a relevant role. The model was apparently best suited to the negative strategy of blocking undesirable policy rather than generating something positive. Moreover, it was extremely vulnerable to the acts of those who acted by strategic rules—the old ruling party and the new partners of the Federal Republic of Germany parties. It seems that a convincing model for the generation of legitimacy was attained at the cost of all strategic efficacy. By the time a constitution was actually generated, the groups that could have creatively utilized it under the new, and admittedly very difficult, circumstances were politically powerless.

4. *Veil of Ignorance*

To the extent that constitution making must involve participants capable of taking strategic action and making decisions that can be enforced, and participants of political, and not merely civil, society, the primary body can only involve a public sphere with significant formal, material, and temporal limits. It is for this reason that a Rawlsian veil of ignorance, rather than a model of undistorted communication, seems to be the best source of the claim that political society can make for the legitimacy of its constituent activity. While no participants clearly raised this requirement, the Round Tables sought to portray their activities as if they operated under a modified veil of ignorance resembling Rawls's constitutional convention, rather

---

59 *See* Preuss, Round Table, *supra* note 4. Revelations concerning the self-aggrandizement of leading figures represented an important turning point in the German Democratic Republic, where previously there had been little cynical insight into the corruption of the ruling elite.

60 Die Verfassung der DDR [Constitution] [Verf] art. 135 (G.D.R.).

than than his original position.[61] Since the model involves primarily a *virtual* and not actual process of coming to an agreement, it can be tested first and foremost by the results of constitution making, by the successful institutionalization into a new set of procedures of the first principle of justice: in essence liberal rights under the particular conditions of a given society, with a specific history and with specific endowments. But the admitted difficulty of deriving a determinate result from such a limiting condition of a just constitution,[62] and even more, the further variability resulting from adding (which Rawls does not) the procedures of the democratic operation of power, makes the legitimation of a constitutional document through its contents alone unconvincing. Eventually, perhaps traditionalization of the text could supply what is missing. In the beginning, however, the process of constitution making that led to some choices rather than others itself had to be justified. Inevitably, then, aspects of the idea of the veil of ignorance came to be applied to the *actual* constitution-making procedure itself. This could not, of course, mean that the participants could ever be strictly Rawlsian—entirely ignorant about the conditions of particular individuals, including themselves. But they were forced to argue as if they were, excluding arguments in terms of self-interest in favor of others based on principles.[63] Such rules of discourse inevitably affect the result. Compromise and bargaining were naturally admitted, but only around divergences of opinion and not explicitly articulated interest. It helped that the parties to the various Eastern European round tables were not linked to clearly identifiable social constituencies representing specific interests, but were rather representative of diverse political philosophies. Even their specific interests as parties were less suspect to the extent that there was good reason to believe that the participants could be seriously mistaken concerning them. In the case of the Hungarian debate about electoral rules, each party clearly sought to institutionalize what it imagined was its particular interest. The fact that they were actually and obviously ignorant concerning outcomes of such rules[64] made the result-

---

61 JOHN RAWLS, THEORY OF JUSTICE 195-96 (1971). According to Rawls, this version of the veil of ignorance allows the knowledge of the principles of justice and of social theory, and also the facts of the given society, and of the existence therein of diverging political views. The constitution-makers are to remain in doubt only about their personal economic and social situation.

62 *Id.* at 200-01.

63 Jon Elster, *Constitutionalism in Eastern Europe: An Introduction*, 58 U. CHI. L. REV. 447 (1991).

64 Three out of the six major parties were clearly wrong about which electoral system favored them; the two most bitter antagonists, the Free Democrats and the Communists, each favored individual mandates which turned out to favor neither.

ing compromise still fit, if only barely, under the veil of ignorance. Indeed, the best democratic arguments could be marshalled behind a mixed system of proportional representation and individual mandates, combining both a relatively accurate representation of the voters' wishes with the responsibility individual representatives owe to their constituencies.[65]What immediately became illegitimate was a form of agreement based on the linking of anticipatory knowledge with the power capable of bringing about results in line with particular interests. When the veil of ignorance was lifted, when an agreement was made which clearly indicated specific winners and losers, as in the case of the presumed deal between the conservative parties and the Communists concerning the presidency, it was possible to delegitimate and defeat the outcome. The argument concerning the veil of ignorance indicates only the minimum conditions for a process of legitimation, a threshold beyond which the penetration of the constituent process by probable future political constellations of interests cannot go. Constitution making by working parliaments that enact fundamental law by qualified majorities alone will not be able to stay within even this threshold. At the same time, I do not believe that the minimum conditions, indicated by the idea of a veil of ignorance, will suffice to legitimate constitutions and constitutionalism in the turbulent period to come. In Hungary, too, the relinking of major dissident groups with a wider public during the intense discussion around the petition campaign and referendum concerning the presidency played a major role in producing at least some democratic legitimacy for the new constitution beyond the minimum generated by the procedures of the Round Table. If the public was not allowed to consequentially discuss and the electorate was barred from voting on the whole constitutional draft, at least discussion, debate, and voting could take place regarding its truly controversial parts. Paradoxically, the Round Table agreements vastly benefitted from a campaign that partially reversed them.

As I have argued, the central constitution-making body can only be held to minimum requirements of legitimacy, and can produce, at best, and as Rawls understood, a liberal version of constitutionalism. In order to generate greater democratic legitimacy, the constitution-making process must include other processes, involve other instances that can bring in the discursively open public spaces of civil society. While provisional constitutions will suffice to guide the work of the

---

65 One could say, of course, that such a system would increase the mandates of the largest parties, and eliminate those of the smallest. Yet no party could know for sure which they would be, and indeed two signers of the accords failed to make the four percent threshold.

transition, constitutions worth keeping for a long time should not be produced without lengthy and organized public discussion before both drafting and final ratification. To be sure, the pluralism of the process should not fragment the process of decision as it did in Hungary. To avoid this result, the various groups should not have parallel constitution-making *power*, and a unified procedural decision-making mechanism (which could include more than one group or body) must be achieved. But there is no reason to limit in time and content the enlightened *influence* of concerned publics and organized or associated constituencies that are deeply concerned. Only such a discussion can counteract the self-defeating hubris of the legislature or even a constituent assembly, to be the sole source of law.

D.   *The* Constituant *in the* Constitué

Finally, I return to my original question concerning whether democratic constitutionalism or dualistic politics may be able to incorporate some of the political spirit of the remarkable transitions in settled constitutions. Considering today's Hungarian politics, it remains a mistake to confine, as did Ackerman, the idea of extraordinary public politics to the constitutional track, or even to confine constitutional politics to the amendment process. The current battle for the freedom of the press and media in Hungary pits the organizations of civil society against the government, and at issue are both rules of normal and constitutional politics. All the same, much civil courage is demanded on the side of journalists and their supporters. The defense of the presidency and of the Constitutional Court against parts of the ruling coalition do involve constitutional politics, but this defense must take place even if new constitutional provisions defining their roles of these public law institutions cannot now be produced.

Nevertheless, while extraordinary politics of public involvement can occur on various levels, the politics of constitution creation and revision has a greater affinity with this politics than any other. While the legitimacy of normal politics today can be attained through a mere defense of rights, constitutional politics cannot produce legitimate constitutions without genuine public discussion. If all politics have elements of the normal and the extraordinary, the center of gravity of constitutional politics alone lies decisively on the side of extraordinary public involvement. And, of all possible forms of constitutional politics, the processes of constitution making and amending are privileged in this context; the former can institutionalize (rather than merely occasion) extraordinary politics as a long term possibility, while the latter in some of its forms is just this politics institutionalized.

CONCLUSION

In conclusion, then, I would like to examine the fate of the amendment process in the few new Eastern European constitutions or constitutional drafts which are available to me. I note the following models:

A. *Democratic Constitutionalist*

As I understand it, the Bulgarian draft retains a complicated version of the two-thirds rule for its own ratification as well as for subsequent revisions.[66] However, it makes important constitutional revisions the task of a grand national assembly elected specifically for that purpose. The document thus makes an important contribution to the theory and practice of democratic constitutionalism.

B. *Monistic Parliamentarian*

As far as I can tell, the Polish law on constitution making and amending remains a two-thirds rule invested in the lower house of parliament.[67] Such a constitution entirely dispenses with democratic constitutionalism, and indeed makes liberal constitutionalism the hostage of contingent electoral outcomes. In Poland, the upper house has no constitution-making prerogative, although it, too, drew up a draft constitution.

C. *Antinomic (Parliamentary vs. Plebiscitary)*

The Hungarian Constitution as revised in 1989 and 1990 contains the two-thirds rule for constitutional revision as well as altering laws which are linked to constitutional provisions, such as fundamental rights.[68] At the same time, referenda, as defined by Act XVII of February 1989 (which itself can only be changed by a two-thirds

---

[66] Constitution of the Republic of Bulgaria arts. 153-163 (draft 1991).

[67] This information is according to Zbigniew A. Pelczynski, who was one of two foreign advisors to the Constitutional Committee of Seym, the Polish committee of the lower house. Jon Elster, relying on the account of the other foreign advisor, Andrezj Rapaczynski, writing in Jon Elster, *Constitutional Politics in Poland: A Report on the Constitutional Committee of the Polish Parliament*, 58 U. CHI. L. REV. 595, 605 n.19 (1991) [hereinafter Elster, *Poland*], asserts that two-thirds of both houses plus a non-binding referendum would be needed to pass a new constitution according to a law of "fall 1990." *See* Elster, *supra* note 63, at 467. When we spoke after his lecture at the New School in 1991, Pelczynski told me that this was incorrect.

[68] A MAGYAR KÖZTÁRSASÁG ALKETMÁNYA art. 24(3).

vote), are also capable of modifying the constitution entirely on their own. There is no decisional rule which governs conflicts between these alternative procedures, and, unfortunately, in the one contested case, the Constitutional Court allowed parliament to partially reverse a referendum, while later it permitted the calling of yet another referendum, after parliament again changed the rule in question. This state of affairs allows, but does not combine, two monolithic approaches to constitutional revision, each with a built-in potential for dramatic abuse. Under these conditions, it may not be surprising that some members of the Constitutional Court seem to take the position that since some of the fundamental rights in the constitution are defined as inalienable they are therefore enshrined, and that the court has judicial review with respect to constitutional amendments as well as ordinary legislation. The second claim (not supported by constitutional text), representing, in my view, an understandable judicial overreaction on behalf of liberal constitutionalism against the dangers of parliamentary majoritarianism, would probably open the door to constitutional crises in the near future, except for the fact that the present coalition does not have the two-thirds majority needed for amendments.

D. Dualistic 1 (Combining Parliamentary and Plebiscitary)

The proposed constitution of the former German Democratic Republic combined a two-thirds vote in parliament with subsequent plebiscitary ratification.[69] What is clearly missing from even this option are proposals for the organization of enlightened and public participation before a plebiscite is held. As I understand it, Wyktor Osiatinsky raised this latter possibility in Poland as early as 1990, but apparently without success. On the other hand, going far beyond analogous provisions of the *Grundgesetz*, the German Democratic Republic's draft enshrines several constitutional provisions having to do with the defense of human dignity, the validity of fundamental rights, popular sovereignty, constitutionalism, adherence to international law, legislation exclusively through parliament or referendum, and an independent judiciary.[70] These defensive measures of a broadly understood liberal constitutionalism would bring it into conflict with democratic constitutionalism.

---

[69] VERF art. 100(1) (draft). If Rapaczynski and Elster are right, the current Polish law, at least for the ratification of the new constitution, has a similar structure, with the added element of a national assembly composed of the two houses. *See* Elster, *Poland, supra* note 67 (Rapaczynski's account); Elster, *supra* note 63. The *Volkskammer* was unicameral, both in reality and in the constitutional draft.

[70] VERF art. 100(2) (draft).

E. Dualistic 2 (Combining Centralistic and Federal)

Under the Czech and Slovak constitution of 1968, as amended in 1989-90, constitutional revision requires three-fifths of the lower house elected in national proportional voting, and three-fifths of *each* of the Czech and Slovak sections in the federally elected upper house, giving veto power in effect to three-tenths, or thirty-one, of the deputies of the latter house, if the nations vote as blocks.[71] This model obviously combines the centralistic and federal types of democracy, but maintains, nevertheless, a version of the purely parliamentary process of amendment which also makes constitutional revision extremely difficult. Given the state of the current partially amended constitution, this is a very serious problem indeed. While this method offers little hope for democratic revision of the operation of the two legislatures, at least it also makes it difficult for the legislatures to further restrict democracy—an idea not particularly foreign to some Czech and Slovak deputies. Apparently, however, as in Hungary, federally organized referenda can alter the constitution, leading to an antinomic structure as well.

F. Dualistic 3 (Combining Centralistic and Local)

András Sajó, who has been extremely critical of the parliamentary-statist tendencies of Hungarian constitutional revision procedures, has produced a much-discussed draft, in many ways superior to the existing, provisional constitution.[72] He puts the procedure of constitutional revision into the joint hands of the existing national assembly and that of a second chamber, a territorial assembly, which would be elected by the local assemblies of self-government proportionate to their size.[73] Sajó's revision procedure requires a fifty-one percent vote of the national assembly, and, within sixty days following that vote, ratification or proposed modifications to the amendment be returned to the originating house by a two-thirds vote of the members of the territorial assembly. If neither is possible within sixty days, the national assembly can pass the amendment by a two-thirds vote, con-

---

71 *See* Lloyd Cutler & Herman Schwartz, *Constitutional Reform in Czechoslovakia: E Duobus Unum?*, 58 U. CHI. L. REV. 519, 549 (1991). Elster misstates the rule as involving simple majorities in each of the three cases but miraculously comes up with the right number (31 rather than 38!) needed to block. Elster, *supra* note 63, at 461. The draft constitution produced for President Havel only dilutes the blocking power of each national block, but does not alter it. Cutler & Schwartz, *supra*, at 549-50. In any case the fate of this new draft remains highly uncertain given the existing rules of constitution making.

72 András Sajó, Draft for a Constitution of the Hungarian Republic (1990) (unpublished manuscript on file with author).

73 *Id.* at arts. 92, 93(1).

tingent only upon the the Constitutional Court's opinion on the amendment's constitutionality.[74]

In my view, this proposal heads in the right direction, but still has serious flaws. Why limit the discussion by the constituencies of the territorial assembly to sixty days? Why return at all to the possibility that one and the same national assembly amend the constitution by a two-thirds vote? Why include judicial review of constitutional amendments, and on what bases would the court judge the constitutionality of amendments as against ordinary laws? Why not propose some provision for consultation with those most directly concerned, which may or may not be the local communities represented in the new chamber?

These are, of course, frivolous questions addressed to Sajó's entirely private constitutional draft, which does not even try to raise the question of who is to institute the new constitution. Evidently the Hungarian Parliament is neither in the position to produce a two-thirds vote for any constitution, nor would it, at this time, wish to share its powers with any territorial assembly. Actually, however, I take the proposal very seriously and wish there were many more like it. Hungary has both the advantage of a constitution that works to some extent and the disadvantage of a constitution that has internal difficulties which will continue to accumulate over time. Since the present parliament and possibly the next one will be unable to change it, the idea of democratic and pluralistic constitution-making centered in a body other than parliament has a chance of being accepted, if it were at all advocated. But even that body's deliberations will be sufficiently enlightened and receptive to democratic influence and control only if a long period of public discussion will produce the requisite sensibility. Alternative proposals may make important contributions to this end.

---

[74] *Id.* at art. 124.

IV

The Identity of the Constitutional
Subject and the Search for Authoritative
Constitutional Meaning

GERMAN CONSTITUTIONAL CULTURE
IN TRANSITION

Bernhard Schlink

INTRODUCTION

A country's constitutional culture lives through its constitution. It will be free if the constitution is free, democratic if it is democratic, authoritarian if it is authoritarian. Where a constitutional culture does not exist, a constitution that functions as the basis and standard for state and political life is also lacking. There may be a constitutional facade, but behind it, and in reality, the decisive factors are the program and organization of a state party, the familiar intertwining of a governing clan or the alliances and rivalries of a military junta. These party, family, or military structures are not the actual constitution behind the constitutional facade. A constitution, at least in the modern sense, is a legal ordering of state and political life independent of such structures; its independence is the result of the process of social differentiation, the external and internal differentiation of law.

However, a country's constitutional culture does not emerge only from its written or unwritten constitution. Hardly less important is the way in which the constitution is dealt with by legislation and administration, judicial decision making and legal scholarship. How legislation and administration deal with the constitution essentially depends upon the sort of supervision to which they are subjected by judicial decision making. How this supervising adjudication in turn deals with the constitution, how strictly or laxly it interprets its provisions, and in what spirit it applies them essentially depends upon how legal scholarship deals with the constitution and with judicial decision making.

The relationship between judicial decision making and legal scholarship is an important characteristic of the constitutional culture. Of course, legal scholarship also deals with legislation and administration; it advises, warns, praises and blames, states conditions for legislative and administrative behavior, and acknowledges the consequences of such behavior. However, its discourse with judicial decision making is particularly intense. For judicial decision making depends, to a greater extent than legislation and administration, on legal argumentation and discussion. Judicial decision making has a discursive character, and thus a particularly close relationship to the discourse of legal scholarship.

Judicial decision making and legal scholarship also share a particular obligation to law. It is true that legislation and administration are also obligated to law and that, on the other hand, judicial decision making is not free of political considerations similar to those that determine legislation and administration. However, the manifold shaping tasks and opportunities inherent in legislation and administration are more directly, openly political than the supervisory function of judicial decision making, for which the controlling standard is law.

There arise numerous distinctions here, and the amount of acceptance gained by political arguments, political decisions, and a political consciousness in judicial decision making indicates differences between different constitutional cultures. Constitutional judicial decision making is understood and presented more or less politically. Constitutional legal scholarship can also either take a positivist approach and ignore the political, or focus upon political judgment or subordinate or integrate it in positive norms.

The differences between constitutional cultures are expressed in such divergences, and, also, in the various structures of the relationship between constitutional legal scholarship and constitutional judicial decision making. Does constitutional legal scholarship anticipate constitutional judicial decision making, or does it follow after it, compiling and systematizing? Is constitutional legal scholarship critical or uncritical of constitutional judicial decision making? Does it behave as a loyal servant of the constitutional court or challenge the court with new problems? Does it cultivate the discursive context that links it to constitutional judicial decision making as a protected domain, or extend the discussion to a general social discourse?

The relationship between constitutional legal scholarship and decision making does not differ only between countries. It can also develop and change within the same country; and the country's constitutional culture develops and changes with it. One can observe such a development in the constitutional culture in Germany. It can be seen in the way that constitutional legal scholarship and decision making deal with the constitution, and in the relationship between constitutional legal scholarship and constitutional judicial decision making. It is still in process, and its final result remains open.

The development of Germany's constitutional culture is the subject of this Article. Using fundamental rights as an example, the first part discusses how constitutional legal scholarship and constitutional judicial decision making deal with the constitution, with an in-depth analysis of the change from a view of fundamental rights as rights to a view of them as principles. The second part addresses the changing relationship between constitutional jurisprudence and constitutional decision making. Although it is certain that constitutional jurisprudence has lost the dominant position it once held over the constitutional court (Staatsgerichtshof) during the Weimar Republic, as well as the independence that other disciplines of legal scholarship enjoy from their branches of the judiciary, it is not at all clear what relationship constitutional jurisprudence and today's constitutional court, the Bundesverfassungsgericht, will finally develop with one another. It is also unclear whether, and in what way, future constitutional jurisprudence will succeed in conveying to German society the issues and problems of constitutional law and the constitutional court, and at the same time, will bring the issues and problems of German society to constitutional law and the constitutional court. The following discussion will make some conjectures.

I

Before we can describe and analyze the change in the view of fundamental rights as rights to the view of them as principles, we must ask what rights and principles are and what distinguishes them from each other. There are two answers in legal precedent and jurisprudence. On the one hand, we speak of subjective rights in contrast to objective principles,[1] and, on the other hand, of rights as determinations, in contrast to principles as rules of optimization.[2]

The phrase "fundamental rights as subjective rights" means the characterization of fundamental rights as entitlements of the individual subject, the individual citizen, to be respected by the state in his individual freedoms, to participate as an individual in the practice of state power, or to be considered in the distribution of positions, means, and opportunities. On the other hand, when described as "objective principles," fundamental rights are maxims according to which social relationships, as well as the relationship between state and society, are to be ordered.

Freedom of the press and of broadcasting may illustrate the dif-

---

[1] GEORG HERMES, DAS GRUNDRECHT AUF SCHUTZ VON LEBEN UND GESUNDHEIT 110 (1987); Ernst-Wolfgang Böckenförde, *Grundrechte als Grundsatznormen*, 29 STAAT 1 (1990); Hans D. Jarass, *Grundrechte als Wertentscheidungen bzw. objektivrechtliche Prinzipien in der Rechtsprechung des Bundesverfassungsgerichts*, 110 ARCHIV DES ÖFFENTLICHEN RECHTS [AöR] 363 (1985); Arno Scherzberg, *"Objektiver" Grundrechtssatz und subjektives Grundrecht*, 1989 DEUTSCHES VERWALTUNGSBLATT [DVBL] 1128.

[2] ROBERT ALEXY, THEORIE DER GRUNDRECHTE 71-104 (1986); Robert Alexy, *Grundrechte als subjektive Rechte und als objektive Normen*, 29 STAAT 49 (1990).

ference. As a subjective right, freedom of the press guarantees the individual citizen the freedom to print and publish, while freedom of broadcasting guarantees the right to run radio and television stations. As an objective principle, freedom of the press and freedom of broadcasting demand that the legislature regulate publications, radio, and television so as to allow as many citizens as possible to express, or see expressed, their opinions and inclinations, and to satisfy their need for information. In other words, freedom of the press and of broadcasting, as an objective principle, demands a system of press, radio, and television characterized by varied content and diverse supply.[3]

The freedoms of the press and broadcasting can coexist harmoniously as a subjective right and an objective principle. If many make use of their subjective rights, the diversity of content that the principle demands can emerge by itself. However, the subjective right and objective principle can also conflict with one another. For example, diversity of content may only be achievable through the imposition of some limits on individual rights, such as regulation and control of the press and broadcasting markets. This might involve the breaking up of monopolies, the closing off of access to some citizens, the promoting of access to others, and perhaps the use of subsidies.

The other view of the difference between rights and principles differentiates fundamental rights as determinations from fundamental rights as rules of optimization, and thereby juxtaposes a strict and a relative conception of fundamental rights.[4] Viewing fundamental rights as determinations means that the citizen is entitled to have his freedom respected and to participate in the practice of state power and distribution of positions, means, and opportunities, although the entitlement may be denied to him in exceptional cases. The rule is that the citizen is entitled; the exception lies in the denial of the citizen's entitlements. The exception must be expressly admitted and must be particularly justified, as, for example, when one citizen's claim to his fundamental right conflicts with other citizens' claims to their fundamental rights, or when conflicts arise between fundamental rights and state interests and cannot be settled in any other way.

On the other hand, as rules of optimization, fundamental rights from the outset guarantee the citizen entitlements only in accordance with what is legally and actually possible. In this view, because con-

---

3 For examples of this view of broadcasting freedom expressed in Bundesverfassungsgericht opinions, see Judgment of June 16, 1981, BVerfG, 57 Entscheidungen des Bundesverfassungsgerichts [BVerfGE] 295, 322-24; Judgment of Nov. 4, 1986, BVerfG, 73 BVerfGE 118, 152-60.

4 ALEXY, *supra* note 2, at 71-104.

flicts are unavoidable among fundamental rights, as well as between fundamental rights and state interests, the entitlement to a fundamental right does not go beyond its enforcement in the conflict. The degree of enforcement will be more in one conflict, less in another; it is as much as possible and, to the extent possible, the optimum.

This second difference can also be illustrated with an example. Most constitutions, including the German Grundgesetz, guarantee each citizen a fundamental right to his dwelling; that is, the dwelling may not be entered and searched by state organs unless certain prerequisites are fulfilled, ranging from a judge's decree to the existence of certain clearly defined dangers. When the Bundesverfassungsgericht faced the question of whether protection of the right to a dwelling included not only the home but also business premises, it answered positively. At the same time, for practical reasons, it permitted state entry onto business premises under conditions less strict than those for entry into the dwelling as specified in the Grundgesetz.[5]

This view cannot be reconciled with a strict interpretation of the fundamental right to one's dwelling as a determination. If business premises are included in the concept of a dwelling, then, regardless of practical considerations, they may only be intruded upon in exceptional cases under the conditions expressly permitted by the fundamental right to a dwelling. If business premises are not included in the concept of a dwelling, then the fundamental right to a dwelling is not applicable in the business context. The result is different for the relative conception of the right to a dwelling as a rule of optimization. Optimization of the right to a dwelling means the greatest practical degree of protection of the fundamental right—that is, extension of the dwelling to business premises, but at the same time extension no farther than practical considerations permit.[6]

The two methods of characterizing the different conceptions of fundamental rights each employ differing sets of criteria. The rights/principles model uses a subjective/objective pair of criteria, while the determination/rule of optimization model uses a strict/relative pair of criteria. But they are related to each other from a practical point of view. If the interpretation of fundamental rights as objective principles does not completely replace their significance as subjective rights—that is, if room remains within the framework of the objective principle view for the subjective rights meaning of fundamental rights—then a strict interpretation of fundamental rights as determinations fits badly. However, in an objective principle scheme, the rel-

---

5 Judgment of Oct. 18, 1971, BVerfG, 32 BVerfGE 54, 68-77.
6 ALEXY, *supra* note 2, at 115-17, 256.

ative interpretation, as rules of optimization, fits well. By interpreting fundamental rights according to legal and actual possibilities, rules of optimization can determine the degree to which subjective rights are legally possible within the framework of fundamental rights as objective principles. On the other hand, the strict interpretation of fundamental rights as determinations leaves to the objective principle view of fundamental rights only the area left open by expressly permitted, justified exceptions to guarantees of fundamental rights.

This can once more be illustrated using the example of press and broadcasting freedoms. When freedom of the press and of broadcasting demand drastic regulation and control of the press and broadcasting markets as an objective principle in the interest of diverse content, the most that remains to the individual is a certain limited degree of freedom to print and publish and to run radio and television stations. This certain degree is the relative optimum. On the other hand, strictly understood as subjective rights, press and broadcasting freedoms demand that the individual be able to print and publish, and to run radio and television stations, as long as it is not forbidden to him in exceptional cases; the exceptions must be expressly permitted and require special justification. If the constitution, which guarantees the fundamental rights of press and broadcasting freedom, does not allow exceptions with regard to diversity of content of the press, radio, and television markets, the objective principle cannot operate along with the subjective right.

The German Grundgesetz presents this problem in all its severity. Intrusions upon press and broadcasting freedom may be undertaken in exceptional cases only through so-called general laws—general laws being those that are not geared towards content evaluation or the effects of opinions and information from the point of view of content, but towards a more or less opinion and information neutral point of view, such as that of labor law, construction law, traffic law, or penal law.[7] In this scheme, intrusions upon the individual's press and broadcasting freedom in order to produce diversity of content cannot be justified. On the other hand, if press and broadcasting freedoms are guaranteed not as subjective individual rights but as objective principles in the organization of society, then the creation of diversity of content is not an intrusion upon freedoms that requires justification, but is itself a realization of the principle of freedom.

Before I turn to the consequences for the legal order of interpreting and treating fundamental rights as rights and as principles, a fur-

---

[7] On the concept of the general law, see BODO PIEROTH & BERNHARD SCHLINK, GRUNDRECHTE 153-55 (7th ed. 1991), and references included therein.

ther explanation is necessary. When one speaks of fundamental rights as rights, in contrast to fundamental rights as principles, this does not mean that an interpretation of fundamental rights as rights would be possible without considerations of principle. It means that fundamental rights are not *themselves* principles. However, considerations of principle must be recognized in discussing how far protection of a fundamental right can reach and how intrusions in exceptional cases may be justified.

Let us take once again the right to a dwelling as an example. Whether business premises fall under the term "dwelling," and are therefore encompassed by the fundamental right to a dwelling and its protections, is a question that creates issues of principle involving the function of the fundamental right to a dwelling, the relationship between social and spatial privacy, and the separation and categorization of privacy and the public sphere.[8] In the German tradition of public law, whether or not an intrusion is actually permitted upon the fundamental right to a dwelling, whether narrowly or broadly defined, depends not only on the actual existence of the dangers listed in the constitution as conditions for an intrusion, but also on whether the intrusion is necessary and proper to repel the danger. It must be a means related to the ends sought—this principle of proportionality is decisive in the interpretation and treatment of fundamental rights.[9] However, fundamental rights themselves do not need to become principles. They can remain subjective rights in the strict sense.

II

The consequences of interpreting and treating fundamental rights as rights or as principles become clear when one views the development of decision making by the Bundesverfassungsgericht. This development has been from an interpretation of fundamental rights as rights to an interpretation of fundamental rights as principles. Not that fundamental rights have lost their significance as rights; rather, their significance as principles has become increasingly central.[10]

The cases themselves speak of fundamental rights as values and value decisions, as fundamental value-determining norms, objective

---

[8] *See* Ulrich Battis, *Schutz der Gewerberäume durch Art. 13 GG und Wirtschafts-, Arbeits- und Steueraufsicht—BVerfGE 32, 54*, 13 JURISTISCHE SCHULUNG [JuS] 25 (1973); Prodromos Dagtoglou, *Das Grundrecht der Unverletzlichkeit der Wohnung (Art. 13 GG)*, 15 JuS 753 (1975).

[9] *See* PIEROTH & SCHLINK, *supra* note 7, at 70-75; Bernhard Schlink, *Freiheit durch Eingriffsabwehr—Rekonstruktion der klassischen Grundrechtsfunktion*, 11 EUROPÄISCHE GRUNDRECHTE ZEITSCHRIFT [EuGRZ] 457, 459-61 (1984).

[10] Böckenförde, *supra* note 1, at 4-13; Jarass, *supra* note 1, at 367-69.

fundamental norms, objective legal principles and the like. However, the same thing is always meant—the objective principle, as opposed to the subjective right.[11] The Bundesverfassungsgericht does not speak expressly of principles as rules of optimization. However, constitutional scholarship correctly observes that a relative conception of fundamental rights as rules of optimization harmonizes well with the conception of them as objective principles. The concept of principle, or rule of optimization, was coined especially to categorize the content of fundamental rights resulting from the Bundesverfassungsgericht's development from conceiving of fundamental rights as subjective rights to seeing them as objective principles.[12]

Four problems promoted this development. The first was the problem of the relevance of fundamental rights for private law; the problem called the "third-party effect" in Germany. According to the concepts inherited from the Empire and the Weimar Republic, fundamental rights operate on the citizen's relationship to the state. They protect the citizen's freedom against government intrusion, but do not touch the relationship of citizens to one another. According to these inherited views, how citizens deal with one another as lessors and lessees, employers and employees, sellers and buyers is decided by judges under the relevant civil laws without considering fundamental rights. When, in a spectacular case in the 1950s concerning a call for a boycott, an unacceptable result reached through the use of relevant civil laws was brought before the Bundesverfassungsgericht, the Court for the first time turned to a conception of fundamental rights as objective principles.[13] The Court found that because fundamental rights had importance not only as subjective rights of citizens against the state, but also as society's most important values, they governed the entire legal order, including civil laws that regulated the relationship of citizens to each other. The call for a boycott was protected by the fundamental right to expression of opinion, and its prohibition could not be justified under a correct interpretation of the relevant civil laws that took account of the value of the right to free expression of opinion.

---

11 The changing terminology of the Bundesverfassungsgericht is evidenced in Jarass, *supra* note 1, at 367-69; *see also* ALEXY, *supra* note 2, at 33.

12 This concern is clearly expressed in ALEXY, *supra* note 2, at 115-17, where in discussing the Judgment of Oct. 13, 1971, BVerfG, 32 BVerfGE 54, the author shows how the "difficulties" to which a strict understanding of fundamental rights leads "can be avoided by considering their character as principles." *Id.* at 115. "Based on the principle theory, precisely the protection of fundamental rights that the court guarantees in its decisions can be achieved without constructive problems." *Id.* at 117. However, the fact that fundamental rights exist to cause difficulties and problems for state action gets lost here.

13 Judgment of Jan. 15, 1958, BVerfG, 7 BVerfGE 198 (forbidding call for a boycott of films by an infamous Nazi director as being incompatible with civil laws).

The Bundesverfassungsgericht reversed the prohibition of the call for a boycott. Since then, civil laws and the relationship of citizens to one another have been viewed in the light of fundamental rights, defined as objective principles.[14]

The second problem that promoted the development from subjective rights to objective principles was the relevance of fundamental rights to the formation of government institutions and procedures. Here, too, the ideas inherited from the Empire and the Weimar Republic gave little significance to fundamental rights. This view saw the state's internal structure, with its institutions and procedures, as unaffected by its external relationship to its citizens. When the university reforms of the late 1960s and early 1970s altered the composition and procedures of internal university governing bodies, the change had little influence on the academic freedoms of professors, when understood as subjective rights in the traditional sense. Whatever the composition and procedures of university bodies might have been—whether, for example, the university senate consisted only of professors, or instead, equal numbers of professors, assistants, students, and technical personnel—the decisive factor regarding academic freedom was whether the individual professors could freely determine the subjects, methods, and goals of their research and lessons within the framework of their teaching duties. If they could not, if there were intrusions into their academic freedoms, the intrusions were not mitigated because they were decreed by a body composed solely of professors, as opposed to only one-third or one-fourth professors.

However, to the Bundesverfassungsgericht it seemed unacceptable to leave the organizational form of the university completely to political whim and the experimentation of the legislature.[15] It raised academic freedom from a subjective right to a value-determinative fundamental norm, to an objective principle. The court found that scholarship, as well as the individual scholar, had to be free. Thus, the university's organization had to guarantee that scholarship was not hindered by antischolarly, or even nonscholarly, influences. The Court concluded that professors had to exercise the decisive vote in these bodies. Since this decision, there have been a host of additional decisions that test government institutions and procedures based on

---

[14] Among Bundesverfassungsgericht opinions, see most recently Judgment of July 2, 1990, BVerfG, 81 BVerfGE 242; Judgment of Apr. 2, 1986, BVerfG, 73 BVerfGE 261.

[15] Judgment of May 29, 1973, BVerfG, 35 BVerfGE 79.

fundamental rights—fundamental rights as objective principles.[16]

The third issue that furthered development from the subjective rights view to the objective principles view was the role of government in protecting fundamental rights: whether fundamental rights required the government to take only a passive role in protecting freedoms by not intruding on them, as per the traditional view, or whether the government had a duty to take an active role in protecting freedoms against intrusions by others. The issue arose during the 1970s in the struggle over the criminal treatment of abortion. The legislature had created a scheme that unconditionally legalized abortion in the first trimester, and then legalized it during the following months if certain indicators were present. The Bundesverfassungsgericht considered this insufficient protection of the unborn, who, according to the Court, were better protected by an indicator requirement that applied from the start of pregnancy.[17] The Court considered this increased protection necessary to insure fundamental rights—the fundamental right to life, as a value-determinative fundamental norm and objective principle. Defined as such, this fundamental right required the government not only to refrain from intrusions, but also to support and protect life. Thus, the Court rejected the legislature's arrangement and obliged it to promulgate legislation that applied the criminally stricter indicator arrangement from the start of pregnancy. Two dissenting judges strongly criticized the decision and rejected the objective principle characterization of fundamental rights as a heading under which fundamental rights changed from individual freedoms to a governmental duty of punishment.[18]

The Bundesverfassungsgericht has never again inferred a duty of punishment from a fundamental right. However, it also has never had another opportunity to do so. Whether, now that the legislature is newly interested in abortion as a result of German unification, the Bundesverfassungsgericht will reinforce, weaken, or abandon the legislature's duty of punishment remains to be seen. Regardless, the Court has consistently inferred a governmental duty of protection for fundamental rights, and thus developed a demand for administrative regulations.[19]

---

[16] *See, e.g.*, Judgment of June 14, 1988, BVerfG, 78 BVerfGE 290; Judgment of Feb. 8, 1983, BVerfG, 63 BVerfGE 131; Judgment of Dec. 20, 1979, BVerfG, 53 BVerfGE 30.

[17] Judgment of Feb. 25, 1975, BVerfG, 39 BVerfGE 1.

[18] *Id.* at 67-68.

[19] *See, e.g.*, Judgment of Nov. 30, 1988, BVerfG, 79 BVerfGE 174; Judgment June 14, 1988, BverfG, 78 BVerfGE 290; Judgment of Jan. 14, 1981, BVerfG, 56 BVerfGE 54; Judgment of Dec. 20, 1979, BVerfG, 53 BVerfGE 30; Judgment of Aug. 8, 1978, BVerfG, 49 BVerfGE 89; Judgment of Oct. 16, 1977, BVerfG, 46 BVerfGE 160.

The fourth factor affecting the development of subjective rights to objective principles is the issue of whether fundamental rights only protect against governmental intrusions, or also give rise to claims for governmental services. While this fourth factor has not had quite the same impact on rights development as have the other three factors, its significance as a factor in this development does merit discussion.

Traditionally, to the extent they are not expressly created as rights to services, fundamental rights are only defensive rights. Under the title of the objective principle quality of fundamental rights, however, the Bundesverfassungsgericht has interpreted defensive rights to be service rights, and inferred from these rights entitlements to government support and distribution of positions, means, and opportunities.[20] But the Court has consistently dampened the practical consequences of its decisions on government. It has never demanded that the government release additional budgetary funds to cover these entitlements, but has only required equal distribution of already available means. Thus, in effect, the Court has required precisely that which is already required by equality—no more, and no less.

These four problems are not unrelated. Whether a citizen can appeal to a fundamental right in his relationship with another citizen—whether, for example, an employee whose employer assigns him a task related to weapons production can reject the task, as a pacifist, by referring to his fundamental freedom of conscience[21]—is a problem both of third-party effects and of the duty of protection. It is a third-party effects problem because it is a question of the relevance of freedom of conscience for civil, in this case labor, law and the civil or labor law relationship between employer and employee. But it is also a problem of the duty of protection, because the question arises as to whether the state has the duty to protect the employee's conscience when in conflict with the employer. In addition, the question of protection of activities in accordance with fundamental rights on the one hand, and the regulation of activities in accordance with fundamental rights in government institutions and procedures on the other, are often simply different sides of the same coin. This is not to say that the four problems always flow into one another; but there are always points of contact. Even problems as different as those of the organization of the university and the treatment of the call for a boycott touch

---

20 *See, e.g.*, Judgment of Nov. 3, 1981, BVerfG, 59 BVerfGE 1, 21-29; Judgment of Feb. 8, 1977, BVerfG, 43 BVerfGE 291, 317-25; Judgment of July 18, 1972, BVerfG, 33 BVerfGE 303, 330-38.

21 *See* Judgment of May 24, 1989, BAG [Supreme Labor Court], *reprinted in* 1990 NEUE JURISTISCHE WOCHENSCHRIFT [NJW] 203; *see also* Judgment of Dec. 20, 1984, BAG, *reprinted in* 1985 JURISTEN ZEITUNG [JZ] 1108.

each other on the issue of maintaining freedom in the relationship between citizen and citizen.

This is a common denominator of the various problems and the development described: Fundamental rights no longer protect specific freedoms of citizens against specific government intrusions, as the traditional view expected; they now protect the citizen in his entire existence against an omnipotent and omnipresent state. All law is state law; all relationships between citizens are government regulated relationships. Everything that a citizen may demand or must accept from another citizen, he demands or accepts due to government authorization. In the same way, all of a citizen's actions are relevant to his free development; all such actions are capable of, and in need of, protection as fundamental rights. In this world, where all spheres of freedom are fundamentally protected spheres and all limitations of spheres of freedom are state-sanctioned limitations, every problem of social life is essentially a problem of fundamental rights. This basic omnirelevance of fundamental rights unfolds in the development from subjective rights to objective principles.

Yet this is only a conclusion. It does not explain what triggered and drove this development.

III

The explanation of the development from subjective rights to objective principles is hinted at in the Bundesverfassungsgericht decisions described above, which represent stations in the development from subjective rights to objective principles. In the 1950s, the call for a boycott of the films of a notorious Nazi filmmaker presented an opportunity to assign fundamental rights, as principles, the task of purging the inherited legal order of the ideological baggage of the Empire and the Third Reich. Whatever might have been the wording, history, system, or the sense and purpose of a norm intended by the legislature, it could be reinterpreted by reference to the significance of fundamental rights as values. That which could no longer be corrected and rescued through interpretation could be rejected as null and void by the same reference. Thus, fundamental rights, as principles, affected and legitimized changes in the legal system.

In the decisions on university reform and on reform of criminal treatment of abortion, the issue was also one of a relationship between principles and changes. As subjective rights, neither academic freedom in university reform nor the right to life in the reform of criminal treatment of abortion would have had decisive significance. In both cases, the Bundesverfassungsgericht's conception of these rights as objective principles created the opportunity to lead change in a certain direction.

A look farther back in German history also shows how fundamental rights as objective principles affect and legitimize change, while as subjective rights they rest upon and secure the status quo. Around the middle of the nineteenth century, demands for fundamental rights by the rising bourgeoisie aimed to change society and the legal order, to expose its hierarchical, feudal structure, and transform it into a society of business and acquisition made up of free, equal members. This demand was based on a conception of fundamental rights as objective principles.[22]

However, during the Empire, as the society of business and acquisition was created and the bourgeoisie made its peace with the monarch, the nobility, and the military, the bourgeois view of constitutional law came to see fundamental rights as subjective rights, which protected the status quo from change.[23] In the Weimar Republic, the demand that the legislature change the social order in accordance with fundamental rights stood in opposition to the demand that it leave a society already secured by fundamental rights alone—an objective principle conception of fundamental rights opposing a subjective rights conception.[24] This corresponded with contradictions latent in the Weimar compromise of classes and the lack of homogeneity of the Weimar constitution's fundamental rights.

German history reveals something else as well. When the bourgeoisie was significantly involved in legislation as the class that promoted and academically dealt with fundamental rights, it conceived of fundamental rights more as subjective rights. In contrast, when the bourgeoisie was not significantly involved or, as in the Weimar Republic, feared loss of its involvement, it conceived of them more as objective principles. As objective principles, fundamental rights offered more substance with which to criticize and control the legislature, to instruct it and point it in certain directions.

It is no longer possible to speak of "the bourgeoisie," as in the nineteenth and the first half of the twentieth century. But it remains true that fundamental rights offer more material to be used against the legislature as principles than they do as rights. When the political

---

[22] *See* Hartwig Brandt, *Urrechte und Bürgerrechte im politischen System vor 1848, in* GRUND- UND FREIHEITSRECHTE IM WANDEL VON GESELLSCHAFT UND GESCHICHTE 460, 466-67 (Günter Birtsch 1981); Bodo Pieroth, *Geschichte der Grundrechte,* 1984 JURA 568, 574; Rainer Wahl, *Rechtliche Wirkungen und Funktionen der Grundrechte im deutschen Konstitutionalismus des 19. Jahrhunderts,* 18 STAAT 321, 333 (1979).

[23] Pieroth, *supra* note 22, at 576-77.

[24] Schlink, *supra* note 9, at 458.

struggle against a law has been lost, and the political opponent succeeds in passing his law, the conception of fundamental rights as principles opens a new round of battle—the legal battle before the Bundesverfassungsgericht. Thus, the pathbreaking decisions by the Bundesverfassungsgericht on university reform and the criminal treatment of abortion were issued following bitter political struggles.

This phenomenon relates to a second point regarding the driving force behind the development from subjective right to objective principle: an activist court. The fact that fundamental rights as principles can affect and legitimize change in the legal system, even in the social order, and that they allow political conflicts to be continued on a new legal, but nonparliamentary, level, cannot lead to recognition of fundamental rights as principles unless an activist constitutional court accepts a leading role in this continued political struggle. The court must be willing to affect and legitimize change in the legal system or social order, and thus actualize the significance of fundamental rights as principles. The Bundesverfassungsgericht fully accepted this activist role.[25]

Why this activist role rather than a passive one, such as that played by other constitutional courts? Did there and does there now exist in the Federal Republic of Germany a special need to achieve changes in the legal system or the social order which, if not brought about through politics, required the action of the Bundesverfassungsgericht? Additionally, has there existed a special need to continue political conflicts on the judicial level once they have been fought out on the parliamentary level? Does the Bundesverfassungsgericht's activism respond to this special need?

Special needs rooted in the social, economic, and political characteristics of today's Germany are less responsible for the development described than are the conditions under which political life in Germany began after 1949. Politics had been discredited by the Weimar Republic and the Third Reich, and the old German belief that politics was essentially a dirty business and law a clean one reappeared and gained confirmation. Certainly, the Third Reich had engendered numerous terrible legal decisions. However, the German belief in the purity of law had always differentiated between law in its original and natural state, and that which lawyers and judges make of it. Thus, rather than being shattered by the Third Reich, the German belief in law over politics motivated a return to law as it originally and naturally was—a legal renaissance as a natural law renaissance.

---

[25] On the active role of the Bundesverfassungsgericht, see most recently KLAUS SCHLAICH, DAS BUNDESVERFASSUNGSGERICHT 264-92 (2d ed. 1991), and references therein.

The Bundesverfassungsgericht was especially convincing in representing this legal renaissance because it was a new court, unlike the highest civil and criminal court, the Bundesgerichtshof, whose predecessor was the discredited Reichsgericht. Dirty politics suffered from a deficit of legitimacy, while clean law and its representative, the Bundesverfassungsgericht, enjoyed a legitimacy "surplus." These were the conditions that invited and demanded that the Bundesverfassungsgericht take on an activist role.

This development is interesting not only as a historical reminiscence, but also as an indication of what can be expected of the emerging democratic states of Eastern Europe. There, too, politics has been discredited, and meets with contempt and disinterest. There, too, a constitutional court, occupied by the few honest, wise people it requires, may find a vacuum of legitimacy and encounter expectations and hopes that will lead it to take on an activist role. The faith with which citizens of the former German Democratic Republic view the Bundesverfassungsgericht provides evidence of this potential.

IV

In order to fulfill its activist role, the Bundesverfassungsgericht has driven forward the development from the understanding of fundamental rights as subjective rights to the understanding of them as objective principles. Has this been a negative development? What are, in fact, the fundamental rights of the Grundgesetz: subjective rights or objective principles?

Beyond question, the authors of the Grundgesetz considered its fundamental rights to be subjective rights—protections of personal freedoms through repulsion of state intrusions. After the unfortunate experience with the Weimar Constitution's programmatically broad fundamental rights, which tried and failed not only to secure freedoms through defense against intrusions but also to guarantee government services and the structuring of social relations, the creators of the Grundgesetz consciously limited themselves to guaranteeing fundamental freedoms. Naturally they were guided by principles—that is, maxims—for ordering social relations and the relationship between state and society. However, rather than principles, the Grundgesetz's authors considered fundamental rights to be guarantees of specific freedoms of citizens from specific state intrusions. They considered fundamental rights as necessary, but not sufficient, conditions for a satisfactory ordering of social relations.[26]

---

[26] See Hasso Hofmann, *Die Grundrechte 1789-1949-1989*, 1989 NJW 3177, 3184.

Thus if it were simply a question of the authors' original intent,[27] the question asked above would be easy to answer: Fundamental rights are not actually objective principles, but subjective rights. However, as the authors themselves know, original intent is only of relative significance. They know that their legal texts are introduced into a legal process where interpretations and reinterpretations, and constructions and deconstructions, alternate with one another. The outcome is open, constantly changing, and never more than temporary. The authors' awareness of this legal process overcomes their original intent. Thus, original intent cannot be contrary to textual interpretation because it has anticipated this interpretation. In other words, the authors know what they intend, but they also know that their original intent can only offer the limited authority conveyed by the text; they intend as much of their intentions as the text conveys.

So what does the text of the fundamental rights convey? The answer—and how could it be otherwise?—is ambiguous. According to traditional formulations, nearly all fundamental rights are formulated to repel government intrusions upon freedoms. However, the text of these fundamental rights includes formulations that are concerned not only with freedoms as attached to individuals, but with the freedoms themselves. "Each person has the right . . . freely to express and make known his opinion"[28]—this is a subjective rights formulation. "Freedom of the press and freedom of broadcasting . . . are guaranteed"[29]—this can be understood as an objective principle formulation.

In both cases, and for nearly all fundamental rights, freedoms are protected from state intrusions and limitations. This similarity does not change the fact that they are sometimes formulated more as subjective rights, and at other times more as objective principles. Furthermore, the varying formulations appear to be rather accidental. Thus, while the texts of the fundamental rights may invite interpretation as principles to a greater or lesser degree, they in no way completely reject such an interpretation.

As is the case with looking at the original intent of the authors, looking at the text does not provide much help. In the end, the answer depends on the function assigned to fundamental rights and to the Bundesverfassungsgericht, which is called upon to defend them.

Fundamental rights are open to the most varying interpretations

---

[27] *See* Werner Heun, *Original Intent und Wille des historischen Verfassungsgebers*, 116 AöR 185, 185-209 (1991).

[28] GRUNDGESETZ [Constitution] art. 5, para. 1, cl. 1.

[29] *Id.* at art. 5, para. 1, cl. 2.

when viewed as principles—that is, as maxims for the ordering of social relationships and as rules of optimization. The rule of optimization—as much individual freedom as can be realized in accordance with what is legally and actually possible—is such an open-ended concept that it can justify any state intrusion upon freedoms.[30] Although the Bundesverfassungsgericht does not actually permit every state intrusion, its decision to confirm or reject a particular intrusion may often come as a surprise, pleasant or unpleasant, depending upon one's point of view.

The maxim of the free ordering of social relations and the relationship between state and society is also sufficiently open-ended that, in the political and legal controversies experienced in Germany over reform of the universities, the structure of workers' participation in factories, or regulation of the press and broadcasting mediums, each side could have appealed to fundamental rights as principles.[31] It is true that one position was politically appealing to one point of view, and the other politically appealing to the opposite point of view. In terms of the law, however, the various arguments of principle revealed differences in elegance, but not in legal interpretation. The differences were no longer specifically legal.

I consider this development a loss. In a conception of fundamental rights as principles, determining which fundamental rights will actually be protected by the Bundesverfassungsgericht and which will not is not simply a question of applying a legal methodology. The determination is methodologically incapable of prediction, expectation, or criticism. It can only be guessed at through knowledge of trends in adjudication, judges' personalities and sensitivities, and the political atmosphere within and about the Court.

Furthermore, this loss of certainty is unnecessary. A concept of fundamental rights that simply guarantees subjective rights by repelling state intrusions upon personal freedoms is quite capable of dealing with those societal problems that must be adjudicated in court.[32] Looking once again to the problems that promoted the development from subjective rights to objective principles, it is clear that civil laws cannot be interpreted and implemented under the Grundgesetz's fundamental rights as they were during the Empire and the Third Reich.

---

[30] *See supra* note 12.

[31] The disputes described in the following decisions are most instructive: Judgment of Mar. 24, 1987, BVerfG, 74 BVerfGE 297, 306-10 (broadcasting); Judgment of Nov. 4, 1986, BVerfG, 73 BVerfGE 118, 139-205 (same); Judgment of Mar. 3, 1979, BVerfG, 50 BVerfGE 290, 302-81 (participation); Judgment of Apr. 2, 1974, BVerfG, 37 BVerfGE 79, 89-92 (universities).

[32] For more exact information, see Schlink, *supra* note 9.

However, giving effect to fundamental rights in civil law does not require interpreting them as principles. Instead, it calls for an awareness that the state always intrudes on personal freedoms even in creating civil law relationships among its citizens, and thus must measure itself against protections given to individual freedoms—that is, against fundamental rights as subjective rights. The cases described above provide evidence of this. For example, the judge who forbids one citizen from calling for a boycott of another's films is not applying civil laws that have no bearing on freedoms and intrusions. Rather, in such a case, the state, through the judge's actions, is applying laws in a way that intrudes upon the freedom of expression of one citizen without the exceptional justification required.

By the same token, there is no need to interpret fundamental rights as principles in order to apply them to the structure of government procedures and institutions. For example, whenever the possibility exists that a government procedure will end in an irreparable intrusion, the state must take precautionary measures to sufficiently control the intrusion beforehand, since it cannot be corrected after the fact. In asylum procedures, at the end of which deportation is possible, and in forced auctions, at the end of which property goes irreversibly to the highest bidder, the governing laws demand particularly careful procedures in which the party affected can fully represent its interests.[33]

Here, rather than a passive government duty not to intrude, there exists an affirmative government duty of protection: Where the state can no longer repair damage to fundamental rights once the damage has occurred, the state must protect against its occurrence. Such situations have increased in our technologically advanced world, exposed as it is to technological hazards. Thus, referring to the duty of protection, constitutional adjudication and scholarship rightly make the greatest demand for the duty of protection to be incorporated in the procedures used to build atomic, chemical, biotechnical, and genetics installations, which threaten uncontrollable, irreparable damage.[34]

---

[33] *See* Judgment of May 4, 1982, BVerfG, 60 BVerfGE 348, 358 (regarding asylum); Judgment of Feb. 25, 1981, BVerfG, 56 BVerfGE 216, 242-43 (same); Judgment of Apr. 24, 1979, BVerfG, 51 BVerfGE 150, 156-60 (regarding property law); Judgment of Sept. 27, 1978, BVerfG, 49 BVerfGE 220, 235-39 (same); Judgment of Dec. 7, 1977, BVerfG, 46 BVerfGE 324, 334-35 (same).

[34] In addition to the Bundesverfassungsgericht opinions discussed *supra* note 19, see the recent Judgment of Nov. 6, 1989, VGH Kassel (court of appeals), *reprinted in* 1990 NEUE ZEITSCHRIFT FÜR VERWALTUNGSRECHT [NVwZ] 276, and from the extensive discussion it sparked, Christoph Enders, *Neubegründung des öffentlich-rechtlichen Nachbarschutzes aus der grundrechtlichen Schutzpflicht?*, 115 AöR 610 (1990); Günter Hirsch, *Keine Gentechnik ohne*

These examples can be extended at will. They are evidence that many of the problems which promoted the development from subjective rights to objective principles could also be solved by a strict understanding of fundamental rights as subjective rights. Admittedly, however, only the conception of fundamental rights as principles permits the reconstruction of *every* social and political problem into a problem of fundamental rights.

Some may view the Bundesverfassungsgericht's adjudication of fundamental rights as an additional forum for the treatment of social and political problems, one in which they are dealt with not so much through differences in content, but through their categorization in different forms, removed from political turmoil and thus decided perhaps more calmly and thoughtfully. In this context fundamental rights would be viewed as principles. However, if the function of the Bundesverfassungsgericht's adjudication of fundamental rights is only to secure individual freedoms, then the conception of fundamental rights as principles is inappropriate.

Thus the change from a view of fundamental rights as rights to a view of them as principles is based, in turn, upon a changed view of the function of fundamental rights and the role of the Bundesverfassungsgericht. The function of ensuring individual freedom has become less important. The dominant function is now the creation of an additional forum for the treatment of social and political problems.

This development has been accompanied by yet another change: towards an activist Bundesverfassungsgericht, with a less consistent legal methodology. If the Court considers and treats a wealth of social and political problems as its legitimate domain, it cannot cope with them by virtue of legal methods that convey a systematic constitutional structure. While methodologically convincing decisions still occur every now and again, there are many others that simply arise from the Court's feel for what is indicated by social and political life—for what is accepted and "fits" into the social and political landscape. Decisions thus encompass only the individual cases sub judice, and are expressed and handed down as such. They are also taught to students as such, which is perhaps the best indication that German constitutional law is changing from code-oriented, systematic law to case law.

Gesetz?, 1990 NJW 1445; Peter Preu, *Freiheitsgefährdung durch die Lehre von den grundrechtlichen Schutzpflichten*, 1991 JZ 265; Horst Sendler, *Gesetzes- und Richtervorbehalt im Gentechnikrecht*, 1990 NVwZ 231; Rainer Wahl & Jürgen Masing, *Schutz durch Eingriff*, 1991 JZ 553. *See also* Jürgen Schwab, *Gentechnologie und Immissionsschutzrecht*, 1989 NVwZ 1012.

V

Has constitutional jurisprudence joined in these changes? Does it propel them forward, follow them, or oppose them? Is not constitutional jurisprudence, like jurisprudence in general, traditionally code rather than case oriented in Germany, and thus committed to a method and dogma based on generality, consistency, and system?

German history shows that constitutional jurisprudence or, as it was called back then, the jurisprudence of the law of the state, was not only bound by code orientation, method, and dogma, but also took a leading role in the development and transformation of constitutional law, or law of the state. "Without any assistance, German professors have made the state a legal person."[35] This was how a writer at the beginning of this century characterized a development that had begun before the middle of the nineteenth century, and had shaped the theory of the state as a legal person. The monarch retained only the position of a functionary, and not the role of the sovereign. Though, one may detect in this quotation a degree of scorn for the unworldly armchair scholarship of German professors, the author himself was a German professor. Furthermore, the remark quoted, like all his works, is filled with the proud sense that German law of the state had transformed the absolutist state into the constitutional state, the police state into one based on the rule of law. It is in fact astonishing how far ahead of legislation and legal decision making the newly emergent jurisprudence of the law of the state was in the last century.

This contrasts sharply with today's constitutional scholarship, which is entirely under the "spell" of the Bundesverfassungsgericht. It obtains its material, ideas, and confirmation from the Court's decisions, and attempts to harmonize these decisions into a coherent doctrinal corpus. When this fails, as is increasingly the case, the scholars infer future decisions from past ones, and examine whether one or another solution to a real or hypothetical case is consistent with precedent.

Constitutional scholarship thus thinks and works in the wake of the Bundesverfassungsgericht, rather than ahead of it. The Bundesverfassungsgericht develops central tenets of Germany's constitutional doctrine more or less on the spot, and scholarship then elaborates on them. Thus, the development of the view of fundamental rights as objective principles is mainly a consequence of the decisions of the Bundesverfassungsgericht, and less a result spurred by

---

[35] 1 OTTO MAYER, *Die juristische Person und ihre Verwertbarkeit im öffentlichen Recht, in* FESTGABE P. LABAND 59 (1908).

constitutional scholarship. While some criticism of Bundesverfassungsgericht decisions exist in all this, the criticism tends to protect the existing horizons of constitutional decision making by, for example, defending an established precedent against a new decision or playing a new decision off against established precedent.

These findings can be condensed down to the concept of a Bundesverfassungsgericht positivism which determines constitutional scholarship. This dynamic is not a natural consequence of the relationship between theory and practice, or scholarship and decision making, nor of the special position of the Bundesverfassungsgericht in the German legal and constitutional order. Theory, as other social, cultural, and intellectual disciplines teach, can maintain an extremely critical distance from practice. For example, in the American legal and constitutional order, the United States Supreme Court maintains a position similar to that of the Bundesverfassungsgericht in German society. Yet American constitutional scholarship challenges the Supreme Court more frontally, and if not less respectfully, than at least less gently.

Above all, however, it is the relationship between legal scholarship and decision making in other German legal disciplines that proves that the relationship which now exists between constitutional scholarship and the decisions of the Bundesverfassungsgericht could be different. Neither the decisions of the Bundesgerichtshof in civil and criminal matters nor those of the Bundesverwaltungsgericht are canonized in a form comparable to the decisions of the Bundesverfassungsgericht.

VI

What determines and explains the Bundesverfassungsgericht's influence over constitutional scholarship? What has transpired since the days when jurisprudence of the law of the state could develop an epochal doctrine without any assistance from legislature and decision making?

Since the beginning of the twentieth century, the jurisprudence of the law of the state has taken a different path than legal scholarship generally, especially the scholarship of civil law, under whose characteristic influence it had developed since the middle of the nineteenth century. In civil law, codification of the Bürgerliches Gesetzbuch in 1900 signified a "transition from scholarship to legislation."[36] Dependence on jurisprudential concepts and systems, and their construc-

---

[36] FRANZ WIEACKER, PRIVATRECHTSGESCHICHTE DER NEUZEIT 460 (2d ed. 1967).

tion, became less important than obligations to written law and its interpretation. The so-called jurisprudential positivism (*Rechtspositivismus*) that had prevailed until then was transformed into legal positivism (*Gesetzespositivismus*).

In the law of the state, on the other hand, there was no reason for such a change. Jurisprudence of the law of the state, which had grown up with a codified constitution, produced an early variant of positivism in which dependence on jurisprudential concepts and systems, and their construction, accompanied dependence on the constitution and its interpretation. This relationship was successful because the scanty text of the constitution left considerable freedom of construction. There was no transition from jurisprudential positivism to legal positivism. Most important, there was no transition from scholarship to legislation; scholarship remained dominant in the law of the state.

The situation did not change in the Weimar Republic. During the great Weimar controversies on the tasks, content, and methods of the law of the state, the position of scholarship as the final court of appeal in all questions of law of the state remained unquestioned. This was so despite the fact that the Weimar Republic, unlike the Empire, had a constitutional court. This court, the Staatsgerichtshof, decided few cases, and decided them with reserved caution. The largest, most important case, the dispute between Prussia and the Reich, is today regarded more as a clash between significant Weimar positions on constitutional theory than as an important decision of the Staatsgerichtshof.[37]

During the Third Reich, the self-confidence of the jurisprudence of the law of the state turned into grotesque overestimation of itself—and was also broken. Later interpretations by the authors and others, of essays such as Forsthoff's *Der totale Staat* (The Total State)[38] and Schmitt's *Der Führer schützt das Recht* (The Führer Guards the Law)[39] were attempts to strengthen the state against the National Socialist Party and the law of the state against National Socialist ideology, are were not merely retrospective justifications. Instead, they reflected a self-overestimation that grew out of the unchallenged self-confidence of the jurisprudence of the law of the state. This jurisprudence believed, at least at the beginning of the Third Reich, that it could give the Reich a new, binding, though National Socialist, legal

---

[37] *See* 6 ERNST R. HUBER, DEUTSCHE VERFASSUNGSGESCHICHTE 733-39 (1981); 7 *id.* at 1120-36 (1984).

[38] ERNST FORSTHOFF, DER TOTALE STAAT (1933).

[39] Carl Schmitt, *Der Führer schützt das Recht*, 1934 DEUTSCHE JURISTEN-ZEITUNG 945.

form. But National Socialism was simply not interested, and the jurisprudence of the law of the state sank into insignificance during the Third Reich.[40]

A new epoch for the jurisprudence of the law of the state began with, as well as under, the Grundgesetz. In 1951, the Bundesverfassungsgericht in Karlsruhe had begun to decide cases under the Grundgesetz. Unlike the transition from the imperial constitution to that of the Weimar Republic, and then to the Grundgesetz, the transition from no constitutional court, or a very weak one, to a constitutional court that made far-reaching decisions involving all questions of constitutional life, created a completely new and different context in which to fit the jurisprudence of the law of the state. *Karlsruhe locuta, causa finita*—this remark creates an image of this new situation, in which the Bundesverfassungsgericht speaks ex cathedra and representatives of dethroned constitutional scholarship stand at its feet. The image embodies the concept of Bundesverfassungsgericht positivism.

To summarize the developments, at the end of the previous century, before codification of civil law in the Bürgerliches Gesetzbuch, the jurisprudence of civil law united within itself an "authority that is today divided among various factors: law, high court decisions, major commentaries and textbooks."[41] This authority was reduced by the Bürgerliches Gesetzbuch and through decisions of the Reichsgericht, the highest court dealing with the Bürgerliches Gesetzbuch. In the process, civil law scholarship had to develop a balance between literally complying with written law on the one hand, and injecting constructive significance into it on the other, and also between respect for the decisions of the Reichsgericht and maintaining a critical distance from them.

The jurisprudence of the law of the state could not and did not learn to do this. The letter of the constitution left much room for construction, and without a constitutional court there was no need to reach a respectful but critically distant relationship to court decision making. There were no authorities to balance—the singular authority of constitutional scholarship remained intact.

Granted, this authority possessed from beginning to end a somewhat "ivory tower" character. While the jurisprudence of civil law guided judicial practice even before the Bürgerliches Gesetzbuch, the jurisprudence of the state was faced with a political practice that it

---

[40] *See* Wolfgang Kohl & Michael Stolleis, *Im Bauch des Leviathan*, 1988 NJW 2849, 2850, 2852.

[41] WIEACKER, *supra* note 36, at 446.

could explain but not guide, and to which it occasionally and openly capitulated.[42] However, the authority did remain intact in its unique ivory tower, as it did not have to strike a balance with either extensive codification or the authority of judicial decision making—neither in the Empire nor in the Weimar Republic. Thus, constitutional scholarship took a special place among legal disciplines.[43]

Only under the Grundgesetz and the Bundesverfassungsgericht could constitutional scholarship *begin* its proper relationship to decision making: the correct combination of attention and neglect, reaction and independent anticipation, respect and critical distance. The learning process has not ended. It has been made more difficult since the Bundesverfassungsgericht first began to decide cases, because constitutional scholarship has been tempted, and has often yielded to the temptation, to adapt to the Bundesverfassungsgericht as a sort of junior partner and thus participate in its authority, instead of offsetting its authority as a critical opponent. That is, various constitutional scholars have acted as advisors or representatives in cases before the Bundesverfassungsgericht, as loyal compilers and systematizers of its decisions, even as possible candidates for future positions on the Court. Constitutional scholarship would like to participate in power, and it realizes that the courtiers are rewarded for their service to the royal court by being allowed to influence it.

VII

Thus, constitutional scholarship has offered little opposition to the transformation in the understanding of fundamental rights, and the function of those rights under the Bundesverfassungsgericht. Nor has it opposed the transformation of constitutional law from code-oriented, systematized law to case law. It has mainly accompanied these developments affirmatively.

As a result of this acquiescence, a curious situation has arisen. The Bundesverfassungsgericht has propelled the development of case law forward, and acts in an increasingly open manner politically. In contrast, constitutional scholarship continues the traditional German style of dogmatic legal scholarship that interprets and applies codified law, and then expects judges to be the voice of the law, applying in

---

[42] According to GEORG MEYER & GERHARD ANSCHÜTZ, LEHRBUCH DES DEUTSCHEN STAATSRECHTS 906 (7th ed. 1919), law of the state simply ceased with the Prussian military and constitutional conflict, the greatest conflict of the nineteenth century between the monarch and parliament.

[43] Even the closely related science of administrative law had been confronted since the 1880s with both an increasing wealth of written laws and an increasingly independent, self-confident judiciary, and thus shared the fate of civil rather than constitutional scholarship.

their decisions a law that they have not made, but have simply found. There is no place in this tradition for a scholarly discourse with the Bundesverfassungsgericht that involves political arguments, or concentrates on an individual case, examines how the case's social problem evolved, and addresses whether the problem was correctly solved by the Bundesverfassungsgericht. Nor are the decisions of the Bundesverfassungsgericht methodologically and doctrinally criticized in the way that other branches of legal scholarship criticize the decisions of their high courts. Such criticism would be in keeping with the tradition of dogmatic legal scholarship. But it would demand a critical distance that constitutional scholarship is not used to. It rather canonizes the decisions of the Bundesverfassungsgericht. It reads and interprets these decisions, and their reasoning, as though they were codified law.

Here we can perceive one final transformation. The situation that has emerged is more than curious—it is unstable. A legal and political system cannot long afford uncritical treatment of its constitutional court. Such treatment might be acceptable where legal decisions remained restrained and limited in number. But a constitutional court that frees itself from the text of the constitution, dealing with individual cases in an activist and political manner, requires a critical counterpart.

German constitutional scholarship could provide this counterpart in two ways. First, in the tradition of dogmatic legal scholarship, it could deal as critically with the Bundesverfassungsgericht as do other branches of legal scholarship with their high courts.

However, German constitutional scholarship could attempt a different type of critical behavior, one which confronts the Bundesverfassungsgericht and its concern with individual cases in a broader, more openly political fashion. In this critical approach, constitutional scholarship would determinedly and consistently place cases and decisions at the center of its work. It would investigate the events, interests and conflicts, and the immediate and more distant consequences involved in the cases. The less strictly the Bundesverfassungsgericht's decisions were based on the constitution, the more openly political and ethical they appeared, the more openly constitutional scholarship would confront the political and ethical aspects of the decision. In this way, significant critical potential could be released. Constitutional scholarship could be quite direct in its political and ethical criticism of decisions, and it could define the specific parameters of a decided case in such a way as to clarify the specific and limited significance of the decision. In the context of its political and ethical discourse, constitutional scholarship could address the public as well.

The relationship between constitutional scholarship and the Bundesverfassungsgericht will develop in one of these two directions. The first direction has tradition on its side. In the second, one sees traits of what a European sees in looking at the United States and the relationship between American constitutional scholarship and the Supreme Court. This image of the United States incorporates a view that the American public participates more in the debate on constitutional legal and political questions, constitutional decision making, and appointments to the Supreme Court. Is this a more successful way to convey issues and problems of constitutional law and courts to society, and, in turn, to convey social issues and problems to constitutional law and the constitutional court? Is this what a united Germany, and especially its new states, needs? Finally, is it simply inevitable, with an activist constitutional court, that constitutional scholarship will take this role?

German constitutional culture is undergoing a process of transformation. This can no longer be reversed. However, where a process is in motion, opportunities to structure it arise, even if the direction can no longer be changed. To that extent, the role that fundamental rights and the Bundesverfassungsgericht will play in the future, as well as the influence that constitutional legal scholarship will have upon this role, remains open. Something new is emerging in Germany. Perhaps somewhere between the German tradition of codified, systemized law and the American idea of case law, this "something" will take its form.

CONSTITUTIONAL IDENTITY

George P. Fletcher

Our conventional distinctions—law versus politics, principles versus policies—oversimplify the world of legal adjudication, particularly constitutional adjudication. Supporters of judicial activism gain too much ground from the trivial point that everything a judge does expresses political and moral preferences, and strict constructionists are taken too seriously when they insist that the jurisprudential options reduce legal adjudication to following the drafters' intent or giving free reign to personal values.

Many graduations and nuances inhabit the turf between paradigmatic instances of the nonpolitical and value-free application of rules, on the one hand, and the extra-legal surrender of judges either to private moral judgment or party politics, on the other. Yet we hardly perceive these degrees of law, politics, and morality, for our minds follow the grooves laid out by our well-worn vocabularies.

The aim of this Article is to introduce and clarify a new way of thinking about decisions in close cases, particularly those that address basic issues of constitutional law. When constitutional language fails to offer an unequivocal directive for decision, the recourse of the judge is not always to look "outward" toward overarching principles of political morality. In an illuminating array of cases, the acceptable way to resolve the disputes and to explain the results is to turn "inward" and reflect upon the legal culture in which the dispute is embedded. The way to understand this subcategory of decisions is to interpret them as expressions of the decision makers' constitutional identities.

Some examples are illustrative. In the march of precedents leading to *Miranda v. Arizona*,[1] the Supreme Court had to decide whether it was consistent with our tradition to allow police officers to dominate interrogation sessions without defense lawyers present at the scene of the interrogation. In the 1950s, the prevailing view was that

---

[1] Miranda v. Arizona, 384 U.S. 436 (1966). A more lawyerly statement of the case holding would be that the Court extended the Fifth Amendment privilege against self-incrimination (as applied to the states under the Due Process Clause of the Fourteenth Amendment) to custodial interrogation in the absence of counsel.

confessions generated by aggressive and coercive police interrogation were likely to be unreliable and, therefore, should be excluded.

In a pivotal case leading toward *Miranda*,[2] Justice Frankfurter reasoned that these confessions were excluded not because they "are unlikely to be true[,] but because the methods used . . . offend an underlying principle in the enforcement of our criminal law[.]"[3] Why? Because, as Frankfurter described the American legal system, "ours is an accusatorial and not an inquisitorial system—a system in which the State must establish guilt by evidence independently and freely secured and may not by [its own] coercion prove its charge against an accused out of his own mouth."[4] The point on which Frankfurter's reasoning turned is that Americans are not like *them*— those inquisitorially minded Europeans who are presumably willing to secure confessions at any cost. To Frankfurter, the fact that, with the introduction of public prosecution, the Europeans have a system in which the accusatorial function is separated from fact-finding was meaningless. No, the Court, led by Frankfurter, perceived the Continental tradition as standing for a certain conception of the way in which the state may bear down on the individual in criminal prosecutions. And, he insisted, his adopted country should stay with the Anglo-American way of doing things.

The same way of thinking about law determined the current conservative posture toward abortion in the western part of united Germany. In 1975, the Federal Constitutional Court invalidated a liberal abortion law as a violation of the constitutional provision granting "everyone a right to life."[5] The judges interpreted the term "everyone" broadly to include fetuses because "the historical experience and the moral, humanistic confrontation with National Socialism"[6] required them to bend over backwards to protect life. To the Federal Constitutional Court, the fact that the Third Reich had a conservative position on abortion did not matter.[7] The stigma of Hitler's Final Solution required the court to take a stand in favor of protecting life. The unborn were the beneficiaries of this free-floating anxiety about whether Germans are really sensitive to the value of human existence. As the American Supreme Court sided with the American mode of

---

[2] Rogers v. Richmond, 365 U.S. 534 (1961).

[3] *Id.* at 540-41.

[4] *Id.* at 541. Never mind that the proper contrast would have been between an "adversarial" (common law) and "accusatorial" (Continental) mode of trial.

[5] Judgment of Feb. 25, 1975, BVerfG 39 Entscheidugen des Bundesverfassungsgericht [BVerfGE] 1.

[6] *Id.*

[7] *Id.*

trying criminals, the German court identified itself with what it took to be a humanist, life-affirming current in German culture.

Of course, in these cases the judges might muster arguments of policy and principle about why lawyers should be present at the time of interrogation or why the fetus should enjoy a right to life. But these arguments quickly run dry. Some choice is necessary between competing systems of values, and yet the choice is not one that skeptics have come to call "political" or "discretionary." The choice is rather one of self-realization and self-definition. The identity of a legal system is both reflected and shaped in these pivotal decisions concerning who the judges are and wish to be.

One should not underestimate the element of yearning in these self-definitional constitutional decisions. An illuminating example is the October 1990 decision[8] by the newly constituted Hungarian Constitutional Court to invalidate capital punishment as an "arbitrary punishment"[9] and a violation of the "right-to-life" provisions of the constitution,[10] which had been transplanted by amendment from the International Covenant on Civil and Political Rights[11] to the constitution originally drafted and adopted by the Hungarian Communists. Although the ten academically minded judges on the court wrote long and seemingly serious opinions on capital punishment, they hardly had a convincing argument for their stand. They did not even address the obvious contradiction between their holding and the International Covenant, which explicitly recognizes the legitimacy of capital punishment.[12] Furthermore, their reliance on the supposed "arbitrariness" of the punishment turns out to be no more than a confession that they cannot think of any good arguments for the institution. Of course, there are no good arguments, for they assume—on the basis of superficial statistical analysis—that the death penalty has no deterrent impact and, further, that retribution could not possibly justify taking a life for a life. Below the surface of these inadequate arguments runs a current of yearning to join the "European House," a democratic homeland governed by human rights and an exaltation of human dignity. Abolishing capital punishment, even on the basis of bad legal arguments, is a way of proving that a postsocialist country has an adequate regard for the values now dominant in Western Europe.

---

[8] Judgment of Oct. 24, 1990, Alkotmánybiróság, 1990 Magyar Közlöny [MK.] (Hungarian Gazette) 107.

[9] A MAGYAR KÖZTÁRSASÁG ALKETMÁNYA ch. XII, § 54, para. 1.

[10] *Id*. §§ 54-70.

[11] International Covenant on Civil and Political Rights, U.N. GAOR, 3d Comm., 21st Sess., at 51 (1966).

[12] *Id*. at part III, art. 6.

If this mode of analysis is brought closer to home, one can understand the controversial decisions by the Rehnquist Court on flag burning.[13] In 1989 and 1990, the Court held twice, by five votes to four, that flag burning was a symbolic speech act protected by the First Amendment. Advocates of free speech regard these decisions as self-evidently correct. Yet there are ample signs in these decisions of doctrinal overreaching. There are indeed good grounds for the opposition of the four-vote minority—a minority that, in view of changes in the Court's personnel (Justice Souter for Brennan, Justice Thomas for Marshall), would probably be a six-vote majority if the issue were to come up again.

There are at least three doctrinal hurdles on which the case for First Amendment protection might falter. First, it is not clear that burning a piece of cloth, even the protest burning of a flag, is the type of speech that is addressed by the First Amendment. Second, even if that threshold issue is negotiated, the argument for protection could stumble on the *O'Brien* distinction.[14] Arguably, the prohibition of flag burning speaks only to the means and not the content of the protest, in which case the protestor could well be required to choose another means. The conventional reply runs that the means of protest is bound up with the message, but if this is not true about playing loud music and sleeping in the park (both forms of communication subject to regulation), then it is not self-evidently true about flag burning. Third, even if flag burning is symbolic speech and even if the prohibition against flag burning is regarded as a suppression of speech, the flag might represent the kind of collective interest that warrants a corresponding degree of silence. After all, there are many interests that trump speech—private property, copyright, and reputation to name a few—and one might be forgiven for regarding these interests as less worthy than the people's emotional attachment to their national emblem.

Today, free speech issues generate their fair share of paradox. In the Supreme Court, the temporary majority in *Texas v. Johnson*[15] could not coalesce in the 1989 term behind any other significant issue of civil rights or civil liberties. One finds Justices Scalia and Kennedy voting with the old liberal plurality—Justices Blackmun, Marshall, and Brennan—an odd combination that surely would not come together to protect the interests of either minorities or criminal defend-

---

[13] *See* United States v. Eichman, 496 U.S. 310 (1990); Texas v. Johnson, 491 U.S. 397 (1989).

[14] United States v. O'Brien, 391 U.S. 367 (1968).

[15] 491 U.S. 397 (1989).

ants. Civil liberties may be in decline, but as of 1990 individual freedom still prevailed over the collective interest in national pride.

There is further paradox in the academic community. Arguments that will justify suppressing hate speech that offends minorities and obscenities that degrade women have become doctrinally chic. Yet hardly a voice emerges to uphold the national community's interest in maintaining the emblems of its historic continuity. The idiom of community comes to the lips of the politically correct who seek to suppress offensive speech on university campuses, but the same communitarian vocabulary fails to yield a convincing case for protecting the flag.

This Article does not aim to debate the doctrinal issues of the First Amendment, for the debate about flag burning has little to do either with the history of free speech, or the theory of free speech as a legal category. Behind the doctrinal moves of the Supreme Court's opinions lies an unarticulated sense of what it means to be American and, in particular, what it means to engage in the American way of protest.

The theme of constitutional identity challenges us in this context, for at first blush those that defend the flag, those that wrap themselves in the red, white, and blue, seem to speak for the United States. At a deeper level, however, the American constitutional spirit is expressed in upholding dissent even where, and particularly where, it collides with the collective interest in national pride.

Consider various ways in which one might formulate the conflict in the flag-burning cases. A German lawyer might well formulate the question in the language of duties. According to the Grundgesetz (Basic Law or Constitution),[16] citizens bear constitutional duties as well as rights;[17] organs of the state are endowed with duties as well as powers.[18] For example, Article I of the Grundgesetz prescribes that it is the duty of all state organs to respect and protect human dignity.[19] The doctrine of "third-party effect"[20] implies that individuals bear this Kantian duty as well, even toward objects—such as the dead—that do not, in any ordinary sense, possess rights.

If one starts with the notion of political duty, a duty to respect the emblems of national unity and solidarity can plausibly be attributed to every citizen (and indeed everyone subject to the legal sys-

---

16 GRUNDGESETZ [Constitution] [GG] (F.R.D.).

17 *See, e.g.*, *id*. at ch. I, art. 14.

18 *Id*. at ch. I, art. 1.

19 *Id*. at ch. I, art. 1, para. 1.

20 *See id*. at ch. I, art. 2.

tem). Although this specific duty is not spelled out in German constitutional theory, the implications in the criminal code are patent. Those subject to the criminal code must not only respect the German flag—which is defined in the *Grundgesetz*—they must also act with respect for the various other symbols of the *Bundesrepublik*, including its colors, its code of arms, and its national hymn.[21] This duty is violated not just by symbolic speech, but also by using words, by writing and distributing documents, or by speaking in a public gathering in a way that demeans or makes contemptible (*verächtlich macht*) any of these protected objects.[22] Significantly, the special provision protecting the flag is limited to "officially displayed" flags.[23] The same duty of respect extends to the organs of government, but only if the speech act can be qualified as the first step in an effort to overthrow the constitutional order.[24] These provisions have survived constitutional attack under Article 5 of the *Grundgesetz*,[25] the German analogue of our First Amendment.

American lawyers are likely to recoil at these intrusions on freedom of speech. But even more significant for present purposes is the way German lawyers are likely to formulate the issue as a matter of duty rather than rights. The duty of respect prevails over the right to speak. This seems like a perfectly sensible thing to say—if, of course, one believes that there is a civic duty to respect the flag and the symbols of state power. Yet it is doubtful that an American lawyer could be brought to conceptualize the problem of flag burning as a matter of civic duty rather than of conflicting rights and interests.

The grooves in the American legal mind lead one toward identifying the rights of the individual and the opposing interests of the state or community. There is no slot for duty, no niche for civic responsibility as a constitutional principle. As soon as one begins to think in this American way, the issues take a form that leads liberals to an ineluctable result.

The government's interest in the flag is formulated either too strongly or too weakly. The issue is stated too strongly in the original understanding of the flag desecration statutes, which regarded the flag as a quasi-sacred object subject to be rendered profane by abuse and misuse.[26] The issue is phrased too weakly, when presented as "a sym-

---

21 STRAFGESETZBUCH [Penal Code] [StGB] § 90(a)(1) (F.R.G.).

22 *Id.*

23 *Id.* § 90(a)(2).

24 *Id.* § 90(b).

25 GG ch. I, art. 5.

26 18 U.S.C. § 1700 (1990) (held unconstitutional in United States v. Eichman, 496 U.S.

bol of nationhood and national unity."[27] As liberals aptly respond, torching a piece of painted cloth does not affect the symbol behind the cloth; therefore, this assertion of a state interest simply misses the mark. Either phrased too strongly or too weakly, the state interest asserted against freedom of speech invariably collapses in the face of our regard for the individual right of free expression.

One would be hard-pressed to claim that an idiom of constitutional duties, if transplanted into American English, would generate a different result. However, at least one could think about the problem with a different focus, without concern that requiring a less offensive means of expression would be tantamount to fascist-style claims about collective honor and pride.

Using the phrase "national honor and pride" generates its own characteristic mode of American reaction. Sentiments may be different today, after the explosion of patriotic sentiment during the 1991 Gulf War, but at least at the time of the flag-burning litigation,[28] invoking these values of honor and pride seemed to run against the American constitutional grain. Still, it would be dubious American constitutional rhetoric, then or now, to invoke the values of honor and pride as a basis for regulating and compromising freedom of speech.

Yet our sensing weakness in the government's side of the argument is not the full story. There is something less than transparent about our concern that Johnson and Eichman be able to register their political disaffection by insulting the majority of Americans who have some lingering feeling that the flag is a nearly sacred object. There is, first of all, the obviously exploitative nature of the communication. Burning a piece of cloth, colored red and white and blue, would hardly be a political protest unless other people held the cloth in reverence. The greater the injury, the more intense the communication. In this regard, flag burning resembles hate speech. It makes its point by hurting those who hear it.

What, after all, is the point of letting Johnson and Eichman speak in this way? What good does it do? Their political message is hardly coherent. Granted, they are against patriotism; if they simply told us, we would get the point. No one who believes in the First Amendment could be opposed to their expressing their disaffection in words. Yet it is difficult to see how protecting speech-by-torching en-

---

310 (1990)); TEX. PENAL CODE ANN. § 42.09 (West 1989) (held unconstitutional in Texas v. Johnson, 491 U.S. 397 (1989)).

[27] *Johnson*, 491 U.S. at 407 (language used by the State).

[28] *Eichman*, 496 U.S. at 310; *Johnson*, 491 U.S. at 397.

courages democratic discourse, self-government, the marketplace of ideas, the pursuit of truth, or any other interest that could justify the intangible injury they intentionally inflict on those who value the flag. Yet invoking these group values misses something peculiar in the unusually strong American attachment to freedom of speech.

The way to understand *Johnson* and *Eichman* is to recognize that a value shift has occurred in the structure of the First Amendment. For almost fifty years, from *Barnette*[29] in 1943 to *Smith*[30] in 1990, religion was accepted as the arena in which individuals were particularly entitled to express themselves. Jehovah's Witnesses did not have to salute the flag; Sabbatarians were entitled to unemployment compensation even if they refused work on the Sabbath; the Amish did not have to send their children to public school beyond the eighth grade. Neutral and universal rules could not justify the government's encroachment on these protected spheres of individual and communitarian liberty.

What precisely was the nature of this religious liberty? Religious liberty represents a recognition that believers are subject to conflicting sovereignties, and, therefore, in certain spheres, the state will not force believers to choose Caesar over their commitment to God.[31] In a more secular world, this interest is interpreted to be nothing more than an individual's right to express himself in the arena of conscience. The interest comes to resemble what the German constitution aptly labels the "free flourishing of personality" (*"die freie Entfaltung seiner Persönlichkeit"*).[32]

As soon as the interest in religious freedom is formulated as an expression of personality, then we are embarrassed by the limitation of this freedom to believers. All those who feel strongly about something, all those who experience what we loosely call a commitment of conscience should be able to express themselves freely. In the end, one has no tools for distinguishing the anti-patriotic conscience of Johnson from the anti-public school conscience of the Amish. The locus of special freedom, the rubric under which individuals are exempt from at least some general and nondiscriminatory laws, shifts from one clause of the First Amendment to another, from freedom of religion to freedom of speech.

It was no coincidence that Justice Scalia was the intellectual ar-

---

[29] West Virginia Bd. of Educ. v. Barnette, 319 U.S. 624 (1943).

[30] Employment Div., Dep't of Human Resources v. Smith, 494 U.S. 872 (1990) (the peyote case).

[31] *See, e.g.*, Perry Dane, *The Maps of Sovereignty: A Meditation*, 12 CARDOZO L. REV. 959 (1991) (discussing conflicts between Native American and United States sovereignty).

[32] GG art. 2.

chitect of a revisionist opinion in the peyote case[33]—an opinion that dishonestly dismisses fifty years of free-exercise-of-religion law and provided the indispensable votes in *Johnson*[34] and *Eichman*.[35] The common denominator in Scalia's jurisprudence is that speech, not religion, should be the medium in which individuals express their autonomy from the state and its interests. This position has its antecedents in Justice Jackson's views expressed in his opinions of the early 1940s[36] that led later generations of lawyers to believe the Court's opposition to an obligatory Pledge of Allegiance was based on principles of free speech rather than the free exercise of religious conscience.

One is left, then, with a view of the First Amendment that invests freedom of speech with a particularly heavy burden. The First Amendment is *the* clause in our Constitution that bears the full weight of individual autonomy, the full burden of individuals bearing their souls and expressing their innermost nature in the face of organized demands of conformity and self-restraint. Here is the American spirit at work again, the irreverence of the ongoing American revolution. As Germans are committed to constitutionalizing a right of rebellion against tyranny, the American Revolutionary ethos seeks to domesticate dissent and expressions of conscience as constitutional rights. If the *Smith* decision survives, religion will no longer generate a legal sphere for appeals to higher law, for submissions to conscience, and for resorts to values over which the state has no control. The values of dissent, freedom of the inner self, and the free flourishing of individuals must be borne as emanations of free speech.

At least one can hope that the American regard for dissent continues to flourish. Given tendencies on college campuses today, one might have serious doubts. If those who witness flag burning are offended, their indignation is considered *their* problem, the price they have to pay for a robust democracy. But, if minorities and women are offended in class or on campus, their offense becomes a respectable argument for disciplining students and exerting pressure on "insensitive" faculty. For the time being, however, one can be thankful that the lower federal courts have not succumbed to the new jurisprudence that celebrates individual offense and depreciates the values of academic freedom. Our federal judges still believe that part of what it means to be American is to defend the First Amendment. However,

---

[33] *Smith*, 494 U.S. at 874.

[34] Texas v. Johnson, 491 U.S. 397 (1989).

[35] United States v. Eichman, 496 U.S. 310 (1990).

[36] *See* West Virginia Bd. of Educ. v. Barnette, 319 U.S. 624, 652 (1943); Douglas v. City of Jeannette, 319 U.S. 157, 166 (1943).

in view of the changing membership on the Supreme Court this pattern may not continue. This nation may end up with an unsavory alliance of left and right that promotes dissent neither as a matter of religion nor of speech. Whatever personal doubts one may feel concerning *Johnson* and *Eichman*, there may come a time when the vast majority of Americans look back fondly on an American spirit that takes the inner expressive needs of each individual as its constitutive value.

REACTIONARY CONSTITUTIONAL IDENTITY

Ruti G. Teitel

INTRODUCTION

Comparative constitutionalism today is the study of constitutional change. All over the world, and with breathtaking speed, countries are transitioning to new democratic orders. It is in this context that the United States Constitution celebrates its bicentennial. The world's most enduring constitution has long been the leading model for slow constitutional change. Nonetheless, in recent Supreme Court Terms our constitutional decisionmaking reflects a greater conservatism.[1]

In these comments I maintain that contemporary American constitutional adjudication follows a model directed away from the expansion of individual civil rights and liberties and towards the preservation of the status quo embodied in majoritarian legislation. We are in a process of radical redefinition of the theory of our constitutional democracy. I will suggest that contemporary constitutional

---

[1] There has been much scholarly discussion of the recent conservative direction in politics and in constitutional law. *See, e.g.*, DAVID HELD, MODELS OF DEMOCRACY 243 (1987). The term "conservatism" has been used in a number of senses. Held refers to two understandings of the word: "[A] *laissez-faire* or free market society is the key objective along with a 'minimal state.' The political programme of the New Right includes: the extension of the market to more and more areas of life . . . ." *Id. See also* ROBERT NOZICK, ANARCHY, STATE, AND UTOPIA (1974). Held, however, also notes the existence of another group that "believe[s] in the primacy of tradition, order and authority because [it] fear[s] the social consequences of rampant *laissez-faire* policies." HELD, *supra* at 243 n.1.

With regard to constitutional law, the term has been used in varying senses: Substantively, conservatism has been used to describe a preference for limited government. But it has also been used in a distinctly different sense to describe a theory about the proper sources for constitutional change, including principles favoring tradition, originalism, and arguments for judicial restraint. *See* CHARLES FRIED, ORDER AND LAW: ARGUING THE REAGAN REVOLUTION—A FIRSTHAND ACCOUNT (1991); *see generally* David Chang, *Discriminatory Impact, Affirmative Action, and Innocent Victims: Judicial Conservatism or Conservative Justices?* 91 COLUM. L. REV. 790 (1991); James Boyle, *A Process of Denial: Bork and Post-Modern Conservatism*, 3 YALE J.L. & HUMAN. 263 (1991).

The varying senses of conservatism have led to the problem that conservativism makes a claim for limited government, while opposing expansion of constitutionalism—the very mechanism of our political system for limiting government. Opposition to constitutionalism appears to derive from conservatism in the second sense.

In these comments I will return to the question of what we mean by constitutional democracy. I will show that an analysis of the rhetoric of recent constitutional decisionmaking reveals a strange understanding of constitutionalism as being incompatible with democracy. *See infra* part III.

adjudication embodies a distinct theory of democracy understood not as constitutional but as simply majoritarian.

My comments respond primarily to George Fletcher's paper *Constitutional Identity*, which proposes a principle of constitutional adjudication grounded in culture or national identity.[2] I agree that national identity informs constitutional adjudication, and will pursue this thesis further. I will propose the following relation between national identity and our constitutional adjudication: National identity operates as a justification for, or reactionary argument against progress in constitutional theory. By progress I mean expansion in the protection of individual rights and liberties. I conceive of the emerging principle of American constitutional adjudication as "reactionary constitutional interpretation."[3]

I. TRADITIONAL CONSTITUTIONAL INTERPRETATION

Fletcher proposes the following relation of national identity to constitutional adjudication. "[T]he acceptable way to resolve the disputes and to explain the results is to turn 'inward' and reflect upon the legal culture in which the dispute is embedded."[4]

Fletcher offers a number of examples: a German decision regarding abortion,[5] a Hungarian decision regarding capital punishment,[6] and American decisions concerning police interrogation,[7] flag burning,[8] and religious liberty.[9] These decisions, Fletcher contends, can be

---

[2] George P. Fletcher, *Constitutional Identity*, supra p. 223.

[3] In these comments I am deeply indebted to Albert Hirschman who has described and critiqued reactionary argument as a rhetorical device in political discourse. *See* ALBERT O. HIRSCHMAN, THE RHETORIC OF REACTION (1991). Though Hirschman discusses the role of this rhetoric in political argument, in these comments I maintain it is equally apt in the analysis of recent constitutional decisionmaking.

[4] Fletcher, *supra* note 2, at 223.

[5] Judgment of Feb. 25, 1975, BVerfG [Federal Constitutional Court], 39 Entscheidungen des Bundesverfassungsgerichts BVerfGE 1 (F.R.G.). Judge Barak and Professors Nino, Rousseau and Schlink have addressed the question of the sources of authoritative constitutional meaning. Each of their papers points to principles justifying judicial review, but also constraining constitutional interpretation. I will not address that question directly. *See* Aharon Barak, *Hermeneutics and Constitutional Interpretation*, infra p. 253; Carlos S. Nino, *A Philosophical Reconstruction of Judicial Review*, infra p. 285; Dominique Rousseau, *The Constitutional Judge: Master or Slave of the Constitution?*, infra p. 261; Bernhard Schlink, *German Constitutional Culture in Transition*, supra p. 197.

[6] Judgment of Oct. 24, 1990 (The Death Penalty Case), Alkotmánybíróság [Constitutional Law Court], 1990 Magyar Közlöny [MK.] (Hungarian Gazette) 107 (Hung.) [hereinafter *Death Penalty Case*] (unofficial translation on file at Benjamin N. Cardozo School of Law; pinpoint citations will be to the unofficial translation).

[7] Miranda v. Arizona, 384 U.S. 436 (1966).

[8] United States v. Eichman, 496 U.S. 310 (1990) (recognizing flag burning as protected speech); Texas v. Johnson, 491 U.S. 397 (1989) (same).

[9] Employment Div., Dep't of Human Resources v. Smith, 494 U.S. 872 (1990).

best understood to reflect notions of cultural identity. Just as a German court identifies with a "life-affirming current" in German culture,[10] so too an American court aligns itself with an "American mode" of treating suspects.[11] These decisions, it is suggested, reflect the identity of our national systems.

Put this way, the proposed principle sounds in false dichotomies: constitutional law versus culture or national identity.[12] Yet without such a dichotomy, as a principle of adjudication legal culture appears circular.[13]   Isn't constitutional adjudication itself part of national identity or culture?[14] And is it not particularly so in the case of the United States?[15]

In constitutional decisionmaking, legal tradition and national identity cannot be understood as distinct. The question is how national identity informs constitutional adjudication, and vice versa. The question is a complex one when, as in Eastern Europe or in the United States today, we need to be able to explain substantial constitutional change.

As a practical matter, a principle of constitutional identity does not resolve the questions now before the courts. In a recent case concerning the death penalty, Hungary's high court had before it a choice of identities.[16] In Eastern Europe, generally, the choice of identity is either a return to pre-Stalinist tradition, or westward to a modern European tradition.[17] The Hungarian death penalty decision is not

---

[10] Fletcher, *supra* note 2, at 225.

[11] *Id.* at 224.

[12] Fletcher would criticize law versus politics as a false dichotomy. *See id.* at 223.

[13] Judge Barak also understands constitutional interpretation as expressive of tradition or culture. He refers to the "values and policies that establish the identity of the community." Barak, *supra* note 5, at 256.

[14] Dominique Rousseau offers a sensible understanding of the legitimacy of judicial review: "The control of the constitutionality of laws is legitimate because it produces a definition of democracy that legitimates it." Rousseau, *supra* note 5, at 281. A broader reading of Dominique Rousseau's hypothesis is that constitutional interpretation is best understood as forming part of a broader system of constitutional democracy which the judiciary has a role in creating and which, in turn, affects our understanding of judicial review.

The legitimacy question aside, if this also sounds circular it is because of the hermeneutic problem of attempting to understand the principles of constitutional interpretation independently from the conception of democracy which judicial review itself has a role in creating.

[15] *See* BENJAMIN N. CARDOZO, THE NATURE OF THE JUDICIAL PROCESS (1921); *see generally*, SANFORD LEVINSON, CONSTITUTIONAL FAITH (1988).

[16] *Death Penalty Case, supra* note 6, at 3.

[17] *See* Jon Elster, *Constitutionalism in Eastern Europe: An Introduction*, 58 U. CHI. L. REV. 447, 476-77, 481 (1991) (discussing the attraction of historic pre-communist and contemporary international community models in the Eastern European constitution drafting process).

well explained simply by a principle of constitutional identity.[18]

As in Eastern Europe, the United States is now at a constitutional juncture point. As we celebrate the bicentennial of the world's most enduring constitution, we are in a period of reconstitution in numerous areas: criminal process, privacy, speech, and religion—subjects that imply First, Fourth, Fifth, Sixth, Eighth and Fourteenth Amendment protections.[19] In light of this reconstitution, the question is not how to explain constitutional adjudication generally, but instead how to explain constitutional change.

Fletcher suggests our jurisprudence continues to reflect a tradition of dissent and individual autonomy. The balance, he maintains, still favors "individual freedom" over "collective interest" and "national pride."[20] The recent decisions concerning flag burning, according to Fletcher, continue to reflect an American tradition regarding dissent, privileging speech as the protected medium.[21]

Yet the extent to which the tradition of dissent continues to inform the Rehnquist Court's constitutional adjudication is debatable. I understand the changes in our constitutional jurisprudence to go beyond mere clause-shifting[22] to the very heart of our constitutional identity. My understanding of recent Supreme Court Terms is as a revolution in our constitutional tradition, and relatedly, of our theory of constitutional democracy. I suggest that decisionmaking concerning criminal procedure, and freedom of expression and of conscience reflects an entirely revised constitutional identity.

II.   REACTIONARY CONSTITUTIONAL INTERPRETATION

I suggest the recent change in our constitutional jurisprudence is well explained by a principle I conceive of as "reactionary constitutional interpretation." I will set out elements of the principle of decisionmaking, show how it explains contemporary constitutional adjudication, and finally critique the theory of constitutional democracy underlying the reactionary principle.

---

[18] In the *Death Penalty Case*, the court elected against reversion to its premodern national identity and instead aligned itself with the identity and norms of the European Community. *Death Penalty Case, supra* note 6, at 9-10.

[19] *See infra* part III. There are also other areas in considerable flux.

[20] Fletcher, *supra* note 2 at 227.

[21] *Id.* Though regarding religious liberty, Fletcher would probably concede there has been a limitation and an asserted shift to the protection of speech rights. *Id.* at 230-31 (discussing the peyote decision in Employment Div., Dep't of Human Resources v. Smith, 494 U.S. 872 (1990)).

[22] *Id.* at 227.

My sense is that our constitutional identity had been in steady development,[23] but that in recent Terms this development has stopped short. My interpretation of the new judicial conservatism draws on a thesis of Albert Hirschman's concerning the rhetoric of resistance to political change.[24] In *The Rhetoric of Reaction*, Hirschman describes a number of arguments against political change, and offers a typology of arguments based on reaction to proposed change.[25] One of these he terms the "jeopardy thesis." Under the "jeopardy thesis," the argument against proposed change is that the change involves unacceptable costs by jeopardizing a pre-existing national interest. Recent constitutional decisionmaking reflects this type of "reactionary" argument—an argument resulting from a reaction to proposed constitutional change.[26] The argument is that proposed change jeopardizes majority interests and national tradition.

Questions about constitutional rights are increasingly conceived of as finite zero-sum games.[27] Granting a right to an individual is characterized as, and equated with, taking away an interest from the majority. Or, it is characterized as endangering a prior tradition.

The appeal of zero-sum constitutional analysis is that it offers a constraint in constitutional interpretation. A reactionary approach to constitutional interpretation limits potentially infinitely expandable rights; as such reactionary constitutional analysis offers a response to the interpretivist/noninterpretivist debate which has dominated the past decade. In a curious revisiting of our early political and constitutional history, where reactionary arguments were invoked against the

---

[23] Along the lines described by Dominique Rousseau. *See* Rousseau, *supra* note 5.

[24] HIRSCHMAN, *supra* note 3, at 1-10.

[25] Hirschman terms these: perversity, futility, and jeopardy. *Id.* at 3-8. Contemporary constitutional decisionmaking reflects elements of all of these arguments.

[26] In *The Rhetoric of Reaction*, Hirschman writes about reactionary argument in political discourse. Yet reactionary argument is even more powerful in the adjudicative setting. Principles of adjudication such as stare decisis lend themselves to reactionary arguments. But stare decisis contemplates deference to a judicially recognized interest rather than a simple political interest. For a recent case where the Supreme Court deferred to a political majority over its precedent and the principle of stare decisis, see Payne v. Tennessee 111 S. Ct. 2597 (1991).

[27] *See* HIRSCHMAN, *supra* note 3, at 8, 122; Albert O. Hirschman, *Good News is Not Bad News*, N.Y. REV. BOOKS, Oct. 11, 1990, at 20. Under this model, every action has an equal and opposite reaction. It is a return to a scientific model of law drawing on Newtonian physics. *See* HIRSCHMAN, *supra* note 3, at 8. But reactionary rhetoric in adjudication also draws upon games theory, and a conception of constitutional disputes as two-person games. *See generally* JOHN VON NEUMANN & OSKAR MORGENSTERN, THEORY OF GAMES AND ECONOMIC BEHAVIOR (1964); R. B. BRAITHWAITE, THEORY OF GAMES AS A TOOL FOR THE MORAL PHILOSOPHER (1959). It also draws upon military or conflict theory which has been characterized as "adversarial, zero-sum, and paradoxical." Edward N. Luttwak, *From Geopolitics to Geo-Economics*, THE NAT'L INTEREST, Summer 1990, at 17.

expansion of equality rights—in the name of liberty[28]—today the Supreme Court argues expansion of liberty imperils equality.[29] Liberty is seen as jeopardizing democracy. In other words, constitutionalism—but only at democracy's expense. Yet, constitutionalism ought not be considered to be had at the expense of democracy.

III.   Select Cases in Reactionary Constitutional Interpretation

Below I offer a number of illustrations of the reactionary constitutional interpretation principle. Many decisions reflect this conception and form of analysis. I have selected examples from four subject areas: privacy rights, criminal procedure, freedom of expression, and freedom of conscience.

A.   *Privacy*

In the area of privacy, expanding individual autonomy is characterized as posing a danger to the interests of the people. Perhaps the leading case is *Bowers v. Hardwick*, which rejected a claim to a right of homosexual privacy.[30] In *Bowers*, protecting individual sexual preference was characterized by the Court as a threat to both tradition[31] and majority will.[32]

In *Cruzan v. Director, Missouri Department of Health*, a recent case concerning the right to die, the Court characterized the constitutional question as a conflict between the individual, his or her family, and the interests of the people as reflected in anti-suicide legislation.[33] For the Court, the majority's interest overrode the individual's interest, even though it was the individual's interest in his or her own life which was at issue![34] By giving greater weight to society's longstanding prohibitions against suicide, the balance was stacked in favor of past majorities as tradition. Constitutionalism was understood to conflict with democracy. But that is not the American theory of constitutionalism.

---

28 *See, e.g.*, Plessy v. Ferguson, 163 U.S. 537 (1896).

29 *See, e.g.*, Bowers v. Hardwick, 478 U.S. 186 (1986). *But see* ROBERT A. DAHL, A PREFACE TO ECONOMIC DEMOCRACY 44, 50 (1985) (arguing liberty is not threatened by equality).

30 *Bowers*, 478 U.S. at 186.

31 *Id.* at 192-94.

32 *Id.* at 196. *See also* Robert H. Bork, *Neutral Principles and Some First Amendment Problems*, 47 IND. L.J. 1 (1971) (Bork makes exactly this argument regarding the privacy right at issue in Griswold v. Connecticut, 381 U.S. 479 (1965)).

33 110 S. Ct. 2841 (1990).

34 *Id.* at 2852-53.

B.   *Criminal Process*

In *County of Riverside v. McLaughlin*, the Court held there was no constitutional necessity for a probable cause finding immediately following a warrantless arrest.[35] The Court characterized its task as balancing "competing concerns": the "concerns" of the arrestee versus those of the public.[36] The *McLaughlin* Court found that the arrestee's concerns were trumped by the threat to the people.[37]

In *United States v. Salerno*, the Court for the first time upheld indefinite pretrial detention without a right to bail.[38] Notwithstanding the dissent's invocation of American "tradition" as inapposite to "the police state,"[39] the majority held the "individual's strong interest in liberty" subordinate to the "greater needs of society."[40]

In a case upholding the use of victim impact evidence in the sentencing of a capital defendant,[41] and overruling precedent barring the use of such evidence, Justice Scalia's concurrence declared it a general principle of constitutional adjudication that the "settled practices and expectations of a democratic society should generally not be disturbed by the courts."[42] Judicial protection of Eighth Amendment rights were analyzed as incompatible with democracy.

Decisions in the criminal area are characterized as struggles between individual claims and the interests of the people, locked in an inexorable zero-sum conflict. Democracy is equated with simple majority rule to which individual liberties must be subordinated.[43] Constitutionalism cannot be had at democracy's expense.

C.   *Speech*

Turning to freedom of expression, First Amendment doctrine reflects similar reactionary constitutional interpretation. In *R.A.V. v.*

---

[35] 111 S. Ct. 1661 (1991).

[36] *Id*. at 1668.

[37] The change in constitutional rhetoric is also evidenced in the privacy area, as seen in the abortion debate. A majority of the Court avoids the use of the term "right" regarding choice, but instead uses the term "interest." *See, e.g.,* Planned Parenthood of S.E. Pa. v. Casey, 112 S. Ct. 2791 (1992); Webster v. Reproductive Health Servs., 492 U.S. 490, 520 (1989).

[38] 481 U.S. 739 (1987).

[39] *Id*. at 755 (Marshall, J., dissenting).

[40] *Id*. at 750-51.

[41] Payne v. Tennessee, 111 S. Ct. 2597 (1991).

[42] *Id*. at 2614 (Scalia, J., concurring). *See also* McNeil v. Wisconsin, 111 S. Ct. 2204 (1991) (limiting the right to counsel during a judicial proceeding) (the dissent characterized the decision as revealing "a preference for an inquisitorial system [of justice]." *Id*. at 2212 (Stevens, J., dissenting)).

[43] *See, e.g.,* Arizona v. Fulminante, 111 S. Ct. 1246 (1991); *see also* Barker v. Wingo, 407 U.S. 514, 519 (1972).

City of St. Paul,[44] the majority's opinion invalidating a cross burning statute characterized the interests of the cross burner and the bias crime victim as a zero-sum conflict.[45] According to Justice Scalia's opinion, protecting the victim of bias crimes necessarily implies censorship of the racist speaker.[46] Though *Texas v. Johnson*,[47] a case involving flag burning, upheld individual First Amendment rights, it was by a scant majority.[48] A three Justice dissent declared that the "high purpose[ ] of a democratic society is to legislate against conduct that is regarded as evil and profoundly offensive to the majority of people . . . ."[49]

During the last two Terms, in a large number of cases regarding freedom of speech, the Court has strictly upheld federal, state and municipal legislation over claims of individual expression. In the most notorious of these, *Rust v. Sullivan*, the Court conditioned receipt of governmental financial benefits on limiting the dissemination of information on abortion.[50] *Rust*, however, merely built upon prior precedent. In the previous Term, the Court had upheld city regulations of an outdoor concert[51] and a postal office forum[52] without calling for a compelling, or even a significant governmental justification. Further, in upholding the regulation of nude dancing, Justice Scalia wrote of a "long tradition of laws against public nudity, which have never been thought to run afoul of traditional understanding of 'the freedom of speech.' "[53]

The speech cases, like the privacy and criminal decisions above, characterize constitutional rights as jeopardizing democracy. Constitutionalism—but not at democracy's expense.

---

44 112 S. Ct. 2538 (1992).

45 *Id*. at 2550.

46 "[T]he only interest distinctively served by the content limitation is that of displaying the city council's special hostility towards the particular biases thus singled out." *Id*. As the four Justices in dissent contend, this question need not have been addressed by the majority, as the particular statute at issue was otherwise constitutionally vulnerable. *Id*. at 2550-51 (White, J., dissenting).

47 491 U.S. 397 (1989).

48 Fletcher notes the 5-4 majority in *Johnson*. Fletcher, *supra* note 2, at 226.

49 *Johnson*, 491 U.S. at 435 (Rehnquist, J., dissenting).

50 Rust v. Sullivan, 111 S. Ct. 1759 (1991) (conditioning federal funding on censorship of viewpoint favoring abortion).

51 Ward v. Rock Against Racism, 491 U.S. 781 (1989).

52 United States v. Kokinda, 497 U.S. 720 (1990).

53 Barnes v. Glen Theatre, Inc., 111 S. Ct. 2456, 2464 (1991) (Scalia, J., concurring) The three member plurality referred to the protection of morality as a "substantial government interest." *Id*. at 2462.

D. Religious Liberty

Reactionary argument is perhaps most notable in the area of religion. In the landmark decision *Employment Division v. Smith*, the Court jettisoned established precedent requiring individualized exemptions from political obligations on religious grounds.[54] Overturning a number of cases requiring a compelling state justification to defeat individual religious liberty claims,[55] the Court upheld a state's prohibition on drug use as a condition to unemployment benefits, over the claim to an exemption based upon religious grounds.[56] *Smith* illustrates beautifully the paradoxical thinking characteristic of reactionary constitutional interpretation. For the Court, requiring exemptions on religious liberty grounds jeopardizes democracy: " 'The mere possession of religious convictions which contradict the relevant concerns of a political society does not relieve the citizen from the discharge of political responsibilities.' "[57] To require exemptions as a constitutional matter is considered to threaten democracy: Exemptions nurture pluralism, and pluralism, in turn, is seen as a danger to the rule of law. "Any society adopting such a system would be courting anarchy, but that danger increases in direct proportion to the society's diversity of religious beliefs . . . ."[58]

It is because " 'we are a cosmopolitan nation made up of people of almost every conceivable religious preference,' *and precisely because we value and protect that religious divergence*, we cannot afford the luxury of deeming *presumptively invalid* . . . every regulation that does not protect an interest of the highest order."[59] Expansion of constitutional liberties again is viewed as a threat to democracy.[60]

---

54 494 U.S. 872 (1990).

55 *See, e.g.*, Wisconsin v. Yoder, 406 U.S. 205 (1972); Sherbert v. Verner, 374 U.S. 398 (1963).

56 Fletcher views the case not so much as a step backward for religious dissent but rather as a consolidation of speech rights. Fletcher, *supra* note 2 at 230.

57 *Smith*, 494 U.S. at 879 (quoting Minersville Sch. Dist. Bd. of Educ. v. Gobitis, 310 U.S. 586, 594-95 (1940)).

58 *Id.* at 888.

59 *Id.* (first emphasis added) (citation omitted) (quoting Braunfeld v. Brown, 366 U.S. 599, 606 (1961)). The Court's negative vision of pluralism is further indicated in its telling choice of terms—its reference to religious diversity as "divergence." *Id. See generally*, Richard K. Sherwin, *Rhetorical Pluralism and the Discourse Ideal: Countering* Division of Employment v. Smith, *a Parable of Pagans, Politics, and Majoritarian Rule*, 85 Nw. U. L. Rev. 388, 427-28 (1991).

60 *Compare* West Virginia State Bd. of Educ. v. Barnette, 319 U.S. 624, 630 (1943) ("The freedom asserted by these appellees does not bring them into collision with rights asserted by any other individual. . . . [T]he refusal of these persons to participate in the ceremony [saluting the flag] does not interfere with or deny rights of others to do so.").

Tradition serves a similar function in the Court's adjudication of the establishment clause side of the religion cases. In recent Terms, claims to be free from establishment of religion

E.   *Our Democracy: Majoritarian or Pluralist?*

The above decisions concerning privacy, criminal process, speech and religion reveal an emerging judicial conception of individual rights as fundamentally incompatible and in inexorable conflict with the interests of the political majority. The contemporary constitutional paradox is that the protection of constitutional rights and liberties is no longer considered to strengthen, but instead to endanger democracy. The jeopardy thesis is expressed graphically and ominously in a recent custodial interrogation decision: " 'This Court is forever adding new stories to the temples of constitutional law, and the temples have a way of collapsing when one story too many is added.' "[61]

CONCLUSION

Reactionary judicial analysis employed to resist expansion in the protection of individual rights—in the name of democracy—is a theory of constitutionalism embodying a distinct understanding of democracy. This conception of democracy is one of a democracy of naked majority rule.[62] Further, it is not just simple majoritarianism; in the Court's reliance on tradition, the balance is being struck in favor of past majorities.[63] The message to the fledgling democracies of Latin America and Eastern Europe is that of a shrinking theory of constitutional democracy. The theory of constitutional democracy appears limited to the legitimacy of decisions made by representatives

---

have been repeatedly defeated by asserted interests in majoritarian traditions. *See, e.g.*, Lynch v. Donnelly, 465 U.S. 668, 680-85 (1984) (Christmas displays as traditional, not religious symbols); Marsh v. Chambers, 463 U.S. 783, 786-92 (1983) (legislative prayers as traditional practices); *see also* Ruti Teitel, *Original Intent, History and Levy's Establishment Clause*, 15 LAW & SOC. INQUIRY 591, 605 (1991) ("Inquiry into longstanding history or 'tradition' is the Supreme Court's fundamental standard in the jurisprudence of the religion clauses.").

[61] McNeil v. Wisconsin, 111 S. Ct. 2204, 2211 (1991) (quoting Douglas v. Jeannette, 319 U.S. 157, 181 (1943)) (regarding the right to counsel during a judicial proceeding).

[62] This understanding is expressed repeatedly in Employment Div., Dep't of Human Resources v. Smith, 494 U.S. 872 (1990). In *Smith*, the Court declared it is the "unavoidable consequence of democratic government" that leaves accommodation to the political process. *Id.* at 890. But it also appears in decisionmaking in other areas of constitutional law; in a recent case concerning desegregation in the public schools, Justice Scalia's concurrence presented a conception of democracy as synonymous with electorate choice. *See* Freeman v. Pitts, 112 S. Ct. 1430, 1454 (1992) (Scalia, J., concurring). In its emerging constitutional interpretation, the Court reconstitutes its own role, while simultaneously reconstituting the theory of our democracy generally, as Dominique Rousseau's hypothesis suggests. *See* Rousseau, *supra* note 5, at 281.

[63] This phenomenon has the effect of engendering a constitutional interpretation of greater conservatism. *See* Teitel, *supra* note 60.

fairly chosen. The effect is of a rolling back in constitutionalism.[64]

Even as our society becomes more pluralistic, as we talk of "exploding diversity," and of "minority-majorities," the Court sadly concludes that there is somehow an unavoidable incompatibility between the protection of fundamental individual liberties and majority rule.[65] Our constitutional democracy is being reinterpreted as a reactionary constitutional identity, tilted away from the possibilities of a dynamic national identity.

---

[64] It is a shift in exactly the opposite direction of that in France, as discussed by Dominique Rousseau. *See* Rousseau, *supra* note 5, at 270-73.

[65] As seen in *Smith*, 494 U.S. at 888 ("[the] danger [of anarchy] increases in direct proportion to [a] society's diversity of religious beliefs, and its determination to coerce or suppress none of them."). On the compatibility of constitutionalism and democracy see Stephen Holmes, *Gag Rules or the Politics of Omission, in* CONSTITUTIONALISM AND DEMOCRACY 19 (Jon Elster & Rune Slagstad eds., 1988). On the possibilities of pluralist democracy see ROBERT A. DAHL, DILEMMAS OF PLURALIST DEMOCRACY: AUTONOMY VS. CONTROL (1982).

TOWARD A FIRST AMENDMENT JURISPRUDENCE OF RESPECT: A COMMENT ON GEORGE FLETCHER'S *CONSTITUTIONAL IDENTITY*

Robin West

As is now widely recognized, the emerging debate in the United States legal community over the constitutionality of city ordinances and university disciplinary sanctions designed to deter "hate speech" has generated two sharply polarized understandings of the nature of the First Amendment and the scope of the rights that amendment protects. What Professor Fletcher's Article helps us see is that those understandings, in turn, rest on two very different conceptions of what he labels in his Article as our sense of "constitutional identity."[1] Although largely undefined by Fletcher, we might take his phrase "constitutional identity" to refer to that aspect of our collective and individual self-conception which we owe to our shared constitutional heritage, and which at least on occasion determines outcomes in close constitutional cases in ways that "overarching principles of political morality"[2] do not.

The two understandings of our constitutional identity that seem to bolster these conflicting accounts of the constitutional status of hate speech regulations might be called, however unimaginatively, the "liberal" and the "progressive" paradigm. Part I of this Comment briefly characterizes the two polarized positions on the constitutionality (or unconstitutionality) of hate speech ordinances, emphasizing only the aspects of each account that are central to its implicit conception of our constitutional identity. Part II offers a friendly criticism of the now somewhat standard defense of hate speech regulations proffered by progressives, and suggests what may be a more promising line of analysis, largely because it rests on a truer account of our constitutional identity.

And lastly, this Comment will demonstrate both the strength and limitation of Professor Fletcher's fine Article; namely, that while some explicit or implicit conception of our "constitutional identity"

---

[1] George P. Fletcher, *Constitutional Identity*, *supra* p. 223, 227.

[2] *Id.* at 223.

may be what determines *decisions* about constitutional questions in close cases, the mere articulation of such a conception in no way provides definitive *answers* to those questions. Our "constitutional identity" is surely as contestable and as contested as any particular and vague constitutional phrase or standard, the interpretation of which it may indeed partly determine.

Both the liberal and unquestionably dominant account of free speech, and the correlative liberal argument against the constitutionality of hate speech regulations, are deeply familiar. Both were recently affirmed by the Supreme Court,[3] and both are eloquently spelled out in Professor Fletcher's Article.[4] From a liberal perspective, speech is, for the most part, an *expressive* act engaged in by individuals toward the end of the individual's own self-fulfillment. Expression, as well as the thought and opinion that accompany it, is what gives our lives their individual definition and contour; it is what *individuates* us. Constitutional protection of free speech—including, of course, speech that "offends"—is therefore the means by which the state acknowledges our individual dignity, our moral worth, individual moral responsibility, and autonomy. Like prayer in earlier times, expression of our innermost selves is a vital means of self-fulfillment, and hence is itself a moral act of high order. We each bare our individual, our authentic, our innermost souls when we express ourselves. And, because we value individual souls, we protect and value our speech whatever its context or side effects. Indeed, in his defense of the liberal conception, Professor Fletcher makes explicit the connecting thread between the protection historically provided to religious belief and practice and the modern protection of expression.[5] We protect expression today for essentially the same reason we once protected religion; namely, the constitutive role of expressive religion in earlier times, and expressive speech today, in the development of the individual's personality:

> All those who feel strongly about something, all those who experience what we loosely call a commitment of conscience should be able to express themselves freely. In the end, one has no tools for distinguishing the anti-patriotic conscience of Johnson from the anti-public school conscience of the Amish. The locus of special freedom, the rubric under which individuals are exempt from at least some general and nondiscriminatory laws, shifts from one

---

[3] R.A.V. v. City of St. Paul, Minn., 112 S. Ct. 2538 (1992) (striking down St. Paul's hate speech regulation as content-based and thus violative of the First Amendment).

[4] *See* Fletcher, *supra* note 1, at 226-32.

[5] *Id.* at 230-31.

clause of the First Amendment to another, from freedom of religion to freedom of speech.

. . . .

One is left, then, with a view of the First Amendment that invests freedom of speech with a particularly heavy burden. The First Amendment is *the* clause in our Constitution that bears the full weight of individual autonomy, the full burden of individuals bearing their souls and expressing their innermost nature in the face of organized demands of conformity and self-restraint. Here is the American spirit at work again, the irreverence of the ongoing American revolution. . . . If the *Smith* decision survives, religion will no longer generate a legal sphere for appeals to higher law, for submissions to conscience, and for resorts to values over which the state has no control. The values of dissent, freedom of the inner self, and the free flourishing of individuals must be borne as emanations of free speech.[6]

From the small explosion of scholarly and adversarial writing in defense of the constitutionality of regulations designed to curb hate speech, one can discern, among several other differences from the liberal paradigm, a dramatically different understanding of the nature of speech and of its role in the development of individual personality. Speech, from the progressive perspective, is not essentially *expressive* (whether "free" or not). Rather, speech is essentially *communicative*. It creates a bond, a relationship, or a community that was not there previously between speaker and listener or writer and reader, the creation of which is both the primary purpose and primary consequence of the speech. We may or may not be baring our individual souls when we speak, but what we are almost inevitably doing (willy-nilly or quite consciously) is creating a social soul: a different and transformed community. Therefore, the value of speech and the value of speech acts are importantly dependent upon the quality, and particularly the moral quality, of the relationships and communities they engender. Depending on the context, the content, the motive, and a host of other intangibles, speech might strengthen or enrich communities, but it also might not; speech can perpetuate hierarchies, can further subordinate already relatively disempowered peoples, can censure by shocking or scaring a listener into silence, or can render the responsive speech of the listener less free by injuring his or her dignity and self-esteem. For any of these reasons it may constitute, to use Patricia Williams's telling phrase, "spirit murder,"[7] regardless of whether or not it also, and incidentally, bares the speaker's innermost

---

6 *Id.*

7 PATRICIA J. WILLIAMS, THE ALCHEMY OF RACE AND RIGHTS 73 (1991).

soul. When these spiritually murderous utterances are of little or no positive value, and when they cause the harm which is their primary purpose and most identifying consequence, it is not at all obvious, from this perspective, why we should protect them.[8]

Thus, the progressive who supports these ordinances and regulations is consciously, firmly, and perhaps obsessively focused on the very *consequences* of the speech to which the liberal also deliberately, firmly, and perhaps obsessively, is willfully blind. What the progressive sees as central—the possibly belittling, injurious, endangering, subordinating, spirit murdering consequences of speech—the liberal sees as, at most, incidental "offense." The liberal then views such offense, as may be taken by overly sensitive souls, as not only an insufficient reason for regulating hate speech, but on the contrary a reason to heighten its protection.[9] The progressive views that offense as a serious anti-communitarian injury which sharply undercuts the prima facie reason for protecting speech, and hence a sufficient justification for its regulation.

The progressive conception of speech—motivated by an egalitarian political impulse, but tremendously enriched theoretically by philosophical work on the nature and necessity of interpretation[10]—has in turn given rise to a particular argument for the constitutionality of hate speech regulations. It is that argument which may be incomplete. That defense pits our political commitment to equality against our commitment to liberty, and on the constitutional level pits the Fourteenth Amendment against the First. Speech may liberate the abstract individual, as the liberal insists, but it also may oppress the very concrete and particular members of subordinated groups. Hence, gains in individual liberty—liberty to speak, to print, or to pornograph—have come at the cost of equality, and both are constitutionally protected values. When we liberate the private individual we simultaneously subordinate already oppressed peoples. Our commitment to liberty, then, should be tempered or limited by our commitment to equality.

Constitutionally, the progressive argument continues, the First

---

[8] *See, e.g.*, Richard Delgado, *Words that Wound: A Tort Action for Racial Insults, Epithets, and Name-Calling*, HARV. C.R.-C.L. L. REV. 133 (1982); Charles R. Lawrence III, *If He Hollers Let Him Go: Regulating Racist Speech on Campus*, 1990 DUKE L.J. 431; Mari J. Matsuda, *Public Response to Racist Speech: Considering the Victim's Story*, 87 MICH. L. REV. 2320 (1990).

[9] *See, e.g.*, Ronald Dworkin, *The Coming Battles over Free Speech*, N.Y. REV. BOOKS, June 11, 1992, at 56-58, 61.

[10] *See* STANLEY FISH, IS THERE A TEXT IN THIS CLASS? (1980); STANLEY FISH, DOING WHAT COMES NATURALLY (1989).

Amendment's protection of speech must be read through the prism of the Fourteenth Amendment's more or less explicit promise of equality. We should, therefore, read an additional exception into the First Amendment's protection of speech, an exception motivated by a political quest for equality and sanctioned by the Fourteenth Amendment. Such an exception would allow for regulations, if narrowly and skillfully crafted, of speech that is of little expressive value and which does tremendous subordinating harm. We should read the First Amendment as "balanced by" the Fourteenth, and our commitment to liberty as limited by our commitment to equality.

There are a number of problems with this approach from a liberal perspective, but there are also problems from a progressive perspective. From a progressive perspective, the first problem is simply strategic and goes not to the particular argument, but to the wisdom of advocating hate speech ordinances on equality or any other grounds. Particularly given the Court's recent pronouncement on the subject in *R.A.V. v. City of St. Paul, Minn.*,[11] it seems clear that neither this argument nor any other is likely to succeed, and our failure to sustain these ordinances will have very real consequences. At the very least the failure to sustain these ordinances will further trivialize the harms of speech, and further denigrate its victims both in their own eyes and in the eyes of others. It is belittling, even humiliating, and at least ostracizing to sustain an injury, the infliction of which is constitutionally *protected*, where the Constitution possesses as much power as it does in this culture to create our moral, our social, and our legal identity. To complain of an injury caused by a constitutionally protected act is not just whining over "names that can never hurt me," but is also deeply anti-communitarian in ways in which Fletcher's Article helps to illuminate: Even to voice the complaint is an attack on our collective constitutional identity, as understood and articulated by liberalism.[12] Unsuccessful attempts to sustain such regulations may underscore the marginality and outsider status of victims of speech, simply by emphasizing the high constitutional status of the events which cause the injuries they suffer.

Other problems, however, inhere in the "equality versus liberty" construction of the issues surrounding hate speech regulations favored by progressives, and the conception of our constitutional identity that construction implies. Regardless of what the Court ultimately decides, that progressive construction—that "constitutional identity" and its attendant problems—will persist as a minority or dissident tra-

---

[11]   112 S. Ct. 2538 (1992).
[12]   *See* Fletcher, *supra* note 1, at 227, 231–32.

dition in First Amendment jurisprudence. It is therefore imperative that we do what we can to get it right.

The first problem is rhetorical. In popular consciousness, as well as constitutional history, we never have had a political or moral commitment to equality that comes anywhere near the weight or intensity of our commitment to liberty. To use Fletcher's phrase, liberty is at the heart of our "constitutional identity" in a way which equality has never been. Think of the pledge of allegiance, the Star Spangled Banner, or the grade school ditty "My Country 'Tis of Thee," all of which mention liberty, and none of which mention equality. In any popular standoff between equality and liberty, liberty will triumph in the popular mind as well as in constitutional doctrine. The contemptuous tone of the charge of "political correctness" that accompanies arguments against hate speech regulations and also against diversity and multiculturalism in education,[13] can be attributed, in part, to that simple rhetorical fact. The often apologetic tone of defenders of these ordinances and of victims of such speech is a much sadder reminder.

The second problem is descriptive. The progressive understanding of hate speech as harmful because of its adverse consequences for equality misdescribes, or at least does not fully describe, the problem. For it is not only the *equality* of subordinated persons (or the groups to which they belong) that is damaged by hate speech. It is also *liberty*: the liberty to walk the street, the campus, or the workplace undeterred by fear of harassment; the liberty to speak uncensored by the silencing effects of hate; the freedom to live in a community with others or to live in peace with oneself unshackled by the effects of speech which, perhaps uniquely, injures the listener by reducing her to her materiality by negating her noncorporeal existence and by equating her with her physical being—in short, by murdering her spirit. When we characterize the injury of hate speech as one to equality, rather than to liberty, we saddle ourselves not only with a constitutional argument which may well be unsustainable, but also with a description of the injury that rests on an unnecessarily thin vision of social and political life. Equality is not the only value at stake—it is not the only characteristic of an ideal community to which we ought strive—nor is inequality the only harm or evil we should seek to eradicate. The claim that it is rests on a falsely narrow understanding of the community as constituted *only* by politics, by power, by domination, and by subordination. But there is much more to social life than power, and much more to individual thriving than relative equality.

---

[13] *See, e.g.*, Paul Carrington, *Diversity!*, 1992 UTAH L. REV. (forthcoming Jan. 1993).

Lastly, the standard equality-based defense of hate speech concedes what should be contested: namely, an understanding of our constitutional identity that pits abstract individual rights of liberty and speech against harms sustained by concrete members of particular groups. For if the progressive understanding of speech as essentially communicative, rather than expressive, is right, then liberals are wrong to characterize the problem as a standoff between individual "rights of expression" on the one hand, and the interests of members of subordinated groups protecting against subordinating injuries on the other. If the progressive critique is right, then it is the liberal conception of our shared constitutional identity—a constitutional self-image of a community of individuals freely expressing their innermost souls and possessed of rights to do so, and of group members injured by such expressions and possessed of interests and vulnerabilities—and not its favoring of individuals and rights over groups and interests, that is the flawed premise in the liberal argument against hate speech regulations. We need to challenge that conception, not simply argue for a rebalancing of the rights and interests it posits.

We should at least supplement, if not supplant, the current Fourteenth Amendment/equality defense of hate speech regulations with a reinvigorated, reconstructed interpretation of the First Amendment that would take seriously the progressive understanding not just of the magnitude of the harms caused by hate speech, but also of the nature of speech and of our consequent "constitutional identity." That understanding would construe the "point" of the First Amendment, to use Ronald Dworkin's phrase,[14] as the protection and facilitation of *communication* rather than expression, and the well-functioning community, rather than the soul-baring, expressive individual of conscience, as its inherent ideal. Understood as such, the First Amendment would protect much of what it now protects and be subject to many of the same exceptions as under its liberal interpretation. It would also non-problematically weigh in favor of regulations of speech designed to counter the censorial effects on communication of private concentrations of power, whether those concentrations be racial, economic, or sexual. The First Amendment, understood as protecting communication rather than expression, and communities of speakers and listeners rather than soul-baring individuals, would thus protect the listener and potential speaker who sustains and is transformed by the consequences of speech, whether for better or ill, as well as the hateful utterance and its expressing speaker. Viewed as such, it would protect all participants—speakers, listeners, potential

---

[14] *See* Dworkin, *supra* note 9, at 56.

speakers—against not only ill-founded state efforts to enforce a stifling conformity, but also against malicious private attempts to induce a silence born not of a valued privacy, but of a stultifying and strangling self-hatred.

This is not to argue that such a redirection would drastically improve the chances of sustaining these ordinances in court against a First Amendment attack. It would not obviate the danger and risk to victims of hate speech posed by unsuccessful defenses of the constitutionality of ordinances designed for their protection. It might, however, address some of the other problems that now plague progressive arguments for the constitutionality of hate speech regulations. On a rhetorical level, it would be tremendously helpful to begin to fashion an understanding of the First Amendment as being in alignment, rather than in tension, with both the Fourteenth Amendment and with progressive ends. It could only help progressive political efforts to rest on a non-contradictory "constitutional identity," rather than one characterized by paradox, contradiction, and tension.

More importantly, such a recharacterization of the First Amendment might be truer not only to the nature of the injuries victims of hate speech sustain, but also to the progressive constitutional identity the sufferance of those injuries offends. As Rodney King pleaded in the violent aftermath of the hate crime he suffered, we must learn to "get along"[15] with each other. In our current pluralist, multicultural, multiethnic, severely *crowded* times, the contrasting liberal constitutional identity behind standard First Amendment understandings—that we learn to let each other alone to nurture, express, or bare our own individual souls—is increasingly an unattainable, whether or not desirable goal. Rodney King's plea may not only be expressive of a more appealing political vision—a more desirable constitutional identity—but a more realistic one as well.

---

15 *Riots in Los Angeles: A Plea for Calm*, N.Y. TIMES, May 2, 1992, at 6.

HERMENEUTICS AND CONSTITUTIONAL INTERPRETATION

Aharon Barak

I. THE PROBLEM

I am a judge. For me, a constitution is an operational document. I decide cases by extracting meaning from its text. The process of extracting meaning from the text of the constitution, as with any document, is the process of interpretation, and so the question presented to me is: How do you interpret a constitution? It is not an answer to say "Words have no meaning; do whatever you think politically expedient." Words *do* have meaning. A cigarette is not an elephant. I am a judge, not a politician. I do not have a political agenda; I do not represent a constituency. It is not my role, nor do I desire, to impose my subjective will on the polity. I am required to act judiciously, objectively, consistently, coherently. It is no answer to me to advise, "Think and act prudently, pragmatically, reasonably." What does "prudently" mean? When am I acting "pragmatically"?

It is also no answer to say "Read the text and apply it." To read and apply requires the intermediate step: to construe. The words of a constitution, like the words of any other document, may have several meanings. What meaning should I choose? Words can be applied on different levels of generality and abstraction. Which level should I choose?

It may be said "Choose the level of generality and abstraction that fits the intent of the framers of the constitution." But why should I? Is the purpose of interpretation to further *their* intent? Isn't the purpose of interpretation to further the purpose of the constitution?

In order to know how to read a constitution I must have a better understanding of interpretation. What is "interpretation" and how is it accomplished? I realize soon, that I am faced with similar questions when I read other texts. How does one read a contract, a statute, a will? Do I read a constitution the same way I read a will? Do we not always have to be aware that "it is a constitution we are expounding"? All these documents must be interpreted, but is there a uniform theory for reading them all?

Perhaps the suggestion that I read a constitution in a way that implements the intent of the founding fathers provides the answer. Isn't this the case with wills—one should, perhaps, interpret a will in a manner that implements the intent of the deceased. But then I recall that a contract should be interpreted "objectively," and that the intent of one party should not matter so long as it is not shared by the other party; there are reliance interests to be taken into account. Aren't there reliance interests to be accounted for when one interprets the constitution or a statute?

By now it is clear to me: I need a theory of interpretation. Not a meta-theory—a theory about theories—but a workable theory of how to read a legal text generally and a constitutional text in particular.

Judges, scholars, lawyers, and the public interpret legal texts every day. Most of them reach the same results most of the time. There is law outside the courts. Not every case is a hard case; there are easy cases. Not every case reaches the Supreme Court. There must be a common method—accepted by the legal community—to interpret a legal text.

II. THE TEXT

I start with the text—whether it is a will, a contract, a statute, or a constitution. Interpretation requires that I give it meaning. In adjudicating, the meaning I must give is the "legal" meaning, that is, the normative meaning. My first general rule of interpretation is: one should not give to the text a legal meaning that is not supported by its literal meaning. The literal meaning, or rather the zone of literal meanings, marks the boundary between interpreting an existing text and creating a new one. We must distinguish between text and meaning. As interpreters we can change our understanding of the meaning of the text, but we can't change the text. Legal interpretation is a process of choice of meaning that must be confined to the zone of literal meaning.

The normative force of interpretation derives from the normative force of the text itself. The court's interpretation is not at a normative level above the text or below the text; it is a choice, among different literal meanings of the text. The court's constitutional interpretation is not the supreme law of the land. The court's constitutional interpretation is the legally binding choice of what the Constitution, as supreme law of the land, means.

III.   THE CHOICE

If legal interpretation is a choice within the zone of possible literal meanings of the text, how is this choice to be made? Is there a choice that is "true to the meaning of the text?" Is there a right or wrong choice? My answer is simple: There is no "true" interpretation. There is no "true" meaning. There is only "proper" interpretation. There are different methods or theories for choosing the legally binding meaning of the text, and a choice must be made among these theories. But none of the theories has a claim to truth.

The choice among different methods for extracting legal from literal meaning is not itself an interpretative choice; it is not conducted by rules of interpretation. If the study of hermeneutics teaches anything, it teaches us that hermeneutics cannot tell us which hermeneutical approach to use. The choice among the different methods or theories is a policy choice. Every theory of interpretation is the outcome of noninterpretive considerations. The choice is not the individual exercise of a judge or scholar; it is a choice made by generations of judges and scholars throughout history. These choices determine the nature of the interpretive legal community.

There are legal communities, however, in which there is no consensus on how the choice should be made. The American legal community is one example; it is divided mainly because of the problem of judicial review. The Israeli legal community is another; the failure of consensus can be traced mainly to the problems posed by the transfer from British rule to independence. What, then, can I suggest about the proper choice among thoeries of interpretation in the context of such a divided legal community?

A.   *Purposive Interpretation*

My starting point is the purpose of the law. For me, every law has a purpose. These purposes include, among others, the ethical, social, and economic, objectives that law as a social institution must fulfill. If law has a purpose, and if any specific legal norm has its purpose, then interpretation has to be a tool for effectuating the law's purpose. My theory of interpretation of the legal text recommends the choice within the range of possible literal meanings, of that particular meaning which, more than any other, furthers the purpose of the norm embodied in the text. If one wishes, one can call it "purposive interpretation." Thus, just as the aim of interpreting a will or a contract is to further its purpose, the aim of interpreting a statute or a constitution is to further its purpose. This theory furthers the democratic notions of representative government, separation of powers, and the rule of law. Since it furthers the basic values of the society, it furthers human rights and other values that it is the law's function to fulfill.

Thus, the object of interpretation of a given legal text is to make a choice, within the literal zone, that furthers the purpose of the norm embodied in the text, not the intent of the creator of the text. The purpose of a norm is not a psychological concept. It is a normative concept. It is not something to be "found" or "discovered" in the text. It is a legal concept, an abstraction, a construction, to be created outside the text. In creating this abstraction, the interpreter is not wholly free; but he is not fully bound, either. How then is the purpose established?

B. *Establishment of Purpose*

Among the sources from which the purpose of a legal norm is to be extracted is, first and foremost, the intent of those who created the text. Intent is a tool for understanding purpose. We may call it the "subjective purpose." The relevant intent is the intent concerning the purpose of the norm—it is the general purpose. Usually there will be several purposes with different levels of abstraction. The relevant intent is not aimed at knowing how the creator of the text would solve the problem faced by the interpreter. We do not ask counter factual questions. The relevant intent is aimed at the creator's concept of the general and abstract purpose of the legal norm that was created.

The purpose of the legal norm is not exclusively a "subjective purpose." The legal norm also has "objective purposes." These objective purposes are the ones that the legal community wants to achieve with its norms, and they represent the deep and basic understandings of the legal community. They consist of the values and policies that establish the identity of the community. Their origin is in the past. They were developed by generations of judges and precedents. They are the outcome of history and tradition. They reflect the legal community's understanding of its identity and its diversity.

The subjective purpose and the objective purpose usually coincide. It is usually the subjective purpose of the text's creator to further the objective purposes of the community. But the two kinds of purposes have to be distinguished. The creators of the text may not have had in their mind any of the objective purposes. They may even have had a subjective purpose which is at odds with some objective purpose. What are, then, the interrelationships between these purposes?

There is no "true" answer to that question. It is a policy decision, to be accepted or rejected by the legal community. It cannot be the same answer for all legal texts. You may say, for example, that with regard to wills, the subjective purpose always prevails unless it is illegal. The objective purpose only supplements. You may also claim that as to contracts, the common subjective purpose of the parties prevails, while the objective purpose applies to third parties who have no knowledge of the subjective purpose. Beyond that, absent information on subjective purpose, one may refer to objective purpose.

Where statutes are in question, it seems to me that a subjective purpose embodied in the express words of the statute should prevail over objective purpose. This fits our understanding of the functions of legislators and judges, as well as our notions concerning the separation of power. If the legislature does not like the outcome, the statue can be changed. Still, the objective purpose plays a critical role. It is the criterion by which a choice is made among conflicting subjective purposes; it creates a strong presumption about purpose, and only reliable and convincing evidence of subjective purpose can overcome this presumption. Furthermore, if there are fundamental changes in the outlook of the legal community, including changes brought about by subsequent statutes, the subjective purpose may be found entirely unacceptable. If the subjective purpose conflicts with the objective purpose, and the objective purpose is embodied in the constitutional text, the subjective purpose can result in a declaration that the statute is unconstitutional.

This brings me to the interrelationship between subjective and objective purpose in constitutional interpretation. But before moving on to that subject, it is helpful to make some observations concerning judicial discretion in interpretation.

C. *Judicial Discretion*

"Judicial discretion" is the power of the judge to choose among several interpretative alternatives, each of which is lawful. This definition assumes, of course, that the judge will not act mechanically, but instead will weigh, reflect, test, and study. Yet, this conscious use of the power of thought does not define judicial discretion. Judicial discretion, by definition, is neither an emotional nor a mental state. It is, rather, a normative condition, in which the judge has the freedom to choose among a number of interpretive options.

Any theory of interpretation must assume the existence of judicial discretion. There can be no interpretation without discretion. Interpretive theories differ as to the scope of discretion, but not as to its existence. Subjective theories of interpretation assume discretion, at least as to the level of generality among different subjective purposes. Objective theories of interpretation assume discretion, as to the different levels of objective purposes, and as to the weighing and balancing among conflicting values or principles. Thus, it would be a grave mistake to formulate any theory of interpretation without integrating, as an integral part, a theory of discretion. In fact, the recommendations for the use of judicial discretion form the most important aspects of any interpretive theory. Thus, the choice between subjective and objective purposes in interpretation has to be integrated into a broader concept of judicial discretion. Such integration is especially necessary when the subject is constitutional interpretation, as the basic considerations regarding judicial discretion are constitutional in nature. These considerations raise questions about the role of a judge in a democratic society. The questions are intimately associated with the constitutional role of the judge as interpreter of the constitutional text.

D. *Purposive Constitutional Interpretation*

What is the proper mix of subjective and objective purposes in constitutional interpretation? This too, of course, is a policy decision to be made by the general consensus of the legal community. Absent such consensus, what is the "proper" way to make this choice? Is it the same choice in statutory interpretation as in constitutional interpretation?

The full answer to this question requires more time than I have today, as it raises many fundamental issues. I can only provide a short answer: constitutional interpretation is different from statutory, as well as other legal interpretation. The difference lies in the special character of the constitutional text.

The purpose of the constitutional text is to provide a solid foundation for national existence. It is to embody the basic aspirations of the people. It is to guide future generations by its basic choices. It is to control majorities and protect individual dignity and liberty. All these purposes cannot be fulfilled if the only guide to interpretation is the subjective purposes of the framers of the constitutional text. The constitution will not achieve its purposes if its vision is restricted to the horizons of its founding fathers. Even if we assume the broadest generalizations of subjective purpose, this may not suffice. It may not provide a solid foundation for modern national existence. It may be foreign to the basic aspirations of modern people. It may not be consistent with the dignity and liberty of the modern human being. A constitution must be wiser than its creators.

It is my view, therefore, that in constitutional interpretation, unlike in other legal interpretation, the objective purpose should prevail. However, in the realization of the objective purpose as a normative concept, the past should not be forgotten. The objective purpose is a vision of life, embodied within the zone of literal meaning, that has its origin in the past. It is a reflection of higher values transferred from one generation to another, a fulfillment of basic values embodied in past decisions. It is a carry-over of old traditions into the modern environment. It is the modern understanding shaped by past experiences of the role of the individual in the state.

Of course, such an interpretation restricts the current majority, acting via an ordinary statute. In this respect, a judge exercising this kind of interpretation is acting in a counter-majoritarian fashion. But, so is a judge who interprets the constitutional text according to the subjective purpose of the creator of the text. The legitimacy of any theory of interpretation does not come from the text or from the creator's intent. The legitimacy of every theory of constitutional interpretation—like the legitimacy of the constitution itself—derives from non-legal sources outside the subjective purpose method of interpretation and may also legitimize the objective purpose method of interpretation.

In establishing the purpose of the constitutional norm, the judge has discretion, but not unlimited discretion. It is a discretion rooted in history and tradition. The vision of the judge concerning modern purposes must be compatible with his vision of the historic purposes. The modern purpose must conform to the level of generality already recognized by other judges in modern times. Precedent must generally be respected. A judge should not impose personal values; instead, he should try to reflect the basic values of national life. These values do not represent majority views or minority views; they reflect basic ideals. They should fit comfortably into the coherent and natural development of basic concepts. They should fit the constitutional structure and system, and be continuous with the constitutional scheme. A constitution is not a collection of articles; it is a unified whole to be applied with a broad view. A constitution is an integrated document in which the interpretation of one of the articles requires the interpretation of the whole text.

But there is discretion. In exercising his discretion, a judge is asked to be a historian, a philosopher, and a prophet. The judge may fail. Though his decisions may be final, they are not infallible, and the judge may commit grave mistakes. He may misread the national way of life. He may not strike the proper balance between stability and change. He may further his subjective views, and not the heritage of the system. He may be influenced by temporary, fleeting trends and ideas. Those are the risks that must be taken into account. No theory of interpretation can prevent mistakes. The question is, does my theory of interpretation generally, and my theory of constitutional interpretation in particular, fulfill its purpose? Does the judge as a constitutional interpreter fulfill a proper function in the general constitutional scheme? Does he stand the constitutional trial? I hope the answer is positive, though I realize the challenges this answer faces. As a judge, I should know my limitations. As our elders said, "You would think that I am granting you power? It is slavery that I am imposing on you."

THE CONSTITUTIONAL JUDGE: MASTER OR SLAVE OF THE CONSTITUTION?

Dominique Rousseau

Both positivist and natural law doctrines are based on the assumption that a constitution is a given, a reality both existing apart from the Conseil constitutionnel (the "Constitutional Council" or "Council") and obtruding upon it. Whether created by the state or existing independently of it, constitutional rules of form and substance are considered norms with their own meaning. In other words, none of the constituted powers dictates the meaning of norms, their meaning exists independently. In this context a constitutional judge provides to a legislator a simple reminder of the meaning of the constitutional norm where it may have been misconstrued. The Council adds nothing, creates nothing; it merely applies to Parlement a norm whose meaning constrains Parlement and subjects the legislator to a norm that the Council itself must obey and for which it is only a spokesperson.

Here, then, judicial reasoning resembles mathematical reasoning. Judging comes down to a simple operation of applying the constitutional norm to the law, an operation that derives its method from the syllogism. The judge has no freedom of evaluation, no power of interpretation, since the meaning of the norm is self-contained. This is why the Council does not wield any political power under these doctrines; as Montesquieu expressed it, since judges are just the organ that pronounces the words of the Constitution, their power to judge is practically nil.

The advantage of this point of view is that it exorcises the spectre of the judge's political power and rids us of the very question of the democratic legitimacy of control of the constitutionality of laws. The Council's jurisprudential activity would be political if it were creating a constitutional norm, but since it is only applying a preexisting norm its activity is neutral. The striking disadvantage of this point of view, however, is that it ignores the reality of the juridical task. In order to apply a constitutional provision, the Council must first determine its meaning.

Let us consider two examples:

Article twenty-seven of the French Constitution provides that a member of Parlement may delegate to a deputy the personal right to vote in exceptional circumstances. The Council was expected to censure a certain vote, where the number of "ayes" exceeded the number of deputies present, indicating improper delegation in violation of article twenty-seven. Rather than referring to the express terms of the Constitution, the Council dismissed the action, reasoning that while voting irregularities were apparent, it had not been shown that the final result was affected.[1]

The Council used similar reasoning in a case concerning the validity of a statute. Within each Department, according to article seventy-two of the Constitution, the Prefect, among other things, had power to administer, reform, or invalidate the laws of local communities. In 1982 this control was transferred to a judge, thereby substituting juridical control for administrative control. The Council determined that this was consistent with article seventy-two, even though the text explicitly provided for administrative control; while the Prefect no longer has exclusive power over local laws, a case may still be submitted by the Prefect to the court, thereby continuing the Prefect's role in oversight of community actions.[2]

These examples negate, perhaps definitively, the argument that the constitutional judge is merely "the spokesman of the Constitution." The task of the judge may not be reduced to a simple mechanical operation of application of the Constitution; he does interpret, even if—and herein lies all the theoretical difficulty—his interpretation frequently depends upon the text alone. The questions are, then, What does it mean to interpret? and What is the status of the text?

The argument defended here is that the text does not contain its own hidden meaning or truth that the judge brings to light, deciphers, or recovers by invoking the authors' intention. Invoking the authors' intention is a bit like invoking God; one can make them say whatever one wishes because they are not available to invalidate or corroborate. The text is only a structured arrangement of words to which the judge, in a specific set of circumstances, attributes a meaning; the text's only reality lies in its interpretation. Undoubtedly, the judge's task appears to derive from the text, but if, *when seen as finished work*, the judicial ruling is taken as inferred from the Constitution, *when*

[1] Judgment of Jan. 23, 1987 (*Loi portant diverses mesures d'ordre social*), Con. const., Rec. C.C. 13.

[2] Judgment of Feb. 25, 1982 (*Loi relative aux droits et libertés des communes, des departements et des regions*), Con. const., Rec. C.C. 38.

seen as work in progress, the inference of the judicial ruling is, in fact, impossible, for the text allows numerous interpretations. There is no one strictly correct interpretation but only interpretations made at a given time, in specific political, legal, cultural, or social circumstances.

In order to answer the difficult question posed in the title of this Article, the judge must be considered a master of the Constitution. At the same time, however, the judge is not free to produce whatever interpretation of the Constitution he or she chooses. How then can this unique position of the constitutional judge, the "unfree master" of the Constitution, be reconciled with constitutional requirements? These are the two considerations discussed below.

I. THE CONSTITUTIONAL JUDGE'S INTERPRETATION AS THE PRODUCT OF MULTIPLE, COMPLEX INTERACTIONS

A. *The Techniques of Interpretation*

The main means of constitutional control is textual interpretation. When a statute is challenged in court, claimants always allege that the legislator misinterpreted constitutional principles and that the purpose or effects of the law, as interpreted by those who bring the action, are unconstitutional. In order to respond to these challenges, in a word to declare that a law is or is not consistent with a given constitutional principle, the Council must determine both the meaning of the right or liberty in question and the correct meaning of the disputed law. The interpretation of texts is thus at stake in a constitutional contest in which the interpretations of Parlement, of those bringing the action, and of the Council vie with one another. For the Council, interpretation is an inherently intellectual operation that is indispensable for its exercise of control. Thanks to constitutional interpretation and a meticulous analysis of the content of the statute, the Council can speak out about the consistency of its constitutional rulings. In order to accomplish this task, the Council has gradually evolved three specific interpretive techniques.

1. *The Three Techniques of Interpretation*

The first, the *limiting interpretation*, involves the Council's removing juridical effect from disputable legislative provisions or excluding from among possible interpretations those that would make it contradict the Constitution. Thus, for example, where a claimant takes issue with certain provisions of a statute, the Council may reason that the "provisions are devoid of any legal effect"; by rendering the provisions inoperative, "there are no grounds to declare them inconsistent with the Constitution."[3] Or, the Council may decide that a statute could not possibly have the unconstitutional effect ascribed to it by the claimants.[4]

The second technique is *constructive interpretation*, in which the Council no longer curtails but adds provisions to the law that are designed to make it consistent with the Constitution or make a legal clause convey more meaning than is expressly provided in the text. Thus, when article twenty-nine of the law concerning the prevention of lay-offs orders only that the labor union bringing suit on behalf of a wage-earner must give him notice "in a registered letter with acknowledgement of receipt," the Council assumes that this provision

> implies that the letter must contain all relevant details about the nature and purpose of the current lawsuit, about the full implication of his acceptance, and about his acknowledged right to stop the suit at any point . . . and that the tacit acceptance of the wage-earner may be considered granted only when the union can prove when it brings the suit that the wage-earner personally had thorough knowledge of the letter including the details mentioned above.[5]

None of these specifications is delineated in the text of the law; the Council, through the task of interpretation, added them so that the law may be deemed consistent with the Constitution.[6]

The third technique, *guideline interpretation*, consists of the Council defining and specifying for those authorities responsible for implementing the law, the modes of application necessary for conformity with the Constitution. Thus, in its decision issued on July 28, 1989, the Council first specified the rules of application in a case where several financial and penal sanctions could obtain against the perpetrators of stock exchange misdemeanors, by providing that the

---

[3] Judgment of July 27, 1982 (*Loi portant réforme de la planification*), Con. const., Rec. C.C. 52.

[4] *See, e.g.*, Judgment of Sept. 3, 1986 (*Loi relative à la lutte contre le terrorisme*), Con. const., Rec. C.C. 122; Judgment of Aug. 8, 1985 (*Loi sur l'évolution de la Nouvelle-Calédonie*), Con. const., Rec. C.C. 63; Judgment of Dec. 29, 1984 (*Loi de finances pour 1985*), Con. const., Rec. C.C. 94; Judgment of Jan. 19, 1984 (*Loi relative à l'activité et au contrôle des establissements de credit*), Con. const., Rec. C.C. 23; Judgment of July 19-20, 1983 (*Loi relative à la democratisation du secteur public*), Con. const., Rec. C.C. 49; Judgment of July 19, 1983 (*Loi portant approbation d'une convention fiscale*), Con. const., Rec. C.C. 43.

[5] Judgment of July 25, 1989 (*Loi modifiant le code du travail et relative à la prevention du licenciement économique et au droit à la conversion*), Con. const., Journal Office [J.O.], July 28, 1989, at 9503.

[6] *See, e.g.*, Judgment of Jan. 19, 1984 (*Loi relative à l'activité et au contrôle des establissements de credit*), Con. const., Rec. C.C. 23; Judgment of Jan. 19-20, 1981 (*Loi reforçant la sécurité et protegeant la liberté des personnes*), Con. const., Rec. C.C. 15; Judgment of July 20, 1977 (*Loi de finances rectificative pour 1961*), Con. const., Rec. C.C. 39.

total amount of sanctions must not in these cases exceed "the highest amount of one of the sanctions incurred." The Council immediately added a directive of application by asking "the competent administrative and legal authorities to pay careful heed to the fulfillment of this demand in the implementation of these provisions."[7]

Whatever the technique, the Constitutional Council does exert its control through an interpretation of the statute whose scope it limits, whose provisions it completes, and whose modes of application it specifies. Because of its judicial and political implications, this means of control raises many problems.

2. *The Clear Error* (l'erreur manifeste) *Standard*

The Council's use of "clear error" as a standard for control over the legislator's awareness of the facts, circumstances or situations forming the bases of a statute, appears for the first time implicitly in its decision issued on January 19-20, 1981 and explicitly in its decision issued on January 16, 1982: "[T]he legislator's assessment of the necessity of nationalizations decided by the law which is under examination by the Constitutional Council could not be challenged *in the absence of unmistakable error*."[8]

Since that decision, the Council has regularly used this means of control of facts both to underscore the legislator's awareness of the severity and need for disciplinary measures regarding the unacceptable features[9] and the length of time during which valid provisions remain temporarily applicable;[10] this means also helps the Council to find out whether Parlement has made an error in its weighing of contextual distinctions that might justify an infringement on the principle of equality. The Council ensures that decisions, such as where the threshold from which professional property is exempt from the surtax on great wealth belongs,[11] or regarding the setting of different age limits for various classes of civil servants,[12] do not arise from obviously flawed judgments.

In the same way, the clear error standard is systematically used

---

[7] Judgment of July 28, 1989 (*Loi relative à la transparence du marche financier*), Con. const., J.O., Aug. 1, 1989, at 9678.

[8] Judgment of Jan. 16, 1982 (*Loi de nationalisation*), Con. const., Rec. C.C. 18 (emphasis added).

[9] Judgment of July 25, 1984 (*Loi modifiant la loi du 29 juillet 1982 sur la communication audiovisuelle*), Con. const., Rec. C.C. 55.

[10] Judgment of July 24, 1985 (*Loi portant diverses dispositions d'ordre social*), Con. const., Rec. C.C. 56.

[11] Judgment of Dec. 29, 1983 (*Loi de finance pour 1984*), Con. const., Rec. C.C. 67.

[12] Judgment of Sept. 12, 1984 (*Loi relative à la limité d'age dans la fonction publique et le secteur public*), Con. const., Rec. C.C. 73.

to control the various aspects of delineating voting district boundaries, variations in representation from district to district, and fairness in determining district boundaries.[13] This method is not only procedural; in fact, the Council does not hesitate to censure legislative judgments that seem substantively flawed. For example, in its decision issued on August 8, 1985, the Council raised the point that the number of councillors set by the legislators for the four regions of New Caledonia rested upon a clear error in the estimation of each region's demographics.[14]

With the clear error standard, the Council thus introduces control of proportionality in disputed constitutional claims. This clearly springs from the wording of recent decisions in which the Council examined in turn whether statutes set up "an *obvious disproportion* between the offense and the punishment incurred,"[15] or create *excessively disproportionate* gaps in representation between election districts;[16] further, the Council criticized, in matters of amnesty, "provisions which *obviously exceed the limits* which respect for the Constitution imposes on the legislator."[17]

But the idea of proportionality was already present in the decision issued on February 16, 1982.[18] As a general rule, the Council

---

[13] Judgment of July 7, 1987 (*Loi modifiant l'organisation administrative et le régime électoral de la ville de Marseille*), Con. const., Rec. C.C. 41; Judgment of Nov. 18, 1986 (*Loi relative à la delimitation de circonscriptions pour l'élections des députés*), Con. const., Rec. C.C. 167; Judgment of July 1-2, 1986 (*Loi relative à l'élection de députés, et autorisant le Gouvernment à délimiter par ordonnance les circonscriptions électorales*), Con. const., Rec. C.C. 78; Judgment of Aug. 23, 1985 (*Loi sur l'évolution de la Nouvelle-Calédonie*), Con. const., Rec. C.C. 70; Judgment of Aug. 8, 1985 (*Loi sur l'évolution de la Nouvelle-Calédonie*), Con. const., Rec. C.C. 63.

[14] Judgment of Aug. 8, 1985 (*Loi sur l'évolution de la Nouvelle-Calédonie*), Con. const., Rec. C.C. 63. See also the decision issued on January 7, 1988, in which the Council holds that the particular situation the legislator had conceded to certain categories of Credit Agricole shareholders "excessively undermines the principle of equality." Judgment of Jan. 7, 1988 (*Loi relative à la mutualisation de la Caisse nationale de crédit agricole*), Con. const., Rec. C.C. 17. In the decision issued on December 30, 1987, the Council determined that by prescribing that the fiscal fine incurred in the case of a disclosure of a person's income will equal the amount of the income disclosed, the legislator has issued a sanction that assumes "an obviously disproportionate character." Judgment of Dec. 30, 1987 (*Loi de finances pour 1988*), Con. const., Rec. C.C. 63; *see also* Judgment of July 20, 1988 (*Loi portant amnistie*), Con. const., Rec. C.C. 119.

[15] Judgment of Sept. 3, 1986 (*Loi relative à la lutte contre la criminalité et la délinquance*), Con. const., Rec. C.C. 130 (emphasis added).

[16] Judgment of July 7, 1987 (*Loi modifiant l'organisation administrative et le régime électoral de la ville de Marseille*), Con. const., Rec. C.C. 41 (emphasis added).

[17] Judgment of July 20, 1988 (*Loi portant amnistie*), Con. const., Rec. C.C. 119 (emphasis added).

[18] Judgment of Feb. 16, 1982 (*Loi portant réforme de la planification*), Con. const., Rec. C.C. 52. The Council actually is of the opinion that there is no clear error about the necessity of acts of nationalization "since it has not been proven that the currently worked out transfers

always ascertains whether the legislator's threats to a constitutional right are not so severe that its meaning and implication would be distorted.[19] In other words, the clear error standard allows the Council to weigh, on one hand, the common interest sought by the statute and on the other hand, the threats to a given constitutional principle; depending on the result, whether or not the Council judges the threats to be disproportionate or excessive with respect to the interest sought by the legislator, the statute will be declared consistent or inconsistent with the Constitution. Recall the decision of July 28, 1989,[20] where the Council applied the principle of proportionality to establish a constructive interpretation that would save the constitutionality of a statute: Where concurrent sanctions are imposed the total must not exceed the highest of any individual sanction.[21]

With the evolution of such a method, isn't the control of constitutionality constrained by political exigencies? More specifically, are nationalizations violative of constitutional property rights, or are they bad politics?

B. *The Logic of the Task of Interpretation*

1. *The Constitutional Judge, Participant in a System of Concurrent Enunciation of Norms*

Inevitably an instrument of control, the interpretation of the law causes the Council, as a further consequence, to take part in the workings of Parlement. Undoubtedly, these interpretive techniques have the primary effect of seeming to respect the will of the legislator since the statute, as interpreted by the Council, is declared to be in conformity with the Constitution. One could even support the view that if it refused to limit the disputed provisions of one statute or to fix and round out the scope of another, the Council might be led often to invalidate statutes and oppose Parlement. Moreover, it is plausible that in order to avoid having to declare a law invalid, which always appears as a repudiation of majoritarianism (and hence as a political ploy of the opposition), the Council would prefer to "save" the law—and the face of its authors—by interpreting it so that it is consistent with the Constitution. The techniques of interpretation are thus a

---

of property and companies would *restrain* the scope of private property and freedom of enterprise *so much* that it would contradict the provisions of article 17 of the 1789 Declaration."

[19] *See, e.g.*, Judgment of July 4, 1989 (*Loi modifiant la loi #86-912 du 6 août 1986 relative aux modalités d'application des privations*), Con. const., J.O., July 5, 1989, at 8383.

[20] *Supra*, note 7 and accompanying text.

[21] *Id.*; *see also* Judgment of Jan. 17, 1989 (*Loi modifiant la loi du 30 septembre 1986 relative à la liberté de communication*), Con. const., J.O., Jan. 18, 1989, at 757.

way for the Council not only to sidestep direct political conflicts with Parlement and the government,[22] but also to manage the various constraints weighing it down. By taking into account the relevant constitutional principle (legal constraint), the political importance of the text submitted for its examination, the political context, the number of invalidations already declared against the same majority, the Council can in effect moderate its censure; either it interprets the statute using one of the three techniques set forth above and does not censure it, or it abandons these techniques and finally invalidates the law.[23] Surely the techniques of consistent interpretation give the Council a broad scope of inquiry in the legitimate use of its powers.

The techniques also allow the Council to engage in legislative work because the cost of avoiding invalidation and direct conflict with Parlement is the Council's remodeling of the statute. The Council devalues certain legislative provisions, keeping their wording intact but merely as declarations of intentions without binding legal value, even though the legislator had conferred it on them;[24] at other times it adds details that did not appear in the text approved by Parlement.[25] The statute declared constitutional is not precisely the one adopted by the legislator; it has been reinterpreted by the Council, modified by cuts or the introduction of new rules.

These modifications are all the more important in that the statute can only be applied by taking into account the Council's interpretative cuts or additions. The Council in fact forcefully upholds their binding nature. Thus, for example, the decision of July 25, 1989 provides that in order to be constitutional, a union may may not bring suit on behalf of a member without his permission (*mandat*) unless the letter giving the member notice of the suit contains all the terms set forth by the Council.[26] Elsewhere it declares that "any other in-

---

[22] The term "government" in this Article refers to the French Prime Minister and certain members of Parlement selected to serve as cabinet members. These individuals remain members of Parlement while functioning as executive officials.

[23] For example, in the decision issued on January 17, 1979, the Council found that a legislative provision forcing the government to table a bill violates the Constitution. Judgment of Jan. 17, 1979 (*Loi portant approbation d'un rapport sur l'adaptation du VIIe Plan*), Con. const., Rec. C.C. 26. It later determined to neutralize that provision, to deprive it of legal effect thereby avoiding its censure. Judgment of July 27, 1982 (*Loi portant réforme de la planification*), Con. const., Rec. C.C. 52.

[24] Judgment of July 27, 1982 (*Loi portant réforme de la planification*), Con. const., Rec. C.C. 52.

[25] *Supra*, note 5 and accompanying text.

[26] Judgment of July 25, 1989 (*Loi modifiant le code du travail et relative à la prevention du licenciement économique et au droit à la conversion*), Con. const., J.O., July 28, 1989, at 9503; *supra*, note 5 and accompanying text.

terpretation would violate the Constitution"[27] or that "this interpretation is the condition precedent for the constitutionality of the provisions under consideration."[28] In each instance, the Council indicates that the law is constitutional only by virtue of the modifications that it has introduced; occasionally, following the example of the Italian constitutional court, it even introduces the interpretations it has formulated into the holding.

In this sense, the control of the self-contained constitutionality of law, through the task of interpretation of texts such control inevitably implies, makes the Council a colegislator without in the least removing from the Council its role of constitutional judge. And this situation is not unique to France; it is the same for all foreign constitutional courts.

The Council is a jurisdiction that engages in a game-like power struggle with other institutions of different types; the whole of this dynamic defines what may be called a system of competitive articulation of norms. The development of the law today is in fact the result of competition among three rival institutions: the government, which originates almost all legislative texts and oversees the assemblies' agenda; Parlement, which debates, amends, and passes the bill; and lastly the Constitutional Council, which can round out the law, specify its modes of application, suppress some of its provisions or nullify others. These institutions are competitive in the sense that each of them evaluates the text based on different procedures, preoccupations, and legitimacy: the government, on the basis of the confidence in its majority and with the help of the administration, transforms its political program into bills; the legislature, on the basis of voter confidence, debates the context and content of the texts in a public and adversarial manner; and the Council, on the basis of the French people's solemnly proclaimed attachment to human rights and to the principles of national sovereignty (as defined in the Declaration of 1789, upheld and enlarged by the 1946 Preamble),[29] assesses and verifies the content of the law in secret and according to legal reasoning. Each institution thus contributes to the shaping of the general will.

Considering its institutional status and especially article sixty-two of the Constitution, which prescribes that the Council's decisions "are binding upon public, administrative and juridical authorities,"

---

[27] Judgment of Oct. 10-11, 1984 (*Loi visant à limiter la concentration et a assurer la transparence financiere et le pluralisme des enterprises de presse*), Con. const., J.O., Oct. 13, 1984, at 3200.

[28] *Id.*

[29] Judgment of Jan. 16, 1982 (*Loi de nationalisation*), Con. const., Rec. C.C. 18.

does not the Council, within this competitive system of stating norms, enjoy a privileged status that allows it always to impose its own interpretation? In theory it does, but in practice the Council's interpretation is never the result of a totally free or arbitrary choice. It is the product of a series of constraints, of a game pitting several players against one another: legislators, who during the legislative debate and in the argumentation of the case give a glimpse of their own interpretation of the constitutional text; law professors, who in their commentaries endeavor to define the relevant meaning; special interest groups interested in the disputed statute, each of which provides its own reading; journalists, specialized or not, who try to assess the reaction of public opinion to a given interpretation, and so forth. Yet another constraint is the Council's jurisprudence itself insofar as its prior decisions, when they exist, limit its power of interpretation. In order to have its interpretations considered objective by the public and by the administrative and judicial authorities, the Council must be consistent in its decisions; its interpretations cannot vary, and they must respect a coherent and consistent relationship. Moreover, the Council's jurisprudence, like the petitioners in any given case, must remain faithful to the doctrine in order not to stray too far afield.[30]

The Council, therefore, is not unrestrained in its interpretation. It must integrate or at least remain aware of competing exegeses. Its legitimacy as an interpreter depends on this because beyond its constitutional basis, the Council's legitimacy also is built upon the legal and political community's acknowledgment of its jurisprudence. To establish such recognition, the Council, the government, and Parlement must structure a relationship in which, despite the institutional status of the Council, the others can agree in whole or in part with the reasoning behind its decisions. Without this recognition, the Council would risk provoking the hostility of the very institutions needed to assure its own legitimacy.[31]

2. *The Constitution, an Open Space*

It is precisely this juridical task that makes the Constitution a

---

[30] Thus, in its decision issued July 8, 1989 concerning the right of union officials to be reinstated following dismissal for serious misconduct, the Council cited an interpretation given in its July 20, 1988 decision dealing with the same issue. Judgment of July 8, 1989 (*Loi portant amnistie*), Con. const., J.O., July 11, 1989, at 8734.

[31] Each time an interpretation strays too far from the *opinio juris*, the Council's very legitimacy, not simply its decision, is vigorously contested; note, for example, the reactions of the President of the National Assembly and the Senate after the ruling on the "Seguin amendment." Judgment of Jan. 23, 1987 (*Loi portant diverses mesures d'ordre social*), Con. const., Rec. C.C. 13.

living document, constantly being created or evolving, because the selection of a meaning is never definitive; the interpretation of a text,
captured at any given moment, can always vary. If this phenomenon
is familiar in civil and administrative law because the passage of time
allows us to recall the sometimes tremendous evolutions in meaning
that judges have etched upon the clauses of the Code or general principles of law, it is equally true in constitutional matters. This is simply because the Constitutional Council does not have a monopoly on
interpretation any more than judicial or administrative jurisdictions
do. This interpretation is the heart of the competitive articulation of
norms.[32] In this complex give-and-take of meanings, the competition
between those who wish to have their meaning prevail is never even,
inasmuch as each draws a different degree of authority according to
its status. This authority and status could vary, however, according
to the political and legal circumstances to whose development they
contribute. It is a fact that the Constitution at the outset grants to the
Council a privileged place, but its legitimacy as an interpreter, over
and above its constitutional foundation, depends on the recognition of
its jurisprudence by the community of legal experts.[33]

In other words, interpretation, the logic of juridical work, is not
the result of a choice of meaning freely made by the Council, but
rather of a power struggle between rival institutions. That is why interpretation is never set down and anchored once and for all; it
evolves and changes with the fluctuations in the power struggle,
although the different modes of operation of the Council and of the
community of legal experts account for the fact that this process is
not fulfilled all at once. Under certain circumstances, the Council
might reject an analysis of the content and consequences of a given
constitutional principle, yet may accept that analysis when the circumstances have altered. Why give up on a doctrine likely to influence the Council gradually or impose an interpretation upon it or lead
the court to change through suitable commentaries of successive decisions? Perhaps we should see in this light the acceptance of President
Luchaire's interpretation, which convinced the Council to abandon its
1978 jurisprudence in 1985 and accept the idea that "an established
law can be usefully contested upon an examination of legislative acts

---

[32] See supra section B1.

[33] It would be more precise to speak of a community of concerned professionals—academ-
ics, politicians, etc. See Phillipe Jestaz, La jurisprudence: réflexions sur un malentendu, 1987
DALLOZ ch. 3.

that modify it, complete it, or touch upon its subject matter,"[34] or the Council's acceptance, based upon undisputed doctrinal analysis, of Professor René Capitant's argument in favor of broadening the interpretation of article fifty-three to include the hypothesis relating to the secession of territories.[35]

On the whole, the unending competition between different interpretations prevents the Constitution's text from becoming dead or fixed at the very moment it is produced. As the regulator of this competition, the constitutional judge brings the text to life by constantly adapting it to the new demands that political life generates. In this sense, the logic of juridical work changes the Constitution from a closed, sealed document into a space that is wide open to the ongoing creation of laws.

Unlike closed constitutions, where new laws are often affirmed by profound political and legal upheavals, the existence of a constitutional court ushers in a public space constantly open to accept new liberties. However, there is one condition; the Council's partners must be actively involved. More than anything, it would be unacceptable to posit, as Dean Favoreu seems to wish, that "as soon as the constitutional judge's decision is issued, the debate ceases."[36] Although the Council calms political life, it must not lull it to sleep! Legal professionals—professors, lawyers—should constantly engage in debate with political experts—sociologists, historians, and philosophers—to find in the evolution of social thought the aspirations or claims that deserve recognition as rights. They must also, by fitting these claims into a legal framework, facilitate the adjustment of these rights to the jurisprudential charter of freedoms; in addition, they must engage in dialogue to encourage the Council to abandon or modify its jurisprudence in order to recognize new rights while invoking their consistency and compatability with existing principles. Last but not least, they must continue to ponder the political meanings of modernity operating in the Declarations. Indeed, more than an enumeration of rights, do not these meanings denote an "unravelling" of law and power, the origin and recognition of debate, of the conflict of opinions, as the only legitimate instrument to authorize human rights in the future? In other words, the philosophy of human rights, from which the Council wishes to draw its legitimacy, still poses an ongo-

---

[34] Judgment of Jan. 25, 1985 (*Loi relative à l'état d'urgence en Nouvelle-Calédonie et dépendances*), Con. const., Rec. C.C. 43.

[35] Judgment of Dec. 30, 1975, Con. const., Rec. C.C. 28.

[36] Louis Favoreu, *Actualité et légitimité du contrôle juridictionnel des lois en Europe Occidentale*, 1984 REVUE DE DROIT PUBLIC ET DE LA SCIENCE POLITIQUE 1195.

ing question about law because it abolishes any idea of a single authority invested with the power to pronounce laws with definitive certainty; these rights are constantly at the heart of discussions from which they obtain their recognition as rights.

But if there is debate about interpretations put forth by the judge at any one time, the compatability of principles worked out, or the claims to be recognized as new rights, and so forth, this can only be upon the condition that the Council takes part in the expansion of democracy by defining a space open to the ongoing creation of rights. Only by recognizing in the basic texts the right to have these rights would the Council unleash "an adventure whose course is unpredictable."[37]

II.   CONSTITUTIONAL DEMOCRACY: THE BASIS OF THE LEGITIMACY OF CONSTITUTIONAL JUSTICE

To question the legitimacy of constitutional justice is to question the definition of democracy. Either a fundamental definition exists— an a priori definition—in which we must confront the legitimacy of constitutional justice, or democracy is defined by the continuous action of the institutions that give it life and we must assess the special contribution of constitutional justice. According to the second hypothesis, I propose to show that the classical "shape" of majoritarian democracy is fading, giving way to the shape of constitutional democracy which legitimates the role of the the constitutional judge.

A.   The Classical Shape of Majoritarian Democracy

1.   The Criteria of Majoritarian Democracy

The first criterion of majoritarian democracy is simply the exercise of power by the majority elected by the people. In this conception of democracy, the principle of the people's sovereignty tolerates no limitations. Since the citizens have freely expressed themselves and since an arithmetic majority has resulted from the elections, the majority gains the political power to legislate and govern. The loser, the minority or minorities, must respect democracy by deferring to the verdict of the polls, and must grant to the winner the right to express the general will. Democracy is assessed at the origin of power: universal suffrage. This explains the great importance of election procedures because the system's quality depends on these forms: equality of the candidates, control of electoral expenses, propaganda

---

[37] Claude Lefort, *Les droits de l'homme et l'État-providence, in* ESSAIS SUR LA POLITIQUE 31, 51 (1986).

methods, and obviously the fairness of the electoral system. The true constitution is the mode of vote, and the example of the United Kingdom is typical in this respect; the true constitutional law is the electoral law. It would be inconceivable for the constitutional judges to control the legislative work of the elected representatives of the sovereign nation; the only possible control is the kind wielded by the people themselves at the polls, either by changing the majority if they disapprove of its performance, or by reelecting the majority if they approve of its politics. But between elections, the majority must be able to make its decisions freely.

The second criterion of majoritarian democracy is the separation of powers. The first criterion might lead us to believe that in this form of democracy, the guarantee of citizens' rights and liberties is forgotten when the power of the majority is boldly asserted. This is not the case, however; only political freedom and protection of rights are considered the inevitable consequence of a limitation of power resulting from the separation of power. In order for liberty to be respected, as Montesquieu wrote, "the same man or the same body of principals or nobles or of the people must not wield these three powers—making laws, executing public resolutions and judging crimes or disputes between individuals."[38] By thus dividing the powers, each becomes a counterbalance, each limits and balances the others, protects its interests against the competition of the others, and the whole automatically produces legislation which is well-reasoned, moderate, and respectful of the Constitution. Passing bills violative of citizens' liberties is rendered impossible because of the division of the legislative body into two houses; each house has an interest in maintaining its own authority and possesses the means necessary to prevent or impede any abusive pretentions of the other. Through the mechanism of the separation of powers, they check each other, thereby creating, as Louvet de la Somme expressed it, "the strongest possible guarantee of the strict observance of the Constitution."[39]

2. Criticism of Majority Democracy

Constitutional experiences, comparative observation, and doctrinal reflection[40] have gradually revealed the practical impossibility of obtaining from the separation of powers the expected political goals:

---

[38] MONTESQUIEU, XI DE L'ÉSPRIT DES LOIS ch. 6 (Robert Derathé ed., Garnier Frères 1973) (1748).

[39] Louvet de la Somme, untitled, GAZETTE NATIONALE, Aug. 17, 1795, at 1329.

[40] MICHEL TROPER, LA SÉPARATION DES POUVOIRS ET L'HISTOIRE CONSTITUTIONNELLE FRANÇAISE 205 (1980).

neither the division of power, nor its limitation, nor political freedom. However, constitutional experts have long debated the relative merits of flexible versus rigid separation of powers. Whatever the constitutional organization of public authorities and their relationships may be, the unity of state power was always reestablished in the executive through the majoritarian game of conferring to the winning party and its leader the authority over normative power. Separation of powers no longer exists when the legislative majority aligns with the government and when the President of the Republic himself belongs to this majority. This phenomenon is not unique to France, nor peculiar to this type of separation of powers; it can be found in Portugal, Sweden, Spain, Germany, the United Kingdom, and Austria even though these countries have different constitutions. In these countries the head of state is the prime minister but because of the logic of the electoral system, he or she is in fact elected by the people. Then, because of the control of its parliamentary majority, the system transforms Parlement in a parallel way into a chamber that registers the people's political will.

The second criticism concerns the relationship between government and governed implied by majoritarian democracy. Since its principle is the power of those elected by majority, it follows that the general will is assimilated by the majority will: more precisely, by the will of the legislative and governmental majority. In this way, the majority representatives become the sovereign's equal and, as shown by Carré de Malberg,[41] even take on the role of sovereign. Indeed, in this conception of democracy, the will of the people is identified with and merged into the will of the majority representatives; by definition there cannot be any other general will than the one expressed by the representatives since the people's will cannot exist independently, separate from the representatives' will. The political relationship thus established, this identity of governed and government, deprives the former of autonomous means of expression and intervention, transforming democracy into a delegation-renunciation of individuals' powers without the compensating counterpart of an institutionalized right of inspection by the citizens of the representatives' activity.

The extreme representative effects of this political logic are even greater because of the phenomenon of disciplined and stable majority alliances. In earlier republics, the frequent changes and reversals of legislative and governmental alliances implied that during one legislative session, all of the principal parties were at one time or another empowered. Under these conditions, the law was inevitably the result

---

41 Carré de Malberg, *La loi, expression de la volonté general*, 1987 ECONOMICA.

of compromises between the different trends of opinion; thus, it could be considered the expression of the general will and not that of a majority, since no airtight boundary existed between majority and minority. Today, when alliances are tighter and more stable over time, the minorities are left out of the elaboration of the law. They do intervene, but only to a lesser degree and the law appears more clearly as the expression of the majority's will alone.

By becoming more of a charter of rights and liberties than a text defining the relationships between public authorities, the Constitution shapes a new democratic configuration.

B.   *The New Face of Constitutional Democracy*

1.   *The Criteria of Constitutional Democracy*

The first criterion of constitutional democracy is to enhance— meaning to place out of harm's way or to consecrate—human rights and liberties. The popular origin of power is not enough to consider a system democratic because universal suffrage might allow a majority to emerge that could use its numerical advantage to restrain, limit, or even suppress civil rights. And so the law, as the expression of this majority will, is not in itself the ultimate legal means of guaranteeing the rights of the governed. Constitutional democracy is not the power of the majority because there can exist an absolutism of "the several," or a legislative absolutism similar to the absolutism (under the *Ancien regime*) "of one alone" or a royal absolutism. For the same reason, constitutional democracy is no more the power of the law than was the former absolutism. It is the power of the Constitution insofar as the Constitution, according to article sixteen of the 1789 Declaration, assumes the guarantee of rights, that is, the guarantee that parliamentary law respects rights, principles, and liberties of constitutional value. In this way, constitutional democracy is defined by the exercise of permanent control over the activity of the government, including the elected representatives, in order to compel public authorities to respect human rights and liberties.

The second criterion, naturally, is the existence of a constitutional judge. In fact, the judge is the instrument of a double mutation in the relationship between governed and government. First, by making the Constitution into a jurisprudential charter of rights and liberties, the judge breaks the identity of governed-government to the extent that this charter constitutes for the former a space for recognition, autonomous to that of the latter. Individuals' rights and liberties are no longer mingled with the will of the representatives, they are distinct from them. This separation places two groups—constituents and representatives—in a position of exteriority; theoretically, it allows for the exercise of a right of inspection, or a check by the governed on the government's activities. Second, constitutional jurisdiction is the institution which in practice supports this differentiation insofar as it verifies the legislative work of representatives with regard to the rights and liberties that the French people have solemnly consecrated. The best example is certainly the decision issued on January 16, 1982 concerning nationalizations, in which the Council explicitly reminds the representatives that it is "the French people who approved, in the referenda of October 13, 1946 and September 28, 1958, the texts that confer constitutional value on the principles and rights proclaimed in 1789," in particular the right of ownership.[42] So, the differentiation between representatives and those they represent can be translated into institutional terms: the representatives "have" parliamentary and executive institutions; those they represent "have" the Council. The control over the constitutionality of laws is what allows for the imposition upon the agents of the state respect for the rights of the governed between one election and the next. But is such control legitimate?

2. The Social Elaboration of the Legitimacy of Constitutional Justice

The question of the legitimacy of the Council's role is inevitable given current trends of thought. Indeed, according to the classic presentation, democratic logic improves when the rules related to devolution, organization, and exercise of political power depend on neither the good will of a single man or group nor on the simple existence of tradition, custom, heredity, or brute force. In this sense, constitutional movement can be confused with the democratic claim insofar as the Constitution is precisely the written text that explicitly and solemnly organizes political power and binds the state's agents and activity to legal rules.

But legal logic implies that for the surrender of politics to law to be perfect, there also must be a system of sanctions, applicable to all who do not abide by the rules. This is where the problem arises, because in constitutional matters, the agent—burdened by the control and the threat of sanction—is the legislator elected by the people. Thus, the creation and role of the Council within the very process of elaborating laws, satisfy legal logic but clash with democratic logic, which presupposes that the laws express the will of the sovereign peo-

---

[42] Judgment of Jan. 16, 1982 (*Loi de nationalisation*), Con. const., Rec. C.C. 18.

ple. Is the democratic system not subverted in its philosophy and institutional mechanisms when a body composed of non-elected members has life-and-death power over the laws voted upon by the people's elected representatives (according to a formula created in 1795 during the debate on the *jurie constitutionnel*)? Asked in these terms, the question of the legitimacy of the control of constitutionality is insoluble because it is wrapped in a perfect dilemma: Either there is no control of the laws, and the democratic principle must tolerate the assaults of a legislator's decisions that are contrary to liberties and infringe on the Constitution adopted by the people, or there *is* control of the laws, and the democratic principle must likewise tolerate the gradual submission of the will of the people's elected representatives to an institution without elective legitimacy.

This question and this dilemma steadily fuel the doctrinal and political discussions about constitutional justice; they were present as early as 1789, reappear in 1795 with the Sieyès project, during the Third Republic with the various proposals of Charles Benoist, in 1946 with the Constitutional Committee, and once again in 1958 with the creation of the Constitutional Council. In August 1986 they even provoked a defensive reaction of the political class against the position held by this institution in the French constitutional system. If the legitimacy of an institution depends on common belief in its social value, the Council today profits by this belief, strengthened after a period of constitutional, political, social, and doctrinal evolution.

First, a *constitutional* evolution, since the Council derives part of its legitimacy in the increased imbalance of powers. The election of the Chief of State through direct universal suffrage, the Gaullist, then Gaullian custom of the institutions, the majority reality, and the discipline of parliamentary groups have gradually reduced Parlement's role; it is no longer the site of decisions but rather the place where, solemnly and in the ritual of debates whose results each participant knows will not be altered by them, the decisions desired and conceived elsewhere (that is to say in the Élysée and at Matignon) are registered. The separation of powers between the executive and legislative branches, which the *Anciens* considered the very foundation of political freedom because it established a mechanism of weight and counterweight limiting the state's power, has had its day. Whatever the exact nature of the constitutional text may be, the unity of the state's power is reconstructed upon the executive (president or prime minister), thanks to the majority political logic granting the authority over normative power to the winning party and its leader. In light of the silence and weakness of Parlement, the Council appears as the only place in which the government's legislative will may be effectively discussed. The decline in confrontation between government and Parlement corresponds to the increase in confrontation between the executive and the Council, the latter thus appearing as the modern counterweight in a new constitutional balance.

Next, a *political* evolution, insofar as the Council profits from the disrepute currently undermining political institutions. The public's opinion of politicians is undeniably negative, and the conviction (which used to be limited to traditional social categories) that they are more concerned with their own ambitions and personal interests than with real problems, is widely held. This rejection not only of the political class but also of politics is seen in growing disaffection with respect to unions and traditional political parties,[43] in a strong rate of abstention from voting notable in its recurrence,[44] and in the electoral success of special interest groups challenging the partisan game (environmentalists, for example). Additionally, there is increased mistrust of Parlement, and even more mistrust of deputies deemed "not very conscientious" by fifty-two percent of the French and "rather honest" by only fifty percent.[45] Therefore it is not surprising that public opinion transfers its trust to institutions like the Constitutional Council, which supervise the activities of the political class whose sincerity we no longer trust. The Council is thus perceived as the instrument of civil society versus political society, a perception which, considering the weakness of belief in the virtue of politics, becomes a self-fulfilling prophecy.

A *social* evolution as well, since this rejection of politics translates in public opinion as a promotion of ethical values, a rediscovery of human rights as a moral principle correctly applied to all political power. In this conflict between morality and politics, "the public understands," writes Dean Georges Vedel, "that the Council holds sacred the intangibility of principles" against a legislator who, for partisan reasons, might wish to call them into question again.[46]

The *doctrine*, finally, has recently undertaken to base the legiti-

---

[43] At the time of the June 18, 1989 European election, the three major parties together received only slightly more than half the vote, that is, one-fourth of the total electorate. For the last several years the number of union and party members has steadily decreased or remained stable at a very weak level.

[44] The rate of abstention was thirty-four percent in the June 1988 legislative elections, sixty percent in the November 6, 1988 referendum, twenty-seven percent in the 1989 municipal elections, and fifty-one percent in the European elections.

[45] See the survey conducted jointly by SOFRES and *Le Monde*. *Les Français n'accordent à leurs députés qu'une confiance limitée*, LE MONDE, July 15, 1989, at 12.

[46] George Vedel, *Le Conseil constitutionnel, gardien du droit positif ou défenseur de la transcendance des droits de l'homme*, 1988 POUVOIRS 149 n.45.

macy of the Council in the law, in particular by seeking to demonstrate that its creative role in the elaboration of laws is not against the democratic principle and that the dilemma raised above is a false dilemma.

The most interesting, and apparently the most paradoxical, justification is perhaps the one which, as in Jean-Jacques Rousseau's political theory, looks for the foundations of a legitimation of the legislator's authority. For the author of *The Social Contract*,[47] the only true democracy is direct democracy where the common will is expressed by the citizens without mediation; this democracy is inevitably "upstanding" since the people always want what is good and can never be unjust to themselves. Once reality imposes recourse to representation, the qualities Rousseau attributed to the people and their works alone were automatically transferred to the legislators and their work. Wrongly so, because legislators form a mediating body whose individual ego is in opposition to the communal ego of the people; it therefore develops its own individual will, independent of the people's will. This individual will is in fact even opposed to the people's will since its "ongoing effort," "its inherent and inevitable vice" is to try ceaselessly to usurp sovereignty. In short, the representatives' will is not the people's will, and therefore there is no infringement of democratic principle or of the prerogatives of the sovereign people when establishing mechanisms to oversee representatives. Rousseau himself thought of a few such mechanisms: imperative writ, regular meetings of citizens' assemblies, frequent replacement of deputies, popular ratification, and so forth. Today, the verification of the constitutionality of laws logically follows from this notion because by controlling the legislator's will, the Council does not control the people's will, insofar as it can be ascertained. Moreover, it can even be the instrument which allows citizens, if not to recover their sovereignty, at least to exert a semipermanent control over the work of their representatives.

The way the Council conceives of its role adds a certain force to this theoretical presentation. In fact, in its famous decision issued on January 16, 1982, in order to confer full constitutional value to the principles of 1789, it placed the will of the sovereign people in opposition to the will of the representatives: "*[T]he French people,*" it states, "*in the May 5, 1946 referendum have rejected* a new Declaration of the Rights of Man allowing a statement of principles different from

---

[47] JEAN-JACQUES ROUSSEAU, THE SOCIAL CONTRACT bk. 2, chs. 3-4, bk. 3 (Maurice Cranston trans., Penguin 1968) (1762).

those proclaimed in 1789,"[48] and "on the contrary, *in the referenda of October 13, 1946 and September 28, 1958, the French people have approved* texts conferring constitutional value upon the principles and rights proclaimed in 1789."[49]

Undoubtedly, the Council is not the institution that will bring about the democracy dear to Jean-Jacques, nor is it the opposite. It is more precisely the instrument of a renewed form of democracy, "constitutional democracy," wherein elected representatives lose their monopoly over the expression of norms and citizens gain a power of intervention.

CONCLUSION

Unlike doctrines that base the legitimacy of constitutional justice on an a priori definition of democracy, most often formulated before the origin of constitutional justice, the hypothesis proposed here is the following: *The control of the constitutionality of laws is legitimate because it produces a definition of democracy that legitimates it.* So, the issue is not to connect democratic truth with the mechanism of control of the constitutionality of laws, but to show which democratic truth this mechanism makes possible and which legitimates it in return.

As a matter of fact, the history of institutions and ideas tends to show that every technology of power, every new organization of power, every creation of a new institution, gives rise to a new discourse that is in sync with the new relation of power, that articulates its truth and therefore makes it natural and legitimate. Thus, at the end of the eighteenth century, the claim, and later the setting up after 1789, of new mechanisms of power come complete with new words—social contract instead of imperium, citizen instead of subject, the nation's sovereignty instead of divine right, equality instead of class privilege—and new discourse, the most significant of which is the Declaration of August 26, 1789. Far from being a superfluous text, it is indispensable to the current political process since it generates the principles necessary to establish as natural the restructuring of society and the attribution of legislative power to the National Assembly; at the same time, the text disqualifies the former organization of power and royal legitimacy. In other words, the new authority—the National Assembly—is legitimate because it produced the discourse—the Declaration of 1789—which legitimates it. Later, the introduc-

---

[48] Judgment of Jan. 16, 1982 (*Loi de nationalisation*), Con. const., Rec. C.C. 18 (emphasis added).

[49] *Id.*

tion of new mechanisms—direct universal suffrage, political parties, the Administration—produced in a similar way modifications of discourse suited to legitimate them: the 1946 Preamble, social democracy, the welfare state, and so forth.

It is the same today with constitutional justice. Its birth and growth occur in a country and at a time in which, despite the governmental instability of prior republics, the legitimacy of the legislature and of the law remain widely dominant. Within this representation of democracy, the mechanism of control of the constitutionality of laws is undoubtedly illegitimate, even more so because it developed outside the letter of the 1958 Constitution. It was meant to protect the government from Parlement's infringements and it turned into a technique to protect human rights and minorities against the abuses of governmental majority. However, it is precisely this mechanism which will produce a new representation of democracy that will, in turn, devalue the old one by establishing the legitimacy of the restructuring of the institutional landscape on the principle of the preeminence of the Constitution and, therefore, of the Constitutional Council.

With successive touches, it will give its input to this new representation of democracy: "[I]n the exercise of his competency, the legislator could not be exempted from respecting the principles and rules of constitutional value which are imposed on all the agents of the state;"[50] "the law expresses the general will only in its regard for the Constitution;"[51] "the necessity for pluralism in the currents of ideas and opinions forms the basis of democracy."[52] With these words and these shifts in meaning, the Council constructs a definition of democracy different from the preceeding period, but conforming to the new allocation of power.[53] "The law is the expression of the general will" was the discourse creating, and at the same time legitimating, Parlement, the legislative power of the sole representatives of the nation. Today, "the law expresses the general will only as far as it respects the

---

50 Judgment of Jan. 16, 1982 (*Loi de nationalisation*), Con. const., Rec. C.C. 18.

51 Judgment of Aug. 23, 1985 (*Loi sur l'évolution de la Nouvelle-Calédonie*), Con. const., Rec. C.C. 70.

52 Judgment of Jan. 11, 1990 (*Loi relative à la limitation de dépenses électorales et à la clarification des activités politiques*), Con. const., J.O., Jan. 13, 1990, at 573.

53 The doctrine likewise shares in the reformulation of modern democratic requirements, thereby reinforcing the Council's very task. *See, e.g.*, LAURENT COHEN-TANUGI, LA MÉTAMORPHOSE DE LA DÉMOCRATIE (1989); LAURENT COHEN-TANUGI, LE DROIT SANS L'ÉTAT (1985); JEAN-MARC VARAUT, LE DROIT AU DROIT (1986). On the philosophical point of view, see, for example, BLANDINE BARRET-KRIEGEL, LE DROITS DE L'HOMME ET LE DROIT NATUREL (1989); LUC FERRY & ALAIN RENAUT, PHILOSOPHIE POLITIQUE (1985); CLAUDE LEFORT, ESSAIS SUR LE POLITIQUE (1986).

Constitution" is the discourse creating, and at the same time legitimating, the Council's authority to participate in the elaboration of
law by making sure that it respects constitutional rules. Since democracy is no longer defined only by simple majority power to make law
but also by the requisite respect for constitutional rights and liberties,
the Council's role becomes perfectly legitimate according to that definition of democracy. However, this latest definition is not, in and of
itself, "more true" than the one before: It merely articulates the truth
of the new institutional and political system of actualizing the general
will.

A PHILOSOPHICAL RECONSTRUCTION OF JUDICIAL REVIEW

Carlos Santiago Nino

I. The Old Problem Again

The power of the courts to review the constitutionality of legal norms such as statutes or decrees enacted by the democratic branches is one of the central features of constitutional or liberal democracies. This concept was introduced, under the modality of concrete and corrective control, by Justice Marshall in the 1803 case of *Marbury v. Madison*.[1] Judicial review spread in the same form to many Latin American countries. In Argentina, it was accepted for the first time by the Supreme Court in 1887 in the case *Sojo*.[2] In Europe, judicial review was introduced after the First World War by a special Constitutional Tribunal, in the Austrian Constitution of 1918 and the Weimar Constitution of 1919.[3] And judicial review was reintroduced on the Continent in almost all the post-Second World War constitutions.[4]

Judicial review is the main mechanism protecting individual rights against the political powers that may ignore or undermine those rights. It protects individual rights even when the political powers respond directly or indirectly to popular will. Judicial review of the constitutionality of legislation thus creates a balance between the collective will and interests of the people, and the fundamental rights of each individual.

Notwithstanding its crucial role in defining a constitutional democracy, judicial review's justification is rather mysterious (as attested to by the host of works devoted to the subject). Judges—particularly superior court judges, like the justices of a supreme court or a constitutional tribunal—usually are not directly subject to the democratic process since they are generally not popularly elected but

---

[1] Marbury v. Madison, 5 U.S. (1 Cranch) 137 (1803).

[2] 32 Fallos 125 (1887).

[3] Hans Kelsen greatly influenced both of these constitutions. Thus, judicial review was introduced as an abstract and preventative doctrine.

[4] Examples include the Italian Constitution of 1948, the Bonn Constitution of 1949, the French Constitution of 1958, the Portuguese Constitution of 1976, and the Spanish Constitution of 1978.

285

appointed by a popularly elected branch of government. Furthermore, in most cases, they are not subject to a periodic accounting, nor do they respond directly to public opinion and discussion.

Superior tribunals resembling the United States Supreme Court and most Latin American supreme courts are chosen by the president, with or without advice and consent of the legislature. The judges generally have life tenure, subject to impeachment for misbehavior. Justices in European-style constitutional tribunals are appointed by political bodies and remain in their position for a definite period. However, European courts' more direct connection with the democratic process still does not make them as accountable to the public as legislative or executive branches of governments. Why should the rather aristocratic judicial branch have the last word on such important questions as the scope of individual rights, the separation of powers or the adequacy of democratic procedures, rather than elected officials who are subject to the permanent control of popular will and opinion? This problem, the *counter-majoritarian difficulty* of judicial review,[5] has received much more attention from North American scholars in the last decade than from scholars elsewhere in the world. This difficulty calls into question the very principle of division of powers, ascribing to judges the role of applying decisions of the democratic organs, without any corresponding popular accountability.[6]

In this Article I offer a philosophical foundation for judicial review which will determine its limits and scope, answering the countermajoritarian difficulty in a way that in some ways differs from previous analyses by other scholars. My arguments will go through several steps and exhibit a dialectical structure. First, I shall examine an argument which offers an obvious justification for judicial review. After rejecting that argument, I shall offer a second one that goes even further, grounding the absolute subjection of democratic branches to judicial control. Given the paradoxical nature of the argument, I shall offer a third which questions any possibility of judicial review of democratic decisions. Finally, I shall present three arguments which offer exceptions to this denial of judicial review, advancing toward a theory of the judicial control of democratic decisions which involves both important restraints and significant leeway.

My arguments will employ, when necessary, tools of conceptual

---

[5] *See* ALEXANDER M. BICKEL, THE LEAST DANGEROUS BRANCH: THE SUPREME COURT AT THE BAR OF POLITICS (1962).

[6] *See* MONTESQUIEU, THE SPIRIT OF LAWS (David Wallace Carrithers ed., 1952) (the text of this edition is Thomas Nugent's translation (London, Nourse 1750) of the first French edition (Geneva, Barillot 1748)).

and logical analysis that seem to be out of fashion among constitutional scholars writing in the United States, as I think that they are useful in illuminating some frequent quandaries. The aim of this work could be described as the dismantling of the institutional arrangement of judicial review to reveal its logical and conceptual structure, thus preparing the way for a more robust reconstruction. The partial conclusions of my analysis may appear wildly implausible to lawyers accustomed to relying upon common sense, but if they can contain their impatience with philosophical free-wheeling speculation, they will find the final account much more acceptable to their sensibilities. My focus will not be on any specific constitution, since I wish to unearth problems and to propose solutions which could be of interest to lawyers in any legal system.

II.   A BROAD RECOGNITION OF JUDICIAL REVIEW: MARSHALL'S "LOGIC" AND KELSEN'S "PROBLEM"

The clearest ground for judicial review was advanced by John Marshall at its very moment of inception.[7] Marshall's justification for judicial review exhibits such a pristine clarity and such an overwhelming cogency that one is tempted to speak of Marshall's "logic." It is still surprising to observe the dexterity with which this military man deployed subtle conceptual distinctions (such as the validity of norms and different normative strata) that only much later were elucidated by scholars of considerable philosophical sophistication such as Hans Kelsen.[8]

It is useful to cite for the thousandth time the relevant paragraphs of Marshall's opinion, which are the vehicle of his logic:

It is a proposition too plain to be contested, that the constitution controls any legislative act repugnant to it; or, that the legislature may alter the constitution by an ordinary act.

Between these alternatives there is no middle ground. The constitution is either a superior, paramount law, unchangeable by ordinary means, or it is on a level with ordinary legislative acts, and like other acts, is alterable when the legislature shall please to alter it.

If the former part of the alternative be true, then a legislative act contrary to the constitution is not law: if the latter part be true, then written constitutions are absurd attempts, on the part of the people, to limit a power, in its own nature illimitable.

Certainly all those who have framed written constitutions

---

7 Marbury v. Madison, 5 U.S. (1 Cranch) 137 (1803).
8 *See* HANS KELSEN, PURE THEORY OF LAW (1934).

contemplate them as forming the fundamental and paramount law of the nation, and consequently the theory of every such government must be, that an act of the legislature, repugnant to the constitution, is void.

This theory is essentially attached to a written constitution, and is consequently to be considered, by this court, as one of the fundamental principles of our society. It is not therefore to be lost sight of in the further consideration of this subject.

If an act of the legislature, repugnant to the constitution, is void, does it, notwithstanding its invalidity, bind the courts, and oblige them to give it effect? Or, in other words, though it be not law, does it constitute a rule as operative as if it was a law? This would be to overthrow in fact what was established in theory; and would seem, at first view, an absurdity too gross to be insisted on. It shall, however, receive a more attentive consideration.

It is emphatically the province and duty of the judicial department to say what the law is. Those who apply the rule to particular cases, must of necessity expound and interpret that rule. If two laws conflict with each other, the courts must decide on the operation of each.

So if a law be in opposition to the constitution; if both the law and the constitution apply to a particular case, so that the court must either decide that case conformably to the law, disregarding the constitution; or conformably to the constitution, disregarding the law; the court must determine which of these conflicting rules governs the case. This is of the very essence of judicial duty.

If then the courts are to regard the constitution; and the constitution is superior to any ordinary act of the legislature; the constitution, and not such ordinary act, must govern the case to which they both apply.

Those then who controvert the principle that the constitution is to be considered, in court, as a paramount law, are reduced to the necessity of maintaining that courts must close their eyes on the constitution, and see only the law.

This doctrine would subvert the very foundation of all written constitutions. It would declare that an act, which, according to the principles and theory of our government, is entirely void; is yet, in practice, completely obligatory. It would declare, that if the legislature shall do what is expressly forbidden, such act, notwithstanding the express prohibition, is in reality effectual. It would be giving to the legislature a practical and real omnipotence, with the same breath which professes to restrict their powers within narrow limits. It is prescribing limits, and declaring that those limits may be passed at pleasure.

That it thus reduces to nothing what we have deemed the

greatest improvement on political institutions—a written constitution—would of itself be sufficient, in America, where written constitutions have been viewed with so much reverence, for rejecting the construction. But the peculiar expressions of the constitution of the United States furnish additional arguments in favor of its rejection.[9]

The logical structure of Marshall's reasoning may be displayed along the following lines:

PREMISE 1: *The duty of the judiciary is to apply the law.*

PREMISE 2: *When there are two contradictory laws the application of one of them excludes that of the other.*

PREMISE 3: *The constitution is the supreme law and the defining criterion of legality for other norms.*

PREMISE 4: *The supremacy of the constitution implies that when it is in conflict with a norm enacted by the legislature, the latter ceases to be valid law.*

PREMISE 5: *The negation of the foregoing premise would imply that the legislature might modify the constitution through an ordinary law, and thus that the constitution is not operative in limiting that legislature.*

PREMISE 6: *The legislature is limited by the constitution.*

PREMISE 7: *If a law is not valid then it lacks binding force.*

CONCLUSION: *If an enactment of the legislature is contrary to the constitution it is not binding upon the judicial power.*

This reasoning seems to be fully valid. Thus, if the supremacy of the constitution is recognized, judicial review seems to necessarily follow: judges should not apply legislative enactments which are contrary to the constitution. This conclusion would apply to any legal system with a supreme constitution. When judicial review does not exist, as is the case in the British legal system, this logically implies that the system not only lacks a written constitution, as is evident, but that it lacks a constitution at all! The logical necessity of judicial review that follows from *Marbury v. Madison* has rarely been commented on by constitutional scholars, who instead devote their energies to the legitimacy of judicial review. Nevertheless, if Marshall's logic were cogent, these scholars would be wasting their time, since what is logically necessary does not need an evaluative justification, unless that justification addressed the presupposition of the logical necessity, that is, the supremacy of the constitution.

However, I believe that Marshall's logic is not so solid, after all.

---

[9] *Marbury*, 5 U.S. at 177-78.

In order to display the flaws in his analysis, I refer to a problem faced by Kelsen when he drew the implications of a conceptual scheme similar to that of Marshall's.[10] This contrast is attractive, since Kelsen paralleled Marshall in his influence on the introduction of judicial review.

Kelsen depicted the structure of a legal system as a pyramid. At the top is the *Grundnorm*, or fundamental norm, which is a presupposition of legal thinking that validates the ultimate positive norms or laws of the system (the positive constitution of a country).[11] In turn, the constitution validates the derivative norms (legislative statutes) which are enacted in conformity with the prescriptions concerning the competent official, procedure, and content of the former norms. The derivative norms determine the validity of lower norms enacted in conformity with them (administrative decrees, municipal ordinances, and so forth). Finally, the bottom of the pyramid is formed by individual norms, which refer to particular persons and acts such as administrative orders, judicial decisions, or contracts, enacted in conformity with the prescriptions of controlling superior norms. If a prescription is enacted without following the requirements of competent official, procedure, and content established by valid higher norms, it is not a valid norm of that system.

The recursive criterion of validity that Kelsen offers for the lower norms of the system establishes that a norm is valid when it satisfies the conditions established by a higher valid norm of the legal system. The validity of the ultimate norms of the system is determined by the application to the fundamental norm. A law is valid for Kelsen (according to the characterizations he offers in his successive works) if it "exists as such," has "binding force," and belongs to the legal system.[12]

However, when Kelsen deploys this conceptual structure for the case of conflicts of norms or laws of different hierarchy such as unconstitutional statutes or illegal ordinances, he encounters a substantial difficulty, which I deem "Kelsen's problem." The foregoing conceptual scheme implies that it is enough for a lower norm to contradict a higher norm—either in enactment or in substance—for it to lack validity and thus not belong to the legal system, or as Marshall asserted, for it not to exist as law.[13]

---

[10] KELSEN, *supra* note 8.

[11] *Id.* at 221-78.

[12] *See* CARLOS S. NINO, LA VALIDEZ DEL DERECHO (1985) (discussing the ambiguities and problems of these characterizations of validity).

[13] *Marbury*, 5 U.S. at 177-78.

Nevertheless, unlike Marshall, Kelsen perceived that this does not respond to the phenomenology of legal thinking. Many statutes or other laws that objectively contradict constitutional clauses are considered by jurists to be valid and binding laws. This occurs in several situations: with regard to the effects of an unconstitutional statute prior to its being declared unconstitutional; in legal systems (like Argentina's) where judicial decisions, even those declaring a statute unconstitutional, have no *erga omnes* effects because they are only applicable to the specific facts of the cases; when courts mistakenly declare constitutional a statute which is obviously not so; in legal systems in which there is no judicial review (like Great Britain's); or when judicial review does exist but it is not used to overturn a particular statute.

These situations are theoretically different. For instance, if there is no procedure for challenging the constitutionality of statutes, the supremacy of the constitution may be in doubt, and when a judge or a superior court mistakenly declares a statute constitutional, an epistemological problem arises about how and by whom constitutionality is to be objectively determined. However, despite their relevant differences, all these situations present the problem that the notion of legal validity and normative hierarchy deployed by Marshall and Kelsen do not coincide with legal thinking. For instance, one could be convinced that a statute that declares homosexual acts among adults punishable, objectively violates the Liberty Clause of the Fourteenth Amendment of the United States Constitution. But it is quite different to believe that the statute has no binding force or that a imprisonment under that statute would be analogous to an illegal kidnapping.[14] Most lawyers would not draw these inferences from the fact that a statute is objectively unconstitutional, regardless of Marshall's and Kelsen's characterizations.

Kelsen resorted to two theoretical devices in order to try to solve his problem. The first was the adoption of the subjectivist approach towards the validity of legal norms, maintaining that the validity of a norm depended upon its being declared so by a judge.[15] This was a highly unfortunate theoretical step. If the validity of a legal norm or law depended not on the objective satisfaction of the conditions established by superior legal norms, but on a *judge's declaration* that it satisfies those requirements, the concept of validity would not be available to the judges themselves to justify their own decision about

---

14 This would be especially true since the United States Supreme Court declared just such a statute constitutional in Bowers v. Hardwick, 478 U.S. 186 (1986).

15 KELSEN, *supra* note 8, at 73-74.

whether or not to apply a legal norm (this is the same criticism that is usually made of the realist conceptualization of law). As Joseph Raz stated,[16] Kelsen here confused the fact of whether a law is or is not valid (and thus whether the decision of a judge which applies it is correct or not) with the fact that a judge's decision, correct or not, has binding force and constitutes *res judicata*, according to other norms of the system.

The second theoretical device which Kelsen used to try to solve the problem of the discrepancy between the application of his concept of legal validity and the usual conclusions of legal thinking, was the "alternative tacit clause."[17] Kelsen's idea was simply that if ordinary legal thinking considers that, under certain circumstances, a statute is valid and binding despite contradicting an express clause of a valid superior norm, then it must be because legal thinking is assuming that there is a tacit clause in the higher law other than the express clause whose stipulations are violated by the inferior norm. This tacit clause would authorize the enactment of the lower norm despite its contradiction with the explicit text. Hence, higher norms have disjunctive terms: the explicit stipulated conditions for the enactment of lower norms and the tacit authorization to enact norms without complying with the former conditions. Kelsen makes it clear that this does not mean that the conformity with the tacit clause is of the same value as conformity with express clauses. The legal system generally favors the explicit text, establishing sanctions or nullification procedures when the inferior norm or law departs from it. However, a lower norm's conformity with the tacit clause of the higher norm explains why the lower norm might be considered to be valid even when infringing on the explicit formulation of the higher norm.

Unless properly qualified, the Kelsenian device of the alternative tacit clause is truly disconcerting and inadmissible. It seems absurd to suppose that a constitution authorizes the enactment of statutes with any content whatsoever. A constitution gives a certain content priority to some laws over others by establishing mechanisms of sanction and nullification (even if these mechanisms will not be employed). However, it is not easy to perceive the meaning of laws whose total content is so broad as to be vacuous. Moreover, if we take into account the logical interdependence of the requirements of authority, procedure, and content (since an authority operates legitimately when it adheres to its prescribed procedure and when it enacts certain norms and not others), the alternative tacit clause would en-

---

16 JOSEPH RAZ, PRACTICAL REASON AND NORMS 129-30 (1975).
17 KELSEN, *supra* note 8, at 193-276.

compass not only the content, but also the procedure and the authority established by higher norms. Thus, according to Kelsen's proposal, any norm or law enacted, through any procedure and with any content would be a valid norm of any legal system, since its enactment would be authorized by the tacit clause of any norm of competence of that system.

The confusion that Kelsen creates has been partially adumbrated by Eugenio Bulygin, who maintains that there are two meanings of "validity" that Kelsen does not correctly distinguish, and that both these meanings are relevant to norms which contradict the requirements of higher norms.[18] The first meaning of validity concerns *membership* of a norm in a legal system, and the other is the meaning which refers to the *binding force* of the norm in question, in relation to other norms of the legal system. A norm may not belong to the legal system and nevertheless, in certain cases, its application may be obligatory according to norms of that very system. For instance, rules of private international law may declare the laws of a foreign legal system obligatory in certain cases. According to Bulygin, the same is true of unconstitutional statutes; they are invalid in the sense that they do not belong to the legal system, since they do not satisfy the conditions for their enactment established by higher norms of the system.[19] Nevertheless, their observance and application may be obligatory if they are not nullified in the way established by the same system.

However, Kelsen's problem is deeper than Bulygin perceives. Kelsen is not fully aware that his dominant concept of validity is not membership of a norm in a legal system but the "specific existence of norms" or "binding force."[20] This implies that a norm is only valid when what it prescribes should be done, that is, when it is permissible to go from describing that some authority has prescribed "x should be done," to the normative proposition that x should be done. Certainly for Kelsen, this shift from the descriptive dimension to the normative one presupposes the existence of the basic norm. This shift suggests that the first legislator's prescription should be obeyed, and allows us to predicate the same with regard to derivative prescriptions. In this way, according to Kelsen, the basic norm allows us to describe legal reality as genuine normative phenomena and not as mere successive prescriptions. The predication that a law is valid, in the sense that it should be observed or that it has binding force, transmits itself to both

---

18 Eugenio Bulygin, *Sentencia judicial y creación de derecho, in* LA LEY 1240-307.
19 *Id.*
20 NINO, *supra* note 12.

authorized legal norms and legal norms, the observance of which is declared obligatory by the law in question, even when their enactment is not authorized. However, according to the generally accepted notion, the predication of *membership* of a norm or law in a legal system requires that the enactment of the norm be authorized by another higher norm in that system. This means that the central concept of validity in Kelsen's theory (binding force) is not coextensive with membership of a norm in a legal system. There are binding norms for a certain legal system that do not belong to that system. However, Kelsen assumes that coextensiveness exists between membership and bindingness, hence the obscurity of his many references to the validity of legal norms. And when he confronts the critical case of an unconstitutional statute—which makes evident that there *are* valid and binding norms that do not belong to a legal system—he strains his theory of coextensiveness by alleging that higher norms tacitly *authorize* the enactment of those binding norms (which would belong to the system).

How is this logical conundrum relevant to the subject of judicial review? Because the resolution of "Kelsen's problem" shows the lack of cogency of "Marshall's logic." The mere fact that the enactment of a statute does not satisfy the constitutional conditions does not necessarily mean that a statute is not valid in the sense of obligation or binding force (this was perceived by Marshall as a *conceptual* possibility). It may be that legal systems include norms that make it obligatory to observe and to apply, if some conditions obtain or do not obtain, unconstitutional statutes such as the one in question—this may happen with regard to foreign laws, for example. In fact, even legal systems that provide broad procedures of judicial review—like those in the United States or Argentina—nevertheless require courts to apply unconstitutional statutes that have not yet been so declared, either because of mistakes or lack of review by the court.

The thesis is that there are norms in the legal system that under certain circumstances establish the validity or binding force of unconstitutional statutes or illegal administrative ordinances. This thesis supports Kelsen's alternative tacit clause. However, the differences between Kelsen's idea and my thesis follow: First, norms which grant validity to unconstitutional or illegal enactments do not *authorize* such enactments but merely declare that there is an *obligation* to apply and observe the resulting statute. Secondly, these norms are not *necessary* components of every legal system; they are only *positive* and *contingent* parts of some systems, not explicitly enacted but rather generated in a tacit and customary way. These norms may exist in a system, and if they do, they may have different contents. It is conceivable that a legal system does not make obligatory a law that contradicts the conditions of its enactment. Lastly, norms that require the application of illegal enactments generally discriminate between laws, contrary to Kelsen's thesis. Along with negative conditions such as statutes not declared unconstitutional by a corresponding court, the norms in question must satisfy a certain positive condition. However vague the implicit positive condition is, it is nevertheless real and operative; that is, the norm in question should enjoy a certain color or appearance of legality. This theory has been proposed by Constantineau in his famous doctrine of de facto laws,[21] which describes an extreme case of supposedly valid norms whose enactments have not been authorized. For an unconstitutional statute to be obligatory before it is declared so, the statute must not be *obviously* unconstitutional; it must appear to satisfy the established conditions for enacting norms in the legal system.

The foregoing discussion demonstrates that a norm may not be a "law of the system" (according to conditions established by the constitution) but it still may be obligatory according to tacit contingent clauses of that constitution. Marshall would agree with this assertion in cases where the Supreme Court has wrongly declared an unconstitutional law to be so or where it has yet to declare such a law unconstitutional. Likewise, tacit clauses of the constitution may establish that judges, including the Supreme Court justices, are obliged to apply a law if it is not abrogated either by the authority that enacted it or by a different coequal political body. The former system currently exists in England, Holland, and Finland, and existed in France before the establishment of the Constitutional Council. The latter system exists in most of the rest of present day Europe. Therefore, Marshall's logic breaks down between Premises 4 and 7 of my reconstruction of his argument.[22] Premise 4 states that the supremacy of the Constitution implies that a contrary law is not valid (defining valid as membership in a legal system). If "valid" means instead that the application of and obedience to the law is obligatory, then a law that contradicts the Constitution is not necessarily invalid. The denial of the invalidity of a law contradictory to the Constitution does not necessarily imply, as Premise 5 states, that the Constitution does not limit Congress (in the sense that Congress could modify the Constitution by an ordinary law). Congress may be prohibited by the Constitution to enact certain

---

[21] *See* ALBERT CONSTANTINEAU, PUBLIC OFFICERS AND THE DE FACTO DOCTRINE (1866).

[22] *Supra* p. 803.

laws but, if such a law is enacted, the application and observance of this law by the courts and the citizenry may be obligatory until Congress itself abrogates this law.[23] Consequently, Congress may be limited by the Constitution, as Premise 6 states, but this limitation does not imply that constitutionality must be judged by courts and that courts are exempt from the obligation to abide by these subsequent enactments. Premise 7 equivocates on the meaning of "validity." If validity means membership in a legal system, which implies the satisfaction of the conditions established for its creation by other norms of the system, the fact that a norm is invalid does not imply that it is also invalid in the sense that its application and observance is not obligatory. Hence, the conclusion of Marshall's reasoning is flawed. A law that contradicts the Constitution could still be applied by the judicial power, depending on what the other norms implicit in the system provide under the circumstances.

Marshall could reply that a constitution that requires judges to apply unconstitutional statutes destroys itself as an immutable instrument for limiting government and converts itself into ordinary law. But this reply confuses a logical problem with a practical one. It is logically possible for a constitution—like the British and former French Constitutions—to prohibit Parliament from enacting certain norms, even when there is no governmental body authorized to abrogate or to nullify the norms enacted in violation of that prohibition.

A contrary conclusion can only be reached by assuming that every obligation implies a sanction or a remedy. However, this assumption is not plausible; even Kelsen admits to a weak concept of obligation that does not presuppose further sanctions as it applies to the obligation of judges to apply sanctions for certain acts.[24] The practical efficacy of an obligation to sanction depends upon individual decisions as to how to comply with that obligation. But if the conceptual stipulation that there is no obligation without sanction or remedy is used to solve practical problems, then we create a paradox: an infinite circle of such sanctions or remedies.

Of course, it is possible that the remedy to unconstitutional laws does not have to be effectuated by judicial review. This remedy may be effected by a political body, a popular decision (such as a referendum), or through a mechanism of review so diffuse that each and every citizen would be authorized to disobey an unconstitutional law.

---

23 This assumes a concept of legal obligation that does not require sanctions for its enforcement but rather requires the conditions set forth by scholars like H.L.A. Hart. *See* H.L.A. HART, THE CONCEPT OF LAW (1961).

24 KELSEN, *supra* note 8, at 25.

Therefore, a system without judicial review and with a supreme constitution is not a logical impossibility. The main flaw of this argument lies in Premises 4 and 5. The power of judicial review is a contingent arrangement of certain legal systems, which may or may not exist even when the system contains a supreme constitution.

However, it is possible to construct another argument in support of judicial review, with implications even more far-reaching than those of Marshall's logic.

III.   AN EVEN BROADER BASIS FOR JUDICIAL REVIEW: THE NATURE OF LEGAL REASONING AND LANGUAGE

The present argument does not depend, like Marshall's logic, on the contingent fact that a constitution is supreme with regard to enactments of the legislature; the present argument applies to any legal system, since it is based on the logical features of legal reasoning and the language of the law. If these arguments are valid, the current preoccupation with the legitimacy of judicial review would be superfluous, since it would follow as a matter of logical necessity. I think the following arguments are valid but I believe that they are neutralized by another valid, but opposing argument which will be explained in the next section. These arguments in combination call for a radical transformation in the current preoccupations of legal scholarship.

I believe the proposition I advocate is so central for the comprehension of legal phenomena that I have deemed it "the fundamental theorem of legal philosophy."[25] The proposition asserts that legal norms do not by themselves constitute operative reasons for justifying actions and decisions (like those of judges) unless they are conceived as deriving from moral judgments—normative propositions that exhibit the distinctive traits of autonomy, justificatory finality, universability, generality, supervenience, and publicity.[26]

The schematic outlines of the quasi-formal demonstration supports my stated proposition. A legal norm or a law may be conceived of as a legal norm,[27] as a linguistic act,[28] or as a text, in the way that jurists assume that the same norms may have different interpretations. Under none of these three concepts of law may the law itself or its description serve as an operative reason for justifying an action or a decision. The explanation of this is very simple; under these concepts,

---

[25] See NINO, *supra* note 12; for a more succinct account, see CARLOS S. NINO, THE ETHICS OF HUMAN RIGHTS 16 (1991).

[26] *Id.* at 38-82.

[27] See HART, *supra* note 23, at 204-10.

[28] See JOHN AUSTIN, THE PROVINCE OF JURISPRUDENCE DETERMINED 9 (1971).

legal norms or laws are factual events or entities, and neither facts nor their descriptions allow for a justification of an action or a decision. A normative judgment (the content of the decision or the volition determining the action) cannot be derived from facts or their descriptions. This is no more than an application of the Humean principle about the logical hiatus between what "is" (factual judgments) and what "ought" (value judgments) to be. In simpler form, the facts or entities comprised by the law are compatible with any action or decision which is adopted. There is no pragmatic inconsistency between describing a social practice prohibiting x while deciding that x should be done or directly doing x.

However, Kelsen identifies legal norms not with social practices, speech acts, or texts but with *normative judgments* (propositions which predicate that a conduct ought to be, ought not to be, or may be, done). These propositions constitute the internal aspect of those practices, the locutionary content of those acts, or the meaning of those texts. A normative judgment constitutes by itself an operative reason, as it is valid or true, and it cannot be asserted without a pragmatical inconsistency when the action that the judgment prohibits or condemns is done.

However, if we intend to justify a decision, on the basis of a normative proposition (for instance, *"He who kills another ought to be punished,"* or *"The omission to pay two months of rent gives the owner the right to evict the tenant"*) then the question arises as to whether the normative proposition is a *legal* norm or *law*. Kelsen's response might be that we know the proposition is a law because of the proposition's content. A legal norm distinguishes itself from other normative propositions, such as moral or religious ones, because the conduct that the proposition predicates is a coercive act or sanction. The previously mentioned examples satisfy this definition but Kelsen's reply is inadequate. In the first place, there are many norms which are evidently legal, yet do not establish sanctions. Secondly (and this has not been generally perceived), there may be religious or moral norms which permit coercive acts (for example, moral theories and principles that justify punishment).

The alternative to distinguishing legal norms from other normative propositions on the basis of content is distinguishing on the basis of *origin*. In effect, it is plausible to maintain that a normative judgment is a law because of its enactment by a certain authority or its establishment by certain social practice. In both cases, it is relevant that the authority controls, and the social practice regulates, the quasi-monopoly of coercion. However, once this premise is accepted, a difficulty immediately arises; if a legal norm is a normative judgment that we accept because of its enactment by a certain authority or its establishment by a certain social practice, then the *legal norm cannot be an operative reason for justifying a decision*. This is so because the law in question could only operate as a premise of practical reasoning if it is accepted together with a more basic premise: Laws or legal norms are derived from the social practice or the prescription which establishes that law. Once we perceive this, we are in the same situation as the descriptive notions of a legal norm or a law, since it is impossible to derive from a premise that describes a practice or a prescription establishing a law, the normative judgment constituting that law which allows us to justify an action or a decision. When a judgment like "He who kills another ought to be punished" is conceived as a legal normative judgment because it is derived from the premise "Legislator L has prescribed 'He who kills another ought to be punished,' " a further implicit premise is presupposed which allows that derivation, the premise that *"Legislator L ought to be obeyed"* (or *"Legislator L is a legitimate authority,"* or *"Legislator L has power to enact valid laws"*).

However, when the conclusion that legal reasoning is justified only because it is based on a major premise like "Legislator L ought to be obeyed," one should ask what sort of proposition is contained within that premise. The story must be repeated again; whether it is a legal norm or a law does not depend on its content but on its origin, but to have the distinctive origin of legal norms one must accept a pair of premises: *"Legislator R has prescribed that legislator L ought to be obeyed"* and *"Legislator R ought to be obeyed."* The same question may be asked of the last proposition but this kind of question cannot be raised indefinitely. A moment arrives when it is necessary to accept the proposition that an authority or social practice ought to be obeyed not because of the origin of the formulation of that proposition, but because of its intrinsic merits. But a normative judgment which is not accepted for reasons of authority but for reasons of the validity of its content is precisely a moral judgment. This kind of acceptance of a normative proposition exhibits the feature of *autonomy* that Kant[29] has held to be distinctive of the adoption of moral norms. This implies that a legal norm or law only justifies the practical reasoning of judges and other social actors insofar as it is accepted by virtue of a moral judgment that grants legitimacy to certain authority and a descriptive judgment of the prescriptions of that author-

---

[29] IMMANUEL KANT, FUNDAMENTACIÓN DE LA METAFÍSICA DE LAS COSTUMBRES 89 (M. Garcia Morente trans., 1977).

ity. This conclusion constitutes the fundamental theorem of legal theory. (Kelsen also maintains that the force or validity of a legal norm is grounded in a preexisting basic norm that has not been enacted by any authority.[30] However, Kelsen neutralizes the moral character of the acceptance of the basic norm by arguing that in legal reasoning that norm is only *presupposed* and not genuinely accepted. But this can only be applied to the reasoning of legal theorists or scholars who need not justify any real decision or action. If judges and other social actors merely hypothetically adopted the basic norm the conclusions extracted from it would be also hypothetical and thus would not justify an action or decision.)

This theorem implies that legal discourse is not an autonomous species but rather a special modality of moral discourse, what Robert Alexis calls the *Besonderesfall* thesis.[31] In fact, this theorem is easily demonstrated by example: in Argentina there is a debate about whether the Constitution or international covenants should prevail when the two conflict. Advocates of the former view cite article twenty-seven of the Constitution, which states that international agreements should conform to the principles of public law contained in the Constitution.[32] At the same time, advocates of the latter view rely on the Vienna Convention of 1969, which establishes that states cannot justify noncompliance with a treaty because it contradicts the laws of the municipal legal system. Curiously, these two positions are completely circular. The supporters of the supremacy of the Constitution base their position in the Constitution while the supporters of the priority of international conventions ground their position in an international convention! This demonstrates the obvious truth that the validity of a certain legal system cannot be merely grounded in rules of that legal system, but must be derived from external principles. This conclusion is perhaps what supporters of natural law have wanted to stress throughout the history of legal philosophy, but they have been so clumsy in their presentation that their thesis appeared to suggest that there cannot be a descriptive concept of law, even for the purposes of *explaining* a legal system, without attempting to use it for *justifying* decisions.[33]

The implications of this theorem for the discussion of judicial review are as follows: a judge cannot justify any decision on the basis of a legal norm, such as a congressional statute, if he does not ground

---

[30] KELSEN, *supra* note 8, at 193-221.
[31] ROBERT ALEXIS, A THEORY OF LEGAL ARGUMENTATION (1989).
[32] CONSTITUCIÓN ARGENTINA art. 27.
[33] *See* Carlos S. Nino, *Dworkin and Legal Positivism*, 89 MIND 519 (1980).

the legitimacy of that norm, either explicitly or implicitly, upon some *moral* principles (in a broad sense of the expression). These moral principles establish the conditions of authority, procedure, and content which ground the duty to obey and apply a certain law.

If the constitution is conceived of as the expression of those moral principles which grant legitimacy to the laws or legal norms of lower hierarchy, rather than as a social practice or a document resulting from such practice under a descriptive concept, then under a normative concept we must conclude that *judges cannot but review the constitutionality of legal norms.* This does not depend on the type of legal system or constitution but is merely a question of logic.[34] A judge can not justify a statute enacted by the legislature by relying on that statute if she does not assume, explicitly or implicitly, judgments on the moral legitimacy of the authority of the legislature and on the fact that the fundamental rights which condition that authority have not been violated by the enactment.

Although this theorem is a sufficient justification for judicial review of an extremely wide scope, there is an alternative parallel argument that is based on the nature of *the language of law.*

I oversimplified my argument by stating that a normative judgment of "He who kills another ought to be punished" must derive in the first place from a descriptive judgment *"Legislator L prescribes 'He who kills another ought to be punished.'"* But, in addition to these two judgments, there are intermediate premises that must be intercalated to obviate the need for the quotation marks surrounding Legislator *L*'s proposition. This allows the proposition to be employed directly in the derivative premise. These additional premises allow us to interpret the text and decide which conducts are covered by them.

The interpretation of text involves a series of successive steps, several of which implicitly resort to premises of evaluative character. The first step establishes the general criterion for understanding the legal material that justifies a decision. For instance, one must decide whether meaning must be derived from the creator's intent, common linguistic usages, or combination of these two. This step requires some evaluative hypothesis regarding the function of legislation and the judiciary's position on such legislation. The second step empirically verifies the factual data from the first step as it relates to the

---

[34] The necessary structure of justificatory practical reasoning can only rely on norms enacted by certain authorities if the legitimacy of that authority has been previously grounded in certain basic principles—like the constitutional ones—which are accepted because of their intrinsic validity and not because they originate in some other authority.

intention of the legislator or to the linguistic conventions of the community. The third step involves choosing between an ambiguous text and the limitation of vague propositions, then attempting to resolve semantic vagueness and syntactic ambiguities by applying the criterion adopted in the first step. The fourth step extracts the relevant logical consequences from the norms which have been identified through the previous steps. Finally, in order to surmount the newly revealed logical interdeterminacies—like lacunae, contradictions, and redundancies—one must resort to evaluative hypotheses. The evaluative character considerations of interpretive process that must be resorted to in steps one, three, and partially in steps four and five, cannot be replaced by legal norms or laws. If such replacement is attempted—as may be convenient—the difficulty of interpreting the interpretive legal norms will remain. The process of interpretation always resorts to moral judgments in a broad sense, since they must be accepted because of their intrinsic merits and not because of their establishment by a certain authority.

If we view the constitution normatively, as a set of valid principles delineating the functions, goals, and limits of basic authorities and social practices, we may conclude that the review of the constitutionality of statutes and other laws is unavoidable in the process of interpreting the legal materials that other moral principles indicate are relevant. To move from a premise that describes a relevant practice or an authoritative prescription to the normative proposition justifying her decision, a judge applying a law cannot avoid taking into account evaluative considerations (which are part of the constitution when it is normatively conceived). Considerations such as legislative goals, the disparate intentions of lawmakers, popular reactions and contextual circumstances, are all evaluative or moral in character.

Therefore, there are two parallel reasons for grounding the broadest possible judicial review of constitutionality: one is related to the structure of justificatory practical reasoning, while the other is related to the nature of legal language. If the constitution is conceived as generating justificatory reasons, and thus is not viewed in descriptive terms like a text or a practice, then it must be viewed as a set of valid principles. These principles may or may not coincide with what the text or the practice in force establishes about the legitimacy of certain state authorities, their functions and goals, their limits in relation to the fundamental rights of individuals, the balance between the values of justice and security and certainty, and the proper division between several expressions of popular sovereignty. Under this normative concept of constitution, judges inescapably resort to constitutional principles when they decide how to apply and interpret a certain law. If the interpretation of a law is not justified by those principles, then the law does not constitute an operative reason for adopting a certain decision.

This justification for judicial review has been accomplished by replacing the descriptive concept of a constitution with a normative concept of *a moral or an ideal constitution*.[35]

It may appear that this conceptual twist changes the whole nature of judicial review so radically that we are no longer justifying the same institution; I shall subsequently take steps to soothe this discomfort, but for the moment, allow that this approach to the constitution does not seem at first sight to be so phenomenologically strange. Despite references to the four corners of the document and the will of the founding fathers, most judges treat the constitution as a set of valid principles and procedures *per se* regardless of the grounds for that validity. As legal realists have always emphasized, judges seldom feel obliged to apply a constitutional clause of which they truly disapprove. In most cases, the radical uncertainties referred to by legal language analysis, potentiated by such broadly phrased documents as constitutions, allow judges to resort to the principles and procedures they deem valid, while avoiding the more complicated and disputable moral justification by dressing these principles in authoritative garments.

The previous argument is a two-edged sword. A positive or historical constitution cannot serve as the operative reason for reviewing other laws. The decision to apply or to reject a certain law can only be justified on the basis of operative reasons constituted by valid, autonomously accepted, moral principles. Thus, identifying the constitution with such principles under a normative rather than descriptive concept, we reach the conclusion that the broadest judicial review of the constitutionality of laws is not only possible, but necessary.

However, the unrestricted breadth that this combination of arguments ascribes to judicial review casts doubt upon its plausibility. Given the dominant role that these arguments grant to evaluative considerations, which determine the acceptance and interpretation of laws, it is possible to doubt the relevance of laws themselves in the justificatory practical reasoning of judges and other social actors.

The first argument that we have examined leads us to the para-

---

[35] A descriptive concept of a constitution refers to either a positive social practice, the speech acts which generate it, or the document that is the result of it, while a moral constitution is a set of valid evaluative principles and procedures enshrined in a document that may or may not coincide with those prescribed by that practice.

dox I have deemed elsewhere the "irrelevance of the government and its laws."[36] If legal norm or law must be derived from valid moral principles to justify an action or decision, why not to look for the justification of such action and decision in those moral principles? Do we need a government and its laws? This is the kind of reasoning, grounded in the necessary autonomy of justificatory reasons, that has led authors like Robert Paul Wolff to defend philosophical anarchism—the position that no government or other source of heteronomous reasons is justified.[37] If the government acts in a morally correct way and enacts the laws required by the moral principles which justify them, those laws are superfluous. If the government acts contrary to moral principles because of malice or mistake, its laws should not be taken into account. The only laws that might have some significance are those that solve coordination problems between morally indifferent or equivalent situations, because any solution will be justified as long as one is achieved: for example, traffic laws which establish the direction of circulation.

This paradox may be resolved with a twofold answer. First, laws often fill gaps that are not covered by moral principles. As Thomas Aquinas maintained, positive law is related to natural law—my moral principles—not only by specification but by derivation as well.[38] Second, the moral justification for laws generally does not include substantive questions, but rather, *procedural* questions. Since the relevant moral principles generally limit themselves to determining the conditions for the selection of political authority and the procedure under which it must act, the satisfaction of these procedural questions allows us to justify the resulting norms. However, it is not easy to see how the gaps of moral principles can be filled without resorting to other moral principles and to detect moral principles which take certain procedures as *ultimately* relevant. For instance, most of the theories justifying democracy are of a procedural character only in the first instance. The relevant procedures are then justified in light of some substantive right such as autonomy or utility, the materialization of which could in principle be determined independently of the procedure in question. However, since legal norms generally affect important moral values, any procedural moral justification of such norms would have to enjoy great weight in order to justify deviations from the maximum satisfaction of those values.

---

[36] CARLOS S. NINO, ÉTICA Y DERECHOS HUMANOS (1989); *see also* CARLOS S. NINO, THE COMPLEX CONSTITUTION (forthcoming 1993).

[37] *See* ROBERT PAUL WOLF, IN DEFENSE OF ANARCHY (1970).

[38] ST. THOMAS AQUINAS, SUMMA THEOLOGICA, Question 90, Article 3, *in* BASIC WRITINGS OF SAINT THOMAS AQUINAS 745 (Anton C. Pegis ed., 1945).

The second argument regarding the interpretation of legal language also questions the relevance of the government and its laws. If we abstract the valuative steps of the process of interpretation that we have analyzed so far, it appears that the only "hard datum" that conditions the process of interpretation—even this is determined by the moral considerations—consists of texts or conducts, that is, a series of graphs or of bodily movements. Given the general criteria for ascribing meaning to such entities or events, the alternatives for cleaning up the imprecisions and ambiguities of those meanings, and the variants for overcoming logical uncertainties, it is clear that the texts and conducts in question may be associated with any propositional content according to the valuative principles that are assumed in each one of the corresponding steps. Hart replies to those who are skeptical about rules (like legal realists) that the fact that there are "cases of penumbra" does not preclude areas of full clarity in the application of the norms.[39] However, that does not take into account that the distinction between areas of penumbra and clarity presupposes a choice between diverse criteria of interpretation, and this cannot be accomplished without engaging in extralegal considerations.

These two arguments demonstrate that judges enjoy extremely broad power to decide the constitutionality of laws in light of valuative basic standards that could be conceived of as part of an ideal constitution.[40] However, these arguments justify an extraordinary scope of judicial review. They lead to extreme legal nihilism, which makes the conclusion of critical legal scholars look pale in comparison. These arguments are so powerful that they have a boomerang effect on the rationale for judicial review; the legal power of *judges* over the citizenry is put in question when the basis for that power (laws and their interpretation) depends on evaluative premises which might be different than the premises adopted by those judges.

In what follows, I shall analyze an argument that questions some presuppositions of the previous ones and which has, thus, an opposite impact upon the justification of judicial review.

IV. A RADICAL IMPUGNATION OF JUDICIAL REVIEW: DEMOCRACY AND ITS EPISTEMIC RELIABILITY

The nucleus of the argument in favor of legal nihilism is as follows: If by force of logic, one needs to resort to moral principles for laws that justify actions and decisions, those laws are irrelevant since

---

[39] HART, *supra* note 23, at 103-07.

[40] This refers to a normative constitution, which is based upon inherently valid principles and procedures rather than a written text.

those moral principles may themselves justify an action or decision in the case at stake. This argument assumes a position that is not nihilistic toward *moral principles* themselves. If moral principles were only a mask for tastes, interests, or psychological inclinations, then it would not be possible to justify an action or decision. But if this extreme moral skepticism were accepted, the endeavor to justify judicial review (which does more than merely describe positive regulations) would not make sense. Nor would it be possible to explain how a law may justify actions and decisions.

However, the previous argument for legal nihilism contains a more questionable assumption. Any person, including a judge, may have independent access to the *knowledge* of evaluative principles which allows us to justify an action or decision. In other words, this argument presupposes an *epistemic individualism* in the moral sphere. This position, which has its roots in Plato, is assumed by many contemporary philosophers. I believe that John Rawls tacitly adopts the assumption that by mere individual reflection and "reflective equilibrium" an individual can gain access to the knowledge of valid principles of social morality.[41]

Some philosophers adopt opposite stances, in the tradition of the Sophists, and perhaps continued by Rousseau and by Republican movements.[42] Jürgen Habermas, following ideas of Karl-Otto Apel,[43] maintains that only through communicative interaction is it possible to have access to the knowledge of valid moral standards and overcome the conditioning and the false consciousness that individuals are subject to as a result of their insertion in productive relationships. This position of *epistemic collectivism*, which sometimes gets confused with an ontological thesis about the truth of moral standards rather than about knowledge, presupposes that the collective practice of discussion or communication is what *exclusively* provides access to intersubjective valid moral principles.

Neither of these two positions is satisfactory. The first leads to the paradox of the moral irrelevance of government and, hence, either to anarchy or tyranny, depending on the balance of powers between those who reach diverse moral conclusions. For example, if I were

---

[41] JOHN RAWLS, A THEORY OF JUSTICE (1971). I develop this argument in CARLOS S. NINO, EL CONSTRUCTIVISMO ÉTICO (1989). Of course, I am not referring to the later work of Rawls which proclaims an "epistemic abstinency" about moral issues.

[42] With regard to Republicanism, see Frank Michelman, *Law's Republic*, 97 YALE L.J. 1493 (1988); Cass R. Sunstein, *Beyond the Republican Revival*, 97 YALE L.J. 1539 (1988).

[43] JÜRGEN HABERMAS, *Ética del discurso: Notas sobre un programa de fundamentaciòn, in* CONCIENCIA MORAL Y ACCIÒN COMUNICATIVA (1985); KARL-OTTO APEL, THE TRANSFORMATION OF PHILOSOPHY (Glyn Adey & David Frisby trans., 1980).

stronger than the rest of my community I would establish a tyranny, not because I believe that *my* government is morally relevant, but because I believe that my moral judgments are valid while opposite ones are not. Epistemic individualism also faces the problem of characterizing the validity of social morality principles. If it depends on the hypothetical acceptability of such principles under conditions of impartiality, rationality, and knowledge of the relevant facts (according to the presuppositions of our practice of moral discussion), then it is extremely improbable that individual reflection can lead to valid standards of intersubjective morality. An individual cannot impartially represent the interests of all individuals who are affected, and cannot overcome the deficiencies in information and reasoning in isolation. It is plausible to maintain that, in general, an individual best understands her own self-interest when the interests are not only based on her desires but also on her decisions about the relative weight of those interests.

Epistemic collectivism raises a different objection. Communicative interaction consists of both expressing the *interests* of the individual participants and, more fundamentally, of formulating propositions about what the *principles* are that impartially contemplate those interests. These propositions should be accepted after discussion in which the participants successfully reach an agreement. When these principles are introduced they are not random proposals, but rather, they are asserted as true or valid, and the discussion is an attempt to demonstrate the principles' acceptance under impartial conditions and if their acceptability leaves aside relevant interests. This process requires a characterization of the validity of intersubjective moral standards, which must be independent of the *results* of the discussion. Otherwise, it would be meaningless to allege the validity of the principles proposed *during* the discussion itself, when a consensus has not yet been reached. Additionally, the process presupposes that the participants have some *title* that demonstrates their access to the knowledge of whether the requirements for moral validity have been satisfied. Without such a title, the participants' interventions in the debate would only be presumptuous chatter without meaning, not respectable opinions which might indeed be right and obtain general support. A participant's reputation of impartiality, rationality, and knowledge of the facts increases the weight of her opinions given her greater access to moral truth. Even when the discussion ends in agreement, a dissenter may request that the discussion be reopened to prove herself to be right. Therefore, epistemic collectivism cannot explain the nature of the *input* that feeds the discussion or forces its reopening.

Given the deficiencies of both epistemic individualism and collectivism, I subscribe to the intermediate position of *epistemic constructivism*.[44] This thesis maintains that the process of collective discussion and decision among all parties concerned in a conflict has considerably greater reliability in accessing valid principles of intersubjective morality than individual reflection, for the reasons set forth against epistemic individualism in the preceding text. Unlike epistemic collectivism, this thesis does not maintain that the process of collective discussion and decision is the *exclusive* means of moral knowledge and it does not completely discount the possibility that the requirements of impartiality, rationality, and knowledge may be satisfied through individual reflection. Epistemic constructivism emphasizes, however, that it is unlikely that individual reflection will obtain correct solutions, since without the participation of the people concerned, their real, subjective interests and the weight they should be given would be distorted. The ascription of diverse degrees of reliability to the method of collective discussion and decision, and to individual reflection, has important implications. The conclusion that the former is epistemically superior to the latter leads us to observe its results even in those individual cases in which we are sure that our individual reflection is correct and the collective result is wrong. Otherwise, individual reflection would prevail in every case and the method of collective discussion, that by hypothesis is in general more reliable, would wither away. Even when this second order epistemic reason can justify *observing* the collective outcome, our individual reflection provides a reason for asking for the reopening of a discussion to present our arguments in an attempt to change the decision.

The greatest difficulty in applying these considerations to the political system is that even though the democratic procedures of electing authorities and solving substantive issues closely resembles the informal process of collective deliberation and consensual decision, it nevertheless contains crucial differences. Most importantly, an informal discussion, such as an everyday discussion to resolve a conflict, is only over when we arrive at a *unanimous* agreement. Democracy, on the other hand, operates by simple majority rule. This simple majority replaces unanimity when discussion must be concluded, or when the result of the discussion would implicitly benefit those who favor maintaining the status quo when the time for change is at hand. This also applies to qualified majorities. The passage from

---

[44] NINO, *supra* note 12, at 245.

unanimity to simple majority implies a qualitative jump; a unanimous consensus is the functional equivalent of impartiality (because the unanimous consensus implies that the relevant interests have been attended to under the presupposition that each one is the best judge of her own interests), while a majority may discriminate against the interests of a minority.

However, when we compare the latter risks with those involved in other procedures of collective decision making, dictatorship, or elitism, the procedure of collective discussion and majoritarian decision presents various features that generate a greater tendency towards the adoption of impartial solutions than those other procedures.[45] In the first place, all concerned participate in the debate, with the possibility of expounding their interests. Second, after letting their interests be known, the participants must *justify* their proposals to each other, which implies that they must show that those proposals derive from universal principles that would be accepted by an impartial, rational, and knowledgeable person, considerably constraining the proposals that may be plausibly presented. Third, the need to encourage the support of the majority of other participants—given the uncertain outcome created by the possibility of majoritarian voting—leads to the contemplation of as many interests as possible. Fourth, formal structure at the collective level projects the tendency towards impartiality that the democratic process generates at the individual level. For instance, Condorcet's theorem implies that when individuals are likely to arrive at correct solutions, then as more individuals support a solution, the more likely it is that the solution is correct.[46]

Thus, despite the risk of partiality against minorities, the democratic process probably leads to more correct intersubjective moral solutions than any of the alternative methods of collective decision making. Even experts and moral philosophers cannot match the judgment of the people concerned in appraising the proper weight of their own interests. Many dictatorships, such as those that were frequent in Latin America, did not always lack expertise or good intentions. However, the leaders were completely blind to the interests of people with whom they did not need to interact. This account of the value that is predicated *in general* on the democratic method justifies that its results be observed in each particular case. As individual reflection corrects its mistakes less reliably than the democratic method,

---

[45] *Id*. at 248.

[46] This is demonstrated by Condorcet's famous theorem. JEANE-ANTOINE NICOLAS DE CARITAT, MARQUIS DE CONDORCET, ESSAI SUR L'APPLICATION DE L'ANALYSE À LA PROBABILITÉ DES DECISIONS PENDUES À LA PLURALITÉ DES VOIX 1785 (1985).

it is not legitimate to resort to the former for discarding the results of the latter in the cases where we are sure that the collective decision is wrong. To do so would undermine the efficacy of the democratic method of conflict resolution, thereby frustrating the conclusion that it is the most reliable method to reach correct solutions.

Certainly, the epistemic capacity of the democratic process would be greater or lesser depending on how close it comes to the strictures of the original process of moral discussion which determine its inherent tendency towards impartiality. These strictures include participation in the deliberation and in the decision of all those concerned; freedom to present all points of view and a relative equality of the participants; concentration on the justification of proposals that tend to offer different ways of balancing the interests at stake on the basis of principles which are impartially acceptable, regardless of other traits like their being prescribed by some convention or authority; and achievement of the widest consensus possible. Naturally, this implies a program of institutional reforms in order to maximize the epistemic value of democracy.[47]

This justification of democracy allows us to overcome the paradox of the moral irrelevance of government and its laws. Even when only moral principles and not legal norms (conceived of as prescriptions or social practices) provide reasons for actions, if the legal norms have a democratic origin then they provide reasons to *believe* that there are reasons to act. Given this, it is morally justified to act according to norms that have been enacted by the collective procedure of discussion and decision, despite the fact that our individual reflection might indicate to us the existence of opposite reasons.

This vision of democracy serves also to confront the second skeptical argument with regard to law, that of interpretive indeterminacies. If we ascribe epistemic value to democratic discussion and consensus, that value lies not in a text or a social practice but in the propositional content that has been the object of the discussion and the consensus. Thus, not the text or practice in itself, but the intentions of those who proposed the norms and their propositional attitudes are relevant for determining the *meaning* of a text or a practice. The consensus formed out of those intentions enjoys the presumption of validity granted by the democratic process.[48]

---

47 See CARLOS S. NINO, FUNDAMENTOS DE DERECHO CONSTITUCIONAL (1992), in which I suggest such a program.

48 Of course, a problem arises regarding the passage of time and the resultant weakening of the epistemic value of the consensus on some normative proposition, given the fact that the interests involved change as circumstances and their bearers change. This might be tackled

One could object to the conclusion of the present argument on the basis that it ignores the existence of *individual rights*, the main function of which is precisely to contain majoritarian decisions in order to protect the interests of isolated individuals and minorities. The idea of a liberal democracy is based on the premise that certain rights cannot be trespassed even by majoritarian decisions. These individual rights should be protected by mechanisms such as judicial review, which lie outside the very democratic political process. This seems to be part of Ronald Dworkin's argument, which is based on the distinction between policies and principles.[49] For Dworkin, policies define collective objectives (such as national defense or a clean environment) which are goods valued aggregatively and not individually. Principles establish rights which protect situations and whose value takes into account the distribution and the individualization of the goods involved. They constitute a barrier or limit against the pursuit of a collective objective, so that a reason based on that objective cannot override a reason based on a right. According to Dworkin, the rationale for the idea that certain decisions are to be made through the democratic process is basically related to policies, since that rationale refers to the need to balance diverse interests and to the inconvenience of retroactive determinations.[50] On the other hand, this does not apply to decisions made on the basis of principles that do not require a balance of interests and have an atemporal validity. Judges, according to Dworkin, should fundamentally decide on the basis of principles that establish rights and not on the basis of policies.

However, I think that the vision of rights as limiting democracy, either conceptually or evaluatively, is not plausible. From the conceptual point of view, rights constitute a protection of individual *interests* that set forth barriers against considerations grounded on the interests of others or of the social whole. If I have a right to *x*, this right by definition cannot be displaced by the mere consideration that the interests of the majority would be promoted if I were deprived of *x*. But from this we cannot infer that rights are barriers against majoritarian *decisions*. There is no logical inconsistency in stating that the only authority competent to recognize and enforce rights is that of majoritarian origin. Of course, someone might maintain that majoritarian decisions tend to benefit majoritarian interests. How-

---

through the idea of a changing tacit consensus, which certainly would have an impact on the interpretive question.

[49] RONALD DWORKIN, TAKING RIGHTS SERIOUSLY ch. 4 (1977).

[50] *Id.* at 97.

ever, this is a factual and a moral question and is not imposed by the logic of the concept of rights.

Dworkin's thesis must be appraised in this moral and factual context and not as a conceptual conclusion. However, it should be noted that Dworkin seems to assume that there is ample space for the operation of policies that establish collective objectives without colliding with rights, a space which is occupied by the political process exempted from judicial control. This can well be questioned if one supports a *robust* theory of rights, according to which those rights can be violated not only by positive acts but also by omissions.[51] In this case, rights occupy almost all the moral space, leaving very little room for policies and thus, according to Dworkin's thesis, for the unrestrained operation of the majority. This combines with the present view of democracy, which conceives of democracy as dealing with intersubjective moral issues and not merely as a process of aggregating interests as the opposite pluralist vision holds.[52]

It is possible to answer pragmatically the objection that majorities can be, and often are, tempted to suppress individual or minority rights. There is no guarantee that another minority or isolated individuals are not similarly tempted, unless their interests coincide with the minority whose rights are at stake. Judges are those isolated individuals. In most democratic systems judges are not appointed through a process of collective discussion and majoritarian decision, nor are their actions the subject of collective discussion (especially life-tenured judges). Therefore, a judge's decision does not enjoy the epistemic value that accrues to the collective discussion process. The discussion inherent in the judicial process limits itself to those directly affected by the conflict at trial. Those who may be affected by the general principles employed to solve that conflict do not participate. Additionally, the conflict is solved by a third person alien to it. This disassociation may be a considerable advantage in terms of impartiality when the conflict encompasses only few people, but when the decision affects interests of a multitude of individuals (as those resolved by judges generally do) whose experiences cannot be represented by an isolated individual, this disassociation is not possible.

Thus, we confront again the famous counter-majoritarian difficulty: What guarantee is there that judges who have not been directly elected through the democratic process, whose indirect democratic origin of authority dilutes with time, and who are not obliged to involve themselves in collective deliberation, are in a better epistemic

---

[51] See NINO, *supra* note 12, at 199.
[52] See NINO, *supra* note 25, at 243.

position than democratically accountable legislators to decide according to impartial principles, even when those principles establish rights against the majority interests?

This difficulty cannot be overcome by relying on the democratic origin of the constitution itself, the principles of which are used to exert judicial review. There are several reasons for rejecting this alternative. In the first place, most stable contemporary constitutions have been enacted by exceedingly undemocratic procedures, at least compared to the democratic procedure for adopting statutes and other legal enactments which are sometimes disqualified in the light of the constitution. Second, even when the foregoing point does not apply, as is the case with the Spanish Constitution, the very stability of a constitution requires that the democratic consensus obtained at the time of its enactment becomes progressively more irrelevant with the passing of time, since decades or even centuries later that consensus no longer correlates with the interests of the present majority. This objection may be answered by resorting to the idea of a tacit present consensus, but the very fact that a stable constitution cannot be modified by simple majorities produces a majoritarian consensus against some constitutional clauses. Lastly, this rigidity of the constitution might be justified as an attempt of the majority to protect itself in a paternalistic way.[53]

Using the democratic legitimacy of current constitutional norms to justify employing them in judicial review in order to disqualify laws of democratic origin applies also to the *dualist* conception of Bruce Ackerman.[54] He maintains that there are two levels of political action: the constitutional level, the rare moments of extended popular debate and political mobilization and the consequent democratic legitimacy given by the ample consensus reached in those moments;[55] and the day-to-day political level, in which most citizens do not participate and which thus enjoys a lower level of legitimacy. The results of the latter should be subject to the constraints established by the former. It is the role of judges to ensure that constitutional politics prevail over day-to-day politics. Ackerman presents a theory in which

---

[53] This assumes that the majority that established the original constitution—assuming it was a majority—was in a better condition to impartially decide conflicts affecting the interests of future generations than they would be themselves. This paternalism accurately describes many colonialist justifications. *See* Stephen Holmes, *Precommitment and the Paradox of Democracy, in* CONSTITUTIONALISM AND DEMOCRACY 195 (Jon Elster & Rune Slagstad eds., 1989).

[54] *See, e.g.,* BRUCE ACKERMAN, WE THE PEOPLE 72 (1991).

[55] This type of political mobilization occurred in the United States with the enactment of the Constitution, during post-Civil War Reconstruction, and when the New Deal was proposed by Franklin Delano Roosevelt. *Id.* at 72-84.

constitutional rights emanate from the democratic decisions of constitutional moments and restrain the expressions of normal politics. This theory opposes both a monist view, in which rights depend on a continuous and permanent democratic process, and a fundamentalist conception, in which rights restrain any democratic decision.

Despite the attractiveness of Ackerman's theory, there are reasons to doubt both the greater legitimacy of the norms enacted in the constitutional moments and the idea that judges should be the custodians of that supposed greater legitimacy. In the first place, it is not clear why dualism, or two political tracks, is more accurate than a *continuum* of several degrees of legitimacy determined by the degree of mobilization and debate. Certain issues, such as abortion or discrimination, provoke ample debate and popular protest and have considerable impact on the legal system, even though perhaps not comparable to the constitutional moments Ackerman points out.[56] This distinction can be made in relation to a monist system like Great Britain's where there are different levels of democratic expression, including plebiscites, parliamentary elections, the working of Parliament itself, and local elections. Second, the democratic legitimacy of some of the constitutional moments to which Ackerman refers is highly dubious. The deficiencies in the democratic procedures leading to old stable constitutions had not been expurgated by whatever informal debates and mobilizations surrounded their enactment. Third, the image of the people galvanized and excited by the public spirit in dramatic moments results in questions regarding the epistemic quality of such moments. Where is the space for ample public discussion in such moments? Is discussion and decision by all the participants guaranteed in such moments? Are minority views adequately protected? Perhaps the epistemic quality of democracy is better secured in the less romantic but calmer moments of normal politics. Fourth, the democratic legitimacy of the results of the constitutional moments is also questionable because a simple majority cannot change the status quo when it is protected by entrenched clauses. This necessarily implies that a minority may prevent one of those moments from culminating in actual reform. If there were not these entrenched provisions the system would be a monist one in Ackerman's classification. In the fifth place, the legitimacy of the expressions of normal politics would be questionable as well, since, as Ackerman makes clear, the representativeness of the branches of government is problematic according to his theory.[57] The legitimacy of any government derives

---

[56] *Id.* at 108-13.
[57] *Id.* at 181-83.

from the delegation made during a constitutional moment. Thus, any form of government agreed upon in one of the rare constitutional moments would be legitimate. Sixth, Ackerman does not solve the temporal difficulty of the present legitimacy of a democratic decision made by people who died two centuries ago, especially when it is opposed to the will of present people as expressed in parliamentary elections. What is the difference between this and holding that the people in a distant territory are bound by what a foreign sovereign decides for them? Ackerman's response relies on the diverse quality of the two expressions of popular will given their different degrees of mobilization and debate.[58] However, the higher quality of an expression of will that has zero binding value does not raise that value so high as to equate it with another expression of will of very poor quality but with substantial binding value since it retains some connection to the preferences of the people who are affected by that will. Seventh, as applied to judicial review there is no reason why the will of "We the People" should be preserved by counter-majoritarian organs and not by those who at least have some direct connection with present majorities. Eighth, the subjection of judges to the collective will, no matter what its contents, is implausible as an expression of an ideological variety of legal positivism; to say that freedom of religion or expression could be abolished by a constitutional amendment and that judges should ignore those freedoms or else resign, seems to ignore the fact that sometimes the highest moral duty of a judge is to take advantage of her position and rescue some freedoms and lives.[59] It would be strange to ignore this possibility given the fact that Ackerman does not ascribe epistemic quality to the results of a democratic process. Finally, although the degree of public involvement that democratic politics requires should be a legitimate concern from a nonperfectionist perspective, it is excessive to account for that problem by a bifurcating politics which, according to Ackerman, has given the American people only three opportunities to make themselves directly heard in two centuries of an eventful history.

In concluding this section one may assert that an argument based on the epistemic value of democracy seems to imply a radical rejection of the possibility that judges should exercise judicial review. Whether the constitution is conceived of as a set of morally valid principles and procedures or a historically datable text or practice, nondemocratic organs not directly involved in the democratic process

---

[58] *Id.* at 131-62.

[59] A few judges applied this concept during the last dictatorship in Argentina.

of discussion, such as the judicial branch, should not be able to invalidate statutes or other laws with a genuinely democratic origin.

The previous arguments lead to the conclusion that judges must necessarily rely on the moral principles normatively embodied in the constitution to justify the application and interpretation of the laws. However, that conclusion is neutralized since it indicates that judges have epistemic reasons for recognizing and applying democratically enacted laws, as evidence of the valid moral principles upon which they rely. While an undemocratic positive constitution withers away from the picture, the moral or ideal constitution still *logically* takes priority over democratic legislation for justifying decisions. But, from the *epistemic* point of view, democratic legislation evidences the principles of the ideal constitution. Hence, judicial review of the constitutionality of democratic laws is an expression of epistemic moral elitism, since it supposes that a few nonelected officials, quite removed from the political fray, are better equipped to decide the impartial principles that the laws must satisfy than the very people concerned with those laws (their directly elected representatives).

It might now be appropriate to review the tortuous route that my arguments have followed up to this point. First, I have tried to demonstrate that judicial review is not a logical consequence of having a supreme positive constitution since this fact is compatible with the absence of any form of such review. However, I believe that if the constitution is conceived of as a set of valid moral principles and procedures, rather than as a positive social practice or text, then it seems inevitable that judges resort to it in order to decide the interpretation and application of positive laws. Finally, I have suggested that democratically originated positive laws can operate epistemically to indicate the content of valid moral principles, despite the fact that the structure of a judge's practical reasoning leads her toward a moral or ideal constitution, since positive laws cannot be the ultimate reasons for action. This follows as the democratic procedure generating those laws is a more reliable way to determine the right intersubjective moral principles than the individual reflections of a judge. The positive or real constitution cannot generally serve as a guide to those principles given its relative lack of democratic legitimacy as compared with the continuous working of the legislative process. Therefore, judges, as officeholders originating and operating outside of the process of collective discussion and decision, cannot disqualify the normative outcomes of that process by alleging a better understanding of the moral principles that serve as the basic premises of practical reasoning to justify decisions.

This radical rejection of judicial review enjoys considerable weight since it follows from the only stance that overcomes the exceedingly striking implications of complete legal nihilism. However, the radical extremes that these arguments present cause suspicion about the cogency of the present argument. The extreme democratism implied in this view is self-defeating since, as has been often observed, democracy could eat its own tail if certain conditions were not preserved even by undemocratic means. Besides, the conclusion extracted from the combination of the two arguments, that positive constitutions not generated entirely by democratic procedures are completely irrelevant to justificatory practical reasoning, are entirely counter-intuitive. It seems incredible that the numerous struggles[60] for the respect of a certain positive constitution are in the end absolutely fruitless. For logical reasons, a social practice, the speech acts generating it, or the document which results from it (together, what we take to be a positive constitution) cannot logically play any role in justificatory practical reasoning.

However, I shall not use these intuitions to prove the present argument's falsity (since I think it valid). Instead, I shall heuristically account for those intuitions in order to see whether the argument is subject to certain *conditions*, so that the nonsatisfaction of those conditions establishes the limits of the argument, and thus provides relevant leeway for the recognition of judicial review. I shall focus separately on three different assumptions of the epistemic justification of democratic laws which lead to the denial of judicial review. In each case, the complement of the respective assumption, that is, the proposition that describes the opposite states of affairs, will provide a different foundation for making inroads in the denial of judicial review, leading to the acceptance of diverse kinds of judicial review. The resulting scheme will be a theory of judicial review composed of a denial, which assumes some conditions, and three ample exceptions, based on the nonsatisfaction of those conditions and which will appear far less provocative to ordinary legal conventions than my partial conclusions so far. Additionally, I hope this argument offers a more solid philosophical basis for the institution than common sense alone.

A. The First Exception to the Denial of Judicial Review: Control of Democratic Procedure

The first inroad into the previous denial of judicial review is the easiest to substantiate and may be familiar to many. It springs from

---

60 Such as the efforts for an Argentine Constitution after 1983.

the simple realization that not everything that is called "democracy" is a process with the epistemic quality that makes its enactments a reliable guide to moral principles. Democratic process is not an inorganic and spontaneous activity, but rather is subject to particular rules designed to maximize the epistemic value of that process. Democracy's epistemic value depends on a variety of factors: the breadth of participation in the discussion and decision of those affected by the latter; the freedom of participants to express themselves in the deliberation; the equality of the conditions under which that participation is carried out; the satisfaction of the requirement that the proposals be properly justified; the subsequent concentration of the debate on principles for justifying different balances of interests (not the mere presentation of those interests); the avoidance of majorities frozen around certain interests; the amplitude of the majority supporting the decisions; the time that has passed since the consensus was achieved, and; the reversibility of the decision. The rules of the democratic process insure that these conditions as well as others exist to the maximum degree possible.

The question is: Who safeguards the rules of the democratic process? The democratic process cannot be entirely self-regulated since this would prevent the correction of wrongs brought about only by the departure from rules and conditions which ground the process's epistemic value. This has lead some scholars who examined the counter-majoritarian difficulty, like John Hart Ely, to conceive of the judiciary in its exercise of judicial review as a referee of the democratic process, whose essential mission is to see that the procedural rules and conditions of democratic discussion and decision are not violated.[61]

One could object that judges are not directly affected by the distortions of the democratic system because they are not directly subject to that democratic system. Hence, why should they be better suited than democratic bodies (even with the vices that affect democratic operations) to detect those distortions?

Primarily, since *anybody* has reasons to defer her own moral judgment to the contrary decision by democratic institutions, *anybody* is entitled to determine if and to what degree the conditions that determine that deference (the conditions that ground the epistemic value to the democratic process) are satisfied. A judge has no more legitimacy than any citizen who is applying a legal norm for justifying an action or decision and is compelled by the structure of practical rea-

---

[61] JOHN HART ELY, DEMOCRACY AND DISTRUST: A THEORY OF JUDICIAL REVIEW (1980).

soning to resort to autonomous or moral principles. One can only be relieved of that burden if the conditions for relying on the epistemic quality of the democratic process for detecting those principles are given. This may only be determined by individual reflection and not from the results of the democratic process, since the value of that process is at stake. Therefore, the judge has no alternative but to determine whether the collective process leading to that law satisfied the conditions of democratic legitimacy, just as he has no alternative but to determine how the law originated.

Secondly, since the intervention of the judges is by nature unidirectional, judicial activism is always directed to broaden the democratic process, requiring more participation, more freedom to the parties, more equality, and more concentration on justification. It would be absurd, under this conception of judicial review, for a judge to nullify a law because it was enacted through too broad and equal a process of participation and discussion. Sometimes judges may be, and often are, mistaken in their conclusions about the operations of the democratic system, but the overall effect of a procedural judicial review is the promotion of the conditions that grant to the democratic process its epistemic value.

Many of these conditions are the content of individual rights. Those rights may be deemed "a priori rights" since their value is not determined by the democratic process but is presupposed when the value of the latter is assumed. A certain analogy exists between this determination of a priori rights and the transcendental method through which Kant[62] determined the truth of synthetical a priori propositions.

If experience is a good basis of knowledge, preconditions of experience should also give us some knowledge. Likewise, if democracy is a good basis of moral knowledge, preconditions of democracy should also be part of that moral knowledge. These a priori rights should be respected by the democratic process as a prerequisite of its validity, and it is the mission of judges to guarantee that respect.

Certainly, it is quite a controversial question to determine the range of a priori rights, distinguishing them from a posteriori rights, which are established by the democratic process itself. Some a priori rights are obvious: the active and passive political rights and freedom of expression are clearly central to the working of the democratic system. These rights presuppose other more basic rights, such as the

---

[62] IMMANUEL KANT, CRITICA DE LA RAZOÑ PURA 121 (José de Perojo trans., 1961).

security against arbitrary deprivations of life and limb, and politically motivated freedom of movement.

However, there are other a priori rights that are more controversial. Take the case of the so-called *social* or *welfare* rights. These rights are not antagonistic to the classical individual rights but are the natural extension thereof.[63] This becomes apparent when one recognizes that a classical individual right, like the right to life, is not only violated by positive acts but also by the failure to provide the resources necessary to preserve those rights, like medical attention, food, and shelter. The reluctance to accept that omissions are violations of human rights derives from critically accepting current social conventions which unjustly ignore the ascription of *causal* effects to omissions, by ignoring the duty to act positively to avoid the harm. However, once this stance is accepted the counter-majoritarian difficulty of judicial review becomes much more dramatic, since any political decision may ultimately affect, by action or omission, an individual right. Even if the present procedural approach of judicial review is accepted, its scope would be too broad, since the social and economic conditions of individuals (their level of education, their health, their strength vis-à-vis the pressures of the labor market) are preconditions for free and equal participation in the political process. This again raises the question of why judges should be in a better position than legislators, immersed in the democratic process, to make extremely controversial decisions about how to distribute limited social resources and about how to choose the most adequate social mechanisms to carry out that distribution.

There is no algorithmic formula to solve this question. There are resources so fundamental to the preservation and promotion of human rights that they must be provided as a precondition for the participation in the democratic process, or the quality of this process loses all epistemic value. A starving individual[64] is just as disenfranchised as one who is threatened for his ideas. And each individual that is not free to participate in the democratic process proportionately reduces the epistemic value of that process. However, we must be careful when we interfere with the democratic system for its own protection; otherwise the system could end up being reduced to a minimum expression, limited to cases of social deprivation. If we decide which resources are required as a precondition to the proper working of the democratic system, we prevent that system

---

[63] NINO, *supra* note 12, at 217.

[64] Or a very ill individual, deprived of medical attention, or one lacking the minimum access to mass media to express his own ideas.

from determining the final distribution of those resources. As a result, we could have an epistemically magnificent democratic system that is only allowed to decide a few things.

Therefore, we must confront this tension between the strength and the scope of the democratic process. The more we enhance its epistemic quality by expanding a priori rights so as to cover enough resources to insure freedom and equality of participation, the narrower the range of matters decided by that democratic process. Once a certain threshold is surpassed, the democratic system has some capacity to correct and improve itself because of its inherent tendency toward impartiality, providing people with the preconditions that allow for their equal and free participation. On the other hand, if that threshold is not reached, the vices of the process will intensify, and the character of the solutions promoted by the unequal or constrained participation will lead to further inequalities and restraints on the participation of the people. While there is no exact formula to locate this threshold, there are general guidelines that a judge, or for that matter anybody, must take into account. She must determine whether the vices of the "democratic" system are so serious that they render its epistemic reliability below that enjoyed by the isolated reflection of an individual. If it is positive, then she must act on the basis of her own moral judgment, both in order to solve the case at hand and to promote a course of action that will improve the future epistemic quality of the system. Often these two objectives can be achieved by the same decision. Of course, there is no further epistemic authority with which to guide oneself when deciding whether to defer to the epistemic authority of the democratic system or to decide on the basis of one's own light. This decision about the best epistemic process for achieving just decisions must be made in isolation.

B. The Second Exception to the Denial of Judicial Review: Personal Autonomy

The very justification of democracy that I have alluded to also marks the limits of the value of democracy. Democracy's value is grounded in the greater reliability of the democratic process to arrive at morally correct solutions, as compared to alternative methods of decision making. This depends on the fact that democratic decisions are reached impartially and the process contemplates all the interests affected. The idea of impartiality is, of course, highly complex and controversial. I believe that it includes universability, generality, and notions of the separateness of individuals. But it is clear that not all moral standards or requirements depend on impartiality for their validity. The ideals of a good patriot, of a good soldier, of a responsible parent, of a life devoted to knowledge or beauty, of integrity and honesty, of religious commitments, can only tangentially be associated with the idea of impartiality.

In *The Ethics of Human Right*,[65] I distinguish between two dimensions of morals: public, intersubjective, or social morality, which consists of those standards that evaluate actions for their effects on the interests of individuals other than the agents, and; private, self-regarding, or personal morality, which is constituted by those ideals of personal excellence or virtue that evaluate actions for their effects on the quality of the life or character of the agents themselves. The value of autonomy, which is presupposed in the very practice of moral discourse, allows for the interference with the first dimension of morals, since the free adoption of intersubjective moral standards (which materialized the value of autonomy) may result in some actions which adversely affect the autonomy of other people. If, for instance, freely accepted standards allow the agent to kill or injure others, other people will see curtailed their own possibility of acting on the basis of freely accepted moral standards. Instead, the benefits of complete autonomy implicit in moral discourse do not justify the restriction of the free adoption of self-regarding or personal ideals, because that free adoption cannot result per se in the curtailment of the autonomy of other people, except when it implies the acceptance of an intersubjective moral standard, which allows the action notwithstanding its effect on other people. For instance, if somebody adopts an ideal for his life that includes the killing of other human beings, the interference with it is not justified on the basis of disqualifying that personal ideal, but on the intersubjective standard that allows for pursuing such an ideal.

When we participate in moral discourse we implicitly value the end of that practice (others freely accepting our proposed principle) over the general value of moral autonomy implicit in our practice of moral discourse. We may infer from this the more specific and unrestrained value of personal autonomy (this is the value of the free adoption of ideals of personal excellence and of the life plans based on them). An additional argument to ground this value of personal autonomy is the self-defeating character of imposing personal ideals upon others. Unlike intersubjective moral standards, imposed personal ideals are never fully satisfied since they include free adoption as an essential requirement. The moral standard of a good patriot is not satisfied by people who are coerced into singing the national an-

---

65 NINO, *supra* note 25, at 131.

them.[66] In contrast, the moral standard against killing other people is satisfied when people are coerced into not killing.

Additionally, the validity of personal ideals does not depend on the satisfaction of the requirement of impartiality. Therefore, collective discussion and decision, which are likely to satisfy that requirement, are not substantially more reliable than individual reflection for arriving at morally correct solutions. Possibly the *discussion* of those ideals has some value, since intersubjective confrontation is always useful for increasing our information, overcoming factual errors, and surmounting our conditioning. But certainly the collective *decision* does not enhance the epistemic value of the adopted solution, since the goal is not to achieve a balance between conflicting interests of different individuals.

Therefore, judges have no reason to defer their moral judgment to a democratic statute that *is based on personal ideals of virtue or excellence*. In this case, the epistemic ground which justifies applying democratic norms over the personal judgment of the judge is missing. This contradicts the foregoing arguments, which imply that in matters of personal morality only the judgment of the agent himself is relevant. Consequently, judges ought to revise, and eventually disqualify, "perfectionist" laws and other norms of democratic origin.[67]

Before disqualifying a democratic law because of its perfectionist nature, the rationale or ground by virtue of which it has been enacted must be considered. This is because the concept of personal autonomy leads not to the protection of particular actions, but only to the exclusion of the possibility that they be interfered with *on the basis of some kind of reason*. Recall the extreme example where a personal ideal allows the killing of another; the state or another individual interferes with that action not because they object to the personal ideal on which it is based, but because the action also adopts an unacceptable intersubjective moral standard that permits it. An example of perfectionist legislation is the punishment for the possession of drugs for personal consumption alone. What disqualifies that legislation is that its real ground is the imposition of an ideal of human excellence. If the law's rationale was actually an indirect protection of unwilling third parties, then the soundness of the legislation would be something to be discussed through the democratic process and not the judi-

---

66 This argument was advanced in Argentina against prosecutions for scorn to patriotic symbols.

67 By "perfectionist" laws I mean those laws that attempt to impose on people an ideal of personal virtue or excellence; *see* NINO, *supra* note 25, at 133.

cial one.[68] This demonstrates an element essential to understanding the judicial role in the review of constitutionality. A judge cannot avoid taking into account the genuine reasons behind the legal norms, since this is what constitutes their meaning, determines the rationality of their application to a certain case, and controls their constitutionality.[69]

Of course, this second avenue along which judicial review may proceed has implications for the evaluation of controversial decisions in many diverse forums. The United States Supreme Court decision in *Bowers v. Hardwick*[70] cannot be justified, since the Georgia statute proscribing homosexual behavior was clearly based on perfectionist grounds. In Argentina, this view would support the position of the Supreme Court in *Bazterrica*,[71] which overturned the law punishing the mere possession of drugs. This was subsequently overruled by *Montalvo*.[72] The test for evaluating these decisions is whether the rationale underlying the proscription of the act involves adherence to an ideal of human excellence and the subsequent disqualification of others, or only the adoption of some intersubjective moral standards and general factual hypotheses that should be decided by the political process.

C.   *The Third Exception to the Denial of Judicial Review: The Constitution as a Social Practice*

The previous justifications for judicial review did not ground the relevance of a *positive* constitution, the origin of which is not entirely democratic, for judicial review. The control of the democratic procedure, the first exception, must be done in the light of some *ideal* regarding the workings of democracy, since both the structure of legal practical reasoning and the justification of democracy do not allow judges to recognize the distortions of the democratic procedure that might be enshrined in a positive constitution. To take an extreme example: Why should a judge abide by constitutional norms that restrict the franchise, when the constitution itself was enacted by a restricted constituency? The same question is raised with the protection of personal autonomy: If a judge does not have a constitution that consecrates the value of personal autonomy, such as Argentina's, or

---

[68] This would be so even when the factual basis of this rationally was erroneous.

[69] This connects with the idea of "enantiotel," the requirement that for a crime to be punishable it must produce the risk or harm that the criminal law in question seeks to prevent. *See* CARLOS S. NINO, LOS LÌMITES DE LA RESPONSABILIDAD PENAL (1980).

[70] *Bowers*, 478 U.S. 186.

[71] 308 Fallos 1412 (1990).

[72] 309 Fallos 601 (1990).

even if he has a constitution that denies that value, must he still defer to the democratic process on a question of personal ideals? Given the undemocratic origin of the constitution, a judge cannot resort to a democratic determination expressed there. This would imply a position of intersubjective morality that would allow legislation based on personal ideals. The judge can only disregard what the positive constitution says on matters of personal autonomy. If it coincides with what is required for the respect of that value, then it will be valid but superfluous.

Unlike these two avenues of judicial review, the third is an attempt to salvage the moral relevance of the positive or real constitution, and not merely the ideal or moral one.

This exception to the denial of judicial review differs in that it does not merely evolve out of the analysis of the conditions of the democratic process, but results from a deeper conceptual layer. It stems from a reevaluation of the structure of justificatory practical reasoning. This exception overcomes the conclusion that positive legal norms, including the constitution, are not relevant to that practical reasoning without appealing to the epistemic reliability of democracy.

I propose to examine the constitution, and the legal system that emerges from it, as a social practice or a convention. This involves the regularity of conducts, the critical attitudes toward those conducts, the expectations that others will act in a certain way, the motivations for action, and possibly the goal of the whole practice served by the regularity of actions. These will generally solve problems of coordination, allowing people to converge around some *salient* element of the situation.[73]

There have been many attempts to explain why the constitution and the legal system (understood as a social convention) may be relevant as the content of a premise of a judge's practical reasoning for making a decision. Most of these attempts, despite their different guises, conceal a conventionalist or positivist, and hence, relativist, view of morality (such as the present resurgence of the old communitarian way of thinking).[74] The common objections to this view follow: This view of morality does not take into account the Humean divide between "is" and "ought" when it offers a social convention as the ultimate justification for an action or a decision. This justification ig-

---

[73] See David Lewis's analyses of conventions and social practices, CONVENTION: A PHILOSOPHICAL STUDY (1989); HART, *supra* note 23; DWORKIN, *supra* note 50.

[74] *See* Carlos S. Nino, *The Communitarian Challenge to Liberal Rights*, 8 LAW AND PHIL. 37 (1989); NINO, *supra* note 25, at 83.

nores the fact that the main trait of the *modern* practice of moral discussion is to subject every social arrangement to criticism. Additionally, the fact that *positive* morality necessarily presupposes references to an *ideal* morality is not taken into account. Furthermore, conventionalism cannot explain the position of a minority in a moral dispute, since according to its precepts, that position should be false *by definition*. Lastly, it cannot account for rational moral discussions between groups or societies that practice different conventions.

Ronald Dworkin, among some others, has attempted to defend milder versions of the position that the constitution and the legal system at large, being the result of a collective action extended over time, is relevant for the premises of practical reasoning.[75]

Professor Dworkin's theory suggests that judges should make decisions by taking into account the best principles that have justified the decisions of the past present. He grounds this view of justificatory practical reason, which he calls "a community of principles," in the value of *integrity*, which manifests itself in a society whose officials follow a consistent set of principles. The discussion of this intriguing position merits careful attention. However, I am limited to summarizing my previous criticism[76] to the effect that the value of integrity is not strong enough to justify judges' being tied to defective principles that perpetuate unjust prior decisions. Integrity[77] is valuable as a personal trait, since it shows a depth and breadth in the moral character of the agent that is not exhibited by somebody reacting inconsistently when confronted with different circumstances. But *intersubjective* or *social* integrity loses value (except the superficial one of foreseeability and certainty) unless we personify the society. Dworkin accepts this, except that he says that it does not involve any metaphysical commitment. However, this is not a case of just using an heuristic device or a logical construct, but rather ascribing to the social whole some sort of character or *élan* that is valuable enough to make up for injustice.

My attempt here[78] differs from that of the others in that I shall not try to show that the constitution as a convention is relevant to the *premises* of legal reasoning. Instead, I shall focus on the subject matter of its *conclusion*, the kind of pragmatic normative judgment that culminates the reasoning.

In the above arguments I assumed that the conclusion of a piece

---

[75] *See* RONALD M. DWORKIN, LAW'S EMPIRE 130-35 (1986).

[76] *See* NINO, *supra* note 25, at 100.

[77] I define integrity as acting consistently on the basis of coherent principles.

[78] I developed this view more fully in CARLOS S. NINO, DELIBERATIVE DEMOCRACY AND CONSTITUTIONALISM ch. 5 (forthcoming 1993).

of practical reasoning undertaken by a judge is an *individual* action or decision. For instance, I presuppose that a judge must justify her decision to put someone in jail or evict someone from his house, and that the conduct of the judge does not differ substantially from ours when we make everyday decisions that we must justify on the basis of reasons.

However, there is an essential difference between the actions of persons performing in the context of a legal practice and other actions performed in a nonlegal context. The former are *institutional* actions which are performed as part of the practice of the law within a community. The effect of an action is entirely different when it is performed as part of a social practice, since that effect is determined by a series of expectations and attitudes of that practice. The action of the judge sentencing someone to prison has a wholly different effect than a similar action that I intend to perform.

Participating in a legal practice is analogous to building a cathedral. It would be highly irrational for an architect who is asked to complete part of the cathedral to act as if he himself were building the whole cathedral. He must consider in his choice of style or materials the decisions made in the past and the decisions that will probably be made in the future. Perhaps he must satisfy himself with second-best options that nevertheless better agree with the collective enterprise. Though finally he must rely on aesthetic standards as ultimate reasons, he must apply those standards to the collective work and not only to his contribution. Perhaps his conception of a cathedral, built alone, is impossible to apply to an ongoing collective work. Of course, the architect may decide that the ongoing enterprise is so far away from his preferred aesthetic sensibilities that he is not justified in contributing to it. He may feel obliged to refound the construction of the cathedral, which will often not be successful since others will not agree to his vision of the cathedral but will continue to adhere to the previous one; he may also choose to destroy the present cathedral, or to do nothing at all. However, if he decides that the cathedral under construction is worthwhile according to his aesthetic conception, he must seek ways of contributing to it that insures the continuation of the work, as well as the closest approximation to his preferred conception.

I think that something similar happens in the case of the legal system. The role of the architect is occupied by the constitution makers—legislators, judges, and citizens at large. Except for some exceptional dictators, none have complete control of the whole practice, but only the opportunity of a greater or lesser contribution to its development. The positive constitution may be seen as a successful attempt to lay the foundations of social practice on which the law of a community is built. There may have been many similar attempts to found a legal practice, perhaps sometimes better inspired, that have failed to both constitute the salient element around which the attitudes and expectations of the rest of the agents happen to converge, and provide the basis to coordinate the collective behavior.

Legal actions are the contribution of various individual agents performing converging acts with a collective intention. The decisions of democratic branches, of judges, and even of common citizens benefit from the attitudes and expectations that are part of the practice. This, in turn, generates new attitudes and expectations which in turn impact the result of other actions. The acknowledgement that legal actions are not isolated conduct but pieces of a conventional process modifies the traditional vision of what is the *object* or the *subject matter* of legal practical reasoning. Though it is true that reasoning, in order to have justificatory character, must necessarily start from moral principles (universalizable principles autonomously accepted), their object of application is not isolated actions or decisions, but the legal practice as a whole. This conclusion coincides with Rawls's idea that principles of justice do not apply directly to actions and decisions but to the basic structure of society.[79]

Thus, legal practical reasoning is a two-stage process (as rule-utilitarianism proposes that it should be). First, the justification of the practice as a whole must be determined in the light of autonomous principles of justice and social morality, whether the practice as a whole is justified and is thus morally capable of contributing to its continuation. This valuation should take into account what could be the realistic alternatives to that contribution, like working to undermine the present practice, trying to promote a new one, or doing nothing at all. If the first stage in the practical reasoning results in a positive answer, it is necessary to engage in the second stage of the practical reasoning (the positive answer to the first question could be a *conditional* positive answer, which makes the justification of contributing to the continuation of the practice depend on the possibility of reorienting it toward a closer satisfaction of the moral principles). In the second stage, one decides the best action or decision while allowing the continuation of the practice and the maximization of the satisfaction of the principles found out in the first stage. On many occasions the practice, which includes interpretive conventions, is extremely lax and indeterminate. In these cases, the preservation of the

---

[79] *See* RAWLS, *supra* note 41.

practice is completely compatible with a free search for the satisfaction of the basic moral values. In other cases, the interpretive conventions are rich and unequivocal and provide very little leeway to resort directly to first-stage values. Most often, however, there is a tension between alternatives that would consolidate the practice but would affect its moral quality, and alternatives that produce the opposite result. There is no algorithm to resolve this tension; the general considerations that the agent must take into account to justify a decision on the basis of the law are her moral principles, and that possibility that without a practice she probably cannot make any effective decision at all.

In the context of judicial review, even a democratic decision is an institutional action that has an effect on the framework of a legal practice. Rarely is a democratic decision effective enough to initiate a new legal practice or to substantially reorient the present one. Even constitutional reforms must be generally based on the present constitutional practice in order to provoke the right attitudes, expectations, and conduct. Therefore, the effects of the democratic decision depend on the continuity of the practice. Nevertheless, the decision itself may undermine that continuity, which could reduce the efficacy of other decisions.

Consequently, the role of judges is rather more complex than we have seen thus far. Besides accounting for the epistemic value of democratic decisions, they must preserve the decisions' efficacy, so they remain relevant. Perhaps there are more democratic ways of making decisions that might be irrelevant because they are inefficacious. This involves a double scrutiny: first, the measure to which the democratic decision will reflect the attitudes and expectations that constitute the legal practice; second, the extent to which that decision affects the flux of attitudes and expectations that would render other decisions efficacious. Of course, this also presupposes a valuation of the practice as morally plausible, or a determination of whether the maximization of that moral plausibility requires reorienting the practice.

The historical constitution represents a successful foundation for the present legal practice. If the practice as a whole is morally justifiable when measured against the realistic alternatives, it becomes the main responsibility of judges to insure that constitutional deviations do not undermine the legal practice (foreclosing reorientation or transformation). This is a very complex task since the judge must assume the practice is justified, but also account for the tension between the democratic decision and the value of that practice. However, if the decision is relevant, it is only because of the practice, and the practice may be the result of some past decisions, which may or may not themselves possess democratic validity. Thus, the judge must weigh the conflicting considerations.

Though this exception to the denial of judicial review grounded on the epistemic value of democracy presents difficult problems, it is extremely significant. Many blunt offenses against the most obvious interpretation of the constitutional text by democratic officials cannot be disqualified on the basis that the democratic process is affected, nor can they be disqualified on the basis of personal autonomy by resorting to the central role that the constitutional document, the adhesion to it, and the interpretive conventions forged around it, play in the evolvement of a legal practice (the continuation of which is a precondition of both the democratic process and of the judicial capacity to preserve it and personal autonomy). This explains the relevance—subordinated to moral principles—of positive laws in the context of practical reasoning.

CONCLUSION

After trying to dismantle the institution of judicial review to exhibit the logical bones that underlie its draping, I tried to reconstruct it in a way that respected that basic logical structure. The result of that reconstruction is a theory of judicial review which, I trust, is less alarming to legal common sense, which some of my partial conclusions must have led some to fear. Though there is a general denial of judicial review of the constitutionality of those laws which originate through the democratic process, there are three very significant exceptions to that denial. These exceptions involve deciding whether the enactment of the law respected or will affect in the future the preconditions of the democratic process, including the a priori rights; the disqualification of laws grounded on perfectionist reasons; and the examination of whether the law in question undermines the preservation of morally acceptable legal practice.

I think that this reconstruction, if successful, will achieve several things. First, it will put the institution of judicial review on firmer philosophical ground, one based on an analysis of the structure of justificatory legal reasoning.

There also will be very practical implications of this reconstruction. One of them emerges once we understand that the foregoing considerations have assumed an institutional design in which judges have only an indirect connection with the democratic process. The only option that they face is whether or not to apply a law that may violate the constitution. However, both factors may vary and the conclusions may be different. For instance, a European-style constitutional tribunal, with members who are periodically renewed and who are chosen by different branches representative of popular sovereignty, possesses greater democratic legitimacy than a supreme court, like those of the United States or Argentina, in carrying out the functions of review that emerge from this theory. It is also possible to think of procedures that would ensure that the members of the superior courts that exert judicial review answer periodically to the democratic process, insofar as that does not imply a dependency on those exercising political power, but rather implies the support of a wide consensus constituted independently of that power.

Essentially, there are several judicial responses when confronted with a claim of statutory unconstitutionality. When the instrumental conditions for the protection or promotion of rights that involve the distribution of resources and the establishment of institutions are at stake, perhaps the intervention of the judicial power should not consist in an all-out disqualification of a statute or an administrative order. Rather, judges should be encouraged to adopt measures that will promote public deliberation over the issue within the political organs. For instance, judges may be given a veto power over statutes or measures that lie in the penumbra between a priori conditions for the correct working of the democratic process, and the determinations that must be made through that very process, obliging the legislature to engage in a new discussion and decision to override that veto. This type of system, which is similar to Canada's, deserves to be studied more carefully. Also, with regard to the so-called "unconstitutionality by omission"[80] (the failure of the legislator to implement a constitutional prescription), there should be the possibility of allowing a supreme court to obligate the legislature or one of its commissions to explain the reasons for that omission and whether there is some project under discussion to overcome the lacunae. Through these and other mechanisms,[81] judges would have an active role in contributing to the improvement of the quality of democratic discussion and decision-making, stimulating public debate and promoting more reflective decisions.

Another practical implication of this reconstruction of judicial review would be to promote the judiciary's awareness of the complex considerations of their task. These considerations involve a triad of values that in fact are what constitute the complex idea of *constitutionalism*: first, the observance of the results of a democratic process

---

[80] *See* German Bidart Campos, *Las Omisiones Constitucionales*, EL DERECHO (1988).

[81] Some of these proposals would require constitutional reforms.

of discussion and decision making; second, the respect for some individual rights; third, the preservation of a continuous legal practice (which absorbs the idea of the rule of law).

The first value relates to the epistemic quality of democracy, the second to democracy's limits, given its procedural preconditions and the value of personal autonomy. The third is self-explanatory. All of them derive, as I have tried to show in this study, from structural features of legal reasoning and cognition.

Each of these three elements of constitutionalism that a judge must be aware of in judicial review may be in tension with the other two. The democratic process may undermine a priori rights and the continuation of a solid legal practice. The preservation of individual rights as preconditions for the epistemic value of the democratic process may redound, as we saw, in a considerable narrowing of the scope of that democratic process and in the undermining of a legal practice that is not as favorable to that preservation. The continuation of a solid legal practice may imply disqualifying some democratic decisions which undermine it, or leave unprotected some individual rights that are not recognized by that practice.

But, after some threshold is surpassed, each of these three elements of constitutionalism may become mutually reinforcing. Democracy's epistemic value increases if a priori rights are respected. Also, democracy is benefitted in the efficacy of its decisions if the legal practice, in the context of which the democratic decisions are taken, is consolidated. Individual rights tend to be protected by a well-functioning democratic system and by the observance of the rule of law. The continuation of the legal practice is promoted when that practice harbors the democratic process and a due respect for individual rights.

The more than Herculean task of the judges, and indeed of anyone engaged in justificatory legal reasoning, is to balance these three elements of constitutionalism when they conflict, trying to reach the threshold at which their vicious, debilitating, mutual tensions transform themselves into virtuous, fortifying, mutual support.

V

Freedom, Equality, Individuals, Groups, and the Struggle Between Identity and Difference

PREFERRED GENERATIONS: A PARADOX OF RESTORATION CONSTITUTIONS

András Sajó

I. Preferred Generations in Revolutionary Constitutions

What is the impact of the counterrevolutionary nature of the political, and perhaps social, transition on emerging constitutions, particularly in East-Central Europe and Hungary? This essay discusses the problem in terms of the constitutional self, in particular the generations preferred by the restoration constitution.

Constitutions are associated with revolutions. This platitude is essentially correct, although it has little explanatory power in the case of a number of constitutions which are clearly the result of counterrevolution. Of course, a counterrevolution is often conceived as revolution. Typically, recent events in Eastern and East Central Europe are described as revolutions in the Western press, for example, Czechoslovakia's "Velvet Revolution." Events and the level of violence and mass participation varied greatly from country to country. However, there was limited change in the ruling elite. The Communist party was officially ousted, but the methods of domination, and the overwhelming owners of the state, including its property, have survived the changes so far.[1]

De Maistre may have been wrong when he said that "La contrerevolution ne sera point une revolution contraire, mais le contraire de la revolution."[2] However, this is an insider view of a first class French counterrevolutionary shared by many East and Central Europeans. The constitutional arrangements offered by the emerging new leaders promise a return to the golden glorious past and the "correct and normal European" tradition. Restoration-oriented political leaders claim that East-Central European countries shared this common tradition before the abusive socialist revolution.[3]

---

[1] The Hungarian Parliament passed the Zetenyi Takacs Act in 1991 which retroactively punished murder and high treason committed between 1944 and 1990. The Constitutional Court argued that this treatment was unconstitutional as the new democratic constitutional order is based on full continuity of the legal system and, implicitly, revolutionary justice is unjustified. (There is a statute of limitations for murder in most European countries.)

[2] HANNAH ARENDT, ON REVOLUTION 8 (1963).

[3] I believe that in terms of social power, structures of domination and social structure, and to a lesser extent, legal structure, there is a lesser break with the "Communist" past than was heralded by romantic news analysts.

Of course, the word "revolution" is in disgrace among many political actors of the post-Communist world. This has the obvious advantage of mitigating the radical eccentricities and potential brutality associated with revolution. There is strong emphasis on denying Communist practices which makes it difficult to apply the same summary revolutionary justice the Communists used. Needless to say, those groups which were embittered by revolutions are counterrevolutionary. They feel justified in their use of revolutionary means to seek revenge and justice. In this respect, this is a counterrevolution in the sense of being a reaction to action. In East-Central Europe, counterrevolutionary reaction to action is combined with denial of the previous action—in a sense, the return to "normal."

Constitutions are intended to last, if not for eternity, at least long enough to determine or shape posterity. Of course all constitutions are simply political compromises between those political forces acting at the moment the drafting of the constitution occurs. However, the concerns expressed in a constitution are long term considerations of the parties involved in the compromise. They represent an arrangement which is expected to provide fair opportunities in the future for all those involved in the process and, to a lesser extent, to unknown or not yet existing forces, assuming that these opportunities do not endanger those who are involved in the present constitution making.

Whatever the original meaning of the standard preamble of the early American (state) constitutions and the 1787 Constitution actually was, the Constitution's language can be interpreted as expressing these lasting intentions. The Constitution was honestly created to "secure the Blessings of Liberty to ourselves and our Posterity."[4] The 1787 Constitution was primarily an institutional arrangement; the "Blessings of Liberty to . . . Posterity" was promised through a separation of powers system that was intended to be very difficult to change. It is certainly impossible to change the Constitution without broad participation in the amendment process by all those concerned (including "Posterity").

A lasting arrangement concerning the separation of powers may already considerably determine the field of action on future generations, although one may claim that this arrangement is at least generation-neutral in the sense that it does not give preference to one

---

[4] In many U.S. state constitutions, there is no reference to tranquillity or general welfare, and, on the level of linguistic analysis, it is impossible to determine whether the people of the United States established the Constitution in order to grant all of the protected values of the Preamble to "Posterity," or just the protection of "Liberty." Actually, the Preamble is one of the few passages which was accepted without debate in Philadelphia, except, of course, the reference to the states.

generation over the other. Thomas Jefferson and Thomas Paine (certainly an even more revolutionary personality) did not share that view.[5]

The neutrality argument is weakened when not only separation of powers issues are determined by the Constitution, but other issues are written into it, especially the *value-preferences*[6] of the present generation. Value preferences in constitutions may be formulated as negative barriers to regulation, ("Congress shall make no law . . . .") or, as in France, as positive duties to promote human and civic rights. Constitution makers were ready to grant constitutional status to particular values and interests of the day, or to particular institutions of a society, for example, by establishing state religions and, in corporatist constitutions, by granting special status to the prevailing interests and interest groups of the day.[7] Constitution makers in Europe and elsewhere were not particularly concerned with enacting only those values which may at least claim, if not satisfy, universal and eternal criteria. One may at least argue that constitutional human rights are neutral, but constitutions are increasingly overloaded by privileges and privilege-granting restrictions.

Given these circumstances, one cannot deny that constitutions tend to impose more than just freedom of self-determination on future generations. Future generations are further constrained by preceding generations, as the latter may create constitutional laws which may preempt the possibilities and rights of future generations. The present generation may, in many other institutional and biological ways (such as population control), determine the choices of future generations and impose burdens and obligations on them. Modern science and technology give a dramatic new dimension to this determinative power because of significant advances in genetic engineering, and the climatic, atmospheric and other environmental changes.[8] While one

---

[5] *See* Stephen Holmes, *Precommitment and the Paradox of Democracy, in* CONSTITUTIONALISM AND DEMOCRACY 195 (Jon Elster & Rune Slagstad eds., 1988).

[6] Certainly the separation of powers arrangements reflect, to a considerable extent, value choices. To have a king or to live in a republic was a fundamental value choice in the 18th century; it was certainly the most commonly shared value concern of America's founding fathers.

[7] The Communist constitutions went even further, declaring Communist party political "leadership." KONSTITUTSIIA SSSR (1977) Art. 6 (Constitution of the Union of Soviet Socialist Republics). The leading and guiding force of Soviet society, of all state public organizations, is the Communist party. Despite its potential for offering self-determination, constitutionalism itself is inevitably a burden imposed on future generations. (Although an arrangement under the neutral principles of a constitution may offer a chance for self-determination.)

[8] It is paradoxical to discuss the constitutional limits of these changes in terms of original intent and original will to determine Posterity. Two hundred years ago, it was impossible to

can argue that principles of fairness determine the relations among generations, the impossibility of cooperation between generations makes these relations problematic for the philosopher, and nearly intractable for the lawyer concerned with relations among actual beings. From the lawyer's perspective, obligations or fairness to future generations is just another rhetorical form or symbol similar to public interest and welfare.

One can also argue that the recognition of dignity or of mankind as a legal subject will include future generations. To some extent, the price of being included in the constitutional self is generally based on the denial of certain values and interests to be developed by future generations. In this respect, future generations are subject to the same treatment as minorities or specific groups or social institutions: churches, clubs, etc. Minorities, even if they exist as part of the generation of constitution makers, are included in the constitutionally protected group, as long as they have given up some of their distinctiveness and integrity. They are recognized and perhaps even protected, as long as the protected values fit into the value system of the constitution makers. In this respect, judicial interpretation represents a tacit constitutional adaptation, or limited amendment, to the interests and values of those generations which exist at the time of interpretation.

This indicates that the present generation inevitably imposes its scheme or vision upon future generations, and the constitution-making generation (or the political forces that be) have a particularly strong impact on future generations. In the case of the American revolutionary constitutions, there seems to be a discrepancy between the Constitution and the governmental reality which might develop due to the natural fixation on the first generation's preferences. "Although the Preamble permanently proclaims the Constitution to be the social compact of every succeeding generation, the body of the Constitution has remained essentially the compact of 1787 of the people of 1787 to create the government of 1787. Major, radical amendments followed . . . but there was no attempt . . . to make the Constitution a complete compact for the complete government that the federal government has become."[9]

---

determine Posterity's choices in the sense that the present generations have. It was also neither necessary, nor customary, to consider distribution rights of natural resources as a problem of allocation of rights between generations. Although, genetic engineering (and abortion as reproduction control, especially in the case of a genetically damaged fetus) is primarily a matter of the relationship between individuals and individual rights, it has a serious impact on future generations.

[9] LOUIS HENKIN, THE AGE OF RIGHTS 94 (1990).

It is perhaps fair to say that the constitution-making generation is the preferred generation. In ulterior (future) constitutional interpretation (including "interpretation" by the legislature) the present generation prevails over the future. The rights or positions of the future generations are protected only to the extent that these generations fit into the existing constitutional self. This self is sometimes apparently neutral (in concepts of citizenship) and sometimes is all but neutral, especially when the constitutional definition of the self is aggravated by the missionary visions of the founding fathers.

Nation state constitutions are inclined to grant rights to qualified citizens of the nation—only to "good" Hungarians or "good" Spaniards. This restrictive inclusion may have serious practical consequences, both for present and future generations, in such areas as language use rights, as determined by or based on the constitution. For example, if the constitution was drafted at a time when interest in the assimilation of different nationalities into one nation prevailed, a future generation composed of ardent nationalists or of people with strong and varied ethnic identities would be severely restricted. Michael Walzer suggests:

> Admission and exclusion are at the core of communal independence. They suggest the deepest meaning of self-determination. Without them, there could not be *communities of character, historically stable, ongoing associations of men and women with some special commitment to one another and some special sense of their common life.*[10]

There is a paternal interest in the hypothetical inclusion of the future generations of one's kin. This has an inevitable element of perpetuating the actual arrangements and inclusions. Parents know better what is good for their children and they like their own aspirations realized through a predetermined system of education. If (parental) affection determines constitutional inclusion then this again may have lasting constitutional consequences. The descendants of those excluded at the time of constitution making will not be easily included without constitutional amendments. Blacks and American Indians are among the obvious examples.[11] In Germany, third generation descendants of Turkish immigrants are still excluded, notwithstanding the fact that both they and their parents were born in Germany.

---

[10] MICHAEL WALZER, SPHERES OF JUSTICE: A DEFENSE OF PLURALISM AND EQUALITY 62 (1983) (emphasis added).

[11] In the case of black slaves, inclusion required a revolutionary amendment; in the case of American Indians, there is a tendency of some gradual and paternalistic inclusion, although their status still reflects elements of the original exclusion. *Cf.* LAURENCE H. TRIBE, AMERICAN CONSTITUTIONAL LAW 1471-74 (2d ed. 1988).

This generation-related constitutional self problem may have very practical consequences. In a number of cases the United States Supreme Court had to strike down legislation which limited benefits to residents (or resident aliens) with "insufficient" time of residency.[12] Moreover, the Court has recognized the states' right to discriminate on the basis of citizenship "to preserve the basic conception of a political community."[13]

There are certain inherent difficulties in discussing, in terms of inclusion in the community, future generations' exclusion or inclusion in the founders' constitutional scheme.[14]

In the case of future generations, there is one-way communication or unilateral speech; future generations cannot engage in present discussions or dialogues, nor participate in community, individual or constitutional self-formation. On the other hand, they cannot escape participation in a dialogue which was started by the constitution-framing generation, and they have to use a language created by the founders. However, arguments made on their behalf do or may have a role in the actual dialogue between the founders and the interpreters of the present generation.[15] In this respect, they may be considered members of a community, and at least their ghosts may participate in a constitutional dialogue through the voices of those who claim to act on behalf of future generations, or are considered to be their guardians. Guardians may have an individual reality as parents or institution-like educators or legislators, professionally concerned with the future of our youth as the Communist doctrine and the common law would state.

---

[12] *See, e.g.*, Zobel v. Williams, 457 U.S. 55 (1982); Dunn v. Blumstein, 405 U.S. 330, 344 (1972); Oregon v. Mitchell, 400 U.S. 112, 118-19 (1970).

[13] *Blumstein*, 405 U.S. at 344. *See generally* EMILY R. GILL, TWO CONCEPTS OF LIBERALISM: ALIENS AND THE POLITICAL COMMUNITY (unpublished manuscript on file with the author, 1990).

[14] Modern constitutions rarely express clear rules of exclusion and inclusion, partly because they are typically creatures of equality-based systems. It is evident from constitutional practices that constitutions are devices used to disguise inequality based on exclusion in an era of universal equality. In constitutional systems, this was often achieved by silence or constitutional gags. Stephen Holmes, *Gag Rules or the Politics of Omission*, in CONSTITUTIONALISM AND DEMOCRACY 19 (Jon Elster & Rune Slagstad eds., 1988). In the present era, there is more openness in this respect. The German *Grundgesetz*, for example, is relatively clear on who qualifies as a citizen.

[15] For a constitutional application of the Habermasian concept of dialogue, see MICHEL ROSENFELD, AFFIRMATIVE ACTION AND JUSTICE (1991). It is a fascinating problem how an intergenerational dialogue can develop and create justice among present and future generations.

II. THE SPECIAL FEATURE OF RESTORATION CONSTITUTIONS

Counterrevolutionary (or more properly restoration) constitutions may well constitute the majority of constitutions, but the idea of modern constitution is eminently a revolutionary idea, revolutionary in the sense of being a revolution's creation. Modern revolutionary constitutions are intended to be blueprints for the future. Restoration constitutions represent a return to the past while avoiding the possibility that what happened will "unhappen." After a major revolution, there is neither serious willingness nor any real possibility to return to the status quo ante, and, for example, reinstate the prerevolutionary constitution. There are a number of reasons for this. Time has elapsed. New social and political relations have emerged which make impossible a total restoration. Moreover, the original imperfection of the ex ante constitution cannot be denied anymore. Revolutionary changes in the constitution occur when fundamental flaws in the constitutional arrangements prevent a more "organic" development.

One may argue that all this is irrelevant in East-Central Europe, where the revolution and the Communist constitutions were imposed by the Red Army. This is not to say, however, that the pre-Communist constitutions were adequate.[16] A return to those constitutions in terms of their direct application was not a serious option in any of the region's countries. Even a return to the quite advanced Masaryk Constitution in Czechoslovakia seems impossible in view of Slovak and other minority concerns. If there is anything "revolutionary" in the present post-Communist situation, it is the belief of the emerging elite that they are really *constituting* a new fabric of politics.

Constitution making includes the power, legitimation, and mandate to restructure the political sphere and, in particular, to create a new structure of powers which is intended to serve, as usual, those who happen to be the framers.[17]

---

[16] The *Grundgesetz* is particularly interesting in this respect. The reasons for not reinstating the Weimar Constitution in 1949 were more than sovereignty issues. It was a shared belief that the imperfections of the Weimar political system needed to be remedied.

It is not surprising that some of the solutions of the Weimar Constitution which were (even technically) maintained resulted in the survival of certain institutional privileges not supported by the Nazis (for example, those of the churches). These privileges and the property restoration clause seem to be the most important visible element of restoration in the *Grundgesetz*.

[17] The lack of a stable constitutional arrangement or the delay in creating constitutions is due to the struggle to control the constitution-making process. However, in Hungary, where there is a more established uncontested conservative power monopoly, the conservatives prefer to make subconstitutional changes in the political structure slowly; this will increase their power to the extent that they can dictate a constitution at a latter stage. Therefore, while in all the other countries there is an open political struggle to create a constitution, open constitu-

This self-confidence is vanishing, and justly so. If one needs further proof that there was no genuine revolution in East-Central Europe, and that only liberating rebellions are happening so far,[18] one should consider the difficulties of constitution making (or delaying), the decreasing wish of the elites, and the growing disinterest of the public in this respect.[19]

An unconditional return to the past was impossible in East-Central Europe in 1989. Even today it seems impossible. There were and are reasons and forces which make some kind of restoration after the collapse of communism attractive and compelling. First, one of the most important sources of intellectual resistance to communism was a "glorious past"-oriented nationalism. During the Hungarian round table talks of 1989, the 1946 system of "weak" presidency was used as a model and as a compelling argument. The 1946 model represented both national tradition and sufficient return to the denied past. This was compelling enough to make it legitimate for Communist government and opposition groups alike. In Poland there is continuous reference to Pilsudski's Constitution (or to Pilsudski's reaction to the 1920 Constitution) and to the United States Constitution.[20] The move for a *return* to the monarchy is gaining popularity in Romania, as well as in Serbia and Russia.[21]

The second reason that restoration or past-oriented constitutional thinking seems attractive is related to the semi-modernized nature of these societies. A partial return to past constitutional structures makes the modernization of political, and perhaps social, structures of these countries less compelling; it offers legitimate protection from menacing modernization. The simple transplant or adaptation of the constitution of an existing Western democracy seems to be unacceptable to those who fear modernization. These status quo interests, supported by nationalist concepts, have no other choice but

---

tional amendments are not discussed in Hungary. Human and political (individual) rights are less subject to the power struggle, partly because most political forces and parties currently need the degree of credibility associated with being Europeans.

[18] The distinction between rebellion and revolution ending in constitution obviously relates back to Arendt. ARENDT, *supra* note 2, at 143.

My position is obviously influenced by Arendt. Following her argument, it is highly improbable that these liberation effects will result in genuine constitutions and constitutionalism. However, based on the international interdependence of Europe today, one cannot exclude that possibility in some of the East-Central European countries.

[19] Participation in 1992 Hungarian elections never exceeded 32%.

[20] Jon Elster, *Constitutionalism in Eastern Europe: An Introduction*, 58 U. CHI. L. REV. 447, 475 (1991).

[21] *See* David Binder, *As Yugoslavia Boils, Serbs Hail a Would-be King*, N.Y. TIMES, Oct. 7, 1991, at A9; Claus Offe, *Strong Causes, Weak Cures*, E. EUR. CONST. REV., Spring 1992, at 21.

to turn to ideas such as organic development and national character, and, inevitably, to models of the past. Nationalistic traditionalism serves, of course, as legitimation and justification for a nationalistic-exclusive, or national-constitutional system (as opposed to universalistic constitutionalism). However, nationalism, with its own irrationality, is not simply an ideological outcome of antimodernization. It has its own compelling force. Nationalism is a highly respected, nearly uncontested value of the community. (Or at least it is generally believed to have this status.) Nationalistic concerns may have a conservative impact of their own on forces which may otherwise be interested in "Western-type" modernization.[22]

Given this compelling drive to restore past values and virtues, it becomes very difficult *not* to restore past relations. It is in this context that the paradox of the supremacy of past generations over the present generation of constitution makers occurs. At least in Hungary, the concerns of past generations may prevail in constitutional considerations and value choices, to the disadvantage of the present generation. In the present moment of transition in East-Central Europe, most of the crucial constitutional issues are related to the issue of the real constitutional self to be created. It is not yet clear which present communities and institutions are to be included in the constitutional self and what the tolerance will be vis à vis those groups which will not be included.

In some cases the search for a constitutional identity is overt, as in the case of Slovakia.[23] Most of these definitions resulting in exclusion are, however, silent. They enjoy the benefits of nonarticulateness or a "constitutional gag."[24] To some extent, all actors have to accept the universalistic-rights language of western constitutionalism. But constitution makers are in a privileged situation. They have a considerable freedom to allocate rights even if they use apparently neutral criteria. The post-Communist era is considered an exceptional period in which the application of universal criteria may help the former Communists and other malefactors. Therefore, the constitution makers have a special obligation (or justification): They have to remedy the Communist past. Thus, universal rules apply only to the extent that they do not undermine the special constitutional mandate of the framers to undo communism. A restoration constitution of a post-Communist regime has to be a combination of universal neutral con-

---

[22] This contradiction is very obvious in modernization-inspired privatization, where contradicting legislation reflects emerging restrictions based on xenophobia.

[23] Slovakia finally declared its independence after 1992 elections.

[24] Holmes, *supra* note 14.

stitutionalist rules and special rules (exceptions) and institutional settings which are intended to make a break with the past.[25]

A crucial element in the determination of the constitutional self under these conditions of restoration is the issue of the relevant generation: Is the present generation the point of reference or is it the constitutional self of the past, a quasi-imaginary, or past self of a semiretired generation? The problem is certainly obscured by the usual veil of a constitutional gag. Yet it is a veil full of holes. At least in Hungary, there is a clear conflict over who should pay the costs of reprivatization and compensation: A past generation (including former owners, victims of communism, and established churches) with previously strong economic and political power or a younger, propertyless generation. The result is a conflict of generations, although it can be interpreted as a conflict between expropriated owners and propertyless classes.[26]

The creation of a constitutional self which refers to past generations (and inclusion rules as practiced by those unspecified generations) is not limited strictly to property issues. Restoration of church privileges is another element of this struggle, although once again the problem is primarily conceived of as a restoration issue.[27] The belief in the past "normalcy" of church intervention in secular affairs (for example, abortion, censorship or education) is to be interpreted as an attempt to determine the lives of present and unborn generations according to the values of an older generation, or worse, according to the values of a past generation which never existed except as blessed memory.

This memory is certainly the expression of the values, including

---

[25] This is not to say that a "normal" western constitutional system is neutral and nonexclusive. It may be more tolerant towards those excluded, but even that may not be true if emigration to Western Europe continues and cultural heterogeneity increases once again.

[26] Support can also be found for reprivatization among members of the younger generations.

[27] Many argue that property arrangements are not constitutional issues, or that reprivatization is a problem of access to property which is not a constitutionally protected right. Epstein's analysis makes these objections problematic. RICHARD EPSTEIN, TAKINGS (1985). Accepting his analysis, the present approach to property allocation is of fundamental constitutional importance as it will determine, in the long run, admissible government action.

Regardless of its title, the principles of "original distribution" are used to determine the fate of the constitution as well as the future of a constitutional system; one cannot have a firm constitutional system without an independent class of secure owners. Moreover, it is in the process of inclusion in the class of private owners that inclusion in the constitutional self is realized. It is very telling that in a number of countries there were serious attempts to exclude nonresident prior owners from reprivatization (for example, in Romania, and originally in the Czech and Slovak Republics). In this country recent legislation seems to include nonresidents. It is even more important for constitutional developments that are the ground of reprivatization and exclusion from reprivatization.

the dreams and nightmares, of a present generation, although one which is perhaps composed primarily of the elderly and middle-aged. However imaginary and unspecific the reference point is, the past generations' concern remains very important and politically efficient precisely because of its ambiguity. The vagueness of the past generations' values enables some of the differences between the actual values of the "retired generation" and those actually imposed or advocated by this same group, to go unnoticed, and, therefore, makes some consensus more likely. In Hungary certain prewar attitudes were transmitted to postwar generations. There is a wish to return to authentic (national) values which were forgotten and denied even by those who shared those values. Contrary to the American revolution, whose return to the good old tradition of common law entitlement had a liberalizing effect, tradition in East-Central Europe is hardly ever liberal or liberating.

Certainly, East-European counterrevolutions, just like revolutions in the eighteenth century, tend to legitimate themselves as the restoration of the good old virtues. The rhetoric of the American revolution is full of references to the status of the revolutionaries' British ancestors. But the founding fathers were rather unequivocal when they had to define themselves as sources of something radically new.

The struggle for the constitutional self in terms of a preferred generation has so far been primarily a constitutional struggle; legislation of constitutional relevance and creative constitutional interpretation are deeply involved in the search and *determination* of the constitutional self.[28]

III.   THE HUNGARIAN CASE

Of course, the language of the present debate is not predominantly generational. The debate deals with reprivatization and compensation, with punishing politicians and others who are considered responsible for Communist sins and mistakes. The constitutional is-

---

[28] The emerging preferred generation issue may have direct consequences on citizenship/ inclusion. A return to the pre-Communist self may involve the recognition of the citizenship of nonresident nationals. In Hungary, it may involve citizenship of Transylvanian Magyars. The social burden of such a recognition is obvious, even for the past-oriented nationalist politicians; some of their more outspoken exponents insist that Transylvanian Magyars shall remain Magyars within Transylvania. The famous "return clause" of the *Grundgesetz* at the time of its enactment may have seemed to be a present generations-oriented determination of the German constitutional self. Today, there is growing concern with this provision among German constitutional lawyers because of its clear past generation preferences and the related burdens which fall upon the present generation of Germans in terms of costs of "return."

sues are takings, government liabilities, and governmental power to allocate government property. In the political justice cases, the primary constitutional issue is retroactivity.[29] In the case of church reprivatization-compensation, the separation of church and state and the right to education is constitutionally arguable.[30] Reference in these issues is made mostly to the constitution in effect,[31] although, in a discreet way, it is inevitable to discuss and measure constitutionality in terms of the past constitution. The government, at least in Hungary, seems to interpret its constitutional duties of legislation as being related to the past. Past injustices are to be remedied and the measure of those injustices is to be found in the imaginary constitution of past values and hierarchies. One cannot avoid that kind of reference to a past, or imaginary, constitution and to its constitutional self—a semipast generation with its traditional values, if restoration and continuation or at least *constitutional complicity* with the past is what is desired. If the constitutional debate concerns pre-Communist nationalizations, it is nearly inevitable that sooner or later one must evaluate the constitutionality of those takings in light of the constitution under which they occurred.

As it happens, it is extremely difficult to evaluate these problems under the pre-Communist constitutional arrangements for the simple reason that there was no constitutional regime that could be used as a standard of evaluation. In Hungary, the post-1920 period is a series of unconstitutional arrangements. The more democratic period of 1945-47, which offers a natural continuity for restoration, is obscured by Russian influence and the limited national sovereignty of an occupied state. Once again, it is better to rely on an imaginary past and its constitution. The Hungarian feudal tradition of an unwritten constitution, raised to the level of national character and virtue, is obviously very attractive to conservative government forces, partly because it justifies government inaction in constitution making, and partly because it obscures governmental responsibilities.[32] The problem is that

---

29 The question primarily concerns the ability of parliament to repeal the statute of limitations after it has tolled.

30 Act XXXII of 1991. There is a constitutional complaint, submitted in the summer of 1991, pending in the Constitutional Court.

31 The constitutional identity issue is further complicated by the fact that the Constitutional Court is generally much less inclined to believe in the past constitutional self than is evidenced by the prevailing mood among the majority in Parliament. Chief Justice Solyom stated in obiter dicta that he was applying the invisible constitution. 23 Alkotmánybíróság 37 (1990). This constitution does not seem to be the traditional unwritten one.

32 The idea of an unwritten constitutional tradition was quite attractive during the last period under communism. Minister of Justice Kulcsar, who was responsible for shaping a

the political practices of the constitution-formation period are easily promoted as constitutional virtues.

An analysis of the Hungarian reprivatization legislation and its constitutional review shows that because of the restoration commitment there is a strong tendency to give preference to past generations (and their descendants). Of course, the outcome is not clear, and to some extent the outcomes are limited. It is difficult to imagine a constitutional preference completely oriented to past generations, as this would antagonize present generations. However, that danger is diminished to the extent that present generation groups benefit from the past-oriented redistribution. The outcome may not seem justified in terms of social utility, but it is certainly the expected outcome under the logic of collective action,[33] in which a relatively small group with specific interests generally prevails against the diverse interests of the majority.[34]

The conservative coalition government, following suggestions of the only "historical" party, passed legislation in 1992 which provided for the return of some land to previous (small) landowners while at the same time other classes of previous owners were offered as compensation vouchers which represent a fraction of the value of the original titles. This preference shown a certain group of the past, with its emphasis on a constitutional priority of landed property over capital, was declared unconstitutional by the Constitutional Court as containing arbitrary discrimination.[35] Some elements of discretion in further compensation legislation survived,[36] particularly in the 1992 law on compensation for deprivation of personal freedom. This law provides that approximately four times more compensation shall be paid to the

---

constitutional system under Communist rule, had deep respect for Hungarian unwritten constitutionalism.

Traditional views are presumably shared by conservatives and some liberals: It is more traditional to have a set of cardinal or fundamental laws which represent a constitutional tradition than to have an inorganic systematic charter. The consequence of such an approach, in terms of constitutional identity, remains past-generations oriented.

[33] MANCUR OLSON, LOGIC OF COLLECTIVE ACTION (1971).

[34] Of course, the true test will be the referendum. However, the rules of the referendum favor the previous owners with strong interests. The quorum for a valid referendum is fifty percent participation of all franchised citizens.

[35] 27 Alkotmánybíróság 73 (1991); 16 Alkotmánybíróság 58 (1991); 28 Alkotmánybíróság 88 (1991).

[36] The revised Compensation Act (Act XXV of 1991) followed the suggestions of the Court as to the deadlines of further compensation. Nevertheless, the solution itself seems to be unconstitutional, as it discriminates against Jews, Hungarian Germans, and, most probably, the owners of large estates. By the time these groups will receive equal opportunities, the resources (cover) will be preempted, as they cannot participate in the land auction on their previous land. In fact, the second law in question (compensation for illegal takings that occurred between 1939 and 1949) was passed with considerable delay.

successors of those who died in Russian internment camps than due to German deportation.[37] On one hand, the Hungarian Government is not responsible for the deportation of the Jews, while on the other hand the prisoners of war are recognized as war heroes.[38] The historical continuity with past constitutional values is striking.

The government and the Constitutional Court agree that the express constitutional mandate of creating a market economy is to be interpreted as a governmental freedom. The only limit that applies to government decisions in the allocation of state property is the avoidance of unjustified (arbitrary) discrimination. The proposition that the state should not be more restricted in its use of government property during the post-socialist transition was never the subject of serious discussion. Shortly after passage of the Compensation Act, an act concerning previous church property was passed. This act gives churches, as previous land-owners, the right to reclaim their properties.[39] The reason given for such obviously differential treatment is twofold: first, the State wants the Church to function independently as required by the constitutional provision on the separation of church and state; second, the Church does not possess the financial means to provide for its material independence. In fact, this constitutional arrangement provides the basis for the partial restoration of a prerevolutionary constitutional institution.

The Court and the majority in Parliament share the belief that they must uphold the constitutional principle of private property protection. On the other hand, it would be economic suicide to return property to the original owners under past generation-oriented reasoning—that the *authentic subject* of constitutional property rights are "original owners." The Court tries to mediate in the conflict through the application of the concept of *novatio* and emphasis on the unique nature of transition. It denies reprivatization duties but it maintains the validity of compensation duties, allocating some of its burdens to certain generations and social groups. Some of the privileged groups are similar in composition to prerevolutionary privileged groups.

A less expensive and more "constitutional" solution might have been achieved through a constitutional amendment which would have considered the past nationalizations as injustices without remedies.

---

[37] On the compensation of those unjustly deprived of their life because of political reasons (Act XXXII of 1992). While the families of dead prisoners of war receive three years compensation, deported persons only receive eight months. This case is pending before the Constitutional Court.

[38] The case will be brought to the Constitutional Court.

[39] *Id.* (except land but this not clearly indicated).

Some partial compensation might have been offered, at the same time denying all previous titles. A similar approach was acceptable to the German *Bundesverfassungsgericht*, which has recognized that the pre-1949 Soviet expropriations in East Germany and their recent "recognition" by the German Unification Treaty are not inconsistent with the *Grundgesetz*, or at least there is no obligation to return the confiscated assets, although compensation obligations exist.[40] As mentioned earlier there are "natural" limits to restoration (including rendering justice to victims, henchmen, and collaborators). The further the restoration goes, the higher its social costs are. In what is perhaps the most well-known counterrevolutionary restoration constitution, the *Chartre Constitutionelle* of Louis XVIII, there was a stipulation of inviolability of private property. This inviolability insured that "former ecclesiastic landed property acquired legally by civilians during the revolutionary period [as] fully secured . . . ."[41] The Hungarian leaders of today may lack the wisdom of the returning Bourbons.

IV. CONCLUSION

To the extent that the present Hungarian *coquetterie* will end up in a firm constitutional arrangement within or without the text of its constitution, Hungary will represent a theoretically interesting case of the problem of the constitutional self. It is a case where the constitutional self is to a great extent based not on exclusion or inclusion of those who were the contemporaries of the founders, but more on an imaginary self, offering adjustment possibilities and identification with an ill-defined ghost.

The constitutional prevalence of the founders' generation vis à vis the other generations, and that of the present generation (as it exists at the moment of legislation or constitutional interpretation) vis à vis future generations, is inevitable. It may be considered fair as

---

[40] Judgment of Apr. 23, 1991 BVerfG [Federal Constitutional Court], 84 Entscheidungen des Bundesverfassungsgerichts 90. The express position of the Hungarian government is similar to the German principle, however, the Hungarians do not seem inclined to seriously consider the pragmatic German approach. This approach was expressly stated in the East and West German Joint Government Declaration (June 15, 1990) that led to the Unification Treaty: to solve existing property claims "a socially supportable conciliation of different interest is to be found." While in Hungary under the new law, a very complicated land reprivatization or redistribution takes place.

On the other hand, the Germans accept the return of nonindustrial property to those who have the original title. This is more in favor of the former West Germany than past generations.

[41] ROBERT A. KANN, THE PROBLEM OF RESTORATION: A STUDY IN COMPARATIVE POLITICAL HISTORY 331 (1968).

long as it creates or does not hinder equality between generations. In a different justification supported by John Stuart Mill, a constitutional arrangement is fair as long as posterity maintains its capacity of public participation.[42]

If the constitution prefers an (imaginary) prefoundation generation, its values will prevail against all future generations, and it will be extremely difficult, though not impossible, to meet requirements of fairness and constitutionalism. (Constitutionalism here means fair and potentially equal restraints on future democracies.) Property arrangements giving prima facie preferential treatment to past generations' values do not meet these principles of neutrality. Property allocations may preempt rights (potential claims) of future generations; and in our case most people in the present generation will be excluded without sufficient constitutional justification.[43]

There are other negative consequences of having a past generation as the constitutional self. First, there will be no identifiable set of values and, therefore, the possible tyranny of the founders is replaced by the always possible arbitrariness of powerful interpreters. Second, the constitutional system may become backward looking and incapable of change, resulting in high costs for all present and future generations. Such arrangements may end, as Howard Mumford Jones remarked in a different context, in "pursuing a phantom and embracing a delusion."[44]

---

[42] *Cf.* Holmes, *supra* note 5, at 233.

[43] *See* BRUCE ACKERMAN, SOCIAL JUSTICE IN THE LIBERAL STATE 112 (1980); OBLIGATIONS TO FUTURE GENERATIONS (Richard Sikora & Brian Barry eds., 1978); RESPONSIBILITIES TO FUTURE GENERATIONS (Ernest Partridge ed., 1981); Gregory S. Kavka, *The Paradox of Future Individuals*, 11 PHIL. & PUB. AFF. 93 (1982); Derek Parfit, *Future Generations: Future Problems*, 11 PHIL. & PUB. AFF. 113 (1982).

Based on some of the philosophical discussions of obligations toward future generations, it is difficult to establish such obligations, especially if these are related to a possible number and limitation of numbers of future beings.

It is interesting to note that the original constitutional concern of making the constitution binding for future generations may be replaced by a new natural law concern for the unborn. Of course, this may be a logical conclusion of the 18th century concern. If a generation, through constitutional choices, cannot avoid creating (imposing) duties and constraints for future generations, then there might be a certain requirement of reciprocity. David Gauthier explains that under conditions of mutual unconcern, rational morality does not suggest cooperation. Therefore, respect for rights as cooperation is possible only among contemporaries. "[M]oral relationships among persons of different generations require an affective basis." DAVID GAUTHIER, MORALS BY AGREEMENT 298 (1986). Is affection a constitutional principle? Sentiments (for example, brotherhood) turned out to be vicious. On the other hand, Gauthier uses Burke's argument that a society is based on a contract among past, present, and future generations. "The generations of humankind do not march on and off the stage of life in a body, with but one generation on stage at any time." GAUTHIER, *supra*, at 299.

[44] ARENDT, *supra* note 2, at 124 (quoting HOWARD MUMFORD JONES, THE PURSUIT OF HAPPINESS 16 (1953)).

It is well known how vehemently Thomas Jefferson and Thomas Paine objected to the privileges of the generation which has created a constitution: "The vanity and presumption of government beyond the grave, is the most ridiculous and insolent of tyrannies."[45] According to Hannah Arendt, Jefferson's insistence on granting every generation the right to choose the form of government it believes to be most promotive of its happiness reflects Jefferson's interest in maintaining a scheme which enables the people to engage in the peaceful expression of opinion. In this light, the present desire to create constitutional arrangements which *ab initio* govern from the grave is nothing but an attempt to exclude the public from that discourse.

---

[45] THOMAS PAINE, THE RIGHTS OF MAN 63 (Henry Collins ed., Penguin 1969) (1791).

FREE SPEECH AND THE CULTURAL CONTINGENCY OF CONSTITUTIONAL CATEGORIES

Frederick Schauer

I

Constitutionalism is about many things, but one of the things that constitutionalism is about is the existence of second-order reasons for refraining from doing what we have good first-order reasons to do. Even what would otherwise be the best of policy choices will be unconstitutional[1] if it falls within the boundaries of a category of unconstitutional actions. Thus, even though it might under some circumstances be desirable in custody determinations to take race into account in order to make a decision in the best interests of the child, doing so is also an instance of the category of governmentally drawn distinctions based on race, and as such is presumptively impermissible.[2] Although state officials have the responsibility for promoting the interests of the residents of the state they serve, doing so by preferring the interests of those residents over the residents of other states can often be an example of an unconstitutional burden on or discrimination against interstate commerce.[3] And despite the fact that protecting constituents from harm is one of the things that public officials are expected to do, doing so often becomes unconstitutional when the harm stems from communications of a certain sort.[4]

To the extent that constitutionalism thus bars the implementa-

---

[1] I say "be unconstitutional" rather than "be held unconstitutional" because most of what I say here is about the concept of unconstitutionality and not about the mechanisms for determining unconstitutionality or the institutions that provide remedies for unconstitutional actions. As should be apparent, I reject the hyper-Realist thesis that the concept of unconstitutionality is coextensive with judicial determinations of unconstitutionality, for our ability to argue *to* courts and to criticize their conclusions presupposes the lack of conceptual equivalence between the idea of law and the products of the judiciary. *See* H.L.A. HART, THE CONCEPT OF LAW 132-44 (1961). To say this, however, is certainly not to reject Realist empirical accounts of how courts actually behave, for the existence of conceptual space between the concept of law and how courts behave does not say anything about how much law matters in some or all judicial domains.

[2] Palmore v. Sidoti, 466 U.S. 429 (1984).

[3] *E.g.*, New England Power Co. v. New Hampshire, 455 U.S. 331 (1982); Philadelphia v. New Jersey, 437 U.S. 617 (1978); Hughes v. Oklahoma, 441 U.S. 322 (1979); Pennsylvania v. West Virginia, 262 U.S. 553 (1923).

[4] Frisby v. Schultz, 487 U.S. 474 (1988); American Booksellers Ass'n v. Hudnut, 771 F.2d

tion of some otherwise desirable policy choices in the actual or supposed service of larger or more enduring structural, moral, or political values, it serves as a kind of formal rule, standing in the way of what otherwise all things considered ought to be done. Rules, however, constrain only when some act or event falls within what is technically called the "protasis"[5] and what I prefer to call the "factual predicate" of the rule.[6] But terminology aside, I am referring to that part of the rule that designates in hypothetical form the set of facts the actual existence of which triggers the normative pressure of the rule. *If* a car is going more than sixty-five miles per hour in a certain place, *then* its driver is subject to criminal penalties. *If* one is an officer, director, or holder of ten percent or more of the shares of the stock of a registered company, *then* that person may not buy and sell or sell and buy stock in that company in a six month period.[7]

Constitutional constraints can be placed into this structure without great difficulty. *If* government distinguishes among citizens on the basis of race, *then* its action is unconstitutional unless justified by a compelling state interest.[8] *If* the state wishes to search the residence of a citizen, *then* it must normally demonstrate probable cause to a magistrate and secure a search warrant in advance.[9] And although this structural parsing of constitutional constraints may seem strained, it is necessary for my purpose here. For when we disassemble the textual or case law constraints in this manner, we see that much turns on the designation of the descriptive generalization that constitutes the factual predicate of any rule and thus of any constitutional constraint. "Freedom of speech,"[10] "criminal prosecutions,"[11] "classification based on race,"[12] "burden on interstate commerce,"[13] and "establishment of religion,"[14] are all generaliza-

---

323 (7th Cir. 1985), *aff'd without opinion*, 475 U.S. 1001 (1986); Collin v. Smith, 447 F. Supp. 676 (N.D. Ill.), *aff'd*, 578 F.2d 1197 (7th Cir.), *cert. denied*, 439 U.S. 916 (1978).

[5] *See, e.g.*, GIDON GOTTLIEB, THE LOGIC OF CHOICE 39, 43-47 (1968); WILLIAM TWINING & DAVID MIERS, HOW TO DO THINGS WITH RULES 137-40 (2d ed. 1982).

[6] FREDERICK SCHAUER, PLAYING BY THE RULES: A PHILOSOPHICAL EXAMINATION OF RULE-BASED DECISION-MAKING IN LAW AND IN LIFE 23-24 (1991).

[7] Securities Exchange Act of 1934 § 16(b), 15 U.S.C. § 78p(b) (1988). Rules are rarely set out such that the hypothetical character of the factual predicate is so patent, but all rules can nevertheless be transposed into this form.

[8] *See* Loving v. Virginia, 388 U.S. 1 (1967); Korematsu v. United States, 323 U.S. 214 (1944).

[9] U.S. CONST. amend. IV.

[10] *Id.* amend. I.

[11] *Id.* amend. VI.

[12] *See supra* note 8.

[13] *See supra* note 3.

[14] U.S. CONST. amend. I.

tions that can be recast as the factual predicates of constitutional rules. As a result, it turns out that one of the tasks of constitutional decisionmaking is that of making the initial factual/descriptive determination of whether some act or event falls within the contours of the relevant constitutional category.[15]

Stated this way, it becomes easier to comprehend the way in which constitutional decisionmaking is dependent upon the process of descriptive generalization—that is, upon the way in which certain events are seen as (or as not) members of some larger class or category. But from where do these categories come? It is my thesis that for a large group of constitutional categories, the categories come not from linguistically determinate textual provisions, but instead from cultural constructs that determine what events will be considered members of what class. But once put this way, the role played by the process of cultural categorization becomes patent, as does the likelihood that these cultural categories will vary with time and place. This characterization may cast into doubt the recent ease with which constitutional transplantation seems now to be embraced, especially by Americans, but showing that is not my aim. Instead, using freedom of speech as an example, I want to explore the ways in which cultural differences in the categorization of social and political acts may produce large differences in the shape of the constitutional constraints that are dependent on the products of that categorization.

II

The phenomenon I seek to explore is greatest where the degree of linguistic determinacy is least. Although the contours of a constitutional category can and do occasionally diverge from the contours of the meaning (ordinary or technical) of the terms canonically employed to describe it,[16] this phenomenon is rare, both in the United States and elsewhere.[17] Where written constitutions speak in comparatively precise terms—as with the provisions of the United States

---

[15] In other contexts I have referred to this as the "coverage" of a political or constitutional right. *See* FREDERICK SCHAUER, FREE SPEECH: A PHILOSOPHICAL ENQUIRY (1982); Frederick Schauer, *Categories and the First Amendment: A Play in Three Acts*, 34 VAND. L. REV. 265 (1981).

[16] In the American context, see, for example, the Eleventh Amendment cases assimilating within the category of suits against "another State" suits against the plaintiff's own state. Monaco v. Mississippi, 292 U.S. 313 (1934); Hans v. Louisiana, 134 U.S. 1 (1890).

[17] On the comparatively greater willingness of legal cultures other than the United States to adhere to formal or literal legal constraints, see PATRICK ATIYAH & ROBERT S. SUMMERS, FORM AND SUBSTANCE IN ANGLO-AMERICAN LAW (1987); *see also* INTERPRETING STATUTES: A COMPARATIVE STUDY (D. Neil MacCormick & Robert S. Summers eds., 1991).

Constitution specifying the necessary age to hold various offices[18]—
the existence of such crisp language tends to induce in those who apply constitutional constraints (and, consequently, in those who are
subject to those constraints) an understanding of the boundaries of
the constraint that is not very different from the boundaries set by the
meaning of the language itself.[19]

Where the language of a constitutional provision is less determinate, however, the possibility of understanding the constraint in accordance with a well-settled and commonly-shared understanding of
the meaning of the words themselves is much smaller. Consequently,
when the factual predicate of a constitutional category is couched in
terms like "cruel and unusual punishments,"[20] "unreasonable
searches and seizures,"[21] "free development of . . . personality,"[22]
"the Family in its constitution and authority,"[23] or "freedom of conscience and religion,"[24] it is inconceivable that linguistic meaning
alone can do much of the work of delineating the contours of the
category the existence of which triggers the application of the constitutional constraint. Here the categorial delineation must come from
elsewhere, and it is just that "elsewhere" that I want to explore
further.

III

I focus on freedom of speech and freedom of the press not only
because this is a substantive area about which I think I know something, but also because the constitutional category tends to be set out
with more or less equivalent indeterminacy in all of the world's constitutional documents.[25] The United States Constitution, of course,

---

[18] U.S. CONST. art. II, § 1, cl. 5 (President must be at least 35); *id.* art. I, § 2, cl. 2 (members of the House of Representatives must be at least 25); *id.* art. I, § 3, cl. 3 (Senators must be
at least 30).

[19] I recognize that this claim is controversial to some, *see* Sanford Levinson, *Law as Litera-
ture,* 60 TEX. L. REV. 373 (1982); Sanford Levinson, *What Do Lawyers Know (And What Do
They Do With Their Knowledge)? Comments on Schauer and Moore,* 58 S. CAL. L. REV. 441
(1985); Mark Tushnet, *A Note on the Revival of Textualism in Constitutional Theory,* 58 S.
CAL. L. REV. 683 (1985), but that is insufficient to dissuade me from making it. *See* Frederick
Schauer, *Easy Cases,* 58 S. CAL. L. REV. 399 (1985).

[20] U.S. CONST. amend. VIII.

[21] *Id.* amend. IV.

[22] GRUNDGESETZ [Constitution] [GG] art. 2 (F.R.G.), *translated in* 6 THE CONSTITU-
TIONS OF THE COUNTRIES OF THE WORLD 79, 88 (Albert P. Blaustein & Gisbert H. Flanz
eds., 1991) [hereinafter WORLD CONSTITUTIONS].

[23] IR. CONST. art. 41.1.2, *translated in* 8 WORLD CONSTITUTIONS, *supra* note 22, at 21, 68-
69.

[24] CAN. CONST. (Constitution Act, 1982) pt. I (Canadian Charter of Rights and Freedoms), art. 2(a).

[25] I believe that much of what I say here is particularly relevant to issues of equality as
well, for here again we are dealing with a right that is (a) textually protected in almost every

prohibits Congress from making laws "abridging the freedom of speech, or of the press,"[26] but this type of characterization is hardly unique. Similar breadth is found almost everywhere else in the world, regardless of the extent and nature of the constitutional protection for freedom of speech and press within the society, and regardless of the degree of freedom that in fact exists for the relevant activities.[27] Thus, explicit limitations on a broadly articulated freedom of expression and communication are absent from the relevant provisions of the Constitution of the People's Republic of Albania, which provides that "[c]itizens enjoy the freedom of speech, the press, organization, association, assembly and public manifestation. The state guarantees the realization of these freedoms, it creates the conditions for them, and makes available the necessary material means."[28] Similarly, the Constitution of the United Republic of Tanzania says that "[w]ithout jeopardizing the laws of the country, everyone is free to express any opinion, to offer his views, and to search for, to receive and to give information and any ideas through any medium . . . and is also free to engage in personal communication without interference."[29]

Other constitutional protections of what appears to be roughly the same right are couched in equally broad language, but contain textually articulated limitations. The Canadian Charter of Rights and Freedoms, for example, protects "freedom of thought, belief, opinion and expression, including freedom of the press and other media of communication,"[30] but provides that these and other rights are "subject only to such reasonable limits prescribed by law as can be demonstrably justified in a free and democratic society."[31] The Constitution of the Republic of Ireland guarantees "the right of the citizens to express freely their convictions and opinions," but allows "the State . . . to ensure that organs of public opinion, such as the radio, the press, the cinema, while preserving their rightful liberty of expression, in-

---

written constitution; (b) protected in quite broad language; and (c) subject to considerable cross-cultural differences in understanding of the concept.

[26] U.S. CONST. amend. I.

[27] The extent of constitutional protection is not the same as the degree of freedom in fact. A small amount of constitutional protection is consistent with considerable freedom in fact if there is little governmental urge to regulate, and a large amount of constitutional protection is consistent with great repression if the constitutional constraints are both flouted regularly and not effectively enforced.

[28] KUSHTETUTE [Constitution] art. 53 (Alb.), *translated in* 1 WORLD CONSTITUTIONS, *supra* note 22, at 1, 12.

[29] KATIBA [Constitution] art. 18.-(1) (Tanz.), *translated in* 19 WORLD CONSTITUTIONS, *supra* note 22, at 9, 14.

[30] CAN. CONST. (Constitution Act, 1982) pt. I (Canadian Charter of Rights and Freedoms), art. 2(b).

[31] *Id.* art. 1.

cluding criticism of Government policy, shall not be used to undermine public order or morality or the authority of the State"; it further provides that the "publication or utterance of blasphemous, seditious, or indecent matter is an offence which shall be punishable in accordance with law."[32]   The draft Bill of Rights of the Natal Provincial Council of the Natal/KwaZulu area of South Africa assures that "[e]veryone shall be entitled to freedom of opinion and expression, which includes the freedom to hold opinions without interference and to seek, receive and impart information and ideas," subject to a constitutional prohibition of "any advocacy of national, racial or religious hatred and aggression between groups that constitutes incitement to discrimination, hostility, violence or political animosity."[33]   The Constitution of the Republic of Paraguay guarantees "[f]reedom of thought and of opinion," "[f]reedom of expression and of information," and the free practice of "[j]ournalism in any of its forms," but also qualifies these rights by forbidding people "to defend crime or violence," "to preach hatred or class struggle among Paraguayans," and to "proclaim disobedience" to the law. Moreover, "[p]ress organs lacking responsible direction shall not be permitted."[34]   There are commensurate qualifications in the Constitution of the State of Cambodia, which provides that "[c]itizens have freedom of speech, freedom of the press, and freedom of assembly," but also that "[n]o one can abuse these rights to the detriment of other people's honor, good mores and the customs of society, public social order, and national security."[35]   And although the Danish Constitution provides that "[a]ny person shall be entitled to publish his thoughts in printing, in writing, and in speech," it provides as well both that anyone doing so may be "held answerable [after publication] in a court of justice," and that "[a]ssociations employing violence, or aiming at attaining their object by violence, by instigation to violence, or by similar punishable influence on people of other views, shall be dissolved by judgment."[36]

An even broader survey of textual provisions on freedom of

---

[32] IR. CONST. art. 40.6.1.i, *translated in* 8 WORLD CONSTITUTIONS, *supra* note 22, at 21, 67-68.

[33] DRAFT BILL OF RIGHTS OF THE KWAZULU NATAL INDABA CONSTITUTION art. 11(1) (Nov. 1986) (on file with the *Cardozo Law Review*). I am grateful to Nelson Kasfir for providing me with a copy of this document.

[34] CONSTITUCION [Constitution] arts. 71, 72, 73 (Para.), *translated in* 14 WORLD CONSTITUTIONS, *supra* note 22, at 1, 10.

[35] RATHATHAMAMUNH [Constitution] art. 37/1 (Cambodia), *translated in* 3 WORLD CONSTITUTIONS, *supra* note 22, at 1, 8.

[36] GRUNDLOV [Constitution] arts. 77, 78(2) (Den.), *translated in* 4 WORLD CONSTITUTIONS, *supra* note 22, at 15, 24.

speech throughout the world would confirm the two lessons that this small sample demonstrates. First, although it is common to attribute the degree of American freedom of speech and press in part to the unqualified (absolute) nature of the language, the correlation is belied throughout much of the rest of the world, where the existence of the qualifications maps poorly against the degree of freedom of speech in fact. Few would suppose, for example, that the degree of freedom of speech in Canada and Denmark, which have strong textual qualifications, is less than that in Albania, which has none at all.[37]

Second, and of more relevance here, no country has taken the path of strong textual determinacy. Although some provisions are slightly more specific than others, majestic indeterminacy is the order of the day, and no national constitution specifies the contours of freedom of speech, press, and opinion with anything approaching the detail that those constitutions often use to express other rights or structures. The Natal/KwaZulu draft Bill of Rights noted above, for example, has extraordinarily detailed provisions relating to criminal procedure,[38] as do the current "competing" versions of the draft Bills of Rights of both the African National Congress[39] and the South African Law Commission.[40] But because this route of comparative precision has been universally rejected for rights of speech and press, the detailed explication of the categories "free speech" or "free expression" or "freedom of opinion" or "freedom of the press" must come from other than even the closest reading of constitutional text.

When we are talking about freedom of speech and freedom to disseminate and receive information, the worldwide indeterminacy of the language is compounded by the practical impossibility of reading

---

[37] Moreover, one of the most qualified provisions of all is Article 10 of the European Convention on Human Rights, which allows restrictions:

> in the interests of national security, territorial integrity or public safety, for the prevention of disorder or crime, for the protection of health or morals, for the protection of the reputation or rights of others, for preventing the disclosure of information received in confidence, or for maintaining the impartiality of the judiciary.

Convention for the Protection of Human Rights and Fundamental Freedoms, *opened for signature* Nov. 4, 1950, 213 U.N.T.S. 221 (entered into force on Sept. 3, 1953). Despite this seemingly exhaustive list (has there ever been a reason for restricting communication that did not fit one of these exclusions?), however, Article 10 is being interpreted with considerable vigor. *See* HURST HANNUM, MATERIALS IN INTERNATIONAL HUMAN RIGHTS AND U.S. CONSTITUTIONAL LAW 46-83 (1985).

[38] DRAFT BILL OF RIGHTS OF THE KWAZULU NATAL INDABA CONSTITUTION art. 4 (Nov. 1986) (on file with the *Cardozo Law Review*).

[39] THE ANC CONSTITUTIONAL COMMITTEE, A BILL OF RIGHTS FOR A NEW SOUTH AFRICA art. 2, at 2-6 (1990).

[40] SOUTH AFRICAN LAW COMMISSION WORKING PAPER 25: GROUP AND HUMAN RIGHTS arts. 6-7 (on file with the *Cardozo Law Review*).

the broad language literally.   A literalist/absolutist reading of "the freedom of speech" is embarrassed by the Securities Act of 1933,[41] the Sherman Antitrust Act,[42] the Federal Trade Commission Act,[43] much of the Model Penal Code,[44] a great deal of product liability law,[45] and a host of other provisions restricting the ability of a communicator to communicate whatever she wants whenever she wants to do it.[46]   Similarly, the equivalent provisions in other national constitutions are unable to cope with the inevitability of communication restriction in any conceivable modern state.   Constitutions that protect, without qualification, the dissemination of information are unlikely to tolerate breaches of confidentiality by lawyers, physicians, and governmental officials; those that protect assembly will necessarily allow a limit on the right to assemble in a major intersection at rush hour; and none seem willing to entertain free speech claims against the application of their laws dealing with truth in advertising or solicitation to bank robbery.

Although the exclusion of these and other topics from the coverage of the First Amendment is on occasion challenged in the United States,[47] free speech claims that are epiphenomenal even by American standards, and that so far have made little headway in the courts, can hardly be taken to represent the standard for thinking outside the United States.   Rather, elsewhere even more than in the United States, and in the United States much more than some people would like to admit, a wide range of communicative activities are generally considered to have, quite simply, nothing whatsoever to do with the constitutionally relevant category of freedom of speech, however broad the textual marking of that category might be.

IV

We are now at the heart of the matter.   It is apparent that every

---

[41] 15 U.S.C. §§ 77a-77bbbb (1988) (an elaborate system of communication control).

[42] 15 U.S.C. § 45 (1988).

[43] 15 U.S.C. §§ 41-77 (1988).

[44] E.g., MODEL PENAL CODE §§ 5.01, 5.02, 5.03 (1980).

[45] E.g., ARIZ. REV. STAT. ANN. § 12-681(3) (1991).

[46] See KENT GREENAWALT, SPEECH, CRIME, AND THE USES OF LANGUAGE (1990); Kent Greenawalt, Speech and Crime, 1980 AM. B. FOUND. RES. J. 645; Frederick Schauer, Mrs. Palsgraf and the First Amendment, 47 WASH. & LEE L. REV. 161 (1990); Steven Shiffrin, The First Amendment and Economic Regulation: Away From a General Theory of the First Amendment, 78 NW. U. L. REV. 1212 (1983); William Van Alstyne, A Graphic Review of the Free Speech Clause, 70 CAL. L. REV. 107 (1982).

[47] See, e.g., SEC v. Wall Street Publishing Inst., Inc., 851 F.2d 365 (D.C. Cir. 1988), cert. denied, 489 U.S. 1066 (1989); Aleta Estreicher, Securities Regulation and the First Amendment, 24 GA. L. REV. 223 (1990); Burt Neuborne, The First Amendment and Government Regulation of Capital Markets, 55 BROOK. L. REV. 5 (1989).

constitutional system needs a descriptive definition of the category "freedom of speech" (or its equivalent), but it is equally apparent that that definition does not and cannot come from the text of the constitution itself. But then, from where does it come?

I want to offer three possible answers to this question, and the three are not mutually exclusive. As with most social phenomena involving causal relationships, the determinants of a constitutional category are likely multiple rather than singular. Insofar as the factors I identify are themselves plausible, it would be surprising if they existed anywhere in isolation, and are likely to operate together to determine the contours of the relevant juridical category.

That factors may coexist does not mean that there is nothing more to be said about their relative weight. Just as we can say with some confidence that drunk drivers have a greater effect on the level of automobile accidents in the United States than do collisions by sober drivers with animals (even though both are contributory factors), so too can we investigate empirically the degree to which the factors I identify here (as well as others) contribute to the formation of constitutional categories of understanding. I will not engage in that empirical inquiry here, but the questions are no less empirical for my own unwillingness to investigate them empirically.[48]

A

With this said, let me start with the first of the three possibilities for the source of the relevant constitutional category: the United States. This is not a silly suggestion, however odd it might at first seem. Start with the proposition that legal categories in general are increasingly transplanted from one culture to another, a phenomenon that would be expected to accelerate as internationalization of communication and culture increases.[49] If this proposition is true (and it might not be), then are there reasons to think that the United States might be a particularly dominant source of transplants in constitutional context?

---

[48] As I become increasingly irritated by the legal professoriate's casualness with the world of empirical fact, I become increasingly willing to make clear where philosophizing ends and where empirical inquiry must begin, or, to reverse the order, to make clear what investigatable (even if not yet investigated) facts undergird normative legal or constitutional or political recommendations.

[49] On the phenomenon, see ALAN WATSON, THE EVOLUTION OF LAW (1985); ALAN WATSON, LEGAL TRANSPLANTS: AN APPROACH TO COMPARATIVE LAW (1974); ALAN WATSON, SOURCES OF LAW, LEGAL CHANGE, AND AMBIGUITY (1984); Rodolfo Sacco, *Legal Formants: A Dynamic Approach to Comparative Law*, 39 AM. J. COMP. L. 1 (1991); Edward M. Wise, *The Transplant of Legal Patterns*, 38 AM. J. COMP. L. 1 (1990 Supp.).

One reason could be the age and apparent success of the United States Constitution and American constitutional adjudication. Here I am not concerned with the normative proposition that the United States Constitution and the American constitutional system *is* a success. If the measure of success is stability under one nominal document, or continuation of the same structure of government for a very long time, or a degree of economic prosperity (which may or may not be causally related to the constitutional system), or the extent of individual rights against governmental overreaching (a rather question-begging criterion), then the American constitutional system must be considered a success. Under other criteria perhaps it is less so. But the measure of success, and the question whether the American constitutional system has indeed been successful, is different from the fact that the American constitutional system seems to be *considered* a success by a large number of other countries either considering constitutional transformations, or considering the ways in which their own constitutional systems could develop. Not only do references to American constitutionalism appear with greater frequency in constitutional documents and decisions in other countries than is the case with other potential external sources of constitutional guidance, but, one often sees explicit reference to the influence of American constitutional doctrines and principles on the development of constitutionalism elsewhere.[50]

In addition to the age of American constitutionalism (and the size of the corpus of materials that has accompanied the aging), American constitutionalists have appeared to be particularly aggressive in promoting the virtues of American constitutionalism and American constitutional doctrines abroad. Whether this is because of the receptiveness such approaches receive, the size of the American constitutional professoriate, the resources available to American constitutionalists but not to others, or other factors, one sees a particular eagerness on the part of American constitutionalists, most recently in Eastern Europe (and can the Constituent Members of the Commonwealth of Independent States[51] be far behind?) actively to promote the virtues of American approaches in other countries.[52]

---

[50] *See, e.g.*, Jacob Dolinger, *The Influence of American Constitutional Law on the Brazilian Legal System*, 38 AM. J. COMP. L. 803 (1990).

[51] On December 8, 1991, the Soviet Union was dissolved and replaced by the Constituent Members of the Commonwealth of Independent States. *See* Serge Schmemann, *Declaring Death of Soviet Union, Russia and 2 Republics Form New Commonwealth*, N.Y. TIMES, Dec. 9, 1991, at A1.

[52] *See, e.g.*, Symposium, *Approaching Democracy: A New Legal Order for Eastern Europe*, 58 U. CHI. L. REV. 439 (1991).

Thus it is far from implausible that the American delineation of a constitutional category might have some influence on the delineation of a similar constitutional category elsewhere. In 1975, for example, the Supreme Court of the United States, reversing previous interpretations, held that commercial advertising was (somewhat) within the contours of the category of freedom of speech, such that now (but not before) the fact of a governmental regulation of business being a restriction on commercial advertising provides a reason for maintaining, sometimes successfully, that it is unconstitutional and impermissible even if it would otherwise be desirable as a policy matter.[53] In 1991, that topic is of considerable concern in Canada,[54] although to the best of my knowledge the possibility that restrictions on advertisements by physicians, pharmacists, lawyers, and real estate agents present a free speech question remains a source of astonishment everywhere else in the world. We could then try to trace the connection between American and Canadian developments, and at least one possibility is that after the adoption of the Canadian Charter of Rights and Freedoms in 1982, Canadian lawyers and judges looked to a large and close source of literature and case law on commensurate provisions. As a result, Canadian lawyers might have used arguments not because they were indigenous to Canada, and not because they were necessarily well-founded, but rather because they were readily known (and thus readily usable by an advocate looking for any source of assistance) from the presence of a large and linguistically proximate constitutional culture immediately to the south.

B

Second, constitutional categories might develop internally within the legal/constitutional organs of the relevant legal/constitutional systems. Theorists of legal change such as Niklas Luhmann and Gunther Teubner have commented on the differentiation and autonomy of legal systems, maintaining that law, like other institutions in highly complex societies, increasingly turns in on itself, developing internal values and methods that take on a life and force of their own.[55] This

---

[53] Virginia State Bd. of Pharmacy v. Virginia Citizens Consumer Council, Inc., 425 U.S. 748 (1976); *see also* Central Hudson Gas & Elec. Corp. v. Public Serv. Comm'n, 447 U.S. 557 (1980); Bates v. State Bar, 433 U.S. 350 (1977); Linmark Assocs., Inc. v. Township of Willingboro, 431 U.S. 85 (1977). The current vitality of the doctrine remains in doubt. Posadas de Puerto Rico Assoc. v. Tourism Co. of Puerto Rico, 478 U.S. 328 (1986).

[54] *See* Attorney Gen. of Quebec v. Irwin Toy, Ltd., [1989] 1 S.C.R. 577; Attorney Gen. of Quebec v. La Chaussure Brown's, [1988] 2 S.C.R. 712; Roger A. Shiner, Freedom of Commercial Expression (May 1991) (unpublished manuscript, on file with the *Cardozo Law Review*).

[55] *See* NIKLAS LUHMANN, A SOCIOLOGICAL THEORY OF LAW (Martin Albrow ed., Elizabeth King-Utz & Martin Albrow trans., 1985); Gunther Teubner, *Substantive and Reflexive*

claim could take a strong or a weak form. In the strong form, the argument would be that the system, like many bureaucratic systems, comes to see its own perpetuation as a value in itself, independent of the values the system was originally designed to serve. In the weaker and perhaps more plausible version, the system seeks to serve its founding values, but increasingly sees those values through the lens of its own values, its own institutions, and its own practices.

It is quite possible that free speech decisionmaking in the United States has taken on some of these features, at least in the weak version, and thus has some of the characteristics to which Teubner refers as "autopoietic."[56] Particular documents—John Stuart Mill's *On Liberty*,[57] John Milton's *Areopagitica*,[58] Alexander Meiklejohn's *Free Speech and Its Relation to Self-Government*,[59] Justice Holmes's dissenting opinion in *Abrams v. United States*[60]—take on canonical importance, certain cases and doctrines become entrenched, styles of argument begin to dominate,[61] and perhaps, over time, preservation of these cases and doctrines begins to be treated as an end in itself rather than as instrumental to some larger goal.

The dynamics of all of this systemic entrenchment are quite vague, not only here but in the literature to which I refer.[62] Still, insofar as the phenomenon exists, we might find out about the delineation of constitutional categories by inquiring about the institutions in which they are delineated. And it is at least possible that just as law may institutionally be differentiated from other social institutions (which are in the same way institutionally differentiated from each other), so too might systems for delineating constitutional categories differentiate themselves in quite similar fashion. Suppose, for example, that at some level of consciousness Canadian courts, for reasons relating to Canadian perceptions of Canadian-American relations, sought to avoid the use of American doctrines, precedents, and

---

Elements in Modern Law, 17 LAW & SOC'Y REV. 239 (1983). *See generally* Richard Lempert, *The Autonomy of Law: Two Visions Compared, in* AUTOPOIETIC LAW 152 (Gunther Teubner ed., 1987).

56 *See supra* note 55; *see also* Gunther Teubner, *Evolution of Autopoietic Law, in* AUTOPOIETIC LAW, *supra* note 55, at 217.

57 JOHN STUART MILL, ON LIBERTY (Geraint L. Williams ed., 1985) (1859).

58 JOHN MILTON, AREOPAGITICA (1644), *reprinted in* 32 GREAT BOOKS OF THE WESTERN WORLD 379 (Robert M. Hutchins ed., Encyclopedia Britannica 1952).

59 Alexander Meiklejohn, *Free Speech and Its Relation to Self-Government, reprinted in* ALEXANDER MEIKLEJOHN, POLITICAL FREEDOM: THE CONSTITUTIONAL POWERS OF THE PEOPLE 3 (1965).

60 250 U.S. 616, 624 (1919) (Holmes, J., dissenting).

61 *See, e.g.*, Frederick Schauer, *Slippery Slopes*, 99 HARV. L. REV. 361 (1985).

62 *See supra* notes 55-56; *see also* Robert Gordon, *Critical Legal Histories*, 36 STAN. L. REV. 57 (1984).

principles, for many of the same reasons that the Irish courts seem reluctant to rely too heavily on English law. Insofar as this is true, the seeds of differentiation may have been planted, and we might expect that Canadian and American free speech doctrines would be increasingly subject to this differentiating force (while at the same time they were subject to numerous integrating forces going in the opposite direction).

C

Finally, constitutional categories may be dependent on a cultural categorization of particular events that varies with cultural experience and cultural history. Consider in this regard the specific question of whether Nazi and neo-Nazi speakers are protected by the pertinent principles of freedom of speech. Assume as well that for one reason or another the society has determined that it will protect the expression of political opinion, even political opinion well outside of the general range of political debate. Although this issue has been discussed most frequently in recent months with respect to a series of decisions of the Supreme Court of Canada,[63] I want to consider instead the comparison between the United States, which permits Nazi speech in applying its free speech principle,[64] and the Federal Republic of Germany, which does not.[65] Indeed, the most interesting German provision is not the relevant provision of the Basic Law,[66] which excludes from constitutional protection those who would seek to overthrow the democratic order, but rather a recent German law making it especially easy to bring actions against those who would deny the existence of the Holocaust, and doing so in quite Nazi-specific terms.[67]

Consider the nature of the argument concerning Nazi speech as it developed in the United States. Although some maintained that protection of the Nazis was itself directly in the center of a desirable

---

[63] See Canada (Human Rights Comm'n) v. Taylor, [1990] 3 S.C.R. 892; Regina v. Andrews, [1990] 3 S.C.R. 870; Regina v. Keegstra, [1990] 3 S.C.R. 697, reversing [1988] 60 Alta. L.R.2d 1 (Ct. App. 1988); see also Regina v. Zundel (No. 2), [1990] 37 O.A.C. 354 (1990).

[64] Collin v. Smith, 447 F. Supp. 676 (N.D. Ill.), aff'd, 578 F.2d 1197 (7th Cir.), cert. denied, 439 U.S. 916 (1978) (court affirmed Nazis' rights to march through Skokie, Illinois, a town with a large population of concentration camp survivors).

[65] See, e.g., Judgment of Apr. 27, 1982, BVerfG, reprinted in 35 NEUE JURISTISCHE WOCHENSCHRIFT [NJW] 1803 (1982); see also Donald Kommers, The Jurisprudence of Free Speech in the United States and the Federal Republic of Germany, 53 S. CAL. L. REV. 657 (1980).

[66] GRUNDGESETZ [Constitution] art. 18 (F.R.G.).

[67] STRAFGESETZBUCH art. 194, translated in Eric Stein, History Against Free Speech: The New German Law Against the "Auschwitz"—And Other—"Lies", 85 MICH. L. REV. 277, 323-24 (1986).

principle of free speech,[68] the common variety of argument was of the slippery slope/where do you draw the line?/camel's nose is in the tent/parade of horribles/foot in the door/thin edge of the wedge variety. That is, many American civil libertarians made with great gusto and considerable success, in court and out, the argument that communications by social democrats, for example, were members of the same category as communications of Nazism by Nazis, such that prohibitions of the latter created an unacceptable risk of the possibility of future prohibitions of the former. The slippery slope argument succeeds not because the instant case (the Nazis) and the danger case (the social democrats) are necessarily actually members of the same category, or necessarily indistinguishable, but because of a fear that for many they are perceived to be members of the same category.[69] Thus, the slippery slope argument, and a wide variety of similar arguments from the long term or greater undesirability of a decision that is desirable in the short term or in the particular case, depends on the empirical premise that in the hands of others a theoretically usable distinction between two theoretically distinguishable cases will break down in practice. Thus, the Skokie litigation[70] in the United States stands as a monument to the existence of a cultural category that includes both Nazis and social democrats, however many other cultural categories there might be that distinguished the two.

Now, consider the reaction to Nazi activities in the Federal Republic of Germany. Quite informally but extensively, I have attempted to raise the same slippery slope/members of the same category argument in Germany that was so successful in the United States, given that Germany does suppress Nazi speech with some vigor. Yet whenever I raise the possibility the reaction is invariably different than in the United States. To some Germans, the possibility that restricting Nazis will lead to restricting, say, Greens, is too remote to worry about. To others, the suggestion is scarcely comprehensible, and it appears that behind both reactions is the view that Nazis simply do not occupy the same category of understanding, in the law or out, with Greens, social democrats, communists, or anyone else. To most Germans, not surprisingly given the history, Nazis are just Nazis, inhabiting their own social, cultural, and historical category, and indeed to many Germans and others the categories of "Nazis" and "political" do not overlap at all. That Nazis instantiate the

---

[68] *See, e.g.*, LEE C. BOLLINGER, THE TOLERANT SOCIETY: FREE SPEECH AND EXTREMIST SPEECH IN AMERICA (1984).

[69] *See* Schauer, *supra* note 61, at 373-76.

[70] *See supra* note 64.

category of the political to more Americans (even while vehemently disagreeing with the political positions of the Nazis) than to Germans again seems hardly surprising.[71] Thus, for Germans it appears that the likelihood that restricting Nazis will lead to restricting Greens is equivalent to the possibility in the United States that requiring the preregistration of securities sales documents under the Securities Act of 1933 will lead to the precensorship of the utterances of fundamentalist Christians like Jerry Falwell or left-wing social critics like Noam Chomsky.

V

If my perceptions are correct (and they might not be), and if those perceptions are somewhat generalizable (and they might not be, even if they are right for this instance), then it appears that the prelegal instantiations of terms like "political" and "free speech" will vary dramatically from culture to culture. Insofar as courts have the responsibility of filling in such general terms based on theories of what constitutional provisions are designed to do, some of the cultural differences will be ameliorated. But where the differences are particularly great, the cultural differences seem likely to be reflected in judicial perceptions as well. Consequently, the involvement of the courts will not dramatically change my deeper point: so long as cultural differences are reflected in categorial differences, differences in the scope of constitutional protections can be expected to vary far more than might be expected merely by inspecting the relevant constitutional language. Thus, if the delineation of broad but still constitutionally relevant categories like "political speech" will vary considerably with cultural history and national variation, then that delineation may indicate that there are likely to be pressures militating against the cross-cultural assimilation of constitutional categories.[72] In obvious and important ways, constitutions deal with centrally important social and political subjects. Thus, it should come as no surprise that necessary constitutional categories contain the kinds of political and social presuppositions that will vary from country to country, just as the categorial status of Nazis varies between the United States and the Federal Republic of Germany. One result of such a theoretical conclusion might be an empirical study of differences in constitutional constraints for the same subjects across na-

---

[71] I explore this theme further in Frederick Schauer, *Exceptions*, 58 U. CHI. L. REV. 871 (1991).

[72] Which, to repeat, is not to deny that there are factors of internalization militating in exactly the opposite direction.

tional boundaries, with Rudolf Schlesinger's Cornell studies being one possible model.[73] But another might be a different American response to the recent spate of international constitution-making. One need not slide into an unacceptable relativism to acknowledge that perhaps American constitutionalists can perform a great service by helping other countries to understand that constitutional constraints rest on culturally contingent social categories. This acknowledgement might in turn lead to recognition of the fact that American constitutionalists can also serve better by helping others to locate and manage their own categories than by trying to get them to accept ours.

---

[73] FORMATION OF CONTRACTS (Rudolf Schlesinger ed., 1968).

THE MULTICULTURAL SELF: QUESTIONS OF SUBJECTIVITY, QUESTIONS OF POWER

M. M. Slaughter

I

Until very recently, national identity both here and abroad has been defined as monocultural, and assimilation of minorities has been the prevailing norm. Assimilation is meant to dissolve cultural difference to create the sense of national identity, e.g., American or French. One of the main instruments of assimilation has been the educational system. Its function has been to socialize students into the national culture and to create them in the image of monocultural national identity.

Many are now demanding that public institutions, particularly schools, reflect the increasing diversity of society, rather than continue their exclusively monocultural focus.[1] These demands range from changes in the curriculum to demands for race-conscious and culture-conscious policies. In France, Muslim girls have demanded the right to wear the hijab (head scarf) in class, in violation of France's strict policy of cultural and religious neutrality.[2] Elsewhere, they have demanded the right to separate schools. In the American context, blacks have demanded the right to attend schools with an "Africa-centered" curriculum; Hispanics seek bilingual, culturally oriented heritage schools.[3] These demands for multiculturalism have been criticized as a kind of racial and ethnic balkanization which violates the ideals of a monocultural and color-blind society.[4]

---

[1] For a range of articles discussing this subject, *see* THE POLITICS OF LIBERAL EDUCATION (Darryl J. Gless & Barbara Herrnstein Smith eds., 1992).

[2] See Edward Cody, *Muslim School Girls Spark French Immigration Debate*, WASHINGTON POST, Oct. 23, 1989, at A17; Associated Press, *Muslim Scarves Stir French School Controversy*, CHICAGO TRIBUNE, Oct. 23, 1989, at 4. In the end, girls were permitted to wear their veils at the discretion of the school principal. Reuters, *Gesture to French Muslims*, N.Y. TIMES, Oct. 26, 1989. In December 1993 France repudiated its toleration of multiculturalism and the hijab was once again banned, this time in the name of cultural homogeneity rather than religious neutrality. Alan Riding, *France, Reversing Course, Fights Immigrants' Refusal to Be French*, N.Y. TIMES, Dec. 5, 1993, Sec. 4, at 4.

[3] Michael Myers, *Afrocentrism = Balkanization*, N.Y. TIMES, June 15, 1993, at 46; Susan Chira, *Rethinking Deliberately Segregated Schools*, N.Y. TIMES, July 11, 1993, Sec. 4, at 20.

[4] ARTHUR SCHLESINGER, THE DISUNITING OF AMERICA: REFLECTIONS OF A MULTICULTURAL SOCIETY (1992).

Multiculturalists argue that the notions of a monocultural national identity and an assimilated majority are mythic constructs which simply stand for white, Eurocentric, and Western. The social reality is, however, that Western nations are culturally heterogeneous, and increasingly so. Monocultural ideology privatizes and silences these heterogeneous differences. In the schools the standard curriculum, or canon, purports to reflect the national cultural identity, but it is in fact the reflection of the dominant white, Eurocentric majority.

Since multiculturalism is a vexed subject, it is important to get definitions and terminology clear. There are two kinds of multiculturalism: one pluralist, the other separatist.[5] Pluralists oppose assimilation and celebrate diversity. They speak of the "rainbow curriculum," the "gorgeous mosaic." Pluralists recognize the existence of difference and want to incorporate it into existing structures—by discussing, for example, cultural groups in textbooks, or by teaching non-white, non-European, non-Western history, literature, art, or music. But although they celebrate diversity, they recognize, along with assimilationists, a basic commonality shared by all. All are the same in their difference. Pluralism equates all differences, all groups. This is symbolically expressed in Justice Powell's statement in *University of California v. Bakke* that America is "a nation of 'minorities'."[6]

Separatists deny the commonalities between racial, religious, and cultural groups. Pointing to obvious social and economic realities, they argue that cultural groups are different in the degree to which they are segmented and isolated from the mainstream or majority. They are different in their difference—by virtue of their nature, history, social power, and the like. To varying degrees, separatists call for public and legal recognition of this segmentation. Blacks are not satisfied, for example, with the incorporation of black history and literature in the standard curriculum and demand separate schools with an African-centered curriculum. Or they demand race-conscious admissions policies in public universities. Muslims demand separate schools for girls. Native Americans demand separate schools to preserve their languages and traditions.

The metaphor of the mosaic nicely reflects this inherent tension between the pluralist and separatist strains of multiculturalism. Pluralists focus on the fact that the pieces of the mosaic are resolved into

---

[5] Bill Ong Hing, *Beyond the Rhetoric of Cultural Pluralism: Addressing the Tension of Separatism and Conflict in an Immigration-Driven Multiracial Society*, 81 CAL. L. REV. 863 (1993).

[6] Regents of the Univ. of Cal. v. Bakke, 438 U.S. 265, 292 (1978).

a unity. Separatists focus on the fact that the pieces are bounded and discrete.

II

Intertwined with the debate between monoculturalism and multiculturalism are discussions of identity. The question is whether the subject is, by its nature, an autonomous, a priori free agent or whether it is constructed by social forces. Discussions of identity thus attempt to derive legal and political policies from the particular nature of the subject that is posited. It is not clear, however, that interrogation of the subject is helpful for making decisions on political and legal questions.

Two separate questions are involved here. The first is whether individual identity is constructed by social discourse and/or power relations, or whether individuals are autonomous creators of their identities. This is the subjectivity question. The second is whether the *legal* or constitutional subject should be an individual (whether autonomous or constructed) or a collectively defined entity. This is the power question.

A. *The Subjectivity Question*

Construction theory asserts that the subject—the individual self-motivated actor or speaker—is not a natural essence but a subject position.[7] Identity is created through hegemonic forces which construct or "write" social categories onto persons through opposition to the other. Thus subjects, e.g., whites, constitute themselves through opposition to others, e.g., blacks. In so doing, they objectify the others and deny them subjectivity, thus marginalizing and silencing them. Subjects then pronounce their difference as natural, normal, and meaningful. They erase the origins of this construction and make the categories appear natural and essential. At the same time, they make the other appear naturally deficient, deviant, and abnormal and thus a proper object for control and/or exclusion.

Social constructionists see groups and their members as produced or written by relations of force. What binds individuals to groups is the sheer power and domination of those opposing them. Foucault, for example, from whom many social constructionists borrow, describes the way in which the homosexual was constructed (and demonized) in the nineteenth century as a category of being, when he

---

[7] *See* MICHEL FOUCAULT, THE HISTORY OF SEXUALITY 92-102 (Robert Hurley trans., 1980).

had previously been simply a person who engaged in certain sexual acts.[8] Heterosexuality was produced as the norm and, simultaneously, homosexuality as deviance.

The classic description of this kind of construction occurs in Sartre's discussion of the relation between anti-Semite and Jew.[9] Anti-Semites attribute to the Jewish other an essence which is defined as everything that Christians or Frenchmen lack, so that everything the Jew does is evil.[10] The Jew has an essence, a substantial form, a metaphysical principle that is the source of the evil.

Sartre exposes the constructed nature of this notion of Jewish essence. He shows that Jews are not a single race. Nor are they a religion. Not only are there secular or atheistic Jews, but for many practicing Jews, religion is only ceremonial or attenuated, a symbolic way of maintaining ties to a lost national past. Neither are Jews a historical community; they have existed for two thousand years in dispersion.[11]

Sartre concludes that Jews do not share an essence or common nature as anti-Semites claim. Rather, Jews get their identity as a group from their "situation" or subject position vis-à-vis non-Jews.[12] Thus, the Jew is "one whom other men consider a Jew . . . ."[13] They *make* the Jew. They "have *created* the Jew."[14] In this position the Jew is subordinated and excluded. He is a creature of the other's making and in his control. His identity comes from the other's perceptions. As a result his actions can only be reactive. Because Jewish identity lies in the eye of the beholder, Jews define themselves and behave "in accordance with the representation made of them."[15] Thus, the Jew's identity is quintessentially that of a victim. This is the common fate of those who are constructed, then essentialized, as others.

The contrary view posits identity not as negativity but as essence. One variation sees the subject as autonomous by nature. This view is the foundation of liberal individualism. Another variation posits a subject whose identity is based on a constitutive culture and/or community, whose essence is a nomos or tradition.

---

[8] *Id.* at 43-44.

[9] *See* JEAN-PAUL SARTRE, ANTI-SEMITE AND JEW 93, 100 (George J. Becker trans., 1948).

[10] *Id.* at 39. Democrats are no better. They do silently what anti-Semites do publicly.

[11] *Id.* at 66-67.

[12] *Id.* at 67, 100-102, 145.

[13] *Id.* at 69.

[14] *Id.* at 68.

[15] *Id.* at 15.

The latter view is embodied in the idea of an Afrocentric culture whose traditions would be taught in the all-black Ujamma schools that were proposed for New York City.[16] The curriculum was to be based on Nguzo Saba, or "Seven Principles," which included purpose, unity, collective responsibility, and economic cooperation instead of Enlightenment values and individualism. It would teach civilization from an African point of view and offer other subjects, such as Swahili and Yoruba, from which the American black tradition is said to derive.

This concept of identity based on community also lies behind Muslim demands for halal food and the hijab in public schools in France and England. These are practices which represent an entire way of life, and through them, that life, culture, and cultural identity are maintained and reproduced. The hijab, for example, is one means by which a Muslim woman expresses pride, loyalty, and deference to a religion and culture she feels essential to her identity. From her point of view, she *takes* the veil. Individual identity rests on identification with and participation in the nomos of the community.

Taking the nomos to be a positive source of identity is a critical difference between constructivist and essentialist views of identity. For example, it is, comparatively speaking, difficult to define Muslims through absence. Muslims believe themselves to be part of the ummah, an actual community of believers who gather at the mosque on Friday, go on the haj, fast during Ramadān, and are bound by sharī'a law.[17] It is a community defined by a nomos, a world of value and a way of life based on the Message given to Mohammed in the Qur'ān. Its history and tradition and the identity of individual members are seen to be the working out or fulfillment of that nomos.

This, then, is a group that defines itself internally through a set of beliefs, traditions, and practices, however that group may be perceived by the dominant majority. However delinquent a Muslim may be, or, for that matter, however fundamentalist, he can still point to a particular cultural unity—the unity of orthodox Islam—as the basis of his identity. This is not to say that Muslims are not discriminated against, nor subordinated, nor unequal in a particular context. Nevertheless, identity is not constituted exclusively as absence, through the gaze of the other; it is difficult to define them as victims.

The constructivist and essentialist positions both have consequences for social transformation. The obvious problem with a con-

---

[16] *See, e.g.*, Joseph Berger, *'Africa-Centered' Proposal Outlined for a Trial School*, N.Y. TIMES, Jan. 22, 1991, at B3.

[17] See H.A.R. GIBB, ISLAM: A HISTORICAL PERSPECTIVE (1986).

structivist view of the individual as victim is that it undercuts empowerment for political action. To the extent that people are defined as, and see themselves as, victims, it denies them power to be self-motivated actors and speakers. Furthermore, to the extent that they are defined by negativity, it prevents them from forming the solidarities needed for political action.

Social constructionists are not, however, complete determinists. They recognize the possibility of resistance. They argue that the self is never really complete or fully present to itself although the dominant group may try to make it appear that way. One is never only, or essentially, a black, Muslim, Jew, or homosexual. Rather, the self is a text written with a multitude of discourses. Political action is directed to resisting the oppression and dominance of official, totalizing discourse. This is accomplished through recognition of the constructed nature of identity as negativity.

Resistance takes place in the interstices of the networks of power where there are skirmishes with local narratives and histories. The point of resistance is to unmask official discourse to publicly reveal the relations of power—of domination and subordination—that lie behind it. A constructionist, for example, would encourage minorities to engage the notion of a monocultural, assimilated national identity to expose the fact that it masks the dominance of white, Western, Eurocentric ideology. Muslim identity would be exposed as the construction of the muftis and mullahs. Thus, Edward Said, a Lebanese Palestinian Christian, argues that he too is included in Islamic culture.[18] Akeel Bilgrami, a nonbeliever of Muslim descent, argues that he is culturally a Muslim; it is only the religious powers that be that define Muslims so as to exclude secular Muslims.[19]

The critical problem with the social constructivist view is that it is subjectivity all the way down. If all are subjects, for example, black and white, all are equally constructed and there is no a priori means of choosing one or another as the proper subjects of political or legal reform. It might be said that reform in principle should always be directed to relieving oppression, but since all are to some degree constructed, all can claim they are to some degree oppressed. Recognition of the constructed nature of the subject in and of itself gives no direction for deciding how to allocate power. Thus there is no way to choose, for example, between disadvantaged or subordinated whites

---

[18] Edward Said, *The Phony Islamic Threat*," N.Y. TIMES, Nov. 21, 1993, Sec. 6, at 62.

[19] Akeel Bilgrami, *What Is a Muslim? Fundamental Commitment and Cultural Identity*, 18 CRITICAL INQUIRY 821 (1992).

and subordinated blacks seeking admission to medical school. Both are constructed and oppressed through relations of power.

A view of identity as nomos, on the other hand, presents obvious problems of determinism. Nevertheless, it does have this virtue: identity does not depend exclusively on forces external to the person or community for empowerment and self-transformation. Rather, the source of subjectivity lies within the nomos of the community. No matter how much the dominant majority may define the Muslim as object, for example, he can still look to Islamic values and the ummah for the source of his subjectivity. Although he might demand that this nomos be translated into public institutions and legal rights, the denial of that public recognition does not deny his identity. He is neither an object, cipher, nor victim. This might, therefore, provide a stronger foundation for political action even though it may require a subordination of individual will for the greater good of the community.

B. *The Power Question*

The definition of the subject is an epistemological question—how one knows and comes to be known. It is not necessarily related to the question of the subject as a unit of social organization or to the *legal* subject, the bearer of rights. In terms of legal and political justice, the question that is more properly raised is not the nature and source of subjectivity but whether the legal subject is the individual or some form of collective entity. This is the question posed by claims to rights for groups and separate group-based institutions.

The constructivist notion of the subject does not ineluctably lead to one or the other. The subject may work within a system of individual rights or seek social transformation through collective action. Essentialist notions of the subject as either autonomous or constituted lead in two different directions also. A notion of the a priori autonomous subject usually leads to a legal regime based on individual rights. A view of the subject as constituted by a community leads to demands for some form of collective rights.

In the American context two cases illustrate the conflict between individual and collective rights. *Martinez v. Santa Clara Pueblo* hinged on a tribal rule whereby the children of tribal women who married non-tribal men were excluded from membership in the tribe.[20] These women could not pass on land to their children, nor

---

[20] Martinez v. Santa Clara Pueblo, 436 U.S. 49 (1978). The lower courts in *Martinez* decided the case on the merits. The district court found for the tribe, the appellate court for Martinez. The Supreme Court decided the case on jurisdictional grounds, holding that the

did the children have a right to live in the Pueblo. Martinez asserted an individual rights claim, arguing that the rule violated the equal protection provision of the Indian Civil Rights Act and that tribal rules should be changed to guarantee her right to choose a husband without penalty. The tribe asserted a group rights claim, arguing that the patrilineal rules were an essential part of its unique culture. In order for that culture to survive, the customs of the community must prevail over individual preference even if that meant gender inequality. The lower courts divided on the cultural issues. The district court ruled in favor of the tribe's group rights claim; the appellate court in favor of Martinez's individual rights claim. The Supreme Court resolved the issue on jurisdictional grounds having no relation to the merits.

Race-conscious laws are another instance in which this conflict is presented. A paradigmatic instance is the *Bakke* case. The University of California sought racial preference rules in admission decisions. That is to say, they sought recognition of racial groups as legal subjects. In holding that racial quotas were unconstitutional, Justice Powell flatly stated that the only subject of legal or constitutional rights was the individual.[21]

One can reach a result favoring the group by either the constructivist or essentialist route. Each offers a justification for why the political unit should not necessarily be limited to the individual. The social constructivist project is helpful where it questions the entire Enlightenment project of individualism as contingent rather than universal and necessary. Thus, while the social constructivist may resist at the local level within a polity based on individual rights, in the struggle against oppression he may also seek transformation of the legal regime so that it recognizes collective rights in order to end oppression. The essentialist justification for group rights also questions the focus on the atomic individual, but the argument is that individuals are by their nature communal beings and need community for self-actualization. Despite the substantial philosophical differences between these concepts, each opens up the individual rights–based legal system to the possibility of distributing power to cultural groups.

III

A theory of the legal subject as individual leads to either assimilationist or pluralist policies. A theory of the legal subject as a collec-

---

Indian Civil Rights Act did not provide a civil cause of action in federal courts. As a result, only tribal courts had jurisdiction to consider Martinez's claim.

21 *Bakke*, 438 U.S. at 318 n.52, 319.

tive entity leads to separatist policies. Separatist solutions flow easily from culture-based, essentialist views of the person. They are often seen as necessary for the realization and perpetuation of the cultural nomos. The classic example is the case of the Amish community, which required vocational education for its children to perpetuate its character as a simple agricultural community modeled on the practices of early Christians.[22]

Separatist solutions like defining the community in terms of a cultural tradition (African, Santa Claran, Muslim, Amish), or in terms of separate public institutions like the Ujamma schools, institutionalize difference. For the essentialists, the goal is to preserve and perpetuate difference. For the constructivists, the goal is ultimately to deinstitutionalize difference as a means of domination. For them, separatist measures would turn dominated objects into subjects, into persons who are actors and speakers, articulating their own self-definition through their own discourse. They see remedies like race-conscious laws as a means of destabilizing the lockstep relations of subject/object, oppressed/oppressor. Arrogating the object to subject position forces upon the dominant subjects the realization that their dominant position is contingent, the result of historical accident and not natural talent and superiority. Thus the goal is to shatter the fiction of their fully realized, natural essence. This, it is hoped, will change the dominant group so that it will cease to regard the subordinate group as a closed, fixed, metaphysical entity. Out of these breaks and fissures in the system of power, new alliances and new solidarities may be formed. If the dichotomies of race are destroyed, for example, new alliances along class lines might be formed.[23] Institutionalization of difference thus becomes the ultimate means of eradicating it.

Assimilationist policies attempt to annihilate difference by recognizing only atomic individuals, i.e., universal subjects shorn of their unique differences. They imply that the only means of attaining equality and fairness and eradicating oppression is to reduce all to a common denominator, e.g., American. As is becoming more and more apparent, the problem is that all are *not* the same and assimilation requires that some must lose their difference. This assumes, of course, that "the same" is willing to open itself up to the reconstructed "different," an assumption that is often dubious. Assimilationist policies are an implicit assertion that difference is a deviation from some implicit norm and that the norm may only be a reflection

---

[22] Wisconsin v. Yoder, 406 U.S. 205 (1972).
[23] *See* KWAME ANTHONY APPIAH, IN MY FATHER'S HOUSE (1992).

of the values and characteristics of those with the power to normalize. Assimilationist norms are, therefore, a form of domination. The price for a ticket out of subordination, e.g., poverty, is giving up minority (cultural, religious, racial) affiliation.

Pluralism is also built on recognition of the individual as the unit of political management or transformation. Pluralism, however, does not actively seek to annihilate difference. It rejects the heavy price demanded by assimilation. Sartre's discussion of the Jew is again a classic for describing the pluralistic perspective. Having described the false, anti-Semitic view of the Jew as a metaphysical entity, Sartre offers what he takes to be the ideal conception. He rejects the classic liberal solution. The liberal "recognizes neither Jew, nor Arab, nor Negro . . . but only man—man always the same in all places. He resolves all collectivities into individual elements. To him . . . a social body [is] a collection of individuals . . . ."[24] The liberal demands rights for them as universal, abstract subjects, "not as concrete and individual products of history."[25]

Sartre, on the other hand, proposes "concrete" liberalism as the civic ideal. Since man as such does not exist, assimilation is an unacceptable violence. It "would mean the annihilation of a spiritual community."[26] Rather, the right to participate in the national enterprise must be granted, e.g., to Jews as Jews, to "concrete persons."[27]

Because pluralism demands acknowledgment of differences, it acts to combat hegemonic forces. It constantly serves as a reminder, for example, that the white and Eurocentric are not the only reality nor are they a given, natural norm. But if pluralism recognizes difference on the one hand, it also works to diminish the power or salience of difference on the other hand. It marginalizes and contains difference in a number of ways. One is to treat difference as an elective affinity, a matter of preference and choice. The choice to identify oneself with a minority community, e.g., black, Italian, Jewish, or Muslim, is regarded as similar to the choice of wearing short skirts or listening to rock and roll.

More important, however, pluralism diminishes the power of difference by treating all differences as equal, when in terms of social positionality they are not. Justice Powell's treatment of the admissions system at the University of California medical school in the *Bakke* case is a perfect example. Having rejected the possibility that

---

24 Sartre, *supra* note 9, at 55.

25 *Id.* at 117.

26 *Id.* at 145.

27 *Id.* at 146.

race alone might be the determining factor in granting admission, Powell went on to praise the Harvard admission scheme that considered race as one factor among many in order to achieve diversity. What is interesting is the list of factors that Harvard considered. Among these were geographical location, social background (the farm boy, the disadvantaged), and special talents (sports, music, etc.).[28]

Considered broadly, this list collapses all distinctions between groups—blacks, Arab-Americans, bassoonists, southerners, gymnasts. All are put on a par and difference is rendered relatively meaningless. More particularly, this pluralist scheme collapses distinctions between racial minorities and members of other ethnic or cultural minorities— "Celtic Irishmen,"[29] Italian-Americans,[30] and the like. It is a painful historical fact, however, that the background of these disparate groups has not been similar. Ethnic minorities with European backgrounds have been able to enter mainstream American society while racial minorities, in part because of past government intervention, have not. In a different vein, by virtue of their unique history, Native American tribes make claims to sovereignty as "peoples," but these claims are ignored and the tribes are treated as just one of the many "similar" minorities.[31] Pluralist treatment of groups effaces these historical differences.

Furthermore, the current socioeconomic situation of these disparate cultural and racial groups is not similar (quite possibly in part because of their historical differences). They are not alike in their degree of segmentation and isolation from mainstream opportunities nor are they alike in the degree to which they wish to enter the mainstream. While the ultimate goal of blacks is for the most part to achieve economic equality, the ultimate goal of many Native Americans is to achieve separate political status. The one seeks inclusion, the other separatism. Pluralism effaces these differences also.

In a culturally heterogeneous society, therefore, pluralism might provide a basis for changes in attitudes and perceptions, although given the way in which it levels differences even that is debatable. But it cannot provide a basis for solving economic, social, or political problems, or for legal reform. Since it focuses on individuals and privatizes difference, it cannot publicly differentiate between differences and cannot rank them. Thus there is no basis for the distribu-

---

[28] *Bakke*, 438 U.S. at 316.

[29] *Id.* at 292.

[30] *Id.* at 316.

[31] Patrick Macklem, *Distributing Sovereignty: Indian Nations and Equality of Peoples*, 45 STAN. L. REV. 1311 (1993).

tion of power. The only basis for such distribution is legal recognition of groups.

If we raise the question as to how minorities are to attain a political voice—or give voice to their differences—we are offered two alternatives. The constructivist view, which defines the other as negativity, is not compelling. While it is not impossible, resistance from within a position of negativity is difficult. A more essentialist view of subjectivity, which looks to a constitutive nomos—identification with a cultural vision within the community—is more self-empowering. This is the move made by Muslims who demand that public institutions be accommodated to their particular needs. It is also the move we see among members of the black community who look to African culture and separate schools with an African curriculum. In these instances, demands for power and legal entitlement flow from the needs of the community for self-realization.

In either case, what is ultimately necessary for treatment of minorities is the realization that individual, autonomy-based justifications for legal entitlement are not sufficient. A national identity and constitutional polity based exclusively on the foundations of Enlightenment individualism are in the end the ultimate fiction and ultimate oppression. In order to combat the ideology of white supremacy and Eurocentrism, Enlightenment ideology will have to be changed or transformed by nondominant cultures. This includes transformation of Enlightenment norms of individualism and assimilation. This points to the formation of a new consciousness and new community which would not be simply a new version of the Enlightenment project. It would be a new tradition that has been shaped by—perhaps founded upon—cultural difference.

VI

On Drawing Constitutional Boundaries

Between Self and Other:

The Role of Property Rights

ON PROPERTY AND CONSTITUTIONALISM

Cass R. Sunstein

INTRODUCTION

It is generally understood that the recent revolutions in Eastern Europe are producing a large-scale transition. It is important, however, to distinguish among the quite different features of the current changes. The new reform movements actually involve three distinct transitions. The first is a transition from a command economy to one based on markets. The second is a transition from a system of one-party domination to democracy. The third is a transition from a system in which government is unconstrained by laws laid down in advance to one of constitutionalism and the rule of law.

Although important work is taking place on all these fronts, participants in current debates generally assume that the three transitions are not closely connected. At the present, and for the foreseeable future, it seems clear that the transition to markets, and the accompanying efforts to promote economic development, will be foremost in the minds of the reformers. Democratization also appears on the agenda, but it usually takes a secondary role. In the meantime, the movement for constitutional reform generally draws little public attention, and indeed has been dwarfed by other matters. In many circles, the drafting of the constitution is thought to involve symbolic or even irrelevant matters having no real connection to the hard pragmatic work of economic and political reform.

I believe that the separation of the three transitions, and the devaluation of constitution-writing, are unfortunate and potentially dangerous mistakes. In fact, the transitions are closely related. The right kind of constitution could play an important role in fueling economic development and democratic reform; indeed, under current conditions, it may be indispensable to them. The wrong kind of constitution—or no constitution at all—could be devastating to progress in both of these areas.

To offer only one example: Firm constitutional protection of property rights, combined with an independent judiciary, is an excellent way of encouraging international investment in one's nation. Such devices should spur domestic investment and initiative as well. Without constitutional protection, there will be a serious obstacle to the necessary economic activity from international and domestic enterprises. Anyone who engages in economic activities in these nations will do so with knowledge that the state may take their property or abrogate their contracts. To say the very least, this will be an obstacle to economic development.

In Eastern Europe, there is a more pressing need for constitutional protection of economic and democratic rights than there was in the United States or the West. In the United States, for example, the process of constitution-making was simplified by the fact that well before that process began, private property, the common law, and civil society were firmly in place. The constitution-makers could build on, and attempt to protect, existing achievements. The market and the institutions of civil society—private intermediate associations operating between the individual and the state, including religious organizations, charitable trusts, local community groups, business enterprises—antedated the Constitution.

The task of constitution-making in Eastern Europe is both more critical and more daunting, precisely because of the absence of well-established institutions protecting market ordering and civil society. The emerging constitutions must not only create the basic governmental structures and protect the conventional catalog of liberal rights, but also concern themselves with the creation of safeguards for the transition to (some version of) market ordering. If they fail to do so, a large amount of the important work will be done on the legislative front, where there may be unique barriers to success. A particular problem is that democratic politics may make it difficult to create real markets, which will produce such transitional problems as inflation and unemployment. Even more fundamentally, the process of constitution-making could become irrelevant to many of the fundamental issues now facing Eastern Europe. There is a serious current danger that the moment of constitutional opportunity will be irretrievably lost; and if it is, both prosperity and democratization will be at risk.

This Essay comes in three parts. Part I briefly discusses the relationships among property, democracy, and economic growth. My principal goal is to show that property should be seen as a political right, one that reduces dependence on the state and creates the kind of security that is indispensable to genuine citizenship in a democracy.

Property rights are not in conflict with democracy; in a variety of ways they help provide the preconditions for self-governance. The creation of private property also serves a number of functions indispensable to economic development.

Part II speculates about the contents of a constitution that is self-consciously designed, as western constitutions have not entirely been, to create a market economy and to promote the institutions of civil society. My particular goal here is to argue that constitutionalism can play a crucial role in protecting both economic development and democratic self-government. A well-drafted constitution can guard against a system in which ownership rights are effectively subject to continuous political revision; such a system reintroduces all of the problems, both economic and democratic, introduced by common ownership of property. Through cataloguing possible provisions, I discuss the possibility of developing a set of economic liberties specifically designed for constitution-making in Eastern Europe. Such a development might ultimately count as one of a range of contributions of the recent events to the theory and practice of constitutionalism, and to the long-overdue integration of economics and constitutionalism.

Part III deals with two problems that cannot be solved through constitution-making. The first problem is that of interpretation. The meaning of any text is a function of interpretive principles, and these cannot be spelled out in the text itself. The second problem is the task of initially allocating entitlements. That task must be undertaken through ordinary legislation, and it will have some surprising effects.

I. PROPERTY, PROSPERITY, DEMOCRACY

We should begin by distinguishing between two sorts of constitutions. Westerners often think that the constitutions of Eastern European countries before the downfall of communism are not constitutions at all. In fact, however, they embody a distinct conception of constitutionalism.[1] Crucially, such constitutions do not distinguish between public and private spheres. They apply their prohibitions and permissions to everyone.

Moreover, such constitutions contain duties as well as rights.

---

[1] I will not explore the extent to which the Eastern European constitutions in the communist era draw on principles of constitutionalism that predated communism. There is no question that the tradition of a protective, sometimes paternalistic state has far more force in Europe than in the United States, and that this tradition is likely to affect constitutionalism after the downfall of communism. For present purposes, I do not inquire whether the communist constitutions departed in important respects from traditional Eastern European conceptions of constitutionalism.

They do not merely grant privileges to citizens, but also impose obligations on them. Finally, and most important of all, the central provisions of these constitutions set out very general social aspirations or commitments. Their provisions are designed to state those aspirations, not to create concrete entitlements that citizens can attempt to vindicate, through an independent judiciary, against government officials. These aspirations include a wide range of "positive" rights.

Thus, for example, the Soviet Constitution includes the right to work,[2] the right to rest and leisure,[3] the right to health protection,[4] and the right to maintenance in old age, sickness, and disability.[5] It imposes on citizens the duty to preserve and protect socialist property and to enhance the power and prestige of the Soviet State.[6] The Polish Constitution includes the right to work,[7] the right to rest and leisure,[8] and the right to health protection.[9] The Romanian Constitution includes the right to leisure,[10] the right to work, including equal pay for equal work and measures for the protection and safety of workers.[11] The Bulgarian Constitution offers the right to a holiday,[12] the right to work,[13] the right to labor safety,[14] the right to social security,[15] and the right to free medical care.[16]

Along each of these dimensions, western constitutions are quite different. The provisions of such constitutions generally apply only to the government, and not to private actors. They do not impose duties. Most important, they aim to create solid individual rights, ones that can be invoked by individual citizens, as of right, in an independent tribunal authorized to bar governmental action. Western constitutions generally do not include broad aspirations. Positive rights are the exception, and when they exist they are usually not subject to judicial enforcement.[17]

The individual rights protected by western constitutions are not,

---

2 KONST. SSSR, art. 40 (1977).
3 *Id.* at art. 41.
4 *Id.* at art. 42.
5 *Id.* at art. 43.
6 *Id.* at art. 62.
7 KONSTYTUCJA [Constitution] art. 68 (Poland).
8 *Id.* at art. 69.
9 *Id.* at art. 70.
10 CONSTITUȚIA [Constitution] art. 19 (Romania).
11 *Id.* at art. 18.
12 KONSTITUTSIA [Constitution] art. 42 (Bulgaria).
13 *Id.* at art. 40.
14 *Id.* at art. 41.
15 *Id.* at art. 43.
16 *Id.* at art. 47.
17 The German Constitution is, in its basic text, not an exception. The Constitutional

of course, limited to private property and economic liberties. They include other political and civil liberties and rights as well, and these are indispensable safeguards. My principal goal here, however, is to explain how constitutionalism might work simultaneously to promote the transition to economic markets and the transition to democracy, and for this reason it will be valuable to focus on the right to private property. In this section I briefly outline some of the functions served by that right. The basic story should be familiar; I recount it here because it seems especially important to keep in mind while exploring the recent wave of constitution-making in Eastern Europe.

A. *Private Property and Economic Prosperity*

It is generally agreed that a system of private property helps to bring about economic prosperity. There are at least four central reasons for this result.[18]

First, the institution of private property[19] creates and takes advantage of the powerful human inclination to bring goods and services to oneself and to people one cares about.[20] This claim does not depend on a proposition about human selfishness. The desire to acquire goods might be deeply altruistic, in the sense that people may want to give their goods to others, including the most vulnerable members of society.

In a system of private property, the gains from the use and cultivation of ownership rights accrue to a designated owner. A system without private property stifles incentives and thus induces both sloth and waste.[21] These points, too, do not depend on especially cynical accounts of human nature. It is necessary only to glance briefly at history, past and present, and to acknowledge that human beings will

---

Court has, however, used the text to create some positive rights. *See* Bernhard Schlink, *German Constitutional Culture in Transition, supra* p. 197, 211-12.

[18] I draw in this section on JEREMY WALDRON, THE RIGHT TO PRIVATE PROPERTY (1988).

[19] As a technical matter, a system of private property should not be identified with a market economy. The distinguishing feature of a market economy is free alienability of ownership rights. The distinctive feature of a system of private property is that individuals are entitled to decide how resources will be used. *See id.* at 60. In practice, however, these closely related ideas tend to go hand-in-hand.

[20] Aristotle made the basic point: "Men pay most attention to what is their own: they care less for what is common; or, at any rate, they care for it only to the extent to which each is individually concerned." *See* ARISTOTLE, POLITICS § 1261, at 44 (Ernest Barker trans., 1946).

[21] This is a claim about the likely facts, not a necessary truth. Powerful social norms may operate as a surrogate for private property, helping to overcome some of the problems discussed in this text. *See* EDNA ULLMANN-MARGALIT, THE EMERGENCE OF NORMS (1977) (discussing norms as solution to collective action problems).

frequently attempt to accumulate resources. Social institutions that appeal to this inclination will increase social productivity.

Second, a system of private property performs a crucial coordinating function. It ensures that the multiple desires of hundreds, thousands, or millions of consumers will be reflected in market outcomes. In this way it protects against the perverse forms of scarcity produced by a command economy. Public officials cannot possibly know what and how much people will want in advance. Official decisions will thus create both too much and too little production. By contrast, a system of ownership rights signals people to devote their productive activity to areas in which that activity is most valued. A command-and-control economy is far inferior in this regard. Nearly every citizen of Eastern Europe has seen multiple illustrations of this tendency.

Third, the institution of private property solves, all at once, a serious collective action problem faced by people in any system without that institution.[22] When property is unowned, no one has a sufficient incentive to use it to its full advantage or to protect it against exploitation. The creation of private property overcomes this problem. It ensures that externalities from use will be internalized by people who are producing either social harms or social benefits.[23]

The point can be made more vivid by a glance at the problem of environmental deterioration. In recent years, it has been increasingly recognized that that problem—especially severe in Eastern Europe but of critical importance in the West as well—is in significant part[24] a product of the collective action problem produced by the fact that the air and water are public goods, that is, collectively rather than privately owned.[25] The consequence is that the environmental costs of polluting activity are widely diffused among the public and not "internalized," or taken into account, by polluters. Because they do not bear the direct cost, polluters lack an incentive to limit their polluting

---

[22] This point is elaborated in Harold Demsetz, *Toward a Theory of Property Rights*, 57 AM. ECON. REV. 347 (1967).

[23] The text uses a pre-Coasian understanding of both harms and benefits, *see* R.H. Coase, *The Problem of Social Cost*, 3 J. L. & ECON. 1 (1960); that is, it assumes that we can know without much reflection what sorts of things are "costs" of what sorts of activities. As Coase would have it, costs should be seen as relational entities produced by acts and omissions by many people and not clearly attributable to any one of them. An understanding that something is a cost of something else looks like a descriptive proposition, but it must actually be justified on moral grounds.

[24] This is not, of course, the only possible understanding of the environmental problem. There are other, noneconomic reasons to think that the level of pollution is too high. *See, e.g.*, STEVEN KELMAN, WHAT PRICE INCENTIVES? (1981).

[25] Garrett Hardin, *The Tragedy of the Commons*, 162 SCIENCE 1243 (1968).

activity. This system creates a built-in tendency toward excessive pollution levels.

A system without private property can be understood as a massive version of this unfortunate state of affairs. If property is unowned, everyone has an incentive to exploit it, and no one has an incentive to use it to its full advantage. Activity levels will have no relationship to their actual social costs and benefits.[26] Ownership rights overcome this difficulty. They operate like a well-functioning system of environmental law; they ensure that people have incentives to take account of both the benefits and the harms of what they do. This is an exceedingly important task for a constitutional democracy.

Finally, a system of private property creates the kind of stability and protection of expectations that are preconditions for investment and initiative, from both international and domestic sources. A company deciding whether to invest in a country will have a greater incentive to do so if it knows that its investment will be protected, and that government confiscation is prohibited by the nation's highest law. A citizen who is seeking to begin a business will be far more likely to do so if he can operate against a secure and stable background, protected against the vicissitudes of government policy. In this way, too, economic development can be facilitated by property rights.

B. *Property and Democracy*

The connection between property and prosperity may be reasonably well understood, but the right to private property has not always been considered a precondition for democracy. On the contrary, private property has frequently been thought to present an obstacle to democracy, and for this reason is sometimes deemed highly objectionable, or perhaps at best an institution necessary for economic growth and therefore to be reluctantly accepted despite its corrosive effects on the democratic process.[27]

There is indeed some tension between a system of property rights and a system of democracy. If property rights are secure, there is a firm limit on what the democratic process is entitled to do. In this sense, the tension is a real and enduring one. Notably, a new market

---

[26] I do not mean to endorse here the economic conception of costs and benefits, which is based on private willingness to pay and which will be unacceptable for many purposes. By any valuation, however, a system of collective ownership threatens to create the dangers mentioned in the text.

[27] I do not deal here with the relationship between individual development and property rights, though I believe that property rights do in fact promote that goal. For a good discussion, see WALDRON, *supra* note 18, at 343-89.

economy will likely impose conspicuous short-term costs[28]—unemployment and inflation—and in the emerging Eastern European democracies, there will probably be a continuous temptation to slow the transition to markets, or perhaps to reject it altogether. For this reason, the simultaneous transition to democracy and to economic markets—without the protection of constitutionalism—will be exceptionally difficult.

In important respects, however, it is quite plausible to think that the right to a stable system of property rights—one with which the state will interfere only occasionally or in a limited way, with a provision for compensation—is actually necessary to democracy and not opposed to it at all.

The most fundamental point about the relationship between property and democracy is that a right to own private property has an important and salutary effect on the citizens' relationship with the state and—equally important—on their understanding of that relationship. Because of this effect, it can be seen as a necessary precondition for the status of citizenship. Personal security and personal independence from the government are guaranteed in a system in which rights of ownership are protected through public institutions.

This theme has played a large role in republican thought. In the republican view, the status of the citizen implies a measure of independence from government power. This view was often associated with exclusionary practices—as, for example, in the notion that people without property should not be allowed to vote. One may deplore the exclusion without rejecting the proposition that a democratic state should attempt to give citizens a sense of independence from the state itself. In fact, the republican tradition, read in light of modern understandings, argues not for an abolition of private property, but instead for a system that attempts to ensure that everyone has some.

In this sense, the ownership of private property is closely associated with the role of law.[29] Both of these create a realm of private autonomy in which the citizenry can operate without fear of public

---

28 And long-term ones as well.

29 FRIEDRICK A. HAYEK, THE ROAD TO SERFDOM (1944). Initially Hayek's discussion of this point seems exceptionally confusing. He identifies markets and property on the one hand with the rule of law on the other; but the rule of law seems to imply not necessarily markets and property, but instead firm constraints on official discretion and institutions to enforce those constraints. Such constraints can be created with or without property; a command economy can set down clear rules in advance. Consider some of the American law of environmental protection, which relies on command-and-control methods, but which usually does not delegate open-ended authority to bureaucrats. But the identification seems more plausible in light of the considerations discussed in the text.

intrusion. That realm is indispensable to the public sphere itself. Only people with a degree of security from the state are able to participate without fear, and with independence, in democratic deliberations. In this sense, a sharp, legally-produced distinction between the private and the public can usefully serve the public sphere. Contrary to a conventional understanding, it need not harm it at all.[30]

Even more fundamentally, the division between private and public spheres is hard to defend or even to understand if it is treated as a metaphysical one, or as a claim that public power is not behind the private sphere. But if we understand the division as a political one, to be justified in public terms, it becomes both intelligible and indispensable. The (legal) creation of a private sphere, undertaken by the state, is a key element of the process of creating civil society and market ordering. If these can be justified, the private sphere itself becomes unproblematic, at least in the abstract. Of course its particular content can always be criticized, and is frequently subject to democratic redefinition.

The creation of private property can also be connected with the traditional proscription against punishment under vague laws or punishment without laws at all.[31] That proscription is designed to provide the citizenry with a wall of personal security, creating zones of freedom in which people can operate without fear. A system of private property performs closely related functions.

A central point here is that in a state in which private property does not exist, citizens are dependent on the good will of government officials, almost on a daily basis.[32] Whatever they have is a privilege and not a right. They come to the state as supplicants or beggars rather than as rightholders. Any challenge to the state may be stifled or driven underground by virtue of the fact that serious challenges could result in the withdrawal of the goods that give people basic security. A right to private property, free from government interference, is in this sense a necessary basis for a democracy.

In American law, the unconstitutional conditions doctrine operates as a response to this concern in the context of funding, licensing, and employment.[33] The government may not use its power to grant

---

[30] Cf. Stephen Holmes, *Gag Rules or the Politics of Omission*, in CONSTITUTIONALISM AND DEMOCRACY 19 (Jon Elster & Rune Slagstad eds., 1988).

[31] See the classic discussion in LON L. FULLER, THE MORALITY OF LAW (1964).

[32] The demoralizing effects of such regimes are well known to citizens of Communist nations, and indeed to visitors as well. Continuous dependence on government officials has a range of predictable corrosive effects on both character and spirit—a worthy subject of inquiry for a modern Tocqueville.

[33] *See generally* Kathleen M. Sullivan, *Unconstitutional Conditions*, 102 HARV. L. REV.

(say) welfare benefits as a way to pressure the exercise of free speech rights. In fact, the creation of property rights should be seen as an unconstitutional conditions doctrine writ very large. The idea is that government may not use its power over property to pressure rights in general; the existence of property rights generates a strong barrier against this form of pressure, just as the unconstitutional conditions doctrine provides a degree of insulation in narrower settings.

There is a more particular sense in which private property helps to promote resistance to government. If government owns the presses, or the means of distribution, freedom of speech cannot easily exist. Indeed, if government owns the newspaper itself, or distributes it in its discretion, there will be serious problems for the system of free expression. More generally, private ownership facilitates the kind of security on which diversity and pluralism depend. Political censorship may be altogether unnecessary if it is understood that current holdings are vulnerable to state control.

The final point is that one of the best ways to destroy a democratic system is to ensure that the distribution of wealth and resources is unstable and constantly vulnerable to reevaluation by the political process. A high degree of stability is necessary to allow people to plan their affairs, to reduce the effects of factional or interest group power in government, to promote investment, and to prevent the political process from breaking down by attempting to resolve enormous, emotionally laden issues about who is entitled to what. Stability and security—a sense of context—are important individual and collective goods. A system in which property rights are open to continuous readjustment will produce serious harm.[34]

In addition, government control of property—through constant readjustment of property rights—simply reintroduces the collective action problem originally solved by property rights. Public choice theory can be seen in part as a generalization of this simple insight.

Like the right to freedom of religious conscience,[35] moreover, the right to property helps create a flourishing civil society, an intermediate level between the government and the individual. The development of a civil society can in turn be understood as a mechanism both for creating economic prosperity and for promoting democratic self-governance. A constitutional system that respects private property

---

1413 (1989); Richard A. Epstein, *Unconstitutional Conditions, State Power, and the Limits of Consent*, 102 HARV. L. REV. 4 (1988).

[34] For this reason the embrace of "context-smashing" in ROBERTO M. UNGER, POLITICS: A WORK IN CONSTRUCTIVE SOCIAL THEORY (1987), seems most puzzling.

[35] *Cf.* Holmes, *supra* note 30.

should be regarded not as an effort to oppose liberal rights to collective self-government, but instead as a way of fortifying democratic processes.

I have not dealt with the question of redistribution. In the West, enthusiasm for property rights is often thought to entail a reluctance to allow redistribution, or (worse) complete indifference to the poor. The proper response is twofold. First, property rights help create wealth, and greater wealth will often benefit the most vulnerable as well. Time and again it has been shown that economic growth does more than welfare and employment programs to benefit the disadvantaged. Of course, growth does not do everything, and it must be supplemented. The second point, then, is that welfare and employment programs are a necessary part of any system of property rights. Such rights are best defended in self-consciously instrumental terms, because of the good things that they do. When they do not accomplish good, or enough good, they must be accompanied by other social strategies. Indeed, it is important to ensure not merely that everyone has a right to private property, but also that everyone has private property. Property rights without property ownership involve a degree of dependence that is debilitating to citizenship.

Properly understood, the defense of property rights is a defense of programs of redistribution as well. These programs are not designed to produce economic equality—a truly disastrous goal—but instead to bring about at least rough equality of opportunity and, even more important, freedom from desperate conditions, or from circumstances that impede basic human functioning.[36]

II. PROPERTY AND CONSTITUTION-MAKING

I have said that the task of economic development cannot be rigidly separated from the task of constitution-making. Without constitutional protection of property rights, there will be continuous pressure to adjust distributions of property on an ad hoc basis. When a group of people acquires a good deal of money, it will be tempting to tax them heavily. When another group verges on bankruptcy, there will be a temptation to subsidize them. After the fact, these steps may seem fair or even necessary; but if everyone knows that government might respond in this way, there will be a powerful deterrent to the development of a market economy. No citizen—and no international or domestic investor—can be secure of his immunity from the state.

---

[36] *See* Martha C. Nussbaum, *Aristotelian Social Democracy, in* LIBERALISM AND THE GOOD 203 (R. Bruce Douglass et al. eds., 1990); AMARTYA SEN, COMMODITIES AND CAPABILITIES (1985).

A pervasive risk is that governmental control over property rights will undo the decision, made in the basic system creating such rights, to solve a collective action problem faced by public ownership. If property rights are insecure—if they are subject to continuous governmental examination—the system will approach equivalence to one in which there are no such rights at all. This will introduce all of the problems, described in Part I, to which a system of property rights is supposed to respond. Above all, it will create individual vulnerability to government and at the same time produce both too little and too much use of existing resources. It will deter economic development and impair the movement toward democracy as well.

A. *In General*

I have claimed that a constitution can accomplish a great deal in easing the transition to economic markets and private property. In order for it to do so, constitutional protections must be judicially enforceable—that is, a court must be available to vindicate any rights that the constitution creates. Ordinary citizens must have a general right to raise constitutional objections before an independent tribunal authorized to provide redress. Without judicial review, constitutions tend to be worth little more than the paper on which they are written. They become mere words, or public relations documents, rather than instruments that confer genuine rights. While the efficacy of courts in carrying out social reform is disputable,[37] there can be little doubt that judicially enforceable constitutions can have a significant effect both on real-world results and on legal and social culture in general.[38] To be sure, some nations in the West have prospered with little or nothing in the way of judicial enforcement of constitutions. But these nations benefitted from the background of civil society, market economies, and well-defined property rights. For them, constitutional protections were far less important.

For Eastern Europe in general, the drafting of a constitution appears to pose two especially distinctive challenges. The first is to begin the process of creating a legal culture with firm judicial protection of individual rights. By individual rights I mean, first and foremost, traditional "negative" rights against government, prominent among them property ownership and freedom of contract. It is, of course, misleading to think of these as genuinely negative rights. They de-

---

[37] *See* GERALD N. ROSENBERG, THE HOLLOW HOPE (1991).

[38] Much of the effect is the deterrence of harmful governmental action before the fact, rather than governmental losses in actual litigated cases. The fear of losing in court has often proved a substantial deterrent to government.

pend for their existence on governmental institutions willing to recognize, create, and protect them. But this point is a semantic one; the defense of the traditional rights need not depend on the false claim that they are negative.

The second challenge is to facilitate the creation of a market economy and of a civil society—that is, a realm of private action containing institutions (churches, markets, corporations, labor unions, women's organizations, and so forth) that are independent of the state and minimally constrained by it. Through meeting these challenges, a constitution could simultaneously promote democratic goals and help bring about economic prosperity.

To carry out this task, constitution-makers should avoid three strategies that contain serious risks. All of these strategies are characteristic features of communist constitutionalism. Unfortunately, all of them appear to be influencing current debates in the post-communist era. The draft constitutions tend to replicate the errors of the communist constitutions themselves.[39]

1. *Aspirations*

The first such strategy is to use a constitution as a place for setting out very general social aspirations, or for imposing positive duties on government (such as the provision of a social welfare state including such guarantees as equitable remuneration, leisure time, social security, and occupational safety and health).[40] There are three reasons why this would be a dangerous strategy, at least under current conditions.

First, to state aspirations and impose positive duties—prominent of course in the Soviet Constitution—runs the risk of turning a constitution into something other than a legal document with real-world consequences. It is important to remember that if it is to create rights realistically enforceable in the world, a constitution should not list all things to which a country aspires. It should limit itself, for the most part, to rights that it is genuinely able to enforce. A constitution that creates positive rights is not likely to be subject to judicial enforcement because these rights are vaguely defined, simultaneously involve the interests of numerous people, and depend for their existence on active management of government institutions—something for which judges are ill-suited. The existence of unenforceable rights will in turn tend to destroy the negative rights—freedom of speech, freedom of

---

[39] These draft constitutions are on file with the Center on Constitutionalism in Eastern Europe, University of Chicago Law School, and can be obtained from that Center.

[40] *See supra* notes 2-16.

religion, and so forth—that might otherwise be genuine ones. If some rights are shown to be unenforceable, it is likely that others will be unenforceable as well.

The second problem with positive rights is that they will work against the general current efforts to diminish the sense of entitlement to state protection, and to encourage individual initiative and self-reliance. Both markets and democracy tend to develop these highly salutary characteristics. Sometimes liberal constitutionalism is praised because it responds accurately to "human nature," and does not try to tinker with it. There is undoubtedly something to this idea; efforts fundamentally to revise human character are usually doomed to failure. But liberal constitutionalism might be defended precisely on the ground that it has healthy effects on human character. Markets and democracy tend to create certain types, with many valuable characteristics.[41]

To say this is emphatically not to say that in the post-reform era, nations in Eastern Europe should eliminate social welfare protections and leave their citizens to the vicissitudes of the market. Such a route would be a recipe for disaster, since it would allow for mass suffering of the kind that is unacceptable in any nation. But these protections should be created at the level of ordinary legislation, and subject to democratic discussion, rather than placed in the foundational document.

The third problem with positive rights is that they establish government interference with markets as a constitutional duty. The current trend is to limit such interference, and to establish the preconditions for private markets, free trade, and free contract. To impose a constitutional duty of interference is to move in precisely the wrong direction.

A possible response to these points would be, first, that no constitution without positive rights is likely to be ratified and, second, that constitutions should be understood not merely as a place for setting forth legal rights but also as a forum for the identification of national ideals. The identification might serve educational and other functions; it might inform statutory interpretation. The point suggests that aspirations and positive rights may well belong at least in western constitutions, to encourage political attention to fundamental matters (such as shelter, subsistence, medical care, and environmental quality) and to ensure that statutes are interpreted in the light of a full range

---

[41] *See* JOHN S. MILL, CONSIDERATIONS ON REPRESENTATIVE GOVERNMENT (Oxford University Press ed., 1975) (1861). To say this is not of course to say that all of those characteristics are always good ones.

of social commitments. Ambiguities might therefore be resolved favorably to, for example, environmental protection.

In Eastern Europe, these ideas are less appealing in view of the large cultural shift now underway, and of the unfortunate legacy of communism. But perhaps a section outlining explicitly unenforceable positive rights could enhance the chances of ratification, play a beneficial role in public debate, and accomplish this without compromising the effort to produce genuinely enforceable "negative" rights. At most, any positive rights and aspirations should be understood to be unenforceable.

2. *Duties*

Another strategy, posing similar risks, is to use the constitution as a place for creating "duties" as well as rights. Such duties are not likely to be enforceable through courts. Their statement in a constitution tends to weaken the understanding that the document creates protected rights, with real meaning, against the state. Moreover, countries in Eastern Europe are attempting to eliminate the effects of the notion that the state imposes "duties" on citizens, rather than giving them rights. It may be that in the West, more emphasis on duties would be a good idea. Perhaps the western emphasis on "rights" has harmed social deliberation, especially in the United States, where duties should be taken more seriously.[42] But this is the point from which Eastern Europe ought to be emerging.

3. *No Distinction Between Public and Private Spheres*

Yet another dangerous strategy is to make constitutional provisions binding against private people and private organizations as well as against the state. In almost all western systems, the constitution applies only to the government, not to the people in general. This is extremely important, because it recognizes and helps create a private sphere—a civil society that operates independently of the state. It also frees up private organizations—employers, religious organizations, unions, and so forth—to act as they choose. If the people want to apply particular constitutional provisions to particular private organizations, of course they can do so, through ordinary legislation. But it is a mistake to apply such provisions through the constitution itself. Above all, this strategy works to erase the distinction between the private and public spheres, in a way that would tend to defeat

---

[42] *See* MARY ANN GLENDON, RIGHTS TALK (1991).

current aspirations in Eastern Europe. As noted, that distinction should be enthusiastically embraced on substantive political grounds.

Ironically, these dangers are more serious for the East than for the West. In the United States, for example, the institutions of private property and civil society are firmly in place, and social injustice frequently occurs precisely because of the absence of positive protections and of safeguards against the power of private institutions. The case for a firm right to some forms of social assistance is at least a plausible one in America. Such a right would not seriously jeopardize existing legal and social institutions; it could not possibly threaten the general belief in markets, solid property rights, and civil society.

In systems that are seeking to establish free markets and civil society for the first time, and that already have a strong public commitment to a social welfare state, the relevant considerations point in precisely the opposite direction. A dramatic legal and cultural shift, creating a belief in private property and a respect for markets, is indispensable. It is therefore surprising but true that the case for a strongly negative constitution, protecting market arrangements, is under current conditions powerful in Eastern Europe, even if it is ambiguous in the West.

We might draw a more general conclusion from this discussion. It is often said that constitutions, as a form of higher law, must be compatible with the culture and mores of those whom they regulate. In one sense, however, the opposite is true. Constitutional provisions should be designed to work against precisely those aspects of a country's culture and tradition that are likely to produce harm through that country's ordinary political processes. There is a large difference between the risks of harm faced by a nation committed by culture and history to free markets, and the corresponding risks in a nation committed by culture and history to social security and general state protection. Constitutions should work against the particular nation's most threatening tendencies. This point explains why extremely powerful safeguards against sex discrimination and ethnic and religious oppression are necessary in Eastern Europe (a point that would, however, take me well beyond the scope of this Essay). It is for this reason above all that constitutions designed for one nation are ill-adapted for use by others.

B.   Particular Provisions

In the next few years, it will be critical to develop a set of potential provisions for inclusion as an "economic freedoms" section of proposed constitutions. Indeed, this section could serve as one of the many possible new contributions of current constitution-makers to the general theory and practice of constitutionalism. There is no such section in western constitutions. Its design should be understood not as an effort to export western ideas to Eastern Europe, but instead as an exercise in constitution drafting intended specifically for problems in that part of the world.

I provide in this section a preliminary outline of constitutional provisions that might be adopted in the interest of creating a well-functioning system of property rights and economic markets. The outline amounts to little more than a list; it is intended only to provide a starting point for discussion.

1. *The Rule of Law*

In order to comply with the rule of law, a government must ensure that action may not be taken against citizens unless it has laid down, in advance, a pertinent law. The rule of law requires that any such restriction be clear rather than vague and publicly available rather than secret. It also must operate in the world as it does on the books.[43]

A guarantee of the rule of law is both an economic and a democratic right. It creates a wall of protection around citizens, giving a guarantee of immunity and ensuring that they may engage in productive activity without fear of the state. And by creating this wall of protection, the guarantee creates the kind of security and independence that are prerequisites for the role of a citizen in a democracy.

2. *Protection of Property Against Takings Without Compensation*

Many constitutions contain protections of this kind. The American Constitution embodies this idea in the Fifth Amendment, which says in part, "nor shall private property be taken for public use, without just compensation."[44] A provision of this general sort is indispensable on both economic and democratic grounds. Without such a provision, there is not, in fact or in law, a fully functioning system of private property.

3. *Protection of Property Against Takings Without Due Process*

This is a procedural rather than substantive protection of property. It means that citizens will be provided with a hearing before

---

[43] *See* FULLER, *supra* note 31, at 51-53.
[44] U.S. CONST. amend. V.

government may interfere with their holdings. A provision of this sort accomplishes two tasks.

First, it promotes accurate fact-finding. A hearing before an independent tribunal ensures that property will not be taken capriciously, or on the basis of whim, or for discriminatory or irrelevant reasons. In the hearing, it is necessary to show the facts that would justify a deprivation of property as a matter of law. Second, the right to a hearing carries out an important dignitary and participatory function. To say that people cannot be deprived of property without a hearing is to say that before it acts against them, the government must listen to what they have to say. This constraint improves governmental legitimacy as well. There is considerable evidence that people feel more secure and trustful if government affords them an opportunity to be heard before it undertakes action harmful to their interests.

4. *Protection of Contracts*

a. In General

Many constitutions protect contractual liberty from governmental invasion—as in, for example, a provision to the effect that government shall not pass any "Law impairing the Obligations of Contracts."[45] Constitutional protection of contracts ensures that when citizens engage in economic arrangements, they can do so free from the spectre of governmental intervention. Without this right, there will be a serious deterrent to productive activity.

For those countries that choose this route, there are two central questions. The first is whether the protection applies prospectively, or only retroactively. One might think that the state should be free to create the background against which people enter into agreements, and that therefore there should be no limit on the state's power to set out, in advance, limits on the terms on which people may contract. This is the approach taken in American law, which allows the government to affect contractual ordering however it wishes, so long as it does so in advance.

The second and related question is the extent to which the police power may limit contractual freedom. It is obvious that the state can forbid contracts for murder and assault. It will probably be agreed that the state may forbid contracts to work for less than a certain monthly wage, or for more than a certain number of hours per week. But does this mean that a state can impair a contract retroactively

---

45 U.S. CONST. art. I, §§ 9 & 10.

simply because it believes that the outcome is unfair to one side?[46] If so, freedom of contract becomes a dead letter.

b.   Ban on Wage and Price Controls

Limits on wages and prices—in the form of floors or ceilings—are of course a standard method for interfering with free markets. There is for this reason a plausible argument that Eastern European countries should commit themselves, in advance, to a decision not to take this course, which is often appealing in the short run but extremely destructive for the future.

A particular problem here is that well-organized private groups will frequently seek government assistance, in the form of regulatory laws enabling them to function as a cartel. This strategy might at first glance have a public interest justification, but it can ultimately be disastrous. For example, a system that creates minimum prices for milk may help some milk producers, but it will also create scarcity in an important commodity and also overcharge consumers, many of them likely to be poor. Maximum prices can in turn produce scarcity, often of important commodities.

A system in which government sets minimum and maximum prices will eventually produce many of the economic and democratic problems that Eastern European nations are attempting to solve. The United States has witnessed this very problem with regulation of energy prices; such regulation helped produce the energy crisis of the 1970s.

On the other hand, it is also plausible to think that controls on wages and prices will sometimes be desirable during and after the transition to a market economy. Even in such an economy, legal controls on wages and prices sometimes have at least plausible justifications. The category is not limited to the minimum wage; it includes price supports of various kinds as well. A ban on wage and price controls may be excessively strong medicine for the problem at hand.

---

[46] Sometimes people think that the appropriate remedy for a harsh bargain is to disallow the bargain. But it is not at all clear that this remedy helps the weaker side. Usually someone in bad circumstances will be presented with a range of unfavorable alternatives, and will choose the least unfavorable of them. To disallow this option does nothing to improve the bad circumstances, and simply forces the person to choose the second-least unfavorable option. It is important for the emerging democracies to understand this point. Efforts to close off market options are tempting when those options seem few and produce harsh results, but usually the closing off is an utterly ineffectual remedy.

5. *Occupational Liberty*

a. Protection of Free Entry into Occupations, Trades, and Business

A provision of this sort can be found in the German Constitution.[47] This is a salutary protection against governmental restrictions on an important form of liberty, one that is part and parcel of free labor markets.

It does, however, contain an ambiguity, similar to that arising under the protection of freedom of contract. It seems clear that government can impose certain limits requiring that jobs be performed by people who are trained to do them. It can, for example, ensure that doctors actually know something about medicine, or that lawyers are trained in the law. If this is so, it will be necessary to distinguish between legitimate and illegitimate interferences with free entry into occupations, rather than simply to say that the government has no role to play in this regard. This issue is probably best resolved through judicial interpretation, not in the text itself.

b. The Right to Choose One's Occupation

A provision of this general sort can also be found in the German Constitution.[48] It overlaps a good deal with protection of free entry into trades, and has similar virtues. It also raises a similar interpretive difficulty, involving the legitimacy of provisions designed to ensure that people are genuinely qualified for jobs.

c. Prohibition on Forced Labor

This provision seems indispensable to the emerging Eastern European democracies. It nicely complements the right to choose one's occupation by saying that government cannot require people to engage in work that it prefers them to undertake. It also tends to guarantee free labor markets. Such a provision also carries forward, in a particularly crisp way, the traditional liberal prohibition on slavery, embodied in the general idea that "we were [not] made for one anothers uses."[49]

6. *Prohibition on Government Monopolies (de jure)*

If the goal is to create a market economy, the constitution should say that government may not give itself a legal monopoly over any

---

[47] GRUNDGESETZ [Constitution] [GG] art. 12 (F.R.G.).

[48] *Id.*

[49] JOHN LOCKE, TWO TREATISES ON GOVERNMENT 311 (Peter Laslett ed., 1960).

sector of the economy. A right of exclusive management of agriculture or telecommunications is a sure way to stifle competition and impair economic productivity. Indeed, such a right will reintroduce all of the problems discussed in Part I of this Essay. The government should be banned from embarking on this course.

Under certain narrow conditions, an exception might be permitted—as, for example, where government cannot efficiently perform a certain function unless it creates a monopoly, and where competition is impossible. This is an extremely rare circumstance, however, and a strong burden should be imposed on government to show that it is present in any particular case.

It would probably be a mistake to create a constitutional prohibition on government monopolies that exist in fact but that are not created through law. In the transition from communism, some de facto monopolies are likely, and it is hard to see how a constitutional court can prevent them. Here we encounter one of the limits of constitutionalism: the narrow remedial power of the judiciary.

7. *Nondiscrimination Against Private Enterprises*

It probably follows from what has been said thus far that government should be constrained from imposing special disabilities on private enterprises, that is, from taxing, regulating, or otherwise discouraging private entities from operating on equal terms with official organs. Government might well seek to create such disabilities as a way of insulating itself from competition or of protecting its own instrumentalities. If it does so, it will create severe harms to civil society and to economic markets. A prohibition could accomplish considerable good.

Of course, there will be some hard interpretive questions here. To see whether there is discrimination, one will have to explore whether private and public enterprises are similarly situated. This will not always be an easy question to answer.

8. *The Right to Travel Within the Nation and To and From the Nation*

Protection of the right to travel serves both economic and democratic functions. Especially in a system with some degree of jurisdictional decentralization, the right to travel is a safeguard against oppressive regulation. If citizens can leave, there is a powerful deterrent to such regulation; people are able to "vote with their feet." It is fully plausible to think that in the United States, the right to travel has been one of the greatest safeguards against legislation that is harmful to economic development. The right to travel internally creates a built-in check on tyranny, at least in a federal system. The right to leave one's nation serves the same function. In this sense, the right is simultaneously an economic and a political one.

9.   *The Fiscal Constitution*

It might be appropriate to introduce a series of provisions amounting to a "fiscal constitution," that is, a document designed to regulate institutions dealing with the relationship between government and the economy. Of course, such provisions would overlap with those discussed above. I offer a few examples here. I do not discuss monetary arrangements and institutions because they would call for lengthy discussion, but certainly provisions bearing on those issues will warrant consideration.

a.   Ban on Tariffs and Duties

It has probably been established, through both theory and practice, that tariffs and duties are on balance harmful to the citizens of a nation. Despite this fact, there is constant pressure for these measures, from the usually narrow groups and interests that would benefit from them. Because tariffs and duties would create aggregate harms but short-term and narrow gains, it might be sensible to enact, in advance, a constitutional prohibition against them. The problem with this strategy is that it is at least reasonable to think that tariffs and duties are necessary under some conditions, and perhaps their availability is an important device for government to have while it is negotiating with other nations.

b.   Balanced Budget

In the United States, there has recently been some interest in a constitutional amendment that would require "balanced budgets." The case for such an amendment is not obscure. For legislators or governments with short-term electoral and domestic problems, it may well make sense to spend more than one receives. The dangers of such a course are felt by future generations. A constitutional provision might be directed against this form of myopia.

On reflection, however, it would probably be a mistake to include such a provision in a constitution. A decision not to balance the budget might be the right one in any particular year. The consequences of unbalanced budgets are sharply disputed among economists. It is hardly clear that they are seriously harmful. Moreover, a provision to this effect would not readily be subject to judicial enforcement.

c.   Restrictions on the Taxing Power

A fiscal constitution might also impose restrictions on the power of taxation. Most plausible here would be a ban on retroactive taxation. If government may tax resources accumulated in a period in which they could not be taxed, it should not, consistently with the rule of law, be permitted to introduce a tax that will be imposed retroactively. There are also questions here about possible restrictions on progressivity.

d.   Ban on Controls on Export or Import of Currency

It might well make sense to accompany a right to travel with a prohibition on legal controls on the export or import of currency. Such a prohibition could serve similar functions in guarding against protectionism.

III.   Problems

I have not dealt with two problems of special importance to the emerging Eastern European democracies. The first is that the interpretation of constitutional provisions is of critical importance, and interpretation cannot be entirely constrained by those who write the constitution. I have argued, for example, that a constitution should ensure that private property cannot be taken without just compensation. But a constitution cannot possibly spell out, in advance, what government action must be in order to qualify as a "taking." Because of the limitations of language, that task must be left to judges dealing with particular cases and particular measures. The same point applies to all provisions now under consideration in Eastern Europe and elsewhere. Constitutions set out the broad outlines for decision, but in light of the limitations of words and human foresight, they cannot do much more than that.

More fundamentally, the meaning of any text is a function of interpretive principles. To say that the original understanding is binding, or that there should be an interpretive presumption in favor of property rights, or that courts should minimally intrude into political processes, or that a commitment to constitutional equality is a commitment to the elimination of castes—all these are fully understandable claims, but their contents are rarely "in" any text, and they must be justified in substantive terms. Frequently debates over interpretive principles purport to be semantic; actually they involve the selection, on political and moral grounds, of norms with which to give meaning to constitutional texts. No document can avoid the grant of discretion to interpreters in choosing among various possible norms.

The second problem is that a system of private property has to be created rather than merely recognized. In light of the current experience of Eastern Europe, the notion of *laissez-faire* as a description of markets stands exposed as the conspicuous fiction that it is. Markets depend for their existence not on passivity, but on active governmental choices. Most of those choices cannot be made in a constitution. The movement for privatization—for the creation of property rights—is exceptionally important, and it must accompany the writing and implementation of constitutional rights. The constitution will work against the backdrop of property rights, and it will protect those rights once created; but the act of creation will not occur at the constitutional level.

In Eastern Europe, the problem is especially formidable. It is unfortunate but true that existing ownership rights often have their source in arbitrariness or injustice. Who owns what is a function of past acts, public and private, many of which are irrelevant or unacceptable from the moral point of view. In the West, this fact can be conveniently ignored, because the role of fate, injustice, force, or the state in initial allocations is not really visible. And in important respects this is all to the good; a constant focus on the origins of property rights might make it hard to proceed, day to day, with existing allocations. In Eastern Europe, by contrast, any allocation will be very visible indeed. It will occur all at once or in various steps, but in any case people will see that some people are getting property through government decree, and others are not. The task of allocation is for this reason much more difficult.

Sometimes it is thought that the allocation of initial entitlements "does not matter" in the sense that at least in the absence of transactions costs, people will bargain their way toward the same outcome regardless of that allocation. This basic idea is the fundamental claim behind the Coase theorem.[50] Although the Coase theorem has been highly influential in American law, and has contributed to many major advances in our understanding, the proposition is sometimes false. Its falsehood relates in important ways to current reform efforts in Eastern Europe.

The central point here is that whether people have a preference for a commodity, a right, or anything else is in part a function of

---

[50] *See* Coase, *supra* note 23.

whether the government has allocated it to them in the first instance. There is simply no way to avoid the task of initially allocating an entitlement, and the decision to grant an entitlement to one person frequently makes that person value that entitlement more than he would if the right had been allocated to someone else. (It also makes other people value it less than they otherwise would.) The initial allocation serves to influence, to legitimate, and to reinforce social understandings about presumptive rights of ownership. That allocation has an important causal connection to individual perceptions about the good or right in question.

The point is simply a factual one, and it has received considerable empirical confirmation. The effect on preferences of the initial allocation of a commodity or an entitlement is commonly described as the "endowment effect."[51] The endowment effect has immense importance. It suggests that any initial allocation of an entitlement—and government cannot refuse to make an initial allocation—may well have effects on preferences.

Economists and psychologists have found this effect in many places, including both real exchange experiments and surveys. For example, a recent study showed that people who were allocated certain consumption objects—pens, coffee mugs, and binoculars—placed a much higher valuation on those objects than did those who were required to purchase them.[52] No such effects were observed for money tokens in otherwise identical experiments. In a similar study, some participants were given a mug and others a chocolate bar; both were told that they could exchange one for the other. Participants in a third group, not given a prior entitlement, were told that they could select one or the other; 56% of these selected the candy bar. By contrast, 89% of those initially given the mug refused to trade it for the candy bar, and only 10% of those initially given the candy were willing to trade it for the mug.[53] The different evaluations could not be explained by reference to anything other than the initial endowment.

Studies based on survey research have made similar findings. One such study found differences between payment and compensation

---

[51] It was first so called in Richard Thaler, *Toward a Positive Theory of Consumer Choice*, 1 J. ECON. BEHAV. & ORG. 39, 41 (1980).

[52] Daniel Kahneman et al., *Experimental Tests of the Endowment Effect and the Coase Theorem*, 98 J. POL. ECON. 1325 (1990). *See also* Jack L. Knetsch, *The Endowment Effect and Evidence of Nonreversible Indifference Curves*, 79 AM. ECON. REV. 1277 (1989); Jack L. Knetsch & J.A. Sinden, *Willingness to Pay and Compensation Demanded: Experimental Evidence of an Unexpected Disparity in Measures of Value*, 99 Q. J. ECON. 507 (1984).

[53] Knetsch, *supra* note 52.

valuations of trees in a park of about five to one.[54] When hunters were questioned about the potential destruction of a duck habitat, they said that they would be willing to pay an average of $247 to prevent the loss—but would demand no less than $1044 to accept it.[55] In another study, participants required payments to accept degradation of visibility ranging from five to more than sixteen times higher than their valuations based on their willingness to pay.[56] According to yet another study, the compensation demanded for accepting a new risk of immediate death of .001% was one or two orders of magnitude higher than the amount of willingness to pay to eliminate an existing risk of the same size.[57] A related survey showed similarly large status quo biases in willingness to pay for changes in risks.[58] A powerful status quo bias appears to affect reactions to risks or losses.

In many settings, then, it has been shown that people place a higher value on rights or goods that they currently hold than they place on the same goods when in the hands of others. There are multiple possible explanations for endowment effects. In many cases, endowment effects reflect a genuine preference-shaping consequence from the initial assignment.[59] Endowment effects may reflect an effort to reduce cognitive dissonance. High valuation of what one owns, and low valuation of what one does not, is a means of reducing dissonance, and in some respects it is highly adaptive. Perhaps, too, the initial allocation has an important legitimating effect, suggesting that

---

[54] David S. Brookshire & Don L. Coursey, *Measuring the Value of a Public Good: An Empirical Comparison of Elicitation Procedures*, 77 Am. Econ. Rev. 554, 562-63 (1987).

[55] Judd Hammack & G.M. Brown, Waterfowl and Wetlands: Toward Bioeconomic Analysis 26-27 (1974).

[56] Robert D. Rowe et al., *An Experiment on the Economic Value of Visibility*, 7 J. Envtl. Econ. & Mgmt. 1, 8 (1980).

[57] Thaler, *supra* note 51, at 44.

[58] Thus people were willing to pay $3.78 on average to reduce the risk from an insecticide, but 77% refused to buy the product at any price, however reduced, if the risk level would increase by an equivalent amount. K.P. Viscusi et al., *An Investigation of the Rationality of Consumer Valuations of Multiple Health Risks*, 18 RAND J. Econ. 465, 478 (1987).

[59] Such effects may come from experience; people who use a product or have an entitlement may learn to appreciate its value. The effects may be a product of strategic considerations; someone may be unwilling to give up a right because the concession would reveal weakness in bargaining. Sometimes the effects might be produced by the wealth effect of the initial allocation of the entitlement. Different allocations produce differences in wealth—someone with more entitlements is to that extent richer—and perhaps some allocations have wealth effects sufficiently large to affect the point to which people will bargain.

Such effects might also derive from anticipated after-the-fact regret. People who trade one good for another may think that in the event of disappointment, they will be left not only with a good of uncertain value, but also with a feeling of responsibility for that very fact. Notably, some of these explanations do not depend on real preference changes at all. They account for endowment effects while holding preferences constant. But these sorts of explanations do not appear sufficient.

the entitlement "naturally" belongs where it has been placed, and putting a social burden on even voluntary changes. In some cases the divergence between willingness to pay and willingness to accept is probably a product of the change in social norms brought about by the change in the allocation of the entitlement.[60]

For present purposes, it is not necessary to explain the mechanism behind endowment effects. It is enough to say that the initial allocation has preference-shaping effects and that when this is so, there is no acontextual "preference" with which to do legal or political work.

If all this is correct, large consequences follow. In Eastern Europe, property rights have yet to be allocated in many cases. A series of decisions—not feasibly placed in the constitution—must be made to establish who owns what. The distinguishing feature of a system of freedom of contract is that rights of ownership are alienable. But such a system can operate with quite different initial allocations of rights. Should workers have a presumptive right to be fired only for cause, a right that employers can buy through contract? Or should employers have a presumptive right to fire employees at will, a right that employees can purchase in an agreement? Does the right to own a plant include the right to pollute, subject to an agreement to cease, obtained by neighbors? Or do the neighbors own that right initially, with a provision for purchase from the plant owner? A regime of freedom of contract is consistent with all of these systems. The key point is that the initial allocation will affect the valuation of the rights by both current owners and would be purchasers. And if it does so, the initial allocation will have important consequences for ultimate outcomes.

For transition in Eastern Europe, it is also important to understand that much of governmental behavior—the acts of government and of those who seek to influence it—might well be a product of endowment effects. The point has a range of positive implications; indeed, it helps to explain a number of political outcomes and political behavior. Political participants should be able to exploit endowment effects by attempting to describe the status quo in a way that takes advantage of the phenomenon of status quo bias. So too, political actors are frequently successful when they are able to identify and control the perception of the status quo. One example—prominent in Eastern Europe before and after communism—is provided by con-

---

[60] The endowment effect should probably not be seen as a case of individual irrationality, as has been found in certain reactions to low-probability events or in certain kinds of preference reversals. It is by no means clear that status quo bias is irrational.

stant political efforts to lower expectations by describing the status quo, or the expected status quo, as systemically worse than in fact it is—so that the citizenry will rarely perceive deviations as losses but instead only as gains. The phenomenon occurs during elections, during wars, and during debate over the economy.

With respect to current dilemmas in Eastern Europe, the existence of endowment effects shows the importance of initial entitlements in creating preferences and beliefs. Probably the most that can be said is that the initial allocation should be undertaken democratically and with a firm awareness of the (perhaps surprising) consequences. But the constitution cannot plausibly make that allocation. It can only protect property rights once they have been created. Like the problem of interpretation, the problem of allocating initial entitlements points to important limits in constitutionalism.

CONCLUSION

The three transitions now taking place in Eastern Europe should be brought more closely together. Above all, the task of constitution-making can help facilitate the transitions to economic markets and to democratic self-government. To this end, I have outlined some possible constitutional provisions designed to protect the basic institutions of private property, free markets, and civil society. A similar analysis might be applied to provisions not directly concerned with the protection of markets—including rights to associational liberty; freedom from discrimination on the basis of sex, race, religion, and ethnicity; and rights of political and religious liberty.

The most general point is that with strong constitutional protection of private property and economic markets, nations in Eastern Europe can take an important step on the way to both economic growth and democratic self-government. The connection between private property and prosperity is well understood; the experience of Eastern Europe confirms a less obvious point, involving the contributions of such rights to the security indispensable to citizenship. In this light such rights can be defended not on the ground that they conform to "human nature," but on the contrary as part of a system having salutary rather than destructive effects on human character. Both markets and democracy are most plausibly defended in these terms.

To say this is hardly to challenge programs that redistribute resources, training, or opportunities to the poor or that otherwise protect the vulnerable. The instrumental arguments that justify private property call for efforts to ensure that everyone can have some of it.

These arguments powerfully support government programs supplementing market arrangements.[61]

Without strong constitutional provisions on behalf of property rights, civil society, and markets, there will probably be a substantial temptation to intrude on all of these institutions, and, by so doing, recreate the very problems that such institutions are supposed to solve. In Eastern Europe, the task of constitution-making is more difficult, and far more pressing, than it was in the West, in which a well-established backdrop of rights and institutions was already in place. The ironic conclusion is that the case for a firm negative constitution, and for creation and protection of property rights and free markets, is very strong in Eastern Europe; this is so even if the corresponding case is, in western countries, somewhat ambiguous.

No constitution can make the initial allocations of property rights; this must be left to democratic processes. Moreover, no constitutional text can fully control the process of interpretation, and thus there is always a risk that written documents will be given a meaning other than that which would promote a nation's welfare. But large-scale social change is always accompanied by risks, and the ubiquity of risk provides no reason for resignation or discouragement. A constitution offering firm protection to property rights could do a great deal to ease the transition to markets and democracy.

---

[61] To say this is not, however, to say that such programs should be guaranteed constitutionally. Nor is it to deny that difficult instrumental judgments must be made about the efficacy of different programs, some of which undoubtedly undermine their own goals by creating dependency.

TRANSITIONAL CONSTITUTIONS

Arthur J. Jacobson

Cass Sunstein urges the states of Eastern Europe to protect private property in their constitutions, and do it right away.[1] If they do not, he warns, they will hobble the transition to market economies and disable their citizens from participating in democratic government.[2]

I dispute Professor Sunstein's thesis using two texts: Alfred Chandler's study of the requisites of industrial enterprise, *Scale and Scope: The Dynamics of Industrial Capitalism*,[3] and Shakespeare's drama of constitutional transition, *King Lear*.[4] Chandler's work casts doubt on Professor Sunstein's proposition that the exact constitutional arrangements for private property as we know it in the United States are essential to democracy and a market economy and questions whether private property is the core institution of development even in the United States.[5] A reading of Shakespeare's *King Lear* suggests that Professor Sunstein, like Lear, overvalues the power of words to effect fundamental transformations in political conditions.

Echoing Shakespeare, I propose the idea of a "transitional constitution"—a constitution embodying, embracing, and propelling forward in the basic framework those political paradoxes which the great political forces are unable, for the moment, to resolve in permanent accommodations. A transitional constitution postpones the accommodation of political paradoxes using unstable principles instead for

---

[1] Cass R. Sunstein, *On Property and Constitutionalism*, supra p. 383, 384.

[2] *Id.*

[3] ALFRED D. CHANDLER, JR., SCALE AND SCOPE: THE DYNAMICS OF INDUSTRIAL CAPITALISM (1990).

[4] WILLIAM SHAKESPEARE, KING LEAR (Kenneth Muir, ed., Harvard Univ. Press 1963) [hereinafter KING LEAR].

[5] By "private property," Professor Sunstein means the institution of private property as it exists today in western industrial democracies, where "individuals are entitled to decide how resources will be used." Sunstein, *supra* note 1, at 387 n.19. By this definition, few individuals in the United States could be understood to own private property in the means of production, where in the great bulk of the Fortune 500 corporations, just as in government, officers make management decisions, not "individuals." From the other side of the equation, many officers, both in government and in industry, treat offices like fiefdoms resembling property.

carrying on in the absence of agreement on one or more elements of the basic framework.

The paradox Eastern Europeans must embrace in the first round of constitution making is that establishing capitalist property in the name of efficiency requires abolishing socialist property, despite broad expectations masses of citizens formed in it over the past two generations.[6] In order to transform their political economies, Eastern Europeans must undermine the institution of property in the name of the institution of property—destroy property in order to save it. It would be surprising (and possibly mistaken) if the new constitutions of Eastern Europe did not reflect and acknowledge this paradox. Hence, even if we knew that Eastern Europe was headed towards a private property regime much like our own (which I doubt), it might be appropriate for those nations to adopt transitional constitutions, exactly as we did in 1789.

I.   PROPERTY OR "ORGANIZATIONAL CAPABILITY"?

Chandler's *Scale and Scope* speaks to Professor Sunstein's first point—that failing to protect private property in the new constitutions of Eastern Europe will impair the transition to market economies. Chandler proposes a core of the dynamics of industrial capitalism. He calls this core "the organizational capabilities of the enterprise as a unified whole."[7] According to Chandler,

[t]hese organizational capabilities were the collective physical facilities and human skills as they were organized within the enterprise. They included the physical facilities in each of the many operating units—the factories, offices, laboratories—and the skills of the employees working in such units.[8]

Chandler compares three exemplary approaches to achieving the organizational capabilities for carrying on modern industrial capitalism: the United States,[9] Great Britain,[10] and West Germany.[11]

Chandler argues that in the United States the institutions in which organizational capability flourished were fully in place by World War I, when American "competitive managerial capitalism" was deploying teams of production and separating ownership of capi-

---

6 Almost four generations of citizens in the former Soviet Union were governed under socialist regimes.

7 CHANDLER, *supra* note 3, at 594.

8 *Id.*

9 Chandler terms this regime "competitive managerial capitalism." *See id.* at part II.

10 He terms this system "personal capitalism." *See id.* at part III.

11 He calls the third "cooperative managerial capitalism." *See id.* at part IV.

tal from management of enterprise.[12] Chandler's picture of the institutionalization of organizational capability in the United States bears little resemblance to the ordinary understanding of private property as Professor Sunstein employs it. "Personal capitalism" in Great Britain comes the closest of Chandler's models to a property conception of enterprise. But Chandler points out that the lingering of personal capitalism into our century hampered British capitalists from achieving as much organizational capability as their American and West German counterparts in the same period.[13]

Nothing in Chandler's work suggests that the American, British, and West German approaches exhaust the institutional possibilities for achieving organizational capability. One would be most interested, for example, to hear Chandler's view on Japan, which may be far more relevant to Eastern European conditions than our own system.[14] Certainly, Eastern Europeans shopping for models would want to investigate the Japanese version of organizational capability closely, not only because it is successful, but also because it is even less bound to the usual private property conceptions than our own. At any rate, Chandler would almost certainly agree that the Eastern European political economies could yield new approaches to organizational capability—approaches about which we can know little in advance of their implementation. History, accident, and the peculiarities of the Eastern European situation and the creativity of her peoples will determine the exact form in which those nations achieve, or fail to achieve, the organizational capabilities necessary for modern industrial enterprise.

Take, as an example of the accommodations Eastern European regimes may have to make, Professor Sunstein's suggestion

> that government should be [constitutionally] constrained from imposing special disabilities on private enterprises, that is, from taxing, regulating, or otherwise discouraging private entities from operating on equal terms with official organs.[15]

Like Japanese firms, many enterprises in these formerly socialist regimes undertook to provide health care, housing, schooling, and other services to the families of their workers. Should the new governments insist that these community structures be immediately abolished? It is easy to think of strong reasons not to. A regime might be morally

---

[12] *Id.* at 47-49.

[13] *Id.* at 235-37.

[14] Chandler's remarks on Japan in *Scale and Scope* are sparse and do not attempt to create a model. *See id.* at 616-17.

[15] Sunstein, *supra* note 1, at 403.

unprepared to tolerate the probable suffering which would result from such a restriction. A regime might acknowledge the political reality that employees of socialist enterprises are also voters. It might also wish to use old community structures to experiment with novel forms of organizational capability. Professor Sunstein would allow the state to treat public and private enterprises differently, so long as they are not "similarly situated."[16] Apart from the "hard interpretive questions" to which Professor Sunstein alludes[17] ("hard" is not the word; I prefer "mind-boggling"), the principle of nondiscrimination does not address the issue of whether a government ought to put public enterprises in a situation "justifying" different treatment in the first place. To say that different legal treatment of a bad situation is rational (such as affirmative action) does not lead to the conclusion that the government ought to create the situation. Furthermore, shifting attention from the desirability of the situation to the rationality of the government's legal treatment of it is not necessarily a step forward, however well-intentioned.

Undoubtedly Professor Sunstein would argue that "noneconomic" values are as important in democratic regimes as organizational capability. However, it may be necessary to sacrifice some degree of organizational capability to satisfy these other values. Chief among them in our society is personal autonomy. Professor Sunstein insists on tracing even this value through the right to property.[18] But institutions of property are not the only ones that can support autonomy. Suppose, instead, we traced autonomy through federalism and simple ideas of administrative law. We could conceive of firms as agencies that administer a delegation of power from a central authority, provide these agencies with guaranties of independence, constrain their decision-making powers by some standard of review promulgated by the central authority, and so forth.[19] In other words, we could construct as many of our property concepts as we wished

---

[16] *Id.* Professor Sunstein's tolerance for different treatment flows logically from the principle of nondiscrimination.

[17] *Id.*

[18] *Id.* at 390-91. Professor Sunstein does not say whether autonomy, in his view, would ever conflict with the achievement of organizational capability. Chandler's study provides powerful evidence that it does.

[19] *See* Gerald E. Frug, *The Ideology of Bureaucracy in American Law*, 97 HARV. L. REV. 1276 (1984) (discussing bureaucratic organizations in terms of corporate and administrative law). *See also* Arthur J. Jacobson, *The Private Use of Public Authority: Sovereignty and Associations in the Common Law*, 29 BUFF. L. REV. 599, 600 (1980) ("[t]he law of associations . . . can properly be understood only as a distribution of sovereignty to private persons beyond the precincts of the state apparatus.").

through administrative law and federalism.[20] We need not mention "property" to achieve the benefits of autonomy, nor trace autonomy, as Professor Sunstein does, through the institutions of property alone.[21]

The role of property in our original constitutional framework has been repeatedly contested, and I will not rehearse the debates. Even excluding Jefferson, the Framers differed in their views on the role of property in the Constitution, and those views were not always obvious. In Number 10 of *The Federalist*,[22] Madison made the rights of property derivative from the "faculties of men." "The protection of these faculties," he wrote, "is the first object of government."[23] He does not propose protection of the rights of property as the first object. Faction results because citizens own "different degrees and kinds of property,"[24] and a principal task of government is to manage the clash of factions over the great interests of the republic. Property cannot be protected absolutely, only moderately in a shifting program of careful management. This is clearly not the language of constitutional right.[25]

Madison's realism about the political adjustments the institution of property requires in democratic society is even more appropriate today, when the "degrees and kinds" of property have become even more various. In a political economy dominated by teams of production and the separation of ownership of capital from management of enterprise, constitutional protection of property rights as Professor Sunstein proposes may have only symbolic significance. These symbols may be important in our tradition, but they need not play the same role in others.

Each state must battle out the clashes Madison described on its

---

[20] In a sense, that is exactly how the high-medieval lawyers in our tradition arrived at the concept of property.

[21] My colleague, Michael Herz, has suggested as another analogy, in light of my discussion of *King Lear*, that parents can give children lots of autonomy without necessarily giving them much property, or give them property without necessarily giving them much autonomy, as in *King Lear*.

[22] THE FEDERALIST No. 10 (James Madison).

[23] *Id.* at 131 (Benjamin F. Wright ed., 1961).

[24] *Id.*

[25] Here I must leave aside the poverty of current American theories about property. Unfortunately, we must turn to a different tradition—Hegel's *Philosophy of Right*—to get a decent understanding of property in a modern political economy. He describes at least three strands in the institution of property—the abstract property of legal persons, family capital and the capital of corporations—and the distinct role each strand plays in the political economy of the modern state. *See* G.W.F. HEGEL, PHILOSOPHY OF RIGHT ¶¶ 41-70, 170-72, 199-208, and 250-56 (T.M. Knox trans., 1952) (1942). Hegel rejects attaching a property idea to an office. *See id.* at ¶ 277.

own. Each must come to its own solutions. If the states of Eastern Europe do not, if they bring in carpetbaggers to give them the best advice on the latest constitutional fashions, then they risk achieving only constitutional syncretism—common enough in our century—not real transformation.[26] The Mayans in Chiapas practice their ancient religion under the watchful eyes of the parish priest, using Catholic rite as a secret code. Even if the priest is not aware, the parishioners know what the rite truly signifies.[27] Would the Eastern Europeans be any different were they to adopt all the wonderful Sunsteinian constitutional provisions? They may adopt provisions very much like the ones Professor Sunstein proposes, if only because international financial institutions require it, or because they wish to express revulsion for the ancien regime. But the risk still remains that they will mean something quite different by the provisions, and Professor Sunstein, along with the rest of us, will not know that because we will not know, or care to know, the secret code.

II.   A LESSON IN TRANSITIONAL CONSTITUTIONS

It is probable that the states of Eastern Europe can not immediately resolve all their clashes of faction. They need, and I believe they can have, what I call a "transitional constitution." The second text which addresses this idea is *King Lear*. "Lear," in Scots, means instruction or lesson.[28] This man learned a lesson—a lesson about the difficulties of constitutional transition. What Lear learned, at a terrible cost, was that he overvalued the power of words to effect fundamental political transformation.

Lear's first word in the play is "meantime." "Meantime we shall express our darker purpose."[29] The action of the play takes place "meantime," in a period of transition. Lear is handing over political authority to the husbands of his three daughters.[30] He wishes to divest himself of "rule, interest of territory, cares of state."[31] "['T]is our fast intent," he says, "To shake all cares and business from our age."[32] But he would not give away the *title* of king. After he has

---

[26] Professor Sunstein certainly does not recommend importing American constitutional provisions *in haec verba* into foreign circumstances. He does, however, wish to import what he regards as the functional requisites of our constitutional system, at least in the area of property.

[27] *See* FRANK CANCIAN, ECONOMICS AND PRESTIGE IN A MAYA COMMUNITY: THE RELIGIOUS CARGO SYSTEM IN ZINACANTAN 12 (1965).

[28] 6 THE OXFORD ENGLISH DICTIONARY 156 (3d ed. 1970).

[29] KING LEAR, *supra* note 4, act I, sc. 1, line 36.

[30] Cordelia thus needs to marry in order to get her share of the inheritance.

[31] KING LEAR, *supra* note 4, act I, sc. 1, lines 49-50.

[32] *Id*. at lines 38-39.

given the kingdom to Albany and Cornwall, he says:

> Only we shall retain
> the name, and all the additions to a king;
> the sway, revenue, execution of the rest,
> Beloved sons, be yours . . . .[33]

Lear thinks he can retain the name of king, and that giving away "the sway, revenue, execution of the rest" is of no import—just burdens as far as he is concerned. The play goes on to prove that Lear cannot do what he wishes.[34] Retaining the title of king by itself means nothing. Nor does having "the sway, revenue, execution of the rest" mean anything without the title of king. Having one without the other leads to the very strife Lear sought to avoid by settling the succession prior to his death. In order to perfect a succession, Lear must give up both title of king and "the sway, revenue, execution of the rest."

Also, Lear must surrender them legitimately, according to the laws of succession. Lear violated these laws by holding an auction for his kingdom, the coin for which was his daughters' tokens of love. Lawlessly cutting Cordelia out of her inheritance invalidated the succession. Shakespeare does not mean to dispute the importance of love in establishing legitimacy.[35] Lear's error was to look for professions of love, not love itself, in settling the succession. He overvalues words. What he says to Cordelia, when he casts her out, cannot be true:

> Here I disclaim all my paternal care,
> Propinquity and property of blood,
> And as a stranger to my heart and me
> Hold thee from this for ever.[36]

Lear's fate teaches that you cannot eliminate "[p]ropinquity and property of blood" quite so easily, certainly not by words of disclaimer alone.

---

[33] *Id.* at lines 135-37.

[34] And that he has not done what he said he wishes. My colleague, Professor Paul Shupack, points out that Lear doesn't even give up "the sway, revenue, execution of all the rest," since he banishes Kent immediately after effecting the transfer! *See id.* at lines 154-78.

[35] The subplot of Gloucester, Edgar, and Edmund examines this issue with some care.

[36] *Id.* at lines 113-16. "Cordelia," of course, comes from the Latin for "heart." Cordelia, by the way, suffers from the same problem as her father: she too overvalues words (why not just give the old man the tokens he requires?). *King Lear* stands for an account of justice in which language is in just proportion with feeling. Lear and Cordelia suffer the punishment of those in whom language and feeling are out of whack. *The Dean's December*, Saul Bellow's study of the personal and political consequences of disproportion between language and feeling, is the story of his own Cordelia: Albert Corde. Bellow's Cordelia is also Albany—the husband of Goneril who puts the kingdom back in order. Corde, coincidentally, is dean at a scarcely fictionalized University of Chicago—Professor Sunstein's home institution. *See* SAUL BELLOW, THE DEAN'S DECEMBER (1982).

The lesson of *King Lear* is that the Eastern European regimes cannot get rid of their "[p]ropinquity and property of blood"—their socialist traditions—quite as easily as Professor Sunstein might wish. Must not some transition, some clashing of factions, be embodied in their constitutions?[37] The constitutions the Eastern Europeans produce may not, initially, be to our liking, but they, not we, have to make them. If the new regimes unsettle expectations that millions of their citizens have built up under socialism, how can they expect to settle new expectations? What sort of lesson, what "lear," would they then be teaching?

III.   REFLECTIONS ON THE REVOLUTIONS IN THE UNITED STATES, GERMANY, AND FRANCE

The idea of a transitional constitution is not unusual, and certainly not foreign to our traditions. The United States has had two transitional constitutions: the Articles of Confederation and the Constitution of 1787. The Articles of Confederation was entirely transitional, in that the paradox expressed in it went to the entire frame of government: whether two sovereigns could coexist on a single territory—the paradox of federalism and the nature of national sovereignty. The Constitution of 1787 was partially transitional, in that its paradox—whether men own property or property owns men—affected only certain provisions, not the entire frame of government. Neither document resolved the conflict embodied in it. The paradox of the Articles of Confederation was resolved "peacefully" under the threat of external domination. The paradox of the Constitution of 1787 was resolved only by civil war and, effectively, by a third constitution—the Constitution of 1865-70.

There is no guaranty that ordinary, nonconstitutional politics will be able to peacefully resolve the paradoxes embodied in a transitional constitution, or that a second Madisonian constitutional moment will rescue the failures of ordinary politics without disintegration or violence.[38] The idea of a transitional constitution does not require trust in ordinary politics or faith in a second Madis-

---

[37] Professor Jon Elster agrees that "commitment to standing rules" may not be desirable given the rapid social and economic changes in Eastern Europe. *See* Jon Elster, *Constitutionalism in Eastern Europe: An Introduction*, 58 U. CHI. L. REV. 447, 481 (1991).

[38] I prefer the term "ordinary politics" to Bruce Ackerman's term "normal politics." *See* BRUCE ACKERMAN, WE THE PEOPLE: FOUNDATIONS 171 (1991). The word "normal" implies that constitutional politics are "abnormal," hence "unhealthy," or "not according to norms." Certainly this is one position on constitutional politics, but not the only one. "Ordinary" contrasts with "extraordinary," without loading the normative dice against the "extraordinary politics" of foundational constitutional moments.

onian moment. We have transitional constitutions not because we want them, but because we have no choice given our probable inability to resolve the clashes of factions completely in a single Madisonian moment.

By the same token, few constitutions that are in fact transitional set that forth in the document. The *Grundgesetz*—Basic Law—of the Federal Republic of Germany is one that does. The German parliament adopted it in 1949 as legislation (*Gesetz*), not as a constitution (*Verfassung*), with the specific intent that a true constitution must await the reunification of Germany. But the American Constitution of 1787 did not announce that it was transitional in the sense that the constitution as then written embodied a paradox in the basic framework. Article V's amending power permits, but does not require, a constitution of permanent transition. It is conceivable that the paradox embodied in the Constitution of 1787—whether men own property or property owns men—could have been resolved short of civil war and the Thirteenth Amendment.[39] One could imagine the United States government "taking" the slaves as property for the public purpose of manumitting them, giving the Southern slaveowners "just compensation" for their property. Noxious as the institution of slavery is and was, no one doubted that owning slaves as property was lawful under the laws and Constitution of the United States and of the several states in which slaveowners had land.[40] Had the Northern states agreed with the Southern states to "take" the slaves, free them, and compensate their owners with bonds (with a hefty percentage going to the slaves), then slaves would have been free and the South would have had capital for industrial development, all without formal resolution in a constitutional document.[41] Would the Union have

---

[39] The second tier of amendments—the Fourteenth in 1868 and the Fifteenth in 1870—certainly did more than resolve the paradox of the Constitution of 1787. They dealt primarily with the paradox raised by the fact of insurrection over the first paradox: whether citizens of states are also citizens of the national sovereign, hence incapable of dissolving the constitution by the action of states as if it were an ordinary compact. The Fifteenth Amendment asserts the participation of former slaves as citizens of the national sovereign.

[40] The Emancipation Proclamation, by these lights, was a "taking" without "just compensation." *See* Morris R. Cohen, *Property and Sovereignty*, 13 CORNELL L.Q. 8, 24-25 (1927) (Cohen, however, would not compensate the slave owners). So much for the force of constitutional provisions—in this case the Fifth Amendment—without the support of politics.

[41] Henry Clay proposed a different idea—private purchase of slaves for the purpose of freeing them—attaching it, unfortunately, to a program of voluntary resettlement of emancipated slaves in Africa, Central America or the Western United States. *See* Paul D. Carrington, *Butterfly Effects: The Possibilities of Law Teaching in a Democracy*, 41 DUKE L.J. 741, 770 (1992).

My colleague, Professor El Gates, informs me that Congressman Thatcher of Massachusetts proposed in January of 1800 that slavery might be abolished without injury to slave owners, and that an appropriation be made for that purpose. 6 ANNALS OF CONG., 232, 240

been better off had ordinary politics come up with this "nonconstitutional" solution?[42]

On the other hand, it may be a mistake even to attempt to resolve certain foundational paradoxes through ordinary politics. The Federal Republic of Germany may be making just this mistake. During reunification, many voices in Germany called for a new constitution to replace the *Grundgesetz*, in recognition of the Madisonian moment made possible by the melding of two different social systems. The difficulties Germany is experiencing today may confirm the wisdom of this position.

The evil I am counselling against, and to which I believe Professor Sunstein's project is prey, is making constitutions that express ideal intellectual projects rather than real political solutions hammered by factions into constitutional traditions. Ideal intellectual projects are at best useless — distractions from the hard constitutional bargaining that factions often wish to avoid. At worst, they discredit the whole constitutional project by turning constitutions into mere "words on paper," or by offending the constitutional traditions of the nation that the promoters of the ideal intellectual project think they can neglect or avoid.

Constitutions must do more than merely set down the bargains of faction. They must express our best selves—but they must express *our* selves, not someone else's. It is always a danger sign when a constitution's ideal project drifts too far from the nexus of practical political action, as it did in France in the 1790s, and in Weimar in 1919. A new constitution cannot wipe out an old order by provisions. The ancien regime, the endless series of dependencies and hopes accumulated over generations, will not disappear even in a Madisonian moment. These hopes and dependencies have to be patiently worked through, in a practical politics informed by constitutional vision.

(1851). The House voted 85 to 1 that this section of a larger petition "receive no encouragement or countenance from this house." *Id*. at 244-45. Professor Gates also informs me that the New England Quakers, having manumitted their enslaved servants, made arrangements for compensating them for past services. The idea of compensation being due, not to the masters for loss of labor, but to the slaves for their years of unrequited toil and for the wrong done to both them and to their ancestors appears very early among the Quakers, according to Professor Gates. *See* William Burling, *An Address to the Elders of the Church, in* ALL SLAVE-KEEPERS 7 (Benjamin Lay ed., 1737) (1719).

[42] Implicit in this political fantasy is a broader discussion of the relationship between labor and capital, a less pressing but equally pointed version of the governing paradox. Nonviolent resolution of the slavery version obviously would have affected the labor politics of the Gilded Age. On these matters see William E. Forbath, *The Shaping of the American Labor Movement*, 102 HARV. L. REV. 1109 (1989). On the equation of slavery with labor of any sort, see PLATO, THE STATESMAN (J.B. Skemp trans., 1952).

INDEX

CONTRIBUTORS

ANDREW ARATO is Professor of Sociology, Graduate Faculty, New School for Social Research. He is coauthor of *Civil Society and Social Theory* (1992) and the *Young Lukács and the Origins of Western Marxism* (1979). He has also coedited many volumes, including *The Essential Frankfurt School Reader* (1979) and *Crisis and Reform in Eastern Europe* (1991).

AHARON BARAK is Justice and Vice-President of the Supreme Court of Israel. He has been legal advisor to the Israeli Delegation of Peace Negotiations with Egypt, including the negotiations at Camp David. He was Professor and Dean at the Hebrew University in Jerusalem. He is the author of many books, including *Judicial Discretion* (1989).

JON ELSTER is Professor of Political Science at the University of Chicago and Codirector of the Center for the Study of Constitutionalism in Eastern Europe at the University of Chicago Law School. Among his recent publications are *Local Justice* (1992) and *Political Psychology* (1993). He is currently preparing a book on the constitution-making process in a general, comparative perspective.

GEORGE P. FLETCHER is Cardozo Professor of Jurisprudence at Columbia University School of Law. He is the author of *Rethinking Criminal Law* (1978), *A Crime of Self-Defense: Bernard Goetz and the Law on Trial* (1988), and *Loyalty* (1993).

LOUIS HENKIN is University Professor Emeritus at Columbia University and Chair of the Board of Directors, Columbia University Center for the Study of Human Rights.

ARTHUR J. JACOBSON is the Max Freund Professor of Litigation and Advocacy, Benjamin N. Cardozo School of Law, Yeshiva University.

CARLOS SANTIAGO NINO (died 1993) was Professor of Jurisprudence at the University of Buenos Aires and a former advisor to the president of Argentina. He was the author of many books, including *Introduccion al analisis del derecho* (1982), *La validez del derecho* (1985), and *The Ethics of Human Rights* (1991).

ULRICH K. PREUSS is Professor of Constitutional and Administrative Law at the University of Bremen, Director of the Center for European Law and Policy, Bremen, and member of the Constitutional Court of the State of Bremen. He is the author of many books, including *Revolution, Progress, and Constitution: Towards a New Constitutional Concept* (1994).

DAVID A. J. RICHARDS is Professor of Law at New York University and Director, N.Y.U.'s Program for the Study of Law, Philosophy, and Social Theory. His books include *A Theory of Reasons for Action* (1971), *The Moral Criticism of Law* (1977), *Sex, Drugs, Death and the Law* (1982), *Toleration and the Constitution* (1986), *Foundations of American Constitutionalism* (1989), and *Conscience and the Constitution: History, Theory, and Law of the Reconstruction Amendments* (1993).

MICHEL ROSENFELD is Professor of Law at the Benjamin N. Cardozo School of Law at Yeshiva University and Codirector of the Cardozo–New School Project on Constitutionalism. He is the author of *Affirmative Action and Justice: A Philosophical and Constitutional Inquiry* (1991), and coeditor of *Hegel and Legal Theory* (1991) and *Deconstruction and the Possibility of Justice* (1992).

DOMINIQUE ROUSSEAU is Professor of Law at the University of Montpellier, France. He is also the Director of the Center for Comparative Constitutional and Political Research and a member of the board of the French Society for the Philosophy and Theory of Law and Politics. He is the author of *Droit du contentieux constitutionnel* (3rd ed. 1993) and *La Justice constitutionnelle en Europe* (1992).

ANDRÁS SAJÓ is Professor of Comparative Business Law at the Budapest School of Economics, and Research Director for a program on legal reaction to social problems, Institute of Law, Hungarian Academy of Sciences. He is past Deputy Commissioner for Deregulation and a past member of the Constitution Drafting Committee for Hungary (1988–89). Mr. Sajó's interests include legal philosophy, sociology of law, business law (economic freedom), and environmental law.

FREDERICK SCHAUER is Frank Stanton Professor of the First Amendment, John F. Kennedy School of Government, Harvard University. Formerly Professor of Law at the University of Michigan, he is coeditor of *Legal Theory*, coeditor of *The First Amendment: A Reader* (1992), and author of *Free Speech: A Philosophical Enquiry* (1982), *Playing by the Rules: A Philosophical Examination of Rule-Based Decisionmaking in Law and in Life* (1991), and numerous articles on freedom of speech, constitutional theory, and the philosophy of law.

BERNHARD SCHLINK is Professor of Public Law and of Philosophy of Law, Humboldt University Berlin, and Justice of the Constitutional Court of the State of Nordrhein-Westfalen. He is the author of *Absägung im Verfassungsrecht* (1976), *Die Amtshilfe: Ein Beitrag zu eine Lehre von der Gewaltenteilung in der Verwaltung* (1982), and coauthor of *Grundrechte* (7th ed. 1991).

M. M. SLAUGHTER is Associate Professor of Law at the Benjamin N. Cardozo School of Law at Yeshiva University. She has written on Salman Rushdie, libel, and social history. She is currently working on a project on multiculturalism and law.

CASS R. SUNSTEIN is Karl N. Llewellyn Professor of Jurisprudence at the University of Chicago Law School. He is the author of *After the Rights Revolution: Reconceiving the Regulatory State* (1990), *The Partial Constitution* (1993), and *Democracy and the Problem of Free Speech* (1993).

RUTI G. TEITEL is Associate Professor of Law at New York Law School, where she teaches courses in constitutional and comparative law. She is published widely in American constitutional law and comparative law, specializing in areas of religion and the law, and in law and persecution. She is a contributor to *Transition to Democracy in Latin America: The Role of the Judiciary* (1993). Most recently, Professor Teitel received a United States Institute of

Peace grant for a book project on justice in periods of political transition.

ROBIN WEST is Professor of Law at Georgetown University Law Center. She is the author of *Narrative, Authority and Law* (1993) and *Progressive Constitutionalism: Reconstructing the Fourteenth Amendment* (Duke 1994).